D1419182

By the same author

Sir Arthur Chichester, Lord Deputy of Ireland, 1605–16

The Flight of the Earls

John McCavitt

Gill & Macmillan

Gill & Macmillan Ltd
Hume Avenue, Park West
Dublin 12
with associated companies throughout the world
www.gillmacmillan.ie

Index compiled by Helen Litton
Design and print origination by Carole Lynch
Printed in Malaysia

*The paper used in this book comes from the wood pulp of
managed forests. For every tree felled, at least one tree
is planted, thereby renewing natural resources.*

A catalogue record is available for this book
from the British Library.

1 3 5 4 2

Do mo stóirín,
Siobhann

Contents

Acknowledgments

Completing this book on 'the Flight of the Earls' fulfils an ambition that has taken some twenty years to realise. When I embarked on my Ph.D. thesis in 1983 on the lord deputyship of Sir Arthur Chichester in Ireland, I soon appreciated that I had the material for two books dealing with important events in Irish history in the early seventeenth century. My first book (*Sir Arthur Chichester, Lord Deputy of Ireland, 1605-16*) covered political and administrative developments in Ireland during the early seventeenth century and was essentially targeted at an academic readership. While I can put my hand on my heart and say that writing the chapter on finance in the Chichester book was one of the more rewarding from an academic perspective, I can readily appreciate that there have not been many readers who were riveted by every page. 'The Flight of the Earls', on the other hand, is an absorbing episode, rendering little danger that the reader would lose interest.

Thus *The Flight of the Earls* is pitched primarily for the general reader, straying into the territory of so-called popular history. In so far as is possible, however, I have been careful to avoid embellishing the book to make the long-term background, immediate causes and consequences of 'The Flight of the Earls' more interesting than they were in reality. Truth, as the saying goes, is often stranger than fiction. Many of the tales recorded in these pages testify to events that even the most imaginative writer would have difficulty conjuring up. Indeed, having the opportunity to recount these extraordinary events for a wider readership has been a primary motivating factor in writing this book.

And in bringing this project to fruition debts of gratitude have been run up. Mary McVeigh and the staff of the Local History Library (SELB) in Armagh were particularly helpful. Very late in the day I realised the tremendous value of the Robinson Library in Armagh, where Lorraine Frazer was most obliging. Finally, it is fitting that I also acknowledge the assistance of Crónán Ó Doibhlin and the staff of the Cardinal Ó Fiaich Library in Armagh which now houses the Micheline Kerney Walsh archive.

On a more personal level, my Ph.D. supervisor, Mary O'Dowd, has remained a firm friend and maintained a great interest in my work. With Colm Croker, my copy-editor, I have now completed three projects. Not only do I wish to acknowledge his sterling work on a professional level, but I also appreciate his friendship over the years.

Even closer to home are the debts of gratitude owed to my family circle. Sadly, in the closing months of finishing this book my mother, Eileen, passed away. She would have greatly enjoyed celebrating the achievement of one of her 'student princes'. Thankfully, in my first book, dedicated to her and to my father, Dominic, they had the opportunity of witnessing their investment of so much time and effort in my education reaping a certain dividend.

My young sons, Mark and Niall, having become accustomed to books, books and more books, are no doubt looking forward to a Daddy who has time for some of the more important things in life, like the new set of football posts that I have recently installed in the garden for them (me).

But, it is to my wife, Siobhann, that the final words of appreciation are due. There are not many young women who would have been prepared to spend so many 'holidays' in London while research expeditions were engaged upon to the Public Record Office. At least I can claim, however, that I showed her the sights in Los Angeles, Washington and New York (though there were one or two libraries on the way). Perhaps the greatest tribute that I can pay her is that *The Flight of the Earls* is *our* book, *our* achievement.

John McCavitt
May 2002

INTRODUCTION

Irish history, so often colourful, turbulent, too often tragic, certainly rarely uneventful, is an engaging subject for the reader: young, old, serious student or passingly interested. To varying degrees, therefore, many Irish people, or those of Irish descent, are acquainted with the event which has become known in Irish history as 'the Flight of the Earls'. Such an emotive designation, conjuring up connotations of a precipitate, tragic, perilous escapade tinged with romance and despair, it has been suspected, is an epithet that has been contrived in the distant past by an imaginative writer and passed through history as the received term for the momentous day in September 1607 when Hugh O'Neill, Earl of Tyrone, and Rory O'Donnell, Earl of Tyrconnell, boarded a ship in Lough Swilly bound for the continent, never to return. Peeling back the layers of history to 1607 does not disappoint in this instance, for the departure of Tyrone and Tyrconnell was indeed known at the time as 'the flight of the earls'.[1]

An event shrouded in controversy, the Flight has often been depicted as one of the most enigmatic episodes in Irish history. Explanations for the 'mysterious' Flight of the Earls have, not surprisingly, differed greatly over the years.[2] Conceived as a narrative of compelling human interest to the general reader, it is not the purpose of this book to descend into the trenches of academia and engage in a blow-by-blow scholarly exploration of the causes of the Flight of the Earls. Rather, this book is primarily concerned with contextualising the earls' departure by highlighting the dramatic events that not only preceded the Flight but those that proceeded from it. Of the background events, not the least important was the Nine Years War (1594–1603). A review of this conflict illustrates why the Flight was considered an event of international importance. For instance, it was in recognition of the Earl of Tyrone's achievements during his rebellion against England that Henry IV, the King of France, dubbed him the 'third soldier of his age',[3] quite a compliment when it is considered that there were numerous 'wars of religion' raging throughout Europe. It was to be a direct result of the fact that the Earl of Tyrone cut such an imposing figure on the international stage that his flight from Ireland was to give rise to a major diplomatic crisis. Equally, the contention that Tyrone was forced into exile, and had not voluntarily abandoned his lands and his people, explains why his departure from Ireland was not considered at the time, either by the English or the Irish, with any sense of finality, demarcating the demise of Gaelic Ireland. Rather, it was precisely because Tyrone was so anxious to return to his homeland that he continued to have a huge bearing on events in Ireland as well as on the international stage until his death in 1616. Tyrone's presence on the continent, as it turned out, while at times creating discord in international relations, proved critical as a 'deterrent' in preventing a new outbreak of war between the Spanish and the English. Unfortunately, from his own point of view, the complex diplomatic scenario in Europe resulted in the Spanish deliberately and selfishly 'detaining' him in Rome. Consequently, Tyrone's earnest desire to meet 'death with sword in hand' fighting the English 'heretics' in Ireland was to be frustrated.[4] (It is important to emphasise at this early stage that in the narrative that unfolds the Earl of Tyrone is accorded pre-eminence above Tyrconnell. This is attributable in part to his greater contemporary and historical stature, but also to the fact that the Earl of Tyrconnell died so prematurely after the Flight, whereas Tyrone lived for a further eight years during which time he was to be the focus of much intrigue.)

As to the explanation of the Flight of the Earls which underpins this book, almost twenty years of research leads the present author to the conclusion that the earls had been conspiring and were being conspired against prior to their sudden departure. Crucial to this assessment has been the pioneering work of Micheline Kerney Walsh in continental archives. Kerney Walsh unearthed evidence that lends strong support to the conspiracy theory, that the earls had indeed been involved in treason before the Flight at two levels.[5] On the domestic front, the earls had been plotting with other disaffected Catholic elements, not least in response to a campaign of religious persecution that had been embarked upon by the crown authorities in Ireland in 1605. At the international level, the earls had agreed to a 'treasonable contract' with the Spanish government in return for a healthy financial retainer, promising to renew revolt in Ireland at the request of the Spaniards if required.[6] At the time, English government sources indicated that the earls had been involved in conspiratorial machinations and that Tyrone 'had within him a thousand witnesses testifying that he was deeply engaged in ... secret treasons'.[7] These officials exonerated themselves from any blame for this situation, having proffered no provocation other than that 'the law of England and the ministers thereof were shackles and handlocks unto him [Tyrone] and the garrisons were as pricks in his side'.[8] The earls, by contrast, characterised themselves as offended innocents, forced into departing their native land by the nefarious practices of duplicitous, bloodthirsty English government officials. The Earl of Tyrone later testified that he 'perceived the Lord Deputy [Chichester] very desirous and earnest to aggravate and search out matters against him, touching the staining of his honour and dignity' in order to charge him with 'some forged treason, and thereby to bereave him of his life and living'.[9] The reality of the situation, however, is that neither English government officials nor the earls themselves were entirely blameless for the events that culminated in the dramatic departure of Tyrone and Tyrconnell for the continent and the domestic and international crises that developed as a result.

English government officials in Ireland right up to the very highest levels, it is clear, harboured an intense antipathy for the Earl of Tyrone in the wake of his restoration to favour at the end of the Nine Years War in 1603. This conflict, having at one point threatened to obliterate English power in Ireland, ended with the rebels led by the Earl of Tyrone being 'received to grace and mercy, even out of the jaws of death'.[10] Many leading government figures who had served in the English army during the Irish wars, known at the time as 'servitors', had lost relatives or comrades during the conflict. Of the 475 English captains who had seen action in Ireland, 65 were killed and another 50 were seriously wounded.[11] The Lord Deputy of Ireland at the time of the Flight, Sir Arthur Chichester, had lost a brother in the conflict. Thus the servitors were understandably outraged when the Earl of Tyrone and his confederates had been pardoned at the war's conclusion with the Treaty of Mellifont, having held out long enough to secure a negotiated settlement. As far as the servitors were concerned, the rebels had failed to receive their just punishment. For treason the rebels should have been awarded the sentence of death followed by expropriation of family lands, not rewarded with pardon and restoration of their traditional patrimonies almost in their entirety. Indignation that the rebels had escaped virtually scot-free from punishment compounded the disappointment of the servitors who had the anticipated prize of plantation lands snatched from their grasp. To add insult to injury, Rory O'Donnell had been elevated to the title of Earl of Tyrconnell in 1603 as part of an overall attempt to effect a reconciliation with the leaders of the revolt.[12] While appeasing the earls was considered a political priority in London, the crown administration in Dublin, dominated in large measure by the servitor class, was implacably hostile to them. Relations between crown officials based in Ireland and the northern earls in the post-war situation were at best cool while more often verging on the hypothermic. As a result, there can be little doubt that civil and religious policies were pursued in a provocative manner by the royal administration in Dublin and its officials in the provinces.

So far as the earls were concerned, there can be no underestimating the degree to which they themselves contributed to the predicament in which they found themselves by September 1607. Undoubtedly at times they reacted oversensitively to the most trivial of slights, displaying symptoms of a classic siege mentality. To some extent too — and this applies to Tyrone in particular — there is an impression that they had failed to come to terms with the implications of their substantially weakened military position in the wake of the Nine Years War. Tyrone simply, at least temporarily, no longer carried the independent clout that he once did, and it appears that in his dealings with the English authorities in Ireland, and for that matter the Spanish ones as well, he acted with a deluded sense of importance which his precarious position in the aftermath of the Nine Years War and the fizzling out of the Anglo-Spanish conflict did not justify. And yet, paradoxically, the crux of the matter was that despite his emasculated military capacity, Tyrone continued to enjoy exaggerated sway in London, an influence he seems not to have fully appreciated. King James, by temperament, and his leading officials in London, by financial necessity, were predisposed to humour him rather than resort to aggressive policies, particularly regarding the religious question, that could precipitate renewed hostilities. With hindsight, much more than Tyrone appreciated, his scope for playing off the London and Dublin governments remained considerable even at the time of the dramatic events that culminated with the Flight. In other words, rather than becoming involved in renewed conspiracy, his scope for exerting leverage on London in order to restrain the impulses of the Dublin government was substantial. As it happened, though, instead of seeking external warmth from the London authorities in the face of the chill blasts from the royal officials in Dublin, Tyrone and his associates, including arguably increasing numbers of the Catholic 'Old English' (mainly residing in the Pale and the towns in Munster, and known as such by historical convention from the turn of the seventeenth century), collaborated together. Incubated by a burning resentment towards the persecuting policies of the administration of Lord Deputy Chichester, treasonable plots were hatched.

The association of the Earls of Tyrone and Tyrconnell with alienated elements in Catholic Old English society is one of the more unusual aspects of the circumstances leading up to the Flight. For the most part during the Nine Years War, Tyrone had been unable to enlist support from his co-religionists in the towns of the Pale and Munster. Common religious identity had been insufficient to lead to a conjunction of interests at that time, as centuries of distrust and animosity between the Old English descendants of the Anglo-Norman settlers of the twelfth century (Catholics or not) and the Gaelic Irish were not easily dissipated. Rather, the Catholic townsmen preferred to bide their time in the confident expectation, deluded as it turned out, that the succession of the widely suspected crypto-Catholic James VI of Scotland to the English throne would lead to more sympathetic religious policies. Among the great ironies of the situation preceding the Flight were the proliferating indications that the Old English townsmen were soliciting support from the northern earls in seeking to counteract the persecuting policies of the crown administration in Dublin. Indeed, in the end the northern earls found themselves compromised by the vigour of their support for the Old English. This being so, the support given to the Old English at this time by Tyrone — not a person noted for his selfless altruism — was as much motivated by personal concerns as by religious fervour; his purpose in making common cause against the Protestant authorities was primarily in order to avoid what he quite rightly suspected might be a similar fate, religious repression at the hands of 'heretics'. Besides, by the time of his departure for the continent the Earl of Tyrone was facing a barrage of legal suits challenging his proprietorial position. Having every reason to believe that these cases had been contrived by royal officials, Tyrone had an additional private incentive to conspire against the crown.

Of course, had the Old English Catholics thrown in their lot with the Earl of Tyrone following his spectacular victory at the battle of the Yellow Ford in 1598, the likelihood is that the Flight of the Earls would never have taken place and the course of Irish history would have been very different. And yet implicitly criticising the Catholics of the towns for their lack of foresight by failing to support Tyrone in 1598, given their later sufferings at the hands of the victorious Protestant English, goes against the grain of one of the primary contentions of this book, that determinist views of the situation in Ireland in the late sixteenth and early seventeenth centuries should be avoided. The Catholic townsmen were to be shocked by the hostile treatment meted out to them in the early seventeenth century. What is more, notions that the centralised Tudor (and later Stuart) English state was bound to prevail over the divided Gaelic Irish are misplaced. Ireland was very much a melting-pot throughout this time, and events could have turned out so much differently. And therein lies the fascination of this period. For instance, regardless of the failure of the Catholic townsmen to support Tyrone in 1598, the intervention of the Spanish at Kinsale, had things worked out differently, could just as easily have decisively tilted the war in Tyrone's favour. Fynes Moryson, secretary to Lord Mountjoy, the English general who finally forced Tyrone to come to terms, stressed the enormity of the threat which Tyrone's forces posed and the felicitous nature of English successes, including the ultimately decisive hostilities which occurred at the battle of Kinsale in 1601:

> In this last rebellion [the Nine Years War] I am afraid to remember how little that kingdom wanted of being lost and rent from the English government, for it was not a small disturbance of peace or a light trouble to the state, but the very foundations of the English power in that kingdom were shaken and fearfully tottered, and were preserved from ruin more by the providence of God out of his great mercy (as may appear by the particular affairs at the siege of Kinsale) than by our counsels and remedies.[13]

Overall, a reflection on events during the Nine Years War has a considerable bearing on the circumstances that led up to the Flight of the Earls. In the first instance, such was the scale of the conflict, combined with the expenses incurred by the Anglo-Spanish war on the continent and the high seas, that the English state was in a parlous financial position by the time Elizabeth I died in 1603. It is this fact that accounts for the failure of the English to prosecute the war against Tyrone to a decisive conclusion, preferring instead to opt for a negotiated settlement that made a mockery of the enormous financial and human sacrifices incurred on the English side. Once again Fynes Moryson got to the nub of the issue when he referred to the Mellifont settlement of 1603 as the 'appeasing' of Tyrone.[14] The financial embarrassment of the crown that had dictated this outcome prevailed in the years after 1603 as well, the policy of assuagement becoming much more pronounced, certainly from the point of view of the London government. Thus Tyrone's military might had been substantially reduced by events during the Nine Years War, but English resolve and resources had also been depleted. What is more, Ireland, arguably, had not been convincingly conquered, rather quietened. The vulnerability of the supposed English hegemony in the aftermath of the Nine Years War was revealed by two startling military statistics. For financial reasons the infantry garrison in Ireland had been reduced to less than 900 by 1606, a ludicrously small figure.[15] Furthermore, in 1612, at a time when a pirate menace had been prevalent on the coasts of southern Ireland for some years, and when a powerful fleet of sixteen pirate vessels was actually based in the south of the country, only one or two ships of the English navy were patrolling Irish coasts.[16] At one point even the shipment of royal treasure to Ireland was menaced by pirates.[17]

Tyrone's fate in the wake of the Nine Years War had not been sealed: he was by no means necessarily destined for a life of exile. As Nicholas Canny has demonstrated, the Earl of Tyrone was a 'tenacious man ... a brilliant statesman capable of turning defeat into victory'.[18] Again, as Canny points out, it is a 'myth that eventual flight to the continent was the inevitable consequence of Tyrone's defeat at Kinsale'.[19] So much remained to be played for in the situation that pertained after 1603. It was this very fluidity of affairs in Ireland at this time that contributed to the sense of high drama so manifestly felt by all the participants in the affairs that both precipitated the Flight of the Earls and ensued from it. Sean O'Faolain eloquently warned against the temptations of writing history with the benefit of hindsight:

> In historical records one of the most misleading things is the over-simplifi-
> cation that comes from the historian's foreknowledge of events. Because he
> knows the result beforehand he is inclined to pass quickly over preliminary
> struggles where they were in vain, but where they succeeded to describe them
> with an assurance that nobody at the time can have felt. The story thereby
> becomes more intelligible but less complete: it loses most of the tension and
> all the unpredictability of the time.[20]

And it is precisely the uncertainty of affairs associated with the departure of the northern earls that makes the Flight and its aftermath so intriguing. Not only need the Flight never have occurred, but the return of the Earl of Tyrone to his homeland remained a possibility right up until the time of his death in 1616.

As it was, actual events associated with the Flight of the Earls constitute a fas-cinating story spiced with references to spies, assassins and outlaws, kidnapping and hostage-taking, even references to contemporaneous Robin Hoods as well as a curious incident involving witchcraft. Extramarital affairs, rape and suggestions of homosexual liaisons also feature. Such was the degree to which war reduced people to desperation that there were horrific scenes of cannibalism during the Nine Years War, a conflict which witnessed increasingly desperate crown forces resorting in some areas to mass murder tantamount to genocide. That Ireland was once a refuge for pirate fleets as powerful as any that ever plied the Barbary coasts is little appreciated.[21] To a considerable extent too, the Irish 'diaspora' originated in this period. The early seventeenth century witnessed Irishmen dispersed as far afield as the Netherlands, Spain, Italy, Newfoundland and even the Amazon.[22] As a direct result of events contingent on the Flight of the Earls, Irish soldiers, the original 'wild geese', saw service in Sweden, Denmark, Poland and Russia. So many themes that have resonated throughout much of modern Irish history had distant echoes in the early seventeenth century. Thus the issue of extradition arose directly from the Flight when the English government sought to force continental powers to repatriate the fugitive earls. The English government attempted to disarm (decommission) potentially disloyal elements in Ireland. Catholic abstentionism from political institutions also occurred, and the collection of a 'Catholic rent' was organised. Thus the story of the Flight of the Earls is a tale of epic proportions, an enthralling and momentous episode in the history of Ireland that has lost none of its drama and appeal in the passage of time.

1

'BETTER HANG AT HOME THAN DIE LIKE A DOG IN IRELAND'

The Nine Years War (1594–1603), catapulted Hugh O'Neill, Earl of Tyrone, on to the international stage. At the outbreak of hostilities it was not at once apparent that Tyrone was keen to get involved, or what in fact his aims were when he eventually took up arms. During 1594 it was Red Hugh O'Donnell and Hugh Maguire who carried out sporadic attacks on crown forces, with O'Donnell inflicting the first of what was to prove to be many embarrassing defeats on the English by ambushing a supply column in an engagement that has become famously known as the battle of the Ford of the Biscuits. It was to be 1595 before Tyrone declared his hand by overtly joining the rebels. However, it has been persuasively argued that he had been fighting by 'proxy' since 1594,[1] Red Hugh O'Donnell and Hugh Maguire having undertaken hostilities at his behest or at least with his connivance. That Tyrone hesitated before declaring his hand displayed a reluctance on his part to embark on a war against the English if he could have achieved his objectives in any other way. Exactly what those aims were and why Tyrone had to resort to arms in an attempt to achieve them is a matter of debate. However, Tyrone's career had demonstrated a willingness to co-operate with the crown, having participated in the ruthless suppression of the Desmond rebellion in Munster in the 1580s.[2] The Munster rebels, it is worth noting, had raised the clarion call of Catholicism. Tyrone in the years before the Nine Years War cannot be portrayed as the unsullied champion of 'Catholic Ireland', an heroic patriotic pugilist untarnished by collaboration with the English. Indeed, this could not have been further from the case as he courted crown patronage to be ennobled as Earl of Tyrone. O'Neill was nothing if not shrewd and pragmatic, prepared to avail himself of whatever advantages Gaelic or English customs could offer in his rise to power. The experience of the Nine Years War, however, was to prove that Tyrone's championing of Catholicism, to a large extent a flag of convenience to cover up more selfish concerns at the start, ultimately resulted in his genuine commitment to the cause. The hitherto politique Tyrone was to become tinged with ideology.

The context to Tyrone's ambivalent position astride the English and Gaelic worlds by the mid-1590s is explained by political developments in Ireland since the middle of the sixteenth century. As a result of Henry VIII's assumption of a regal title for Ireland in 1541, there was an understanding that crown policy would endeavour to give substance to the new situation, seeking to ensure that the royal writ ran throughout Ireland. The famous 'surrender and regrant' policy was inaugurated as a means of winning the support of the indigenous Gaelic chieftains for the anglicisation of Ireland. The English system of primogeniture granted legal right of succession to the first-born male, avoiding succession conflicts, though it was a matter of chance whether the first-born was a talented individual or a complete buffoon. Under brehon law, the tanistry system enshrined the right of any male relative of the chieftain to succeed. While gifted individuals very often emerged under this practice, more baneful characteristics pervaded the tanistry mode of succession as individuals resorted to all manner of ruthlessness and scheming designs. It was a measure of the endemic internecine strife which accompanied Gaelic Irish succession struggles that the most gracious compliment which Gaelic chroniclers accorded Cúchonnacht Maguire, a leading participant in the Flight of the Earls, was that he had 'attained the lordship without fraud, deceit, treachery, or fratricide'.[3] In this brutal world, Hugh O'Neill demonstrated that he was no shrinking violet, reputedly having hanged with his own hands a rival, Hugh Gaveloch MacShane.[4] It was against this background that Hugh O'Neill, like many another Irish chieftain, was prepared to avail himself of English titles, Baron of Dungannon initially and later Earl of Tyrone, in order to bolster his stock and that of his immediate family in the power struggles which often convulsed traditional Gaelic society. What O'Neill was not prepared to concede to the English in return, however, was the reciprocative measures assumed in the 'surrender and regrant' process, abidance by English laws, not the least of which were his religious obligations to a Protestant monarch as outlined in the Irish Act of Uniformity of 1560. He much preferred to covet the autonomy offered by his position in Gaelic society, particularly when he reached the pinnacle of being styled 'The O'Neill' in 1595. Tyrone, therefore, was seeking the best of both worlds, preserving his independence while availing of crown patronage to underpin his position.

In its conception the 'surrender and regrant' policy was essentially a policy of inducement, sweetening Gaelic chieftains with titles much as the indigenous populations of the New World were to be enticed by worthless beads and trinkets. However, as religious differences grew ever deeper in Europe, with Elizabeth's excommunication by the Pope in 1570, for instance, there was a greater urgency in advancing the policy of anglicising Ireland. Waiting for the persuasive approach to take root was a luxury that could not be afforded. The activities of land-grabbers among the Protestant New English population in

Ireland who sought to exploit defective land titles, combined with the abrasive conduct of captains in 'frontier' regions, undermined the credibility of the anglicisation process. Besides, securing the conversion of the Irish population to Protestantism was a fundamental objective. To what degree persecution would be employed to achieve this goal was a key issue. The conditions for conflict, therefore, were present and, not surprisingly, a series of hostilities ensued: the Butler revolt of 1569, and then the FitzMaurice rising which ultimately merged into the even more serious Desmond rebellion, 1579–83. In each case the crown authorities managed to reassert control after much blood-letting. The most noteworthy aspect of these hostilities for events associated with the Flight of the Earls and subsequent developments concerned the fate of foreign troops sent to aid the Catholic cause in Munster in 1580. A force of 700 men, mostly Italian, had been raised by the Pope, though it was under-pinned by financial help from Philip II of Spain. Having landed at Smerwick harbour and engaged in extensive efforts to fortify its position, the invasion force was besieged by Lord Grey, the ruthless Irish viceroy at the time. Seeing the futility of their military situation, the Italians engaged in negotiations to be permitted to surrender their position and depart from Ireland. Lord Grey, according to his version of events, had not consented to these terms, intimating to the garrison that they must yield themselves up to his mercy. What he clearly had not impressed upon them was that he was merciless. When the Italians duly emerged from their fortified positions and surrendered their arms, the entire force was massacred.[5] That Tyrone later failed to secure Italian support for an invasion of Ireland following the Flight of the Earls is hardly surprising in the light of these circumstances.

It was to be the last decade of the sixteenth century before the province of Ulster, regarded by crown officials as the 'fountain-head of all rebellion',[6] began to be seriously threatened by the growing power of the English crown in Ireland. Once again the conduct of government officials in the localities queered the pitch of the anglicisation process. The political ambitions and per-sonal affairs of Marshal Bagenal (Sir Henry Bagenal), based at the important English outpost in Ulster, Newry, proved critical in this respect. Bagenal's appointment in 1591 to the position of 'chief commissioner' to enforce the judgments of the nascent assize system in Ulster, which signalled the advance of English judicial practices into the north, has been considered an important juncture.[7] In what has been depicted as a ploy to 'neutralise the marshal's grow-ing power', Tyrone had the temerity to ask for the hand in marriage of Mabel Bagenal, the marshal's sister.[8] Marshal Bagenal, appalled, since he despised Tyrone, brusquely rejected the proposal, only to be even more mortified when Tyrone, having succeeded in wooing the impressionable Mabel, aged about twenty at the time, eloped with her. The fact that the marriage ceremony was conducted by the Protestant Bishop of Meath, and that Mabel was Tyrone's third wife (he having divorced the first and survived the second), demonstrate that Tyrone was far from the paragon of Catholic virtue that some nationalist writers have so anachronistically depicted.[9] (The conventional Catholic mores of the nineteenth century did not apply in the sixteenth, when, for example, divorce was common in the Irish Catholic church.) Tyrone's courtship and elopement with Mabel has been described as 'a matter of power politics, not love. In this case Hugh O'Neill used his great personal charm to inveigle a woman half his age into his confidence and then into his bed.'[10] In the end, far from securing a marriage alliance that would neuter the political ambitions of Sir Henry Bagenal, Tyrone engendered the 'enduring hatred' of the marshal; 'the man whom the earl had hoped to win to his side became his implacable foe'.[11] (The fact that the newly-weds' marital bliss soon evaporated, amidst reports of Tyrone's serial infidelities, compounded matters. Tyrone was far from an ideal husband, his love affairs contributing substantially to the marital problems that occurred with his first three wives.)[12] Consequently, Richard Bagwell's depiction of Mabel as the 'Helen [of Troy] of the Elizabethan wars' is not without some degree of substance.[13] Certainly, following the Flight of the Earls in 1607, Tyrone emphasised the antipathy of Marshal Bagenal as the *casus belli*, describing Bagenal as the 'only man that urged' him to what he described as his 'last troubles', i.e. the Nine Years War.[14] It was a measure of the antagonism that existed between Tyrone and Sir Henry Bagenal that the earl challenged his adversary to trial by combat in 1594 following Bagenal's denunciation of him as a traitor. An Englishman, Captain Thomas Lee, recorded how Tyrone offered

> himself to the marshal (who hath been the chiefest instrument against him), to prove with his sword that he hath most wrongfully accused him; and because it is no conquest for him [Tyrone] to overthrow a man ever held in the world to be of most cowardly behaviour, he will in defence of his innocency allow his adversary to come armed against him naked [unarmed], to encourage him the rather to accept of his challenge. I am bold to say thus much for the earl, because I know his valour, and am persuaded he will perform it.[15]

The personal duel did not materialise, though events were soon to render a head-to-head conflict at the time of the battle of the Yellow Ford in 1598.

Besides Tyrone's 'troubles' with Marshal Bagenal, the reality was that by the 1590s English hegemony was extending ever northwards. While the writ of English law by this stage had only marginally impacted on the north, its potential implications for unco-operative northern chieftains was made apparent when Sir Brian O'Rourke, lord of Leitrim, was arrested in Scotland and extradited to England on treason charges, being executed at Tyburn in 1591.[16] Demonstrated at one jurisdiction removed it may have been, but the royal writ had bared its teeth. Clearly other 'frontier' lords, such as Hugh Maguire in Fermanagh, felt menaced that their turn was next. When, therefore, an English sheriff was appointed to Fermanagh in 1593,[17] alarm bells were set ringing for

Tyrone, Red Hugh O'Donnell and Hugh Maguire. His interests under most immediate threat, Maguire opted to take military action to truncate the advancing tentacles of English control. The initial hostilities centred upon a series of engagements in which the fords of the River Erne were the focal point.[18] Maguire, under most immediate pressure, embarked on a revolt with a raid into Connacht in 1593. The headstrong Maguire's impetuosity was understandable, though Tyrone, who could not restrain him at this stage, was as yet unprepared to join him openly in the field. Maguire's force comprised 1,000 Fermanagh men. Significantly, it was also reputed to include 100 of Tyrone's men, led by the earl's henchman, Henry O'Hagan. Ironically, there-fore, in the circumstances, Lord Deputy Fitzwilliam commissioned Tyrone to reduce Maguire to submission.[19] If the accusations concerning Tyrone's col-lusion with Maguire are true, this would suggest that the earl was experiencing great difficulty in attempting to straddle the ever-widening chasm between the interests of his Gaelic Irish allies and his machinations to seek political advantage by manipulating the English.

Clearly unwilling to engage Maguire, while at the same time living in what the Four Masters (Gaelic Irish chroniclers) described as 'dread of the English',[20] Tyrone attempted to broker a deal to end the hostilities. However, when Maguire later raided Monaghan, Tyrone was confronted with a serious dilemma, not least when Fitzwilliam ordered Marshal Bagenal into the field. Still unwilling to engage the crown forces openly, the Earl of Tyrone joined his brother-in-law in action against Maguire in a bizarre military alliance.[21] Such was the degree of distrust and suspicion which Tyrone and Bagenal harboured towards each other that it has been well remarked of their joint operation that their respective troops were 'uneasy, and seem to have spent as much time watching each other as attacking the enemy'.[22] Maguire was subsequently defeated in what has been termed the 'battle of the Erne Fords'.[23] In the course of the hostilities Tyrone was wounded in the thigh, though he was described by a Gaelic chronicler as being 'pleased thereat, so that the English should not have any suspicion of him'.[24] A burlesque footnote to the drama is provided by the decision of the two brothers-in-law agreeing to lavish praise on each other in their accounts of their exploits. 'Tyrone fulfilled his promise, writing that Bagenal had killed several men with his own hands, though there was, he said afterwards, no evidence of the marshal having killed any man. Bagenal omitted this tribute to Tyrone. The relations between the brothers-in-law had been bad, and their common victory brought about no improvement.'[25] Tyrone's relations with the marshal had, in fact, become even more poisoned. His rivalry with Bagenal was critical to his decision to resort to war, though exactly when he opted for a military solution remains shrouded in mystery. Contemporary Gaelic writers were bewildered by the fact that Tyrone had at first 'sided with the English against his future allies'. English contemporaries, by contrast, 'concluded that O'Neill was simply playing for time and had long since determined to make war on the crown'. A number of modern historians later concurred in characterising the earl as a 'vacillating politician'. However, Hiram Morgan, writing in recent years, disagrees, portraying the earl as a 'shrewd and dissembling politician and a clever manipulator of men'.[26] Interestingly in this respect, Tyrone later claimed that he had been engaged in an *eleven*-year war against the English, suggesting that he had been secretly involved in Maguire's operations.[27] Either way, it is clear that an elaborate web of intrigue enveloped his every move, a feature that was to be just as prominent at the time of the Flight of the Earls in 1607.

Early celebrated encounters of the Nine Years War included the battle of the Ford of the Biscuits in County Fermanagh in 1594, when a supply column consisting of over 600 men was routed by Red Hugh O'Donnell's forces. The English force's supplies of biscuit and small cakes that had fallen into the water in the mêlée gave rise to the naming of the battle. The English admitted that 56 officers and men were killed and 69 wounded, casualties amounting to a quarter of the force. However, as the English did not take account of Irishmen serving with them in the casualty figures, the likelihood is that many more had been killed or wounded.[28] Small-scale by comparison with some of the later battles that ensued, the Ford of the Biscuits was to typify the recurrent military disasters that were to befall English arms in subsequent years. English columns were to find themselves regularly engaged by rebel forces on unfavourable terrain, occasionally with catastrophic results. The Ford of the Biscuits was an important juncture for another reason. 'Still Tyrone concealed his hand' despite 'tension reaching breaking-point' as suspicions about his loyalty continued to abound. And yet, without a safe conduct, his decision to travel to Dublin to face the 'cold glares of the Council' was extraordinary. 'The man's effrontery, as well as his courage, was colossal.'[29] Although he was often regarded as a cautious, foxlike character, there were a number of such instances in his career in which he comported himself as a risk-taker, occasionally prone to acting under the influence of a rush of blood (a trait which may ultimately have played some role in his later decision to flee from Ireland in 1607).

Tyrone may have been reluctant to declare his hand against the crown, but when he did so, the military threat which he constituted to English arms was unprecedently strong for a Gaelic Irish leader. He had been engaged in a patient build-up of his military strength over a prolonged period, a time-honoured strategy of successful generals. Tyrone 'excelled at training and organisation' and was reputed to have embarked on a long-term strategy of training the youth in the arts of warfare, not least by simulating musket practice with wooden replicas. What is more, he utilised the pretext of acquiring lead for the roof of his home at Dungannon as a subterfuge for amassing the raw material required to make a stockpile of ammunition.[30] Tyrone's crafty preparations also included a ruse whereby he pretended to be willing to suppress rebellious elements in Ireland. This entitled him to enlist the military expertise of English 'butter captains' to train his troops, the officers being thus termed because they only had victuals as their 'reward'.[31]

By the time of the next major engagement in the Nine Years War, Tyrone had openly sided with the rebels, the Four Masters remarking that in 1595 the 'entire province of Ulster rose up in one alliance and one union against the English'.[32] The proliferating might of the rebel armies was witnessed at the battle of Clontibret in 1595. On this occasion yet another English military débâcle occurred, even more serious this time. Under the inept generalship of Sir Henry Bagenal, a relief column proceeded to Monaghan fort. On its way back to Newry it was attacked. In the resultant hostilities the Earl of Tyrone was observed surveying the battle close to a stream when 'a knight from the Pale named Seagrave charged across the ford with forty troopers, and both he and O'Neill [Tyrone] splintered their lances against the corselet of the other. Seagrave threw O'Neill to the ground but as they wrestled O'Cahan's son cut off the knight's arm, giving Tyrone time to stab his assailant to death.'[33] Tyrone had had a close personal shave with death, but it was the English army that suffered a serious reverse. Following sustained hostilities, the English army was routed, abandoning in its flight a profusion of 'steeds, of coats of mail, of arms, of various weapons, of wares, of rich raiment, of horses, and hampers of provisions'.[34] As such English reversals multiplied, it is difficult to estimate the degree to which captured weaponry fortified the rebel war effort. English casualties at Clontibret ranged between 140 and over 700, depending on whether English or Irish estimates are to be believed.[35] The likelihood is that casualties were much greater than the English were prepared to admit. Sir Ralph Lane, the English muster-master, acknowledged as much when he remarked that there were 'more hurt men in the late service than was convenient to declare'.[36] The scale of the defeat became apparent when the demoralised English army retreated to Newry and from there was evacuated by sea to Dundalk.[37] Bagenal's ignominious withdrawal was a serious embarrassment to crown arms.

The lesson of Clontibret for the remainder of the war was that it was precisely because royal forces in Ireland adopted such conventional marching tactics against Tyrone's troops that they came so often unstuck during the Nine Years War. Tyrone did not play by the prevailing codes of warfare of the time, but rather devised a devastatingly effective hybrid mixture of traditional Gaelic hit-and-run practices and exploitation of natural terrain with the ingenious use of battlefield fortifications, particularly trenches. At times, as several battles were to demonstrate, his troops were successful fighting in close order against the English. Most importantly of all, however, to the persistent success of the rebel forces was the high degree of professionalism with which Tyrone's musketeers rained a deadly fire on their foe, greatly assisted, of course, by the convenient propensity of the English to march in mass formations. The musket was the great leveller in Anglo-Irish warfare at this time. At the battle of Clontibret Bagenal's men were astounded to be confronted by musketeers 'in red coats like English soldiers'.[38] The Irish proficiency in the use of their firearms was a cause of much regret to Lord Mountjoy's secretary, Fynes Moryson, who regarded the English failure to subdue the rebellion in its infancy as a major blunder. Practice, he implied, made perfect in this instance.[39] For Moryson, the fundamental mistake of the English was in not following the example of the ancient Spartans, 'who made a law, never to make long war with any of their neighbours, but after they had given them one or two foils for strengthening of their subjection, to give them peace, and lead their forces against some other, so keeping their men well trained, and their neighbours rude in the feats of war'.[40] Overall, Moryson had tremendous respect for the Irish as a fighting race, describing them as 'this fierce and clamorous nation'.[41] He singled out the Irish foot-soldiers for particular praise: 'The Irish foot in general are such, as I think, men of more active bodies, more able to suffer cold, heat, hunger and thirst, and whose minds are more void of fear, can hardly be found.'[42] While other English commentators considered the Irish hit-and-run tactics as a form of cowardice, Moryson acknowledged that this reflected Irish military strategy rather than cowardice on the part of the troops, noting how they displayed 'great courage in fighting, and I have seen many of them suffer death with as constant resolution as ever Romans did'.[43]

Having 'burned his feudal boats' by openly engaging crown forces at Clontibret in 1595, Tyrone proceeded to the next logical step on the death of 'The O'Neill', Turlough Luineach O'Neill. The earl was himself inaugurated Turlough's successor as 'The O'Neill' in traditional fashion, with the golden slipper being thrown over his head and the white staff presented to him.[44] Having availed of crown patronage to build up his position in the first place, Tyrone was determined to maximise his power base in traditional Gaelic fashion. The rebel alliance in the north, it is equally clear, was rapidly increasing in strength and was beginning to extend its sphere of influence outside Ulster. This was manifested by the manner in which George Bingham, the English governor of Sligo, met his death in 1595. One Ulick Burke, ensign of Bingham's Irish troops, having been insulted by the brusque Bingham, determined upon his revenge. Realising the growing ascendancy of the northern armies, Burke sought to ingratiate himself with Red Hugh O'Donnell, who had dynastic claims to parts of Connacht, by killing Bingham. Seizing an opportunity when Bingham was 'in an apartment with few attendants, he [Burke] went up to him, and upbraided him with his lawlessness and injustice towards him, and as he did not receive a satisfactory answer, he drew his sword, and struck at him till he severed his head from his neck'.[45]

Following Clontibret, a formidable royal force commanded by the highly experienced Sir John Norris penetrated Ulster as far as Armagh, where the cathedral was fortified.[46] Towers were erected and trenches deepened. Norris proceeded to the River Blackwater, where 'they beheld the fortified camp, and the strong battle-array' of the joint armies of Tyrone and O'Donnell. Rather than engage the Irish, Norris returned to Armagh, only to be followed by the rebel forces, who camped nearby. 'They remained thus face to face for the space of fifteen days' in a tense stand-off which indicated that the two sides were sizing each other up.[47] Norris later returned to victual Armagh once more.

This time he was accompanied by his brother Sir Thomas, the governor of Munster. Having completed its mission, the English army was attacked in the Markethill area by the Irish, 'who proceeded to annoy, shoot, pierce, and spear them, so that they did not suffer them either to sleep or rest quietly for the space of twenty-four hours'.[48] Not a battle in any conventional sense, the hostilities nevertheless marked an important juncture in the development of the war. English morale cannot have been boosted by the fact that both Sir John Norris and his brother Sir Thomas were wounded in the engagements.[49] What is more, while an Irish cavalry attack was beaten off, English commanders considered it a 'portent that they [the Irish] had ventured to attack in such easy country'.[50] That English spirits had been downcast while those of the Irish were correspondingly raised was reflected in the Four Masters' subsequent assertion that it was 'no ordinary gap of danger for them [the English] to go into the province after this'.[51]

There can be little doubt that Tyrone's forces held the upper hand in many of the early engagements of the war — so much so, indeed, that the earl was in a position to sue for favourable terms from Elizabeth I to bring an end to the conflict. Indeed, during the initial stages of 1596, extensive negotiations had been held in this regard, with the prospect of agreement looking favourable. It was at this decisive point that a Spanish envoy, Alonso Cobos, arrived. The Spaniards had begun to appreciate the potential of the Irish hostilities for undermining the English in the wider conflict then taking place on the continent and in the New World. As a result, Cobos endeavoured to do everything in his power to persuade Tyrone and his confederates to persist in the war, even going to the extent of deliberately misleading them about the imminency of military assistance in the form of a Spanish fleet and troops.[52] This was to be the first, though certainly not the last, occasion when the Spanish pretended to be keener to assist Tyrone than they actually were. And indeed, Cobos's diplomatic strategy had the desired effect. Tyrone and his allies abandoned plans for a reconciliation with the English crown and committed themselves as 'vassals' of the King of Spain.[53] As a result, what had largely started out as a localised conflict had metamorphosed into a theatre of operations of the wider 'wars of religion' concurrently raging in Europe. Having committed himself to the international Catholic cause, Tyrone employed the rhetoric of 'faith and fatherland' to try to broaden his appeal to the Anglo-Irish Catholics of the Pale and major towns in Ireland. He was attempting 'for selfish, not altruistic reasons ... to replace the politics of competing lordships with those of the nation'.[54] Progressively, therefore, Tyrone was to find himself becoming enveloped by the crusading ethos of the time. More importantly, the aims of the insurgents had been amplified, the ejection of the Protestant English from Ireland being now a realistic prospect, particularly if the Spanish sent sufficient assistance. And Tyrone was determined that the Spanish would honour their word. He was not going to be content with 'hallowed beads and poor counterfeit jewels, as if we had been petty [West]

Indian kings, that would be pleased with threepenny knives and chains of glass, and the like beggarly presents'.[55] Tyrone's military might, after all, was impressive in its own right. He was able to raise £80,000 a year from Ulster to support his war effort, a massive sum by contemporary standards.[56]

Even without Spanish aid the military alliance of the northern lords was a formidable force. The three key leaders were bound by ties of kinship: the Earl of Tyrone, his brother-in-law, Red Hugh O'Donnell, and his son-in-law, Hugh Maguire. Cyril Falls, in his absorbing account of the Elizabethan wars, memorably evaluated their relative contributions to the war effort:

> The Earl of Tyrone, middle-aged, crafty, patient, but inspiring complete obedience, with the talents of a commander of the Fabian school and a genius for organising successfully an unpromising material, represented its brains and skill. The power to arouse enthusiasm, devotion and fanaticism among the peasantry was represented by Hugh Roe O'Donnell and Hugh Maguire, handsome, attractive, and brilliant creatures, of whom the O'Donnell was perhaps the more talented and the Maguire the sounder.[57]

O'Donnell's background is particularly worth elaborating upon, as it had a bearing on events at the time of the Flight of the Earls. Kidnapped in 1587 as a fourteen-year-old boy by an English captain posing as a wine merchant visiting Tyrconnell, Red Hugh remained a hostage in captivity in Dublin Castle until late December 1590 when a daring escape was organised. Soon recaptured, Red Hugh made a renewed bid for freedom, this time successful, the following year during the Christmas season. The escape of Red Hugh, it has been well observed, 'ranks as one of the great epics in Irish history'.[58] Having been brought to the 'refection house' for a meal, Red Hugh and his fellow-inmates, Henry and Art O'Neill, divested themselves of their robes under pretence of going to relieve themselves in the 'privy house'. In possession of a 'very long rope', the youngsters made good their escape.[59] Inquiries into the escape later emphasised the role of the Earl of Tyrone in orchestrating it. Richard Weston, one of Tyrone's men, was implicated for bringing O'Donnell the silken cord with which he lowered himself out of the castle.[60] 'In the hurry of their flight' Henry O'Neill became separated from the others, who, having waited for him in vain and in 'dread of pursuit', headed south. The young fugitives later paid dearly for having left behind their warm cloaks. Traversing the Wicklow mountains in freezing conditions took a severe toll, not least on Art O'Neill, who had become particularly exhausted, having grown 'very corpulent' during a lengthy period in custody.[61] They were later found by a friendly search-party to all appearances dead, their 'bodies … covered over with white-bordered shrouds of hail-stones freezing around them'. Art O'Neill had in fact died from exposure, and Red Hugh himself was revived only with great difficulty. Saved from death he may have been, but Red Hugh was rendered lame for life as a result of frostbite, both his 'great toes' having to be amputated.[62] Spirited back to Ulster, he was entertained on his way at Mellifont by a 'distinguished English youth', Garrett Moore, considered at the time to be a close friend of the Earl of Tyrone.[63] Mellifont, as it turned out, was a location, and Garrett Moore a personality, which were to feature prominently in later events preceding the Flight of the Earls. What is more, despite his handicap, or more than likely because of it, Red Hugh O'Donnell was to become an implacable foe of the English. As Sean O'Faolain so aptly put it, Red Hugh had 'suffered unforgettable and unforgiveable miseries … and his heart was blazing for revenge'.[64] The train of events leading to outright war certainly accelerated on his return to Tyrconnell. Signalling his determination to meet his enemies 'face to face', O'Donnell soon took decisive action, and the English were speedily expelled from Tyrconnell.[65]

The Irish 'confederates', as they were known, led Queen Elizabeth I, her advisers and generals a merry dance during the years 1596–8. This period was marked by a series of mostly indecisive military engagements interspersed by disingenuous exercises in negotiation with the royal authorities. While English armies, such as that of the tough military leader Lord Burgh, were able to undertake expeditions into Ulster, little serious progress was achieved in prosecuting the war towards a successful conclusion from the perspective of the crown. Rather, Ireland continued to serve as a bottomless pit for men and money, and the hazards and privations suffered by the royal troops were soul-destroying. The state of English morale may be gauged by the contemporary quip among crown forces that their best officers were 'Captains Hunger, Toil, Cold and Sickness'.[66] Symptomatic of the misadventures which plagued the English war effort was the massive explosion which blew apart a wide area of Dublin in 1597, killing over a hundred people. One hundred and forty barrels of gunpowder had been landed and stored in Winetavern Street when

> A spark of fire got into the powder; but from whence that spark proceeded, whether from the heavens or from the earth beneath, is not known; howbeit, the barrels burst into one blazing flame and rapid conflagration (on 13 March), which raised into the air, from their solid foundations and supporting posts, the stone mansions and wooden houses of the street, so that the long beam, the enormous stone, and the man in his corporal shape, were sent whirling into the air.[67]

English misfortune was compounded by the death of Lord Burgh, the formidable Irish viceroy, from the dreaded 'Irish ague' in Newry.[68] Even the one striking English success of the era, the establishment of a fort across the Blackwater by Burgh before he died, was to sow the seeds of the biggest disaster to befall English arms in the course of the war, the battle of the Yellow Ford, 1598.

Captain Williams, the 'stout-hearted and well-tried' Welsh commander of the Blackwater fort, defended his position manfully as Tyrone spared no effort in seeking to capture the fort. A storming party of Irish troops received the sacrament of communion before what turned out to be a suicidal mission. Thirty scaling ladders were seized by the English as the Irish assault was bloodily repulsed.[69] The garrison was then besieged, ultimately being reduced to eating their horses and eventually surviving 'upon herbs growing in the ditches and walls'.[70] Despite the fortitude of the garrison, the Blackwater fort was to become a dangerous liability for the English. The practicalities of military logistics resulted in the fort having to receive supplies by a relieving column. Determination to do so became tantamount to an exercise in proving English virility. The battle of the Yellow Ford culminated from the ill-advised decision to relieve the besieged garrison at the Blackwater rather than permit its commander to sue for terms as some leading figures in the crown administration in Dublin preferred. Some royal officials even suggested that it would have been greatly preferable to abandon the isolated fort at Blackwater rather than run the risk of suffering a major military setback in providing what would be at best temporary relief.[71] Perhaps most inauspiciously of all, when a decision was taken to proceed with the expedition, the Irish Privy Council accepted Marshal Bagenal's intemperate offer to command it. His judgment corroded by a searing personal hatred of his brother-in-law, the Earl of Tyrone, Bagenal was far from the ideal choice. Disillusioned by the earl's affections for two other ladies, his sister Mabel had left her husband and returned to live in Newry, where she died in 1596.[72] The premature death of his sister only served to generate an even deeper antipathy towards Tyrone on the part of the marshal. With hindsight the Irish Privy Council had cause to regret Bagenal's appointment, against whom Tyrone bore a 'deadly hatred'.[73] Militarily a dubious enterprise from the beginning, Bagenal's crusade (as much personal as political) to the Blackwater turned out to be as ill-conceived and ill-starred as the medieval crusades had been. Certainly it turned out to be a disaster of unprecedented proportions for English arms in Ireland. The omens had not been good for the expedition, it was reflected afterwards: 'The Irish also and the English observed that before the defeat of Blackwater [the Yellow Ford], and upon divers like disasters, the wolves were seen to enter the villages and the towns of Ireland.'[74]

In the middle of August 1598 a formidable royal force of some 4,000 foot and over 300 horse led by Marshal Bagenal departed from Newry for their destination, the beleaguered Blackwater fort. On reaching Armagh, they decided to 'leave their victuals, drink, their women and young persons, their horses, baggage, servants and rabble'.[75] Setting out for the Blackwater arrayed in six regiments, Bagenal's army constituted an impressive sight. Tyrone's forces, as a Gaelic account makes clear, had to be rallied in the face of the sound of English 'trumpets and horns and their martial instruments, so that to hear the martial instruments of the strange forces was a cause of terror and dismay'.[76] Nor was the English column a sitting duck for Tyrone's marksmen, experience of previous ambuscades having persuaded the English to make 'battle wings' of their cavalry. Skirmishers on foot provided further cover on the flanks.[77] With the benefit of hindsight, however (although self-exculpation may have influenced this), it was reflected by various English commanders involved in the engagement that the distance between the regiments was imprudently large. (The Four Masters' version of events contradicts this, remarking that the English proceeded in 'close and solid bodies, and in compact, impenetrable squadrons'.)[78] Besides, Bagenal was later condemned for having impetuously taken up his position in the van of the army rather than in the main 'battle'. (Presumably, if the battle of the Yellow Ford had resulted in a victory for the English, Bagenal would have been hailed a hero for his courage.) Even more ominous for the crown forces was the fact that Tyrone had constructed an elaborate defensive system that consisted, reputedly, of a mile-long trench, five feet deep and four feet wide 'with a thorny hedge on the top'.[79] In spite of these drawbacks, however, previous experience had not suggested that such an inordinately large English army had reason to anticipate a rout. Accounts of the battle, for instance, stress that the leading regiments managed to negotiate the trench.[80]

A combination of factors conspired to render a catastrophic setback for English arms. Bagenal's early death, having been shot in the head, clearly had a demoralising effect on the English. For the Irish, by contrast, and for Tyrone in particular, Bagenal's presence on the battlefield served to intensify the ferocity of their assault. According to Fynes Moryson, Tyrone 'pricked forward with rage of envy and settled rancour against the marshal, assailed the English, and, turning his full force against the marshal's person, had the success to kill him.'[81] Apart from the impact of Bagenal's death, further misfortune befell the royal army when a huge artillery piece, known as a 'saker', stuck so inopportunely in the mud at the Yellow Ford (reputedly known as such because of the colour of sand on the river bed at that point). Efforts to recover the saker compromised the steady advance of the forces. When the cumbersome artillery piece was finally dislodged, it happened in circumstances which compounded the series of misfortunes bedevilling the royal army. Rather foolishly, though in the heat of battle, a hard-pressed musketeer with his 'match' still alight made his way to the carts carrying the powder barrels to replenish his supplies, only for a spark to fall from his 'match', thereby igniting the powder barrels. In the huge explosion which followed, the 'great gun which they [the English] carried with them was moved from where it was to another place by the force and conflagration of the dry powder, when it blazed up fiercely to the walls of the heavens'.[82]

All in all, the sequence of events during the battle of the Yellow Ford helps to explain why a rout occurred. Nor were English fortunes improved by the highly dubious conduct of their cavalry, despite protestations that they had been in the thick of the battle. The fact that, in the words of a contemporary, 'few were slain but many ran away'[83] suggests that the cavalry's cowardly conduct contributed to the defeat, not least in failing to attempt to repulse the massed 'charge' of the Irish forces. Indeed, it was precisely this massed 'charge', contrary to the normal reputation of the Irish for 'hit-and-run' tactics so commented upon by English contemporaries, which swung the battle.[84] Lughaidh

Ó Cléirigh, Gaelic chronicler of the life of Red Hugh O'Donnell, observed how the Irish forces engaged the English at close quarters and credited the victory to the 'closeness of the compact order in which their leaders of battle and captains of the fight had placed them'.[85] To some extent this disciplined charge may be attributed to the military skills acquired by Tyrone when serving the crown. The fact that Tyrone later singled out for special praise Pedro Blanco, a Spaniard, in his service since the time Spanish sailors from the Armada were shipwrecked in Ireland in 1588, suggests that the small group of foreign troops in his service may well have contributed to the martial discipline so remarked upon on this occasion.[86] This was a stand-up fight, and the Irish also sustained heavy losses.[87] But it was the English who buckled on this occasion, not least perhaps because the spirits of the Irish forces had been stirred, having been galvanised by a potent mixture of xenophobic and Catholic zeal. The Irish forces were cajoled that they were 'on the side of truth and the others on the side of falsehood, confining you in prisons and beheading you, in order to rob you of your patrimonies. ... Besides, it is easier for you to defend your fatherland against a foreign race of strangers.'[88]

Such was the calamitous nature of the English defeat at the battle of the Yellow Ford that, apart from Bagenal, eighteen 'captains' lost their lives.[89] Somewhere between 600 and 2,500 further casualties were also suffered. The latter figure derived from the rebel viewpoint. The Irish, it is worth bearing in mind, possessed the battlefield afterwards, Tyrone having given orders for the burial of the dead. This figure was also said to comprise 'a great number' who were wounded but managed to flee, only to be 'slaughtered, mangled, mutilated and cut to pieces by those who pursued them'.[90] On the English side, Fynes Moryson admitted that 1,500 troops were killed, though he appears not to have included Irishmen serving in the crown army, who were normally not reckoned among such casualty figures.[91] Other English estimates later revised their admission of casualties from an estimated 2,000 to 600, though it appears that an effort was being made to downplay the enormity of the defeat.[92] The reality was that of an army consisting of some 4,000 infantry as well as several hundred cavalry, only 1,500 managed to make it back to Armagh.[93] Refuge was taken in the cathedral there, though it was to be but a poor sanctuary as it was contemporaneously described as 'more like a stable than a church'.[94]

Such was the shattering nature of Tyrone's victory that when the Lords Justices of Ireland informed the English Privy Council of the defeat, their letter was endorsed 'Haste, haste, haste, post haste'.[95] When news reached England, even the intrepid Earl of Essex responded with a deep sense of foreboding. He described the defeat at the Yellow Ford as 'unhappy news ... from yonder cursed country', acknowledging that Ireland was 'like to be conquered' and, what was even more galling, 'by the son of a smith'.[96] (This latter reference was occasioned by the contemporary questioning of the legitimacy of Hugh O'Neill's parentage. His father, Matthew, was rumoured not to be Conn O'Neill's eldest son but the offspring of a Dundalk blacksmith named Kelly).[97]

The contemporary English chronicler William Camden described the Yellow Ford as the most disastrous defeat ever to befall English arms in Ireland: 'Verily, since the time that they [English] set first footing in Ireland, they never had a greater overthrow.'[98] Ever increasingly the Irish wars were considered a graveyard for English manhood. So apprehensive were royal troops about serving in Ireland that desertions became commonplace. Chester, the port of embarkation for many of the crown forces *en route* to Ireland, had a contemporary proverb: 'Better hang at home than die like a dog in Ireland.'[99]

By the evening of 14 August 1598 Hugh O'Neill, Earl of Tyrone, stood at the zenith of his power, the main English army in Ireland having been slaughtered, captured or put to flight. It is not stated in the contemporary sources whether the lachrymose Tyrone, ever prone to expressing his emotion by tearful outbursts, wept with joy on this the occasion of his most spectacular victory over royal forces. Perhaps he reacted in a more phlegmatic manner, finding himself confronted with the dilemma of deciding whether to capitalise on his victory by trying to persuade Queen Elizabeth to concede him palatinate status in Ulster, or to yield to the temptation of striving for an even greater goal by 'seeking to become prince of Ireland under Spanish tutelage'.[100] Interestingly, 'upon his good successes' it was noted of Tyrone by a hostile English commentator that he 'grew at last so proud, as in a treaty of peace he propounded an article, that it might be lawful for the Irish to build great armed ships for trade, and men of war for the defence of the coast'.[101] In proposing such terms, Tyrone demonstrated an astute awareness of military strategy on a national scale and the fundamental importance of a naval capacity.

That Tyrone was at least holding open an option to negotiate seriously with Elizabeth is indicated by his decision to offer terms to the Blackwater garrison and to permit the demoralised remnant of Bagenal's army to depart from Armagh unhindered, though it was stripped almost entirely of its weaponry.[102] Captain Williams's heroic defence of the Blackwater fort may well have influenced the decision not to attempt to assault or besiege Armagh, where the royal army was based in a well-fortified position and had access to the supplies that had been deposited there before the march to the Blackwater. Besides, victory at the Yellow Ford had come at a heavy price, the rebel army suffering large numbers of casualties. There were so many uncertainties in the situation. How would Elizabeth I react? Would Philip III honour the commitments of his father to send troops to assist the Irish in the event of the war persisting? While Tyrone had made commitments to the Spanish, he was too shrewd to consider that he was irrevocably bound by them. In particular, Bagenal, Tyrone's arch-enemy and arguably the prime instigator of the revolt, had been killed. Perhaps the earl felt that a lasting peace could be concluded with the English following Bagenal's demise. Significantly in this respect, crown supporters in Ireland did not mourn Bagenal's death, because he had 'contended with the Earl of Tyrone, and was in some part a cause that he [Tyrone] went into action, which bred great woe to the true subjects'.[103] On the other hand, there were suspicions among the English that Tyrone's conditional licence of departure for the English army, that they proceed directly to Dundalk without stopping at Newry, was a ruse. Tyrone was reported to have laid an 'ambush' for the English survivors on the route, since 'his determination was to cut them off every one'.[104] It was for this reason that the retreating royal army sought refuge in Newry.[105]

Considerations about Tyrone's strategy at this time belong to the realms of speculation. As it was, there were important short-term ramifications for the English of the militarily calamitous defeat at the Yellow Ford.[106] Most importantly, the conflict spread, reaching the plantation areas of Munster where colonisation had taken place in the wake of the Desmond rebellion of the 1580s.[107] The feeble military resistance offered by the Munster planters enraged royal officials; indeed, it could not have contrasted more with the subsequent resolute reaction of Queen Elizabeth I. As a measure of her determination to exact retribution, she dispatched the royal favourite, the Earl of Essex, commander of the audacious raid on Cadiz in 1596, with an army of some 16,000 troops, 'a staggeringly large force by Elizabethan standards'.[108] Popular expectation that Essex would quell the rebellion in Ireland was intense. The newly appointed Lord Lieutenant departed from London in great state, the streets lined two deep for four miles by cheering crowds.[109] The queen made it clear that she had pulled out all the stops to defeat Tyrone. By his reaction in the aftermath of the Yellow Ford defeat, it was not an expedition that Essex anticipated with relish. The English crown may have decided to treat the rebellion much more seriously, but there was a marked lack of conviction that it could be easily subdued. The only bright side for the English was Tyrone's failure to press home his advantage. This gave rise to the contemporary assertion that 'it was truly said to the Earl of Tyrone, that the Romans said of Hannibal after the defeat of Cannae, thou knewest to overcome, but knewest not to make use of thy victory'.[110] Tyrone's inability to deploy artillery to attack the walled towns, it was reflected afterwards, was considered critical in this respect.[111]

As for Essex's expedition, storms delayed his arrival in Ireland. A ship that had sailed out from Dublin to greet him was engulfed by a tempest, with the loss of the Earl of Kildare and other Irish lords. 'This was an ill-omened start to a disastrous viceroyalty, at a time when as many as twenty thousand Irish may have been in arms against the queen, with the further prospect of Spanish aid.'[112] Misfortune dogged the entire expedition, rendering Essex a figure of ridicule long before his brief sojourn in Ireland ended. A frivolous incident that occurred shortly after his arrival was to be symptomatic of what was to follow on what turned out to be a personally disastrous campaign in Ireland for the cavalier royal favourite. Having finally landed safely in April 1599, and learning of the prodigious feats of military discipline being performed at Drogheda with a regiment of foot by Sir Arthur Chichester, one of the most experienced officers in the newly reconstituted royal army in Ireland, Essex promptly departed for Drogheda on a military exercise to test the metal of Chichester's troops. A cavalry charge was ordered, but Chichester's pikemen refused to flinch. Essex, having proved the most audacious, was unable to wheel about his charger on time and ended up impaling himself against a pike. In the words of a contemporary, 'upon his [Essex's] wheel a saucy fellow with his pike pricked his Lordship (saving your reverence) in the a—e, and made him bleed'. Such was the gaiety of the mood in Essex's entourage at the time that he retired from the scene well satisfied with the professionalism of Chichester's men despite his painful and somewhat humiliating experience.[113] The events at Drogheda, however, were to pale into insignificance beside the much more mortifying misadventures which occurred in later stages of his Irish expedition.

Having landed all his troops, Essex decided, not unreasonably, first of all to consolidate royal control in regions of the south which had fallen into rebel hands. Critics of his decision lambasted him for engaging in what some regarded as a regal 'progress' in which he indulged his own vanity.[114] At any rate, what culminated from this decision was a campaign that ultimately depleted his force by a combination of factors: casualties from skirmishes, deaths and sickness due to disease, as well as the requirement to locate substantial garrisons in the south. It was to be typical of Essex's vainglorious experience in Ireland that a hot skirmish in which he was involved while marching through County Laois became known as 'the Pass of the Plumes', the battlefield being littered with the colourful feathers of the hats of his cavalry.[115] The only major engagement to occur in Ireland during Essex's generalship resulted in another catastrophic defeat for English arms, though Essex himself did not take part in the battle. Sir Donogh O'Connor Sligo, a crown supporter, had been besieged by the forces of Red Hugh O'Donnell at his castle in Collooney. Essex ordered Sir Conyers Clifford, the governor of Connacht, to relieve him. And this Clifford proceeded to attempt to do with a force of some 1,500 infantry and 200 cavalry. Confronted by Irish forces in the Curlew Mountains, Clifford opted to engage them in battle, despite the protestations of his troops that they were starving. Convinced that the Irish forces offered insubstantial opposition, Clifford persuaded his troops to engage the Irish forces first, promising them that there would be plenty of beef that night. Before the evening was out, it was to be 'the story of the Yellow Ford over again', a fierce firefight inducing panic and disorganisation in English ranks.[116] The Four Masters make it plain that this was 'breast-to-breast' battle, not a hit-and-run attack. Indeed, Irish tactics were honed for the battle to hand, the Irish cavalry being 'converted' to infantry, such were the difficulties of the mountainous terrain. In the course of the battle 'the Irish discharged at them [the enemy] terrible showers of beautiful ash-handled javelins, and swarms of sharp arrows, [discharged] from long and strong elastic bows, and volleys of red flashing flames, and of hot leaden balls, from perfectly straight and straight-shooting guns'. Final victory was achieved when the Irish forces converged on the English army 'on every side', once more indicating that close combat rather than fighting at a distance was to prove decisive.[117] There can be no mistaking the serious nature of the defeat inflicted on the English forces, as by their own admission a third of their force had been killed or wounded.[118] Clifford's head was sent to Red Hugh O'Donnell as a present. O'Donnell promptly had it dispatched for O'Connor Sligo's perusal, inducing immediate surrender.[119]

By the time the Lord Lieutenant eventually manoeuvred his forces into a position to be able to engage Tyrone in Ulster he could muster no more than 4,000 men.[120] In these circumstances, it is not surprising that Essex's famous *tête-à-tête* with Tyrone near Ardee, the Irish leader up to his horse's belly in the middle of a river and Essex on the other bank,[121] has given rise to convincing arguments that the viceroy had decided to resort to entreaty rather than force to end Tyrone's rebellion. In the circumstances in which he found himself at the time, reportedly outnumbered by two to one, it may have been a wise decision.[122] A prudent course it may have been, but the fact that Essex frittered away a huge royal army without engaging in a meaningful military engagement has besmirched his reputation as a military leader. 'Even in his day men mocked him that his sword never left its sheath except to create knights.'[123] Elizabeth's anger at Essex's failure knew no bounds, as she made clear in a scorching missive dispatched to the offending viceroy:

> Whereunto we will add this one thing that doth more displease us than any charge or expense that happens, which is, that it must be the Queen of England's fortune (who hath held down the greatest enemy [Spain] she had) to make a base bush-kern be accounted so famous a rebel, as to be a person against whom so many thousands of foot and horse, besides the force of all the nobility of that kingdom must be thought too little to be employed.[124]

The summary of the year 1599 by the Four Masters also threw into sharp relief the negligible impact of the Essex expedition. Ulster was described as 'a still pool, a gentle spring, and a reposing wave, without the fear of battle or incursion, injury or attack, from any other part of Ireland; while every other territory was in awe of them (i.e. of the people of Ulster)'.[125]

Still straddling the height of his power at this time, Tyrone issued a proclamation in which he promised his supporters that

> I will employ myself to the utmost of my power in their defence and for the extirpation of heresy, the planting of the Catholic religion, the delivery of our country of infinite murders, wicked and detestable policies by which this kingdom was hitherto governed, nourished in obscurity and ignorance, maintained in barbarity and incivility and consequently of infinite evils which are too lamentable to be rehearsed.[126]

As Hiram Morgan commented on this remarkable passage, Tyrone had 'turned the ideology of Tudor reform, predicated ostensibly upon the goal of eliminating ignorance and incivility upon its head'.[127] At about the same time as he issued this proclamation Tyrone published his demands of the English in the form of twenty-two articles, summarised by Morgan as follows: 'The implications of these articles, encompassing religion, politics, land and trade, were revolutionary. The full restoration of the Roman Catholic Church was envisaged. All posts in the civil establishment were to be filled with Irishmen with the exception of the governor, bearing the title of viceroy, who should be an earl and a member of the English Privy Council. Legislation discriminating against Irishmen was to be repealed. O'Neill, O'Donnell, Desmond and their confederates were to enjoy their ancestral lands. All Irishmen were to have freedom of travel, trade and employment.'[128]

Although it was dismissed for its 'Utopian' demands by Sir Robert Cecil, it has been argued that this 'manifesto' was not seriously considered as the basis for an agreement with the English, but was instead primarily designed to enlist the support of the Catholic Old English.[129] In particular, Tyrone's championing of the Catholic cause was considered to be a strategem rather than a genuine commitment — at least initially. Even Peter Lombard, a prominent Old English Catholic cleric who supported Tyrone 'freely admitted that O'Neill had begun the war to protect his inheritance and that he had only subsequently taken on the mantle of a religious warrior. This, he asserted, was to the church's advantage because the success of O'Neill's private interests were now irrevocably linked with those of the church.'[130] However, with time, though it is not apparent exactly when, Tyrone became imbued with the crusading spirit which he had earlier exploited in such a calculating fashion. As Sean O'Faolain aptly remarked, Tyrone 'may have thought to use the cry of a religious war as a pennant. It blew out into a banner. The idea ended by taking possession of him as all germinating ideas do, by happy contagion.'[131] Tyrone's problem in trying to instigate a 'national' Catholic revolt against the English, however, ran up against the provincialism of Irish society. The rest of Ireland may have been in awe of the achievements of the Ulstermen, but by implication the success of the northern rebels gave rise to a certain degree of resentment. On top of that, there were serious concerns about Tyrone's ambitions in some quarters, where it was suspected that he was in fact exploiting religion as a subterfuge for securing personal objectives.[132] What is more, the fact that Tyrone had helped to suppress the Desmond rebellion rather than march to the aid of the Catholic crusaders in Munster perhaps came home to roost.

The great conundrum of Essex's campaign in Ireland is what would have happened had he chosen from the outset to direct his entire force to the task of reducing the northern rebels. Certainly, both at the time and since, Essex has been castigated by various critics for failing to do so. And yet this analysis fails to take account of several important considerations. Had Essex aimed at Ulster, there was little chance that Tyrone would have offered battle except on the most favourable of terms — and the Yellow Ford had demonstrated the potentially disastrous consequences for English forces. What is likely is that the depletion of Essex's forces would have occurred even more expeditiously in Ulster, where the primary rebel threat lay. It should also be borne in mind that Essex's successor, Lord Mountjoy, was only able to bring Tyrone to terms after some three years of gruelling campaigns and with the assistance of considerable good fortune on the solitary occasion on which Tyrone was obliging enough to offer battle on ground not of his own choosing (Kinsale). What is more, despite commanding a sizeable army, at one point numbering over 15,000 men, Mountjoy, like Essex before him, was equally constricted by having to deploy troops in garrisons throughout Ireland. As a result, as with Essex, this limited the availability of troops for more general campaigning. Thus, despite commanding such a nominally large force, it was observed in June 1600, not long after his arrival, that Mountjoy 'had not sufficient forces to front Tirone and was therefore fain to retire … and to seek new ways and force certain passages by moonlight'.[133] That Mountjoy had to be circumspect before engaging Tyrone was manifest. Indeed, it was to be the autumn of 1600 before he led a complement of some 3,000 men in a series of minor battles, always on terrain chosen by the rebel commander. Overall, as these engagements in particular were to indicate, while Mountjoy has been described as the 'best general of the war',[134] events were to prove that he was certainly one of the luckiest English commanders ever to have set foot in Ireland.

Essex, by contrast, however much fortune or 'providence' favoured him during his expedition to Cadiz in 1596, found himself almost totally bereft of luck during his Irish foray. 'Ireland exploded the Essex myth.'[135] What was worse, however, were the self-inflicted wounds and humiliations which he etched on his own reputation and fortunes by his mistakes. In the event, the most significant bloodletting that occurred as a result of his campaign was his own. At the outset his bombast had been so bizarrely punctured at the seat of his breeches by an English pikeman at Drogheda. By the end of it frustrations with his Irish service resulted in his equally conceited decision to abandon his post, an ill-considered option that ultimately led to his subsequent beheading on a charge of treason. In returning to England without royal leave, Essex had flaunted convention, storming into the queen's bedchamber on his return to court, compounding the offence of abandoning his command by contravening royal etiquette. Such outrages on convention and royal protocol might have been forgiven by Elizabeth if Essex had returned as the conquering hero proffering Tyrone's head for her delectation.[136] Citing charges, by no means groundless, against factional rivals at court for undermining his expedition fell far short of the justification required for such flagrant disregard for etiquette and dereliction of duty. The activities of his subordinates in attempting to orchestrate what amounted to a *coup d'état* at the royal court, by getting rid of prominent opponents, such as Sir Robert Cecil and Lord Grey de Wilton, were the final straw. Sir Christopher St Lawrence, a dashing if madcap officer, volunteered to assassinate Essex's rivals.[137] As fate would have it, St Lawrence, behaving as erratically as ever, was to play a major role in events leading up to the Flight of the Earls.

Overall then, and despite enormous expenditure, Essex's expedition had turned out to be a hugely embarrassing failure for English arms in Ireland. The argument that the Yellow Ford had rebounded on Tyrone, having served only to galvanise Elizabeth into taking decisive action, is revealed to be suspect. It is true that the queen had pulled out all the stops to provide Essex with such an unusually large army by the standards of the day, but even this force achieved very little. Admittedly too, Elizabeth demonstrated enormous zeal in seeking to atone for the Essex débâcle by revamping the army in Ireland under the command of her new general Lord Mountjoy. But the important point to bear in mind is that England did not have limitless resources, while the Irish war was increasingly acquiring the reputation of being a bottomless pit. These factors were eventually decisive in dictating the ultimate outcome of the war, with the English Secretary of State, Sir Robert Cecil, lamenting: 'How that land of Ire hath exhausted this land of Promise.'[138]

2

'RECEIVED TO GRACE AND MERCY, EVEN OUT OF THE JAWS OF DEATH'

The collective experience of English armies in Ireland during the period 1594–1600, generals, officers and rank and file, was a most unhappy one. At times ill-advised strategy did not help. The establishment of garrisons in the heart of rebel territory, such as the one at the Blackwater, and their maintenance at all costs, was considered almost an act of national pride. But it played into the hands of Tyrone's forces, who capitalised on attacking the vulnerable relief columns that were periodically dispatched. By a hybrid mixture of ambuscade tactics combined with more conventional fighting methods when suitable terrain afforded the opportunity, English armies repeatedly found themselves badly mauled, occasionally suffering annihilation or teetering on the brink of it. Tyrone's success at the Yellow Ford (1598), it has been averred, turned out to be a Pyrrhic victory. Elizabethan England, it has been suggested, finally took the gloves off.[1] The assembly of Essex's formidable force of over 16,000 men, the largest army ever to leave the shores of England during Elizabeth I's reign, was symptomatic of this. Essex's subsequent abject failure has been attributed more to personal eccentricity than an appreciation that even a 'no holds barred' approach might have remained inadequate to prevail in the Irish wars. That Mountjoy, ultimately successful in bringing Tyrone to terms, replicated Essex's supposed mistake of dispersing royal forces has been ignored. Perhaps there has been the familiar temptation to read history backwards and to assume that, since England was in the process of emerging as a military nation of the front rank, success in the Irish wars was a foregone conclusion once they were taken seriously. Similarly, there is a temptation to view the Irish as so hopelessly divided that Ireland's inability at this time to emerge as a nation-state was almost predestined.[2] In both respects, neither eventuality should have been taken for granted. English arms were not bound to prevail in Ireland.[3] Equally, the experience of the Nine Years War, particularly after his spectacular success at the Yellow Ford, demonstrates that Tyrone was able to forge alliances throughout the four provinces, including elements of the Old English Catholics — though, crucially, not among the townsmen. The testimony of Elizabethan commanders in Ireland clearly suggests that they realised that they were engaged in a life-and-death struggle, in which English hegemony in Ireland could have been extinguished. Even Mountjoy, as events were to show, ran the risk of joining his predecessors in personal discomfiture and ignominy.

Mountjoy's numerous close shaves with death during his campaigns in Ireland have been explained as proceeding from design, the intrepid actions of a general seeking to boost the morale of his disconsolate forces.[4] The tale of Mountjoy's flirtations with disaster is remarkable. 'His horse was shot under him; his galloglas, carrying his helmet, had it hit while it was in his hands; his greyhound, trotting at his stirrup, was shot dead. One of his chaplains was killed, and another had his horse killed under him. One of his secretaries was killed, and Fynes Moryson [Mountjoy's secretary, the recorder of these casualties] was hit in the thigh. One of the gentlemen of his chamber was killed, a second wounded, a third unhorsed.'[5] That it could be imagined that such dalliance with death, when all and sundry in the viceroy's immediate vicinity were so exposed to death and injury, was supposedly the product of design is not convincing. This catalogue of near misses for the viceroy (though not for his unfortunate retinue) strongly suggests an alternative explanation, that Mountjoy was by no means the invincible general that he has been so often portrayed as, but rather the proverbial cat with nine lives.[6] Indeed, a series of engagements in the Moyry Pass (Gap of the North) during the autumn of 1600 demonstrates that Mountjoy's army could so easily have met a fate similar to what had befallen Bagenal's force at the Yellow Ford. The nature of the hostilities at the Moyry Pass at that time were determined by a shift in the strategic balance of military affairs which had occurred in Ulster during the previous spring.

During the month of May 1600 Mountjoy made an initial advance into the north with a force of 3,500 to divert Tyrone's attention while the amphibious landing of some 3,000 men led by Sir Henry Docwra at Derry took place.[7] Known then as 'the Derry', the tiny settlement which Docwra now occupied was described by him as

> a place in manner of an island comprehending within it 40 acres of ground, wherein were the ruins of an old abbey, of a bishop's houses, of two churches and at one of the ends of it an old castle, the river called Loughfoyle encompassing it all on one side, and a bog most commonly wet, and not easily passable except in two or three places, dividing it from the main land.[8]

Docwra's outflanking presence was intended by the English to alter the course of the war, a fact not lost on the Earl of Tyrone, who did not earn lightly a contemporary reputation as a formidable general. No longer could the Blackwater be considered a virtually impenetrable barrier to Tyrone's heartland. Caught on the horns of a dilemma, the earl was at first uncertain which way to direct his attention and ended up missing an opportunity to inflict serious casualties on English troops traversing the Moyry Pass, the southern gateway to Ulster.[9] Strategic considerations having changed, Tyrone was forced to reflect on his options for inflicting a serious reverse on the English. It was against this background that he was to opt for springing a trap on Mountjoy the next time the English general ventured the Moyry Pass.

The opportunity arose in October 1600 as Mountjoy set out with an army of less than 3,000 men to establish a fort at Armagh before the winter closed in. Given the lateness of the campaigning year, this was a foolhardy operation. Yet, having been in Ireland since February, Mountjoy clearly found himself under enormous pressure to make a major military move before weather conditions proved prohibitive. Certainly, when the viceroy's force encountered Tyrone's full complement at the Moyry Pass in October, there was tremendous expectation in English ranks that a defining moment had arrived, following so many disappointments, not the least of which had occurred under Essex. There was a palpable sense in the English army that pent-up frustrations would finally be vented. That Tyrone was seeking to capitalise on the burden of expectations weighing on Mountjoy's shoulders is obvious, as he baited the viceroy by notifying him of his intention to confront him at the Moyry Pass, a prospect that Mountjoy at first seemed to relish even though Tyrone was known to have fortified the Pass. Despite this, as the contemporary witness Fynes Moryson noted afterwards, the viceroy had resolved 'to march over him [Tyrone], if he stopped his way, and make him know, that his kern [lightly armed foot-soldiers] could not keep the fortification against the queen's forces'.[10] Mountjoy's bravado soon, wisely, gave way to a sense of realism when he belatedly grasped the gravity of the military predicament confronting his troops. Tyrone's forces had at the first level constructed barricades and trenches made of a combination of stones, turf and palisades. Higher up on the mountain side the Irish had 'plashed' (intertwined) the branches of trees to form a further impediment. The viceroy later reflected that in erecting such fortifications 'these barbarous people had far exceeded their custom and our expectation'.[11] In making such claims, the viceroy was either being disingenuous or reflecting his lack of experience. Tyrone had employed similar tactics at the Yellow Ford, and this, it appears, reveals his intent at the Moyry Pass — the annihilation of Mountjoy's army.[12]

Interspersed by periods of bad weather, the hostilities in the Moyry area dragged on intermittently from 20 September until 8 October 1600, a sustained period of confrontation between the two main armies of the English and Irish. Following his initially intemperate bragging about smashing through the Irish fortifications, the only thing that Mountjoy caught from the inclement weather was a dose of cold feet (or realism). Far from storming the

Irish positions, he proceeded with the utmost caution by initially sending only a reconnoitering party towards the Moyry Pass. The Irish, for their part, repeatedly attempted to goad the English into a full-scale assault. The events that followed approached farce at times, revealing the tragic-comic aspect of war. An early incident began with a party of twenty Irish horsemen riding provocatively to 'within a musket shot' of the English camp. Unable to contain themselves, a group of eight English cavalrymen set off in hot pursuit — straight into a trap. One man was killed, while another was reportedly shot off his horse, having been hit in seven places. Luckily, as the English account of this incident goes, the wounded man retained his presence of mind and

> feigning himself to be dead, suffered them without resistance to strip him of his apparel; by which means they struck not off his head, as their fashion is, but leaving him naked, within half an hour after he returned into our camp, and being now very well recovered, is ready to requite their courtesy, when he shall find them at the like advantage.[13]

Subsequent events proceeded in a similar fashion, the English probing of the Pass continuing cautiously, while the Irish persisted in their efforts to provoke an all-out assault.

Under cover of 'an exceeding great mist' Mountjoy then sent a detachment to explore the Irish positions on 25 September, an operation which at first proceeded according to plan but then went awry. Almost fifty casualties were sustained by the English, most by 'friendly fire', it was claimed, 'the grossness of the mist disabling us to distinguish friends from foes'.[14] It was following this skirmish that extraordinarily violent weather, even by Irish standards, intervened, resulting in a lull in the fighting for some five to six days, during which time Mountjoy's galling experiences at the Pass were compounded when his tent blew down.[15] When hostilities eventually resumed on 2 October, it was with redoubled fury, fuelled no doubt by a fresh onslaught of Irish taunting. According to an English chronicler, the Irish 'reviled our men, as their manner is, calling them cowards for stealing on them in the mist, and asking why they came not again, where they should find them better provided to receive them'. It was during the ferocious engagements which followed that Mountjoy experienced one of his lucky escapes. He had just mounted a hill to monitor the battle, when an officer in his retinue, riding 'hard by' him, was mortally wounded.[16] Overall, English casualties were heavy during this engagement, with an admission of 55 killed and 105 wounded, while the English claimed that some 400 Irish also died.[17] Such was the savage nature of the hostilities that English troops who had taken part reckoned them 'the greatest fight made since the beginning of these wars'.[18]

The engagements at the Moyry Pass had reached their climax. Thereafter they petered out as the sober truth dawned on the English that the Moyry Pass could not be forced and despondency set in. Sir Robert Lovell, writing to the

Earl of Essex (who had yet to be executed) after the events of 2 October, encapsulated this. It was a measure of the low ebb to which English spirits had plummeted that the plight of the troops was so dire that the Irish had even managed to steal their cows, 'so that we are forced to eat our mustard without beef'. Lovell reported an ostensibly confident mood in the English camp, though he revealed the gravest of personal doubts about the English position: 'There is no talk but of passing the Moyerie or lying in the mire, which I think rather; but for myself I doubt not to live and see your lordship as happy as ever you were.' Such was the precarious nature of the English army's position that Lovell's premonition of imminent death was realised quicker than even he may have imagined, as he was killed later on the same day that he had penned his final letter.[19] By 8 October Mountjoy had had enough and retreated to Dundalk. In the words of one of the viceroy's biographers, this was a 'tacit but definite admission of defeat on the part of the English'.[20] Like a shrewd angler who tries every trick in the book to land his catch, Tyrone had not yet finished baiting the benighted English general. Tyrone, surprisingly as it may have seemed at the time, withdrew his troops from the Moyry Pass, offering the English the option to proceed into Ulster without further molestation. Duly availing of what appeared to be a heaven-sent opportunity to achieve his original objective, Mountjoy marched into the north — and into yet an even more ingenious trap. Oblivious to his impending predicament, Mountjoy discovered to his immense frustration that severe weather conditions and a lack of supplies forced him to abandon his objective of establishing a garrison at Armagh. Instead a fort was established at a place that became known as Mountnorris.[21] Such were the privations suffered by the English forces at this time that the fort having just been completed, 'there arose such a boisterous tempest, that all our tents, being rotten with long foul weather, were torn and overturned; amongst which his Lordship's being broader and higher than others, led first the dance'.[22] Mountjoy's mortification must then have known no bounds as he set out for his winter quarters in the Pale, only to find out that Tyrone had re-established his positions on the Moyry Pass. What made matters worse was the jibing of Tyrone, who boasted that he had 'willingly given us leave to go forward [northwards through the Moyry Pass], but would make us dearly buy our return'.[23]

Unable to maintain an army in the field for the winter, Mountjoy was faced with the daunting prospect of launching an all-out assault in order to secure passage through the Moyry Pass, should that route be decided upon. In the circumstances, given the heavy casualties sustained during the probing of the Pass several weeks earlier, the viceroy evidently felt that he had little choice but to opt for humiliation rather than annihilation once again. He declined the opportunity to march over the Irish at the Moyry Pass as some of his troops had so bombastically bragged a matter of weeks previously. That the viceroy was acutely conscious of the potentially calamitous consequences of forcing the Moyry Pass was revealed at a later date when he had a castle built on the Pass, determining to make this way a secure gate and passage to beat this proud rebel out of the north, which is such a stumbling-block to the army whensoever it shall pass, that it is a great grace of God if at one time or another the army be not lost, and consequently the kingdom, but at the least both every time we shall do anything in the north.[24]

The advice of officers, such as Captain Williams, who had substantial experience in Ulster, may well have informed the decisions not to force the Moyry Pass on either occasion. At any rate, like Bagenal before him in the wake of the heavy English losses sustained at the battle of Clontibret in 1595, Mountjoy suffered the abject humiliation of taking the seaward route to Narrow Water Castle (near present-day Warrenpoint), conveying his infantry by boat across to the Carlingford side of the lough, and proceeding to Dundalk in circuitous fashion. Excuses that this decision was taken because of the availability of supplies at Carlingford were nothing more than a fig-leaf that did little to cover the ignominious nature of Mountjoy's retreat. Tyrone, whom the English forces were later to brand as the 'Running Beast' for his cowardice in not facing them in open battle,[25] was not the one 'doing a runner' on this occasion. Rather, it was the English who were scurrying away from the prospect of battle. And they were sensitive to the suggestion that the route had been chosen in order that they should 'steal home'.[26]

Effectively, Mountjoy's army had been reduced to skulking out of Ulster. Tyrone, once he realised that the English had declined to venture the Moyry Pass, immediately sent his forces over the mountains to the slopes of the Fathom mountain in order to harry the retreating English forces. That the decision to effect a crossing at Narrow Water was none other than a desperate measure to escape was revealed by the fact that it was only when the English cavalry units reached Narrow Water that they discovered that crossing the narrow waterway was extremely perilous, dangerous currents prevailing even at low tide. Consequently, the cavalry was sent back to Newry, risking a trip along the entire length of the Fathom mountain in order to rejoin the infantry that had been transferred on boats. To make matters worse, the army had been reduced to such dire straits that these manoeuvres had been conducted by troops who had endured two days of fasting, eking out the small amounts of biscuit, cheese and butter that had been shipped up from Carlingford to replenish their supplies just before they attempted to make their way to the security of the castle at Carlingford.[27] Even this journey, as it turned out, was fraught with danger, Tyrone's forces managing to mount a ferocious assault on the retreating royal army for a period of several hours, during which 'many times neither could they see us nor we them, by reason of the cloud of smoke between us'. Once again English casualties were heavy, the principal victim being George Cranmer, Mountjoy's secretary, the 'only man of note, who (to the unspeakable grief of all that knew him) was shot in the head and died, before the next unto him knew that he was shot'.[28] On this occasion the

English noted that Tyrone was equally fortunate in not having been killed, an English musketeer claiming to have shot the 'next man to Tyrone, on whose shoulder at that time he [Tyrone] leaned'.[29] The transparent inaccuracy of this report was revealed not only by the absurdity of Tyrone's alleged composure at the height of battle, but by how the so-called eyewitness managed to discern this highly unusual passage of events in the midst of what was attested to be such a smoke-filled battlefield. Suspicions that this was a far-fetched tale designed to boost flagging English spirits seem to be justified, not least when it is taken into account that over a fifth of Mountjoy's army had been killed or wounded by the time the English army made it back to the safety of the Pale. English accounts record 200 dead and 400 wounded in the course of the expedition.[30] By the end of 1600, therefore, events had shown that Tyrone's forces, with the advantage of choosing their own ground for the fight, were maintaining their ability to inflict debilitating casualties on royal armies in Ireland that were bigger and better equipped than ever. As for Docwra's highly ambitious amphibious landing at Derry, this still remained bogged down at its location. Not only that, but the cream of Elizabethan generals had variously found themselves floundering in the Irish wars and suffering all manner of frustrations. Mountjoy and his army had only just survived. And the Spanish had not arrived yet.

Before the Spaniards landed at Kinsale in 1601, however, the English were beginning to contrive, albeit piecemeal, a more effective strategy for exerting pressure on Tyrone's forces. In this respect, the contribution of Sir Arthur Chichester, who volunteered, not once but twice, to command the isolated English garrison at Carrickfergus from 1599, should not be underestimated — a quirk of fate, as it turned out, which ultimately contributed significantly to the reduction of Tyrone's war effort. Chichester had strong personal reasons for undertaking such a hazardous mission. His brother, Sir John Chichester, had previously held the Carrickfergus command but had been killed in action in 1597. For the English, the defeat inflicted on the Carrickfergus garrison was particularly embarrassing, not least because the encounter between Sir John Chichester's force (some 350) and an army of Scots (1,300) under Sir James MacDonnell was originally intended to be a parley between the two sides.[31] Clearly MacDonnell, by taking along such a large force, was not prepared to run any risk that he would be tricked by the English. And from his own point of view it was just as well. On encountering the Scots, John Chichester turned to a fellow-officer and jocularly remarked: 'Now, captain, yonder be your old friends. What say you? Shall we charge them?'[32] Whether or not Chichester had premeditated committing an act of treachery is uncertain. As it happened, he soon had cause to regret his decision. Having fared well in the early stages of the subsequent engagement, he became isolated from the main body of his troops and was shot in the head. Disaster then overwhelmed his command, with casualties amounting to 180 dead and between 30 and 40 wounded.[33] A Lieutenant Hart and thirty others managed to escape with their lives by jumping into the sea and swimming across to Island Magee.[34] Sir John's decapitated head was then transported to the camp of the Earl of Tyrone, where it was kicked about like a football.[35] Stunned by yet another major reverse, the English Privy Council attributed the defeat to Sir John Chichester's 'own hazarding'.[36]

It was against this background that Sir Arthur Chichester assumed the Carrickfergus command. He would play a pivotal role during the rest of the war and also in precipitating the Flight of the Earls in 1607. Having seen action against the Spanish Armada in 1588, in many theatres of war on continental Europe, as well as service in the New World with Sir Francis Drake, Chichester was precisely the type of experienced, resourceful officer that the crown required in Ulster. His desire to avenge his brother's humiliating defeat was an added bonus. Chichester soon devised a strategy that would greatly influence the outcome of the war. Recognising that Tyrone's forces held the advantage of striking and retiring at will, he suggested that 'this enemy can never be beaten, but by dwelling and lodging near him and in his country'. In this instance, establishing a network of garrisons with stockpiles of victuals deep in enemy territory was not an end in itself, as had previously been the case, but a means of attaining one. The garrison strategy was to be accompanied by the ruthless application of the tactic of spoliation.[37] As Sir Arthur Chichester once commented, 'a million swords will not do them so much harm as one winter's famine'.[38] Taking the initiative, and probably drawing on his experience as a senior commander of marines under Drake in the New World, Chichester hit upon a method of improvisation that Drake himself would have admired. In order to circumvent the perilous crossing of the River Blackwater, an objective that had proved so disastrous for English arms, he opted for commando raids across Lough Neagh with purpose-built small ships in much the same fashion as Drake had constructed similar vessels for navigating strange waters during his expeditions in the New World.[39] Chichester operated from a base at Massereene on the north-eastern shore of the lough and landed his men close to Dungannon. In May 1601 Chichester described how he launched ruthless raids against the utterly unsuspecting inhabitants in the area who had hither-to been sheltered by the natural defence of the Blackwater, proudly reporting on the depredations that had resulted from an attack using a 'great boat':

> We have killed, burnt, and spoiled all along the Lough within four miles of Dungannon, from whence she [the great boat] returned hither yesterday; in which journeys we have killed above 100 people of all sorts, besides such as were burnt, how many I know not. We spare none of what quality or sex soever, and it hath bred much terror in the people, who heard not a drum, nor saw not a fire there of long time. The last service was upon Patrick O'Quin, whose house and town was burnt, wife, son, children and people slain.[40]

And all this was carried out under the very nose of the Earl of Tyrone, whose encampment, Chichester boasted, was within one mile from where his marauding troops had unleashed their devastating attacks, the smoke from the burnings undoubtedly attracting the rebel chieftain's attentions when it was too late.[41]

Mountjoy soon latched on to Chichester's coat-tails, responding to news of the Carrickfergus commander's operation with considerable enthusiasm — although at this point he seems to have baulked at sanctioning the indiscriminate slaughter of the indigenous populace. Requesting Cecil, the English Secretary of State, to dispatch 200 extra men to Carrickfergus, Mountjoy noted that from there 'we [author's italics] have discovered an important road into the heart of Tyrone as in all likelihood will soon ruin that Archtraitor'.[42] Appreciating the significance of Chichester's flanking tactic, Mountjoy instructed him to abandon his plans to establish a garrison at Toome in favour of one (supplied implicitly across the lough) within five miles of Dungannon. The arrival of the Spanish at Kinsale in September 1601, however, resulted in the ambitious plans of Mountjoy and Chichester being temporarily shelved.[43] A new, potentially even more fatal danger lay elsewhere. The redeployment of English troops reflected this, as many as possible being withdrawn from the north, previously the main theatre of operations, to counter the threat posed by the arrival of over 3,000 highly trained Spanish troops at Kinsale, with the distinct possibility of further reinforcements. As the Engish Privy Council signified, the 'whole burden and hazard of the war' now lay in Munster.[44] Indeed, the battle of Kinsale, it has been well observed, 'when it came to be fought, opened more as a battle of desperation for the English than for the Irish'.[45]

Not everything about the impending battle was so inauspicious for the English. Fate, finally in the Irish wars, was turning in their favour. The original arrangement between the Spanish and Tyrone that an invading force would make its descent on Ireland's southern coast was premised on the existence of widespread rebellion in Munster. However, the conflagration that enveloped the southern province in the wake of the battle of the Yellow Ford had largely been quelled by the time the Spanish arrived. (Thus the efforts of Essex and Mountjoy to secure Munster ultimately paid dividends.) Frantic last-minute attempts by Tyrone and his confederates to have the landing-point switched to a more northerly port proved too late.[46] The prospect, therefore, of the Spanish sweeping northwards on the back of a popular uprising to unite with Tyrone's forces had evaporated. Insufficient numbers had also precluded a Spanish thrust northwards on their own account. Instead the Spaniards' static positioning on the southern tip of Ireland engendered the same strategic conundrum for the Irish forces that had previously confronted English commanders who had had to march to the relief of their northern garrisons, whether at Monaghan or the Blackwater. This time the results were similarly disastrous for the Irish. Overall, the isolation of the Spanish at Kinsale catapulted Tyrone on to the horns of an unenviable dilemma — who to leave in the lurch? Having courted Spanish assistance for so long, could he abandon the Spanish troops at Kinsale and thereby put paid to hopes of further Spanish assistance? But, then, if he did not forsake the Spanish, could he risk exposing his own territory and that of his allies in the north? Chichester had already demonstrated his capacity for causing havoc in his presence, never mind his absence. That this was a serious concern was reflected by the fact that Tyrone rendezvoused with the forces of Randal MacDonnell at Toome in late October 1601 in an endeavour to destroy Chichester's flotilla, a matter of days before departing for Kinsale on 9 November. As it happened, the ever-resourceful Carrickfergus commander foiled his equally shrewd adversary by deliberately scuttling his boats to prevent them being burnt, confident in his ability to resurface them.[47] When he eventually managed to do so, bad weather frustrated several attempts that he subsequently undertook to raid across Lough Neagh.[48]

While the inhabitants of the Dungannon region were to be spared by this stroke of good fortune, it was at the expense of others elsewhere, as Chichester determinedly switched his attack landwards, driving through 'extreme snow' to raid the headquarters of the MacDonnells at Dunluce, 'where I spared neither house, corn, nor creature'.[49] Well aware of the lethal danger posed by Chichester, Tyrone left considerable forces in the north to try to contain him.[50] Although he has been criticised for these Fabian tactics,[51] Tyrone did not want simply to abandon the north. Instead he needed to delay his departure, in spite of the steadily worsening weather, in an attempt to neuter the menace of Chichester's amphibious capability. In view of the size of the threat which Chichester posed to Tyrone's heartland — and to a lesser extent, that posed by Sir Henry Docwra's forces at Derry to the territories of Red Hugh O'Donnell and his allies — it was quite remarkable that the main bulk of the rebel forces dutifully left their native province. As the military historian G. A. Hayes-McCoy has pointed out, there was 'no precedent for this in Irish history, and there are few examples of such happenings in the histories of other countries; Washington could count on few soldiers, of all the thousands who served him, who would leave their homes to fight in other parts of America'.[52] Not only that, but the march of the Ulster army along the entire length of Ireland was a prodigious feat. Hugh O'Donnell's circumvention of an English blocking manoeuvre by a forced march of forty miles over the Slievefelim mountains in atrocious winter weather was a signal military achievement by any standard.[53] Ironically, both achievements contributed to the disaster that was about to befall the confederate Irish army in the coming hostilities. However much Tyrone might preach the doctrine of 'Faith and Fatherland' in an attempt to unite hitherto hostile Catholic factions among the Gaelic Irish and the Anglo-Irish, his Ulstermen were less likely to fight with the same degree of conviction in such a far-flung region when the crunch came. What is more, having undertaken such an exhausting march in bad weather, fatigue must have been a factor. They had just marched the length of Ireland, over 300 miles, much of it through 'enemy' territory, 'wading river after river, often up to the chest'.[54]

The arrival of the Spanish force in Kinsale elicited a completely different response from the English. Mountjoy, contrary to the decision of his Irish counterpart, made hasty preparations to move the main bulk of English forces to Kinsale as soon as the Spanish had landed. Before long the Spanish invaders found themselves besieged. As experienced troops, however, they were not unduly concerned, provided their Irish allies came to their relief. Indeed, as the siege unfolded over weeks and eventually some months, conditions soon favoured the besieged rather than the besiegers. The town of Kinsale offered shelter to the Spaniards. By contrast, living conditions in the English trenches became ever more appalling as the winter progressed, the royal forces becoming depleted progressively by a combination of privations, sickness and desertions. Mountjoy's secretary, Fynes Moryson, recorded how English troops 'died by dozens on an heap, for want of little cherishing with hot meat and warm lodging'.[55] And there was little prospect of relief for the English army. The 'Protestant wind' that so often favoured England in its hour of need did not blow in the right direction. On the contrary, Moryson noted how the prevailing winds, after initially favouring the English, turned westerly and remained so until the crisis at Kinsale was resolved.[56] Provisions for their horses were in equally short supply. It later emerged that had the battle of Kinsale been delayed any longer, the English cavalry — ultimately so decisive in the battle — may not have taken part at all: they were on the verge of being forced to attempt to fight their way through to Cork in search of fodder.[57] Of course, Tyrone and his allies were not aware of the particular predicament of the English cavalry, although they were conscious of the chronic nature of the English privations in general. This knowledge tempted the Irish leaders to contemplate that it would be more profitable to prolong the stalemate rather than risking battle. For a time there was not one siege at Kinsale but effectively two. According to Lughaidh Ó Cléirigh, the biographer of Red Hugh O'Donnell, the English had been reduced to desperate straits:

> The entrails of the horses and the corpses of the dead men lay among the living throughout the ten. in the midst of them, so that there arose an intolerable stench in consequence of the great blasts of air mounting up which arose throughout the camp from the filth and the dirt of the lower part [of the English camp]. It was the idea and opinion of many of themselves that the greater number of them would die if they were let alone without being attacked, owing to the contagion and sickness.[58]

The effects of heavy drinking among the soldiers at the time of the siege of Kinsale should also not be underestimated. Contemporary evidence suggests that there was a prevalence of alcohol addiction during the entire war. Women, in particular, 'and of the best sort', were partial to drinking to excess, being described as 'great drinkers in the time of the rebellion, and with such excess as men could not go beyond them'.[59] Predilection for drink, combined with corruption in English army ranks, had serious repercussions during the siege. Fynes Moryson noted how Irish troops in the service of England preferred 'a little drinking money' from their captains, who colluded with the quarter-masters, rather than be supplied with uniforms. As a result of the 'example' of Irish troops 'not caring to go half naked ... some of the English were drawn to like barbarous baseness. So as in a hard winter siege, as at Kinsale (and like-wise at other times), they died for cold in great numbers, to the grief of all beholders.'[60]

Ó Cléirigh's suggestion that the Irish should have refrained from battle and won by default was not, however, as straightforward as it may seem. That the initiative in forcing a battle was not solely the preserve of the Irish and Spanish is not considered. In other words, would the Irish forces have necessarily fared any better in a set-piece battle had the English launched the attack rather than the other way round? Critically short of supplies, the English would very soon have been forced to resort to resolute action to relieve their situation. Following their unsuccessful attempts over several months to reduce the Spanish garrison at Kinsale, the obvious target for any assault would have been the Irish forces. There was another important factor which was not addressed by Ó Cléirigh. Besieging the English army would soon have caused food and shelter privations for Tyrone's forces as well. What is more, there was also the matter of the obligation to the Spaniards, who were not unnaturally eager to have their own siege raised. Don Juan del Águila, the Spanish commander, reportedly exerted pressure on a reluctant Tyrone and his allies in this respect, promising assistance when hostilities began.[61] Considerable controversy has prevailed since the battle of Kinsale about the role, or lack of it, of the Spanish forces in the proceedings. At the time, Father James Archer, a prominent supporter of the Earl of Tyrone, lambasted del Águila for his inaction: 'Don Juan del Águila has the reputation in other parts of being a brave soldier, but here — and I voice the common opinion of all — he has shown himself the most cowardly and timorous man I have ever seen in my life.'[62] However, as the Gaelic chroniclers, the Four Masters, were to aver, the key to the disaster at Kinsale lay with the poor performance of the rebel forces themselves.[63]

At any rate, a decision was taken to effect a union between the Irish and Spanish forces by a co-ordinated attack on the English army sandwiched in between. In the end only the Irish made a move. As a result of either a mis-understanding or a communication problem, the Spanish did not budge until it was too late. This mishap was but one of several that were to bedevil the Irish manoeuvre. The suggestion that the English were forewarned of the exact timing of the operation has been considered very significant by some. According to a contemporary rumour, an Irish captain with a weakness for drink, Brian MacHugh Óg MacMahon, was unable to obtain any whiskey in the Irish camp. MacMahon sent a messenger to an old acquaintance on the English side, seeking a bottle of whiskey 'for old time's sake'. MacMahon returned the compliment by bidding his acquaintance take special care in the morning, thereby betraying the timing of the Irish attack.[64] Not surprisingly, for his supposed role in the catastrophe MacMahon has not enjoyed a favourable press in Ireland. The wrath of the nationalist historian E. A. D'Alton, writing in the nineteenth century, knew no bounds. He commented that the 'list of Irish traitors is a long one, but our history records no more infamous transaction than this bartering of faith and country for a bottle of whiskey'.[65] However, both the truthfulness of the report of a traitor and the significance of his revelation are both open to question. In any event, that the outcome of the battle of Kinsale was so utterly dependent on such a fortuitous warning for the unsuspecting English camp defies logic. It has been well remarked that 'Mountjoy did not need intercepted letters, or the word of an informer, or the gleanings of spies to warn him of the danger in which he stood. He was in too tight a corner not to watch anxiously at night — every night; defeat for him could mean annihilation.'[66] It is highly unlikely, therefore, that Tyrone was banking on the element of surprise as the key to success.

The view that Tyrone's decision to engage in a pitched battle on open ground for the first time in the war was the key to his downfall, since the Irish were not trained for this type of conventional warfare and were bound to be defeated, does not stand up entirely to scrutiny. The suggestion that Tyrone's option for a 'clean' fight was the source of his undoing is a myth that owes its provenance to the propaganda of English commanders who had to explain away defeat after defeat. Portraying the Irish forces as fleet-footed cowards who would not stand and fight was a caricature that perhaps salved wounded pride, but it was by no means completely accurate. The battle of the Yellow Ford demonstrated that Tyrone's forces were capable of conventional military tactics. On that occasion it was not the Irish who turned tail when the going got tough, but large elements of the English army, including, significantly, the much-vaunted cavalry. It was Tyrone's forces too who held their ground at the Moyry Pass in October 1600: it was the viceroy who declined main battle. Only weeks later Mountjoy had another opportunity to engage the Irish at the Moyry Pass on his return journey from the north, only to forbear battle once more, opting instead to take flight from Newry to Dundalk via Narrow Water and Carlingford. Even today this would be an incongruously circuitous route.[67] Granted, Tyrone's forces profited considerably from ambuscade tactics and employed them as their primary tactic over the course of the war. They would have been very foolish not to do so, for the marching English columns made convenient targets for Irish musketeers who became ever more proficient with their weapons with years of experience. Admittedly too, at the Yellow Ford and the Moyry Pass Tyrone had the advantage of choosing his ground, exploiting the natural terrain. Then again, what general worth his salt would not have done the same? In 1942, for example, Montgomery availed of the sea on one side and the Quattara depression (a salt marsh) on the other to prevent Rommel employing one of his famous flanking manoeuvres during the battle of El Alamein. Tyrone had a flair for choosing his ground well, utilising bogs, woods, hills or mountains to cover for the eventuality of misfortune befalling his troops. At Kinsale it was highly significant that it was the first time that

Tyrone did not have the advantage of choosing his own ground, not least because when things started to go wrong for the Irish there was no fallback position.

As it happened, when Tyrone deployed his troops to march to battle at Kinsale in the early hours of Christmas Eve 1601 (apocalyptically in stormy weather, 'with lightning seen to strike some spears'),[68] they were observed to have done so in conventional order of three 'battles', the van, the main phalanx and the rear. What is more, early skirmishing went well for the Irish, while a charge by some of the English cavalry was successfully repulsed by the Irish main 'battle', eliciting hoots of derision from their ranks. Clearly the 'butter captains' had done their job well.[69] To some extent too, this performance may also have been due in part to the Spaniards in his ranks, whom Tyrone had accredited with playing an important part in his spectacular victory at the Yellow Ford. Similarly, there was nothing very unconventional about Tyrone's defeat. As Tyrone's army proceeded, it was noted afterwards, his three 'battles' had become 'too widely separated', so that when a second cavalry assault by almost the entire complement of the English horse took place, Tyrone's main 'battle' was not in a position to be seconded before his troops gave way and fled. This is strikingly reminiscent of the circumstances in which the English defeat had occurred at the Yellow Ford three years earlier. The two battles had other features in common. The Irish cavalry were conspicuous by their poor performance at Kinsale, recalling Bagenal's situation at the Blackwater. Finally, the accidental explosion of a bag of gunpowder in the midst of the Irish ranks contributed to the disarray that ultimately caused the Irish main 'battle' to disintegrate, once more recalling the gunpowder explosion that had thrown the English ranks into confusion at the Yellow Ford. On top of these mistakes and misfortunes, the Spaniards had not engaged the English simultaneously as planned, thereby allowing the English to concentrate their cavalry on attacking the Irish. However, as the Four Masters commented, the role of the Spanish was to some extent immaterial to the outcome of the battle; it was the uncharacteristically poor performance of the Irish troops that proved critical:

> Manifest was the displeasure of God, and misfortune to the Irish of fine Fodhla, on this occasion; for, previous to this day, a small number of them had more frequently routed many hundreds of the English, than they had fled from them, in the field of battle, in the gap of danger (in every place they had encountered), up to this day.[70]

And when the rout occurred it was complete, the English proving as adept at slaughtering and decapitating the fleeing Irish at Kinsale as the Irish had 'mangled' the bodies of the English at the Yellow Ford. Fynes Moryson recounted that 1,200 rebels lay dead on the battlefield. Perhaps just as significantly for subsequent events in the war, it was recorded that the English laid hold of some 2,000 weapons.[71] Further deaths among the rebels occurred as they retreated northwards, relentlessly pursued, at a time of year when the weather was particularly harsh. Moryson recorded the grim details of Tyrone's retreat: 'Tyrone, in great fear and with a speedy march, hasted out of the province of Munster … losing upon every ford many of his foot, but especially in passing the rivers of Broadwater, of May in Connolagh, and at the Abbey Owney in O'Mulryan's Country; at which fords, the waters being high (as we are informed), he lost above 200 men.'[72]

Tyrone's decision to delay his departure for Kinsale until the dead of winter had returned to haunt him. Having enjoyed a prolonged period of successes, Tyrone's decision-making had suddenly become suspect, and his sway over other chieftains in the confederacy correspondingly weakened. Following Kinsale, there 'prevailed much reproach on reproach, moaning and dejection, melancholy and anguish, in every quarter' of the rebel camp. And when the leaders met to consider their options 'their counsel was hasty, unsteady and precipitate'.[73] The 'subtle, fox-like, and craftily wise' Tyrone, after all, was prone to occasional lapses of judgment in a crisis, a failing that perhaps contributed to his later decision to take flight from Ireland in 1607.[74]

One such precipitate, and ultimately costly, policy resulted in Red Hugh O'Donnell resolving to journey to the Spanish court at the end of 1601 to lobby for a new invasion force. Following Kinsale, O'Donnell was described as being 'seized with great fury, rage, and anxiety of mind; so that he did not sleep or rest soundly for the space of three days and three nights afterwards'.[75] When O'Donnell reached Spain, he made his case vigorously and was not prepared to be fobbed off by vague Spanish promises. He was on the point of returning to the Spanish court 'to know what it was that caused the retarding or delay [in the raising] of the army which he [Philip III] had promised' when he was struck down by sudden illness and subsequent death, allegedly poisoned at the hands of an English assassin who was stalking him.[76] O'Donnell's funeral in Spain was a grand affair, reflecting Spanish appreciation of the manner in which the Irish rebels had tied down large numbers of English troops. 'His body was conveyed to the king's palace at Valladolid in a four-wheeled hearse, surrounded by countless numbers of the king's state officers, council, and guards, with luminous torches and bright flambeaux of beautiful wax-light burning on each side of him.'[77] Events were to prove that this was but to be the first in a succession of grand funerals to be held for the expatriate nobility of Ulster. Red Hugh's loss to the confederate cause was immense. His lustre, along with that of the Earl of Tyrone, had been critical in cementing the rebel alliance. Instead, following Kinsale and Red Hugh's departure for Spain, the rebel chieftains returned to Ulster 'in separate hosts, without ceding the leadership to any one lord' to defend their territories as best they could.[78] The relatively co-ordinated military strategy that had been such a distinctive feature of the rebel confederacy was giving way to narrower interests.

And yet the English success at the battle of Kinsale did not reap the dividends that Mountjoy clearly anticipated. Distraught, undoubtedly, at the disaster that had befallen his forces, Tyrone did not allow despondency to set in, and in fact his troops managed to hold out for fifteen months despite the reverse. For a time, indeed, there was reason to hope that Red Hugh might persuade the Spaniards to return with even greater forces.[79] The rebels offered considerable resilience during 1602: the 'struggle ... was far from broken'.[80] That spring, for instance, while the English claimed success in forcing Tyrone from the Blackwater, it was noted that he had 'fortified and entrenched there with great art'.[81] Mountjoy advanced into Tyrone's heartland very cautiously. In June 1602, on crossing the Blackwater, he made sure to erect a bridge and a fort at the ford, 'which of his own Christian name was called Charlemount' (present-day Charlemont).[82] Chichester meanwhile, having carried out yet another amphibious landing on the shores of Lough Neagh, was assisted in establishing a fort close to Dungannon that could accommodate a garrison of 1,000 infantry and 100 horse. The fort was christened 'Mountjoy'.[83] Surveying the English advance over the Blackwater, Tyrone torched his home at Dungannon,[84] indicating from his point of view that a new and even more mobile mode of operations had been resolved upon. Mountjoy mistakenly interpreted this action as indicating that victory was imminent. The Lord Deputy indicated to his entourage that during the summer of 1602 'he meant to lay the axe to the root of the tree, by prosecuting the Arch-traitor, who had nothing to bear him up but false rumours of Spanish aids. This summer (if ever any) was the time to end the war.'[85] But the war was not prosecuted to a conclusion at that time, for the rebels continued to hold out tenaciously. Far from capitulating, they resisted. A large raiding party commanded by Sir Henry Docwra was set upon by the forces of Cormac MacBaron O'Neill during August 1602. Hostilities were so intense that when both sides ran out of gunpowder, it 'came to the sword and push of pike'.[86] But overall the tide of the war had turned markedly against Tyrone and his allies.

A decisive victory had been achieved at Kinsale, but the rebellion had not been suppressed. In order to achieve this, the English had to resort to a war of attrition over a prolonged period. That depended on pressure being exerted by Mountjoy from the south, Chichester from his base at Carrickfergus, and Docwra from Derry. The wartime performance of Docwra, in particular, was to disappoint his military superiors as well as the queen, who expressed her dissatisfaction.[87] There was little sympathy in royal circles for the fact that Docwra's force was blighted by sickness which spread rapidly through the garrison owing to the 'narrowness' of Derry as a location.[88] Docwra claimed that it was a common experience for a company of 150 men to have as few as twenty-five or thirty fit for active service. Shirking hazardous duty may well have contributed to the sickness figures, though it is clear that from the start Docwra himself was a courageous officer, personally leading his men into the thick of battle. On one occasion, in the heat of a skirmish, Docwra recorded how his horse had been shot 'in two places and fell dead under me'.[89] During another mêlée he was knocked senseless from his mount, having been hit on the head by a 'well-aimed cast of a javelin', and was saved only by his helmet.[90] Even among the Gaelic Irish Docwra was rapidly accruing a reputation as a 'mighty man'.[91] The Four Masters paid him a fulsome tribute when they described him as 'an illustrious knight, of wisdom and prudence, a pillar of battle and conflict'.[92] Writing almost four centuries later, the historian John McGurk concurred, describing Docwra as 'one of the unsung victors' of the Nine Years War.[93] Besides his martial qualities, Docwra also displayed an uncanny knack for the classic ploy of *divide et impera*, soliciting the desertion of Niall Garbh O'Donnell from the rebel cause in 1600. Niall Garbh, a dynastic rival of Red Hugh O'Donnell, was 'promised … in the behalf of the Queen, the whole country of Tirconnell … and my lord Deputy and Council at Dublin did afterwards confirm it unto him under their hands'.[94] Securing Niall Garbh's services proved crucial to the improved performance of Docwra's command. Previous to this the English expeditionary force had been largely confined to its 'narrow prison' base in Derry. Niall Garbh alleviated the supply problem that had been afflicting the English, who were surviving on a diet of 'old victuals … and bitter flesh-meat' that no doubt contributed to the rampant sickness of the garrison.[95] For the Four Masters, Niall Garbh's desertion to the English side played a crucial long-term role in the sequence of events leading up to the Flight of the Earls. Referring to a battle in which Niall Garbh was fighting the forces of Rory O'Donnell, later to become Earl of Tyrconnell, the Gaelic chroniclers lamented: 'Woe is me that these heroes of Kinel-Connell were not united in fight on one side against their enemies, and that they were not at peace; for, while they remained so, they were not banished or driven from their native territories, as they afterwards were!'[96] Before the war ended, the esteem that Docwra generated among the Irish was to prove crucial in winning over Tyrone's son-in-law Donal O'Cahan, another key rebel commander, to the English side.

A grudging respect was not something that Sir Arthur Chichester elicited from his enemies. He was too brutal for that. However, his ruthless streak in prosecuting the war appealed to Queen Elizabeth, who was said to be particularly pleased with his performance.[97] Despite the victory at Kinsale, the English were frustrated in their search for a quick end to the war. In these circumstances, Chichester's uncompromising views fell on receptive ears. In his judgment, Mountjoy and the advisers in his entourage had been too honourable and compassionate in their conduct of the war. Clearly smarting at Mountjoy's refusal to countenance an all-out policy of spoliation in the pre-Kinsale period, Chichester remarked that 'We have too mild spirits and good consciences to be their masters.'[98] In the aftermath of Kinsale, with Tyrone still holding out, Chichester felt vindicated when writing to Cecil, the English Secretary of State, that the 'right way of finishing these rebellions has, as you know, not been taken; but continuance [of the rebellion] has now opened the eyes of those whom misadvice and ill counsel would long have kept in blindness'.[99] Before long the message had got through, and Mountjoy's forces implemented what

Cyril Falls has termed the 'extermination' strategy advocated by Chichester.[100] The scenes of horror unleashed by Mountjoy's adaptation of this policy were gruesome, particularly in regions where Chichester played a significant role in implementing the policy. The Newry area suffered grievously in this respect, not least from cannibalism, a fact attested by English sources. One report noted how three old women had been enticing young children to their camp, where they were 'surprised, killed and eaten'. The women, it is worth noting, were duly executed for their offence,[101] having been exposed by a 'great girl' who had escaped their clutches and had informed some English officers, who found skulls and bones to justify the allegations. Indeed, there were other instances where attempts appear to have been made by English forces to salve guilty consciences for the depredations that had been unleashed. Operating in a wood near Newry, Chichester's forces encountered a peculiar odour:

> ... a great savour, as it were roasting or broiling of flesh; the governor sent out the soldiers to search the wood, and they found a cabin where a woman was dead, and five children by her made fire to her thighs and arms and sides, roasting her flesh and eating it. The governor went to the place to see it, and demanded of them why they did so; they answered they could not get any other meat. It was demanded where their cows were, and they said the English had taken them away. Also it was demanded when the woodkern [rebels] were there, and they answered not in three days before. It was asked of them whether they would have meat or money to relieve them; they answered both meat and money; so the governor commanded to collect a proportion of victuals from among the soldiers' knapsacks, and left it with them, and so departed.[102]

Such was the degree of devastation wrought by the scorched-earth tactic by the end of the war that, according to Fynes Moryson, Mountjoy's secretary, 'no spectacle was more frequent in the ditches of towns and especially in wasted countries, than to see multitudes of these poor people dead with their mouths all coloured green by eating nettles'.[103] The Irish were eventually to claim that 60,000 had perished from famine, a figure impossible to verify, though the profusion of English military reports detailing harrowing scenes of starvation lends it some degree of substantiation.[104]

And yet Tyrone continued to hold out. But by now his leading commanders had begun to desert him. It was at this point that Sir Henry Docwra secured the services of Donal O'Cahan, Tyrone's son-in-law, by promising him formal crown recognition for his territorial claims.[105] (Significantly, in view of the manner in which Chichester exploited O'Cahan after the war ended, he was to describe the chieftain at the time of his submission as 'treacherous'. However, he believed that if Docwra considered that it was worth soliciting O'Cahan's services, then 'it will be profitable to temporise with him until the greatest work be done, after which these petty lords will be dealt withal at pleasure'.)[106] O'Cahan's desertion was a particularly severe body-blow, leaving Tyrone vulnerable to attack on yet another front. Indeed, had O'Cahan remained firm, Tyrone was later to reflect, he believed that he could have held out indefinitely against the English.[107] (The desertion of O'Cahan bequeathed a legacy of bitterness that was to persist after the war ended in 1603 and was to be a key factor in the circumstances leading up to the Flight of the Earls in 1607.) Tyrone's durability in such circumstances was quite remarkable, not least in the face of the determined efforts of Sir Arthur Chichester to hunt him down. After years of frustration, Chichester sounded an optimistic note from his naval base at Massereene on the north-eastern shore of Lough Neagh in June 1602 when he remarked that a policy would be resolved upon to effect a 'speedy course for beating and as I hope beheading that woodkern Tyrone whose time is at an end'.[108] Memories of the fate of his brother John clearly remained a motivating factor. Chichester had already managed to contrive the removal of Sir James MacDonnell, whose forces had been responsible for the death of his brother. With the collusion of Cecil, Chichester was party to a successful plot to poison MacDonnell.[109]

One way or the other, Chichester was determined to exact his revenge on Tyrone too. The earl's predicament had become so perilous that the English believed that he would seek to flee from the country, and precautions were put in place at various coastal locations to prevent this. Meanwhile Chichester had put a bounty on Tyrone's head, in the hope that he would be betrayed by one of his own men.[110] 'A great reward upon the head of Tyrone' had been promised, dead or alive, though the reward would be greater if he could be brought in alive. Clearly the English wanted the satisfaction of subjecting him to a formal trial and execution. However, to the intense frustration of the English, even this strategem failed because the Ulstermen could not be 'induced by any rewards of money or pardons for their own estates and lives, to betray him, no not when themselves were driven to greatest misery, and he forced to hide his head in the woods without any forces, and only was followed by some few of his most trusty vassals'.[111] While no one would turn him in, there was no doubt that Tyrone was under dire pressure. This was epitomised by Mountjoy's seizure of Dungannon and the subsequent smashing to bits of the ancient inauguration stone of the O'Neills at Tullaghogue.[112]

It was during the final year of the war that there is evidence to suggest that Tyrone comported himself as the 'Running Beast' of contemporary English caricature. It was a measure of the rising confidence of the English that the gossip at court was dominated by news that Tyrone was on the point of imminent defeat: 'Out of Ireland we hear nothing, but that Tiron runs up and down distressed, and offers to come in upon any conditions with life.'[113] In evading further decisive engagements, and the ever-increasing likelihood of discomfiture either by death or capture, Tyrone's forces were greatly assisted by the 'fastnesses' of Glenconkeyne and Killetragh, large wooded territories where even the most intrepid of Englishmen feared to tread. Even as late as 1608 the

English were largely unfamiliar with the area. A pioneering viceregal tour of the region at that time inspired Sir John Davies's memorable classical allusion that the 'wild inhabitants wondered as much to see the king's deputy, as the ghosts in Virgil wondered to see Aeneas alive in hell'.[114]

Chichester, however, was determined to run down his prey. Just as Christmas 1602 approached, English forces in Ulster were looking forward to the season's festivities. Josias Bodley and a group of fellow-officers recounted how they had been invited by a friend to spend the 'Nativity' in Lecale, County Down,

> but, as Sir Arthur Chichester, the serjeant-major of the whole army, had convoked us with all our companies at that very moment to fight with Tyrone, who was then in the woods of Glenconkein with much cattle and few fighting men, we could not go at that time to Lecale, but joined the said Sir Arthur, and remained with him for sixteen or seventeen days in the field.[115]

Chichester's pathological determination to deliver the *coup de grâce* was transparent. But in the prevailing circumstances, his enthusiasm was not entirely shared by the rest of the officer corps. Bodley recorded, for instance, that while two engagements took place in the course of the campaign, little 'harm' had been inflicted on the earl's forces. In the event, Bodley could only express his frustration when he depicted Tyrone as 'the worst rascal, and very wary and subtle, and won't be beaten except on good terms'.[116]

Bodley was not the only Englishman to betray a growing sense that Tyrone's rebellion could only be brought to an end on terms, not unconditionally. John Chamberlain, a court gossip, having previously boasted that Tyrone could not hold out much longer, articulated the growing sense of exhaustion percolating English ranks. During February 1603 he noted that a 'Captain Whiddon is come newly out of Ireland very weary of those wars'.[117] To make things worse, Chamberlain observed about the same time that reports suggested that Tyrone 'gathers head again',[118] meaning that his military capacity had managed to resurge somewhat in spite of the merciless onslaught of the English forces. It was against this background that Chamberlain reported at the end of February 1603 that the English Privy Council 'have ben much busied of late about Irish matters, and whether Tiron to be received with the conditions offered him by the Earl of Essex, upon which point he stands, and is thought shall obtain'.[119] Having survived winter in the face of devastating English 'total war' tactics, the prospect of spring and the growing season offered hope that Tyrone's forces could continue to survive in the field. In the face of the unrelenting onslaught of the English forces, the fortitude of Tyrone and his remaining forces in holding out was immense, providing the key to what seemed at the time to be their salvation. They had not won the war, but they had still to be beaten into abject surrender. Besides consuming the cream of England's manhood, the prolonged conflict had cost the English exchequer at least £2 million — a phenomenal sum at the time.[120]

In the end Tyrone was not the only one desperate for a negotiated conclusion to the war. So were the English. It is this explanation of events which accounts for the bitter exchanges between Sir Henry Docwra and Mountjoy at the end of the war, after Mountjoy reneged on promises which had been made both to himself and to O'Cahan. Docwra had been offered the Foyle fisheries by way of reward for his military services, while O'Cahan had been promised a formal grant of lands for deserting Tyrone. In each case Mountjoy had backed down as a result of pressure from the Earl of Tyrone. Reacting to Docwra's vigorous complaints about the fisheries issue, Mountjoy responded: 'You see what promise I have made to my lord of Tyrone, and it is not my private affection to any man living that shall make me break it, because I know it is for the public good.'[121] Exchanges between Mountjoy and Docwra about the failure to honour the promises which had been made to O'Cahan were just as acrimonious. Noted as a man 'very fond of fair play',[122] Docwra was to be every bit as mortified by the treatment accorded O'Cahan. 'How shall I look this man in the face?' he demanded of Mountjoy. Mountjoy's response was far from complimentary to O'Cahan, whom he branded a 'drunken fellow ... so base'. Docwra, to his credit, argued that O'Cahan's character deficiencies were not the point at issue, rather the agreement with him should have been honoured.[123] Despite Docwra's solicitations, O'Cahan's proprietorial claims were rejected out of hand. On hearing the news, O'Cahan 'bade the Devil take all English men, and as many as put their trust in them'.[124] As events turned out, O'Cahan did not take his own advice, once more succumbing to the blandishments of crown officials much less honourable than Docwra in the years preceding the Flight of the Earls.

In the wake of Kinsale, while Tyrone was on the ropes, his successful policy of ducking and weaving had prolonged the war sufficiently for him to be in a position to seek terms. Besides, Elizabeth I was dying. Cecil and her other leading advisers became ever more keenly conscious of the problem of the English succession and the likelihood that it would fall to James VI of Scotland, a monarch suspected by many in English court circles of having connived at Tyrone's rebellion, permitting hired mercenaries and supplies to reach the rebel forces via Scotland. Elizabeth's imminent death, it has been suggested, propelled the English authorities into agreeing to end the war on terms with Tyrone rather than permit the rebel leader to utilise the expedient of offering allegiance to a friendly new monarch and to claim that his quarrel had been with the provocative policies of his predecessor.[125] However, given the exceptionally favourable terms accorded to Tyrone by the English in the Treaty of Mellifont in 1603, it is difficult to envisage how much more propitious they could have been. The essential point is that Elizabeth was being forced to concede terms to Tyrone on her own account, despite her utter detestation of having to do so. Money had prevailed; the English state was not in a position to continue indefinitely with the war; and the stalemate had forced the hand of the ailing monarch. Interestingly in this respect, the English Privy Council admitted that it had been the wars in Ireland rather than in France and Spain which had impoverished England.[126] In the end, as Sir Arthur Chichester so appositely put it, Tyrone had been 'unfortunately and undeservedly ... received to grace and mercy, even out of the jaws of death'.[127]

Coming so soon after the decision to offer terms to Tyrone, the sudden death of Elizabeth I almost ruined the plans of the crown authorities. On Elizabeth's death, Mountjoy's commission as Lord Lieutenant of Ireland officially terminated. Technically, while he waited for a new commission from James I, Mountjoy was in no position to parley with Tyrone. Elizabeth's death having queered the pitch, Mountjoy resorted to a ruse by tricking Tyrone into believing that Elizabeth was still alive. Thus it was that on 30 March 1603 Tyrone formally submitted to a 'dead queen'.[128] It was to be several days before Elizabeth's death was publicly confirmed in Ireland, Tyrone weeping profusely on hearing the news.[129]

On a more positive note for Tyrone was the promulgation of the Act of Oblivion in 1604. Mountjoy had hit upon this device as a means of stabilising the situation in Ireland in the aftermath of the war, promising that all 'offences against the crown' committed before the accession of James I were to be 'pardoned, remitted, and utterly extinguished'.[130] Tyrone had been offered a fresh start.

Before long, however, the practicalities of the situation had undermined Mountjoy's act of statesmanship, and Tyrone was eventually forced to flee from Ireland in fear of his life. While the earl's secret post-war dealings with the Spanish and disaffected Old English Catholics contributed to this outcome, the appointment of Sir Arthur Chichester, his inveterate foe, as Lord Deputy of Ireland in 1605 proved to be of critical importance.

3

THE ABORTED FLIGHT OF AN EARL

The year 1603 marked the conclusion of a convulsive decade of war in Ireland during which time the very survival of English rule in Ireland had been seriously challenged. Lord Mountjoy had finally managed to prevail against the Earl of Tyrone's forces following his victory at the battle of Kinsale. However, Tyrone had not capitulated unconditionally, for he had successfully maintained a spirited rearguard action against a ravaging English military campaign which had resulted in large areas of Ulster being laid waste. Furthermore, at the very point of English military ascendancy the underlying debilitating effect of prolonged years of conflict in Ireland (as well as with Spain) had drained much of the life-blood of England, rendering crown policy anaemic. Tyrone was fully aware of the enervating effect that the war had had on England, noting that the 'English themselves admit that over seventy thousand of their numbers died in action and otherwise, and among these was lost the flower of their nobility and of their soldiers. England then became so poor that, instead of silver, brass money was coined.'[1] Overall, Tyrone signified his awareness that the English had been exhausted by the war.[2] Thus, as the remarkably favourable terms granted to the earl on 30 March 1603 by the Treaty of Mellifont indicated, war-weariness had resulted in the English being unable to press home their military advantage to secure an unconditional capitulation by Irish forces. Tyrone, moreover, had not been forced to seek safety in exile.

That Tyrone had not fled in the inauspicious circumstances preceding the conclusion of the conflict in 1603 demonstrates clearly that, far from becoming resigned to a life abroad, he had decided that his position remained tenable in Ireland. The settlement reached at Mellifont indicated that the English as much as the confederate Irish had become a spent force as a result of sustained conflict. On the English side, this was soon evidenced by the fact that the English army in Ireland was reduced by financial constraints to a skeleton force of just over 1,000 men by 1606.[3] Such was the level of underfunding of the English garrison in Ireland at that time that Lord Deputy Chichester was to remark that 'If the soldiers should be continued as now they are, they would become a scorn and occasion of laughter to this people, rather than a bridle to restrain and keep in awe such as are ill affected.'[4] In the short term, of course, Tyrone had to come to terms with a weakened position, much of his territory having been devastated by the English scorched-earth policy. His military capacity had been greatly reduced. The dynamics of the situation in 1603 illustrated, however, that much remained to be played for as far as the Earl of Tyrone was concerned, not least when the Old English in the Munster towns launched what has become known as the 'recusant revolt' of 1603, a major turning-point in the history of Catholic Ireland. (Recusant was the contemporary term for those who refused to attend the services of the Protestant established church. In other words, at that time Catholic and recusant were interchangeable terms.)

On the death of Elizabeth I in March 1603, James VI of Scotland acceded to the English throne as James I. Though a Protestant, as the son of the Catholic Mary Queen of Scots, James was widely considered in Ireland to be sympathetic to the Catholic cause. He was even rumoured to be a closet Catholic. The Old English Catholics were convinced that religious toleration would be granted. Indeed, such were the expectations attendant on James's accession that they account for the fact that the Old English Catholics generally remained loyal to the English crown during the late war, despite the fact that Tyrone claimed that he had been championing the 'Catholic' cause. Traditional rivals of the Gaelic Irish since the twelfth century, the Old English, descendants of the original Anglo-Norman settlers, may well have suspected, as the contemporary chronicler Fynes Moryson alleged, that Tyrone had been employing the clarion call of religion as 'the cloak of ambition'.[5] Besides, what reason had the Old English to revolt when their objective appeared to be within certain grasp? Religious toleration, they believed, would surely ensue on James's accession. There was no reason to take risks in these circumstances, not least because the horrific experiences of the Catholic crusades of the FitzMaurice revolt and the Desmond rebellion in the 1570s and 1580s in Munster were still fresh in popular memory. The poet Edmund Spenser, an eyewitness to the events, described the horrific scenes of famine:

> Out of every corner of the woods and glens they came creeping forth upon their hands, for their legs could not bear them; they looked anatomies of death; they spake like ghosts crying out of their graves; they did eat of the dead carrions, happy were they could find them; yea, and one another soon after insomuch as the very carcasses they spared not to scrape out of their graves; and if they found a plot of water cress or shamrocks, there they flocked as to a feast for the time, yet not able long to continue there withal; that in short space there were none almost left, and a most populous and plentiful country suddenly left void of man and beast.[6]

Little wonder that the Old English of the Munster towns and elsewhere preferred to sit tight with the sands of time flowing so rapidly in their favour as Elizabeth succumbed to advancing age.

Such was the degree of expectancy that toleration would be granted in 1603 that the recusants in the Munster towns could hardly contain themselves. According to a government account of the ensuing events,

> Upon the first report of Queen Elizabeth's death, the citizens of Waterford, Cork and Limerick, etc., took arms, banished the [Protestant] ministers out of their towns, and in their rooms massing priests were placed, divers of His Majesty's good servants and subjects imprisoned, officers of the army and of justice contemptuously used, the magazines of ammunitions and victuals seized upon, and converted to their own use, forts razed, sundry of His Majesty's soldiers slain; and to be brief, nothing was left undone, what in their malice and weakness they were able to effect.[7]

It was a measure of the recusants' defiance that they proclaimed ancient municipal liberties even as Mountjoy marched south to reassert the authority of the crown administration in Dublin. Refused entry by the residents of Waterford on the basis of a charter granted by King John, Mountjoy was famously to retort that he would 'cut King John's charter … with King James his sword'.[8] The recusant revolt in Munster was soon subdued. However, it had long-term implications. William Meade, the recorder of Cork, had been the ringleader of the recusant revolt in the city. When the revolt was suppressed, Meade achieved folk-hero status, 'preferring that he alone should die for all the citizens, than that all should perish with him, avowed himself the sole instigator and leader of the rebellion and prime mover therein'.[9] He was brought to trial, but a sympathetic jury refused to convict him, though they paid a heavy price. Prosecuted in the Court of Castle Chamber in June 1604, the foreman was fined 1,000 marks, while the individual jurors were fined £500 apiece — huge sums. They were also instructed to parade publicly wearing papers acknowledging their offence of perjury at the 'four courts' being held in Drogheda and at the next general sessions in Cork.[10] Having narrowly escaped with his life, Meade journeyed to the Spanish court in 1603, claiming to be a representative of Irish Catholics who had been delegated to 'represent to Your Majesty [Philip III] their misery, persecutions and troubles'. While the Spanish responded by saying that they were unable to come to the aid of Irish Catholics at that time, Meade was considered a person who 'in case of necessity … could cause many cities of Ireland to rally to its [the Catholic religion's] defence'.[11] The significant point, though, was that a realignment in Old English loyalties, away from the English crown and towards Spain, was taking place.

Mountjoy's robust response had quelled the recusant revolt. As events were to prove, however, the aspirations of the Old English were to be even more cruelly dashed by King James's subsequent record (as they viewed it) of tolerating the persecution of Irish Catholics rather than granting religious toleration. While

James was personally opposed to persecution, he was hamstrung by the complexities of his new position as King of England, a fervently Protestant country. He was bitterly resented by many Englishmen as an interloping Scot. A campaign of character assassination employed allegations of repulsive personal manners, inertia and homosexual tendencies to fabricate an all-round image of a 'lamentable creature'.[12] Even James's legendary passion for the hunt was ridiculed by xenophobic Englishmen, who claimed that 'when hunting, the king did not dismount in order to relieve himself, and so habitually ended the day in a filthy and stinking condition'.[13] In this hostile climate, had James encouraged allegations of favouring popery, there is every possibility that he could have gone the way of his grandson, James II, who was to lose the throne of England. Offering toleration to Irish Catholics, therefore, was out of the question.

Quite apart from the sensitive issue of freedom of worship, the pardoning of Tyrone was a sore point in King James's new kingdom. In 1603 England and Wales were still reeling from the enormous human and financial price that had been paid to subdue Tyrone's revolt. The Earl of Tyrone was to witness this at first hand when he accompanied Mountjoy (soon to be elevated to the title of Earl of Devonshire) on the latter's triumphant return to the court of King James. Tyrone was depicted by an English contemporary as the 'trophy of his [Mountjoy's] former endeavours'.[14] It was to be an eventful journey from the start. The royal ship carrying the illustrious passengers, the *Tramontana*, almost met with disaster in a dense mist as it plied its way from the coast of Ireland. A sudden raucous outcry of seagulls alerted the captain to imminent danger, the rocks off Skerries suddenly looming into sight. A timely manoeuvre by the helmsman averted disaster, but not without the smaller boat tied to the stern actually striking crags protruding from the deep. Rocks of a different type were subsequently to menace Tyrone's safety as he journeyed through Wales. Relatives of dead soldiers, mainly women, hurled stones and mud at Tyrone, Mountjoy having to step in to offer protection.[15]

Tyrone's reception at court was much more hospitable. He even went hunting with James I.[16] Not surprisingly, this provoked outrage. Sir John Harrington, captured this mood when he recounted how

> I have lived ... to see that damnable rebel Tyrone brought to England, honoured, and well liked. ... How I did labour after that knave's destruction! I adventured perils by sea and land, was near starving, ate horseflesh in Munster, and all to quell that man, who now smileth in peace at those who did hazard their lives to destroy him: and now doth Tyrone dare us old commanders with his presence and protection.[17]

The reality was, however, that a lingering dread of Tyrone the bogeyman permeated the entire London administration. The earl may have been forced from the field of battle, but his potential for stirring up renewed conflict was to remain a constant source of anxiety at the court of King James. It was for this reason that James (but not crown officials in Ireland) wished to humour him from the start. This was manifested by Tyrone's success in utilising his visit to court to frustrate a design to have a powerful crown official known as a 'president' created in Ulster, the earl emerging as the 'real victor of the negotiations in London'.[18] Equally apparent, though, was the fact that intrigue enveloped Tyrone's every move. Father James Archer, an Irish Jesuit and known conspirator, was reported to have visited Tyrone at his lodgings in London. This was regarded as an ominous sign.[19] Just as portentously, from an English point of view, was the fact that a petition was signed by 'all the principal men of that kingdom [Ireland] then in England' seeking toleration of religion. It was presented to the king by the Earl of Tyrone.[20] This was hardly the conduct of a cowed leader, a man contemplating a life in exile, but one who had confidence that he had a position to bargain from and was prepared to run risks to protect the interests of the Catholic religion in Ireland. Indeed, as events proved, it was partly because he ran a series of such risks that the Flight of the Earls ultimately took place.

On returning to Ireland, the Earl of Tyrone and his followers had to cope with the devastation that had resulted from war. However else he intended to bring pressure to bear on the crown, there was little prospect of renewed revolt in the short term. In November 1603 Sir Arthur Chichester reported that 'extreme famine' prevailed in the north.[21] By the spring of 1604 the earl was residing with his family at Drogheda, from where he had reportedly petitioned the crown authorities in Dublin to order that all his tenants who had fled from the north should return home.[22] The task of repopulating and replenishing Ulster was about to begin. And at first the indications were that the earl was generally intent on becoming the model citizen. In June 1604 he had co-operated in flushing out rebels and outlaws in Ulster, not even sparing one of his own nephews, whom he hanged. During the subsequent winter of 1604 no part of Ulster was described as so law-abiding as the Earl of Tyrone's territory. He even provided assistance for the victualling of the English garrison in the north.[23] The only incident betraying a lingering hostility to the English administration involved Tyrone utilising his martial law commission to hang one of Sir Henry Docwra's messengers for robbing a priest.[24] This incident reflected the earl's desire to act as defender of the Catholic Church in Ireland, a role which ultimately implicated him in renewed treasonable machinations when a policy of persecution was later embarked upon by the crown authorities. Overall, though, despite this summary execution, the impression prevails that in the early stages after the war Tyrone was quietly rebuilding his position. And while Mountjoy's immediate successor, the aged and infirm Lord Deputy Carey, remained in charge[25] there was little threat to his position, apart from some nagging proprietorial controversies involving certain Englishmen, including army officers, who had acquired abbey lands on his territories by 'underhand' means.[26] His tactic for counteracting the hostility of crown officials in Ireland was apparent from the start. Claiming he could not get 'redress here', Tyrone took his case over the heads of the Dublin administration and made a direct appeal for justice to the English Secretary of State, Robert Cecil, now elevated to the distinction of Viscount Cranbourne.[27] But for financial hardship, Tyrone indicated that he would personally have travelled to England to raise his concerns with the king.[28] Threatening to appeal directly to King James was a tactic that the earl resorted to repeatedly over subsequent years in an endeavour to apply pressure on the Dublin authorities.

Overall, the lethargic pace of crown reforms in Ireland attendant on Carey's period in office, 1603–5, during which time the Lord Deputy was reputedly more concerned with acquiring a personal fortune by dubious methods rather than with the pressing requirements of government,[29] redounded to Tyrone's favour as he sought to reconsolidate his position. Had this situation prevailed for much longer, the fruits of the so-called English conquest of Ireland could soon have dissipated as Tyrone grew stronger. Indeed, it is arguable that Ireland had not been conquered by the English in 1603 but quietened. It would not have been the first time that English 'conquerors' had found their power base receding — witness the gradual reduction in areas once controlled by the original Anglo-Norman settlers of the twelfth century. It is highly significant in this respect that despite the devastation which had occurred during the war, Tyrone's wealth recovered rapidly, his lands being worth almost £3,000 annually by 1610, a huge sum at the time.[30]

The rot pervading the crown administration in Ireland was dramatically arrested by the appointment of Sir Arthur Chichester as Lord Deputy in 1605. In tandem with Sir John Davies, the Irish Attorney General, the new Lord Deputy embarked on a programme to civilise Ireland, to bring the 'benefits and blessings' of English law to the 'ignorant' Irish.[31] Neither Chichester nor Davies, as it happens, were particular role models for advertising civilised, law-abiding behaviour. As a young man Arthur Chichester had had to abscond to Ireland after becoming involved in a local 'faction fight' in his native Devon. The incident was treated sufficiently seriously for him to be summoned before the English Privy Council. Chichester, in disgrace, lay low for a number of years as a result.[32] John Davies's youth was similarly tainted, as he had been expelled from the Middle Temple in London and jailed for a time for having assaulted a fellow law student.[33]

Whatever about Chichester's questionable conduct during his youth, there can be no doubt that after he assumed the deputyship in February 1605 the pace of governmental activity in Dublin suddenly began to proceed at break-neck speed.[34] The backlog of work that had built up owing to the 'retiredness' of Carey and a prolonged period when disease ravaged Ireland was promptly attended to.[35] After that, Chichester could concentrate on his own priorities. Significantly, one of the very first policies resolved upon was embodied in a proclamation forbidding the bearing of arms on pain of confiscation,[36] an overt effort to 'decommission' the weaponry of the 'swordsmen', the semi-professional soldiers who provided much of the basis of the Earl of Tyrone's military might. That the Earl of Tyrone soon found himself coming even more directly within the sights of the martial Lord Deputy was also no surprise. After all, this was the same Chichester who had been a pathological enemy of Tyrone from the days of the Nine Years War, the man who considered it a personal crusade to have Tyrone beheaded. Thus Chichester's appointment dramatically changed the complexion of affairs confronting Tyrone. The new deputy's abrasive, militarily efficient approach soon gave rise to a heightening of tensions. For a time, however, a renewed bout of the plague hampered Chichester's activities, preventing him from returning to Dublin in September 1605 following his tour of much of the province of Ulster.[37] Nonetheless, from the outset of his term of office the Lord Deputy emphasised the need for underpinning the military conquest of Ireland:

> As soon as there is a taste of quiet, the erecting of citadels, castles, forts, planting of towns and corporations, are presently thought a superfluous charge: but without these the kingdom is as open to new rebellion as it was before the last troubles, and as apt to entertain a new Robin Hood as ever in their lives.[38]

Clearly the Lord Deputy feared that a parsimonious royal policy endangered the consolidation of the conquest. Not only that, but it soon became apparent from what quarter Chichester considered that the threat to English hegemony emanated — the northern lords in particular. As it turned out, the Lord Deputy endeavoured to make up for the lack of adequate funding by maintaining close vigilance on those whom he regarded with suspicion.

Confronted by a hostile Lord Deputy who had embarked on a major tour of Ulster during the summer of 1605, the northern lords had to be on their toes in dealing with him. As far as the Earl of Tyrone was concerned, Chichester's immediate objective of seeking to undermine him by creating independent freeholders in Ulster was readily circumvented. The earl simply nominated trusted relatives.[39] The results of Chichester's perambulation through Ulster during 1605 were to prove more menacing for Tyrone in the longer term. Legal officials had spent much time carrying out furtive investigations into Tyrone's proprietorial entitlements. As a result, the rival claims of Donal O'Cahan, Tyrone's son-in-law, were targeted as a potential means of prising a huge wedge of land in the north, known as O'Cahan's country, from Tyrone's control.[40] Unaware of this strategem as yet, the Earl of Tyrone was to find himself embroiled in a head-on collision with the new Lord Deputy before the year 1605 elapsed. A proclamation was issued on 24 October 1605 banishing the Catholic clergy from Ireland and ordering all the laity to attend Protestant services.[41] For the Earl of Tyrone, the self-proclaimed champion of Catholicism in Ireland, Chichester's embarkation on a policy of persecution was to act like a red rag to a bull. Even if, in the initial stages, mainly Old

English Catholic areas were to be targeted by the crown authorities, Tyrone was infuriated by this development, as soon became apparent.

In Chichester's opinion, Old English and Gaelic Irish Catholics were equally disloyal. The cities and towns, which were predominantly Old English, were described as 'infected with the rest' by treasonable intentions.[42] The reality was that the vast majority of the Old English were innately loyal to the crown but were to be antagonised into entertaining treasonable designs by Chichester's campaign of religious persecution. The Lord Deputy could not fathom that the Old English were genuinely predisposed to owe allegiance to the English crown when they would not conform to the established Protestant religion of their king. This was a time when the convention 'one king, one religion' prevailed throughout Europe, whether in Protestant or Catholic countries. The uniqueness of the Old English position was not appreciated, with political, linguistic and cultural ties with the English crown stretching back to the twelfth century. It was precisely this umbilical cord linking the Old English and the crown that underpinned their reluctance to assist Tyrone during the Nine Years War. As far as Chichester and other crown officials were concerned, nonetheless, the descendants of the original English colonists had become corrupted, not least by their religion. This background helps to explain the highly charged exchanges which took place when Sir Patrick Barnewall, a leading Old English spokesman (and, it is worth noting, a brother-in-law of the Earl of Tyrone), was summoned to appear before the Lord Deputy and Council in November 1605 for contumaciously objecting to what has become known as the 'Mandates policy', a campaign of religious persecution which aimed to break the resistance of prominent members of the Catholic laity to conformity. Barnewall having being sentenced to imprisonment, a telling interchange occurred between him and the Lord Deputy:

> 'Well,' said he [Barnewall], 'we must endure as we have endured many other things.'
> 'What mean you by that?' said the deputy; 'what have you endured?'
> 'We have endured', said he [Barnewall], 'the miseries of the late war, and other calamities besides.'
> '*You* endured the miseries of the late war!' said the deputy. 'No, sir, *we* have endured the misery of the war, *we* have lost our blood and our friends, and have indeed endured extreme miseries to suppress the late rebellion, whereof *your* priests ... and *your* wicked religion, was the principal cause.'[43]

The circumstances in which the Mandates policy was launched, therefore, were fraught with tension. 'Mandates' were letters sent in the name of the king to specified individuals ordering them to attend Protestant worship on pain of prerogative punishment, effectively punishment at the discretion of the deputy and government. Chichester decided to begin the policy in Dublin, 'the lantern of this whole kingdom'.[44] Sixteen wealthy individuals, including aldermen, were targeted. On failing to abide by the terms of the Mandates, they were summoned to appear before the Court of Castle Chamber in Dublin, 'a fearsome instrument'.[45] The proceedings were scheduled to take place on 22 November 1605. As it happened, this almost, though not exactly, coincided with news being received from England of the Gunpowder Plot when Guy Fawkes and his fellow Catholic conspirators attempted to assassinate the king and his ministers in parliament. Evidence suggests that Chichester received the news on 20 November but concealed it even from members of the Irish Privy Council until the 22nd.[46] The deputy's purpose was plain. He was going to employ the release of the news for full dramatic effect at the trial of the leading recusants. The proceedings in Castle Chamber were interrupted when letters bearing news of the Gunpowder Plot had supposedly just been received, Chichester ordering 'at that instant' that the Lord Chancellor read them to the assembly.[47] The chilling effect can only be imagined. Certainly the defendants in the dock must have greatly feared the fate that lay in store for them. As events turned out, fines ranging up to the massive sum of £100 were imposed (the normal penalty for recusancy was a fine of one shilling), while they were also imprisoned 'till they conformed themselves'.[48]

Chichester was already notorious for his corrosive hatred of the Catholic religion and particularly its clergy, whom he was determined to eradicate by 'fire and sword',[49] and the receipt of the news of the Gunpowder Plot can only have intensified the fury of his persecuting zeal, a characteristic which earned him a contemporary reputation among Irish Catholics as a reincarnated Nero.[50] The confrontational mood of the deputy pervaded the iconoclastic zeal of the rampaging troops who raided the homes of those penalised in an endeavour to raise the fines that had been levied. A contemporary account provides a graphic illustration of Catholic perceptions of the activities of the troops:

> No doors, no enclosures, no walls can stop them in their course: they are unmoved by the shrieks of the females and by the weeping of the children. Everything is torn open, and whatever is of any value is set aside to be taken away, whatever is worthless is thrown in the streets, and devoted to the flames. Silver cups are called chalices, and gems are designated Agnus Deis, and all are, therefore, carried away. Whatever is for profane uses, they profess to regard as sacred, and bear it off, and whatever is sacred they seize on to desecrate.[51]

Not unnaturally, the Catholic Old English were incensed by such activities. Thoughts were evidently turning towards revolt. It was with immense fortitude, in the circumstances, that Tyrone's brother-in-law Sir Patrick Barnewall articulated their sentiments in a letter to Robert Cecil, now Earl of Salisbury, the English Secretary of State.[52] Barnewall made it clear to Salisbury that 'by this unlawful course of proceeding ... even now are laid down the foundations of some future rebellion'.[53] For raising his head above the parapet in daring to challenge Chichester's conduct and in orchestrating a petition protesting against the Dublin government's penal policy, Barnewall was to serve a lengthy period of imprisonment, first in Ireland before being transferred to England, where he was ultimately incarcerated in the Tower of London.[54]

The Lord Deputy was not in the least concerned by Barnewall's warning. Indeed, that Chichester had been anticipating a violent response to his religious policies was revealed by the fact that he had placed his troops on a high state of alert following his embarkation on the Mandates policy. He had spies 'in all quarters' and troops on alert 'to take any opportunity if it be offered'.[55] Such was the degree of disorder in Dublin precipitated by the deputy's religious policy that Chichester eventually employed a provost marshal in an endeavour to suppress Catholic religious activities. In particular, he was concerned by the 'continual flocking of priests, seminaries and Jesuits into that town, drawing and alluring the citizens there to privy masses and private meetings, notwithstanding many proclamations and warnings given by the deputy and state for the contrary'.[56] Chichester was not one to brook such insolence, and he was prepared to exercise the full weight of martial law to stamp it out. That his strategy was a personally high-risk one was later to be revealed by suggestions that conspirators had targeted him and his right-hand man, Sir Oliver Lambert, for assassination. 'Along with his Lordship [Chichester], or before, the first opportunity will be taken to cut off Sir Oliver Lambert. These two lights thus put out, they fear not any in the kingdom.'[57] But neither the personal dangers involved, nor the reduction of the royal garrison in Ireland to a 'police force' of just over 200 cavalry and less than 900 infantry, could deter the Lord Deputy from persisting with his confrontational approach.[58] Chichester, it must be borne in mind, was a courageous soldier who had made his mark for personal bravery on the international stage. His knighthood had been bestowed on him in 1597 by the French king for valour during a period of military service in Picardy, and he had also distinguished himself in battle during the last voyage of Sir Francis Drake, the doyen of Elizabethan adventurers.[59]

And what of the Earl of Tyrone while the controversy associated with the implementation of the Mandates policy was unfolding? The records show that he was in Dublin at the time. A rumour circulating in England shortly afterwards reported that Tyrone remonstrated with Lord Deputy Chichester about his religious policy, the altercation being so serious that Chichester subsequently decided to arrest him. Forewarned (Tyrone had a reputation for having agents or sympathisers in key positions), the earl hastily decamped from Dublin without the deputy's leave, a signal breach of protocol.[60] That the incident had been a serious one is revealed by the fact that the Dublin government was so worried about Tyrone's behaviour that Sir Toby Caulfield, a senior army officer living in County Tyrone, made repeated efforts to have a 'conference' with the Countess of Tyrone to fathom her husband's intentions. According to Caulfield's account, he failed on several occasions during January

1606 until Tyrone travelled back to the Pale, 'and then she [the Countess of Tyrone] sent for him [Caulfield] chiefly to inquire what he [the Earl of Tyrone] had done in Dublin'.[61] With hindsight, Tyrone's return to the Pale, the heartland of the Old English, but within relatively easy striking distance of a hostile Lord Deputy, may be considered important in the context of the conspiratorial machinations which were to provide the backdrop to the Flight of the Earls. Investigations by the crown authorities into Tyrone's conduct suggested that the earl was a primary participant in a plot involving the Old English to overthrow the Dublin government from the time of the 'powder treason', i.e. November 1605.[62] Significantly, following the Flight, Tyrone admitted that disillusioned Old English Catholics, including the 'principal gentlemen who served the Queen of England against us in the last war', had solicited help from himself and Rory O'Donnell, Earl of Tyrconnell, to counteract the hostile policies of the crown administration. The Earl of Tyrconnell, it was admitted, had had 'secret dealings' with them.[63] A 'league' was then formed whereby all involved swore to 'take up arms and remain faithful to this league ... until the deliverance of their country from heresy and tyranny'. Plans were then set afoot to 'surprise certain places of importance held by the enemy'.[64] Quite apart from the domestic aspect of treason in which the earls were involved, Spanish records show that they were engaged in disloyal practices at an international level as well. From as early as 1604 they were actively engaged in negotiating a 'treasonable contract' with the Spanish authorities whereby, in exchange for receiving a substantial retainer, the Earls of Tyrone and Tyrconnell signified their willingness to embark on a new revolt in Ireland should the Spanish so wish.[65]

Chichester was thus not chasing conspiratorial spectres conjured up by his own rabid imagination. His major problem was that while he suspected the earls, he could not categorically prove their involvement in treason. But it was not for the want of trying. It is this context of uncertainty and suspicion that explains why a worried administration went so far as to resort to the direct strategem of interviewing the countess about her husband's activities. From the point of view of the Dublin government, the marital difficulties that the earl and his countess were then experiencing played into their hands.[66] Sir Niall Garbh O'Donnell, a prominent figure in Ulster society, later recorded that Tyrone had been 'determined to put away his countess' and had gathered all the priests in the area to sanction it. According to Niall Garbh, 'the countess told him [the Earl of Tyrone] plainly, that if he desisted not from such courses against her, she would discover him so far as to infer again to rebellion or to lose his head'.[67] Certainly the conduct of the countess during her conversation with Caulfield confirms that she was intensely unhappy with the earl's treatment of her. She began the conversation by pouring out her heart to Caulfield, using 'many bitter and malicious speeches' against her husband, 'recounting many violences which he had used and done to her in his drunkenness'. Had she the money to buy a hundred cows, she declared, she would leave the earl. Caulfield was delighted at finding her in that 'good humour for his purpose'. Coming straight to the point, Caulfield advised the countess to 'purchase protectors from her husband's tyranny, and to be revenged on him for all his injuries at once' by giving 'secret notice if she knew of any practice the earl had in hand against the peace of that kingdom'. However, Caulfield was to be disappointed by her answer. The countess made it abundantly plain that 'if she knew any such, she would not for all the world, however much she hated him, be known to accuse him of anything that should endanger his life'. She was prepared to acknowledge in general terms, though, that she had heard her husband and his friends 'talk angrily against the king ... and that they hoped the world would be better for them shortly'. Also, interestingly, in view of subsequent events, the countess described the Earl of Tyrconnell, Cúchonnacht Maguire of Fermanagh and other northern lords as 'altogether upon her husband's council'.[68] In retrospect, Caulfield's conduct has attracted considerable historical controversy. Not surprisingly, nationalist writers have roundly condemned these underhand dealings. Sean O'Faolain, in his inimitable style, commented on how Caulfield had been delegated to 'worm himself into the confidence of the countess and trap her into damaging admissions',[69] while C. P. Meehan went even further in affirming that in the 'records of infamy there is no baser exploit than the one referred to'.[70] Writing from a unionist perspective, Cyril Falls astutely observed that Meehan's treatment of the affair omitted all mention of the countess's complaints about 'her husband's brutality and drunkenness'.[71] For what it is worth, Chichester acknowledged the impropriety of the transaction, commenting that it may well have been considered a 'very uncivil and uncommendable part to feed the humour of a woman to learn the secrets of her husband'. However, he justified his decision on the grounds of his 'zeal to the king's safety'.[72]

Following the dramatic incidents contingent upon the launch of the Mandates policy and Tyrone's reaction to it, the sense of crisis abated somewhat during the first half of 1606. In part this resulted from the London government's failure to lend its wholehearted support to the viceroy's religious policy. Fearing the possibility of revolt, Chichester was instructed to moderate his activities. As a result, the pace of the Mandates policy temporarily slackened, with an attendant reduction in tensions.[73] As for the Earl of Tyrone, on the surface he had reverted to the dutiful subject, disingenuously describing Chichester to the king as 'very upright'.[74] He even lent the Dublin government £266.[75] However, by the time the Lord Deputy returned to Ulster during the summer of 1606 the conspiratorial mist rising over Ireland thickened once more. It has been suggested that the death of the Lord Lieutenant of Ireland, the Earl of Devonshire (formerly Lord Mountjoy), in April 1606 deprived Tyrone of his 'supporter' at court.[76] Certainly the immediate events that ensued following the Lord Lieutenant's demise suggested that the vultures were beginning to circle the northern earls. Before long it became clear that prominent individuals were lobbying the London administration to create a 'president' of

Ulster, a powerful official whose appointment would have threatened to undermine Tyrone's position in the north. Chichester was particularly keen to obtain the post for himself.[77] (Interestingly, Tyrone was reputed to have an agent in London, a Jesuit priest operating under an alias, who 'continually' advised the earls of all developments.)[78]

Events since 1603 demonstrate that Devonshire had tempered the aggressive disposition of Chichester's administration. In particular, he was opposed to persecution, this stance being taken for practical as well as ideological reasons. Of religious coercion he remarked in 1603 that 'I am persuaded that a violent course therein will do little good to win men's consciences ... and it is most sure that it will breed a new war.'[79] He also favoured a more gradualist approach to truncating the political power of the Earl of Tyrone.[80] He had, it is true, been fully alert to the dangers which might ensue in event of Tyrone's restoration to his former powerful position, as intimated by the Lord Lieutenant's former secretary, Fynes Moryson:

> This most worthy Lord [Devonshire] cured Ireland from the most desperate estate in which it ever had been, and brought it to the most absolute subjection in which it ever had been since the first conquest thereof by our nation. Yet he left this great work unperfect, and subject to relapse, except his successors should finish the building, whose foundation he had laid, and should polish the stones which he had only rough-hewed.[81]

Clearly Devonshire did not believe that the Mellifont settlement was immutable. Yet at the same time he did not wish to be provocative. The sudden frenzy of speculation about the proposed appointment of an Ulster president coming so soon after his death suggests that it was widely acknowledged at court that there was little prospect that such a post would be established while the Lord Lieutenant retained his influence over Irish affairs.

Regardless of the politics of the situation in England in 1606, the Earl of Tyrone was absolutely determined to do everything in his power to frustrate the designs of his enemies. Considering the establishment of an Ulster presidency as a major threat to his interests, Tyrone wrote to the king in June 1606 expressing his profound dissatisfaction with the proposal.[82] By September the earl had his answer. The English Privy Council instructed Chichester to inform him that 'the king had no thoughts of establishing such a government'.[83] The decision demonstrated that the earl's opinion carried some weight at court. While the London government remained inclined to humour the earl, Chichester and his colleagues in the Irish administration spent the summer of 1606 in Ulster, none too discreetly investigating suggestions that the northern lords, including Tyrone, were involved in planning treason. Chichester's hopes may have been dashed as far as the Ulster presidency was concerned; however, the crafty campaigner had not given up hope of outflanking his old adversary on another front.

For the Irish Attorney General, Sir John Davies, it was a source of great pride that Chichester undertook this important expedition attended by as few as 120 foot and 50 horse, whereas 'in former times (when the state enjoyed the best peace and security) no Lord Deputy did ever venture himself into those parts without an army of eight hundred or one thousand men'.[84] In his desire to praise the achievements of Chichester (and for that matter his own), Davies had conveniently omitted mentioning that the diminutive nature of the Lord Deputy's escort was in large part dictated by the fact that the entire royal garrison amounted to little over 1,000 men. Nevertheless, Davies was correct in stressing Chichester's comportment as a 'confident deputy'.[85] It took a brave man to lead such a small force into Ulster at a time when Ireland had been convulsed by the application of penal laws that had given rise to rumblings of revolt. Not only that, no one was under any illusions about Chichester's abiding hostility to the northern lords. That being acknowledged, the fact remained that the Lord Deputy enjoyed an awesome reputation as a military commander, and he was determined to show that the royal writ ran throughout the country. To this end, two 'notorious' thieves were executed at the first port of call, Monaghan. For Davies, 'their execution struck some terror in the best men of the country; for the beef, which they eat in their houses, is for the most part stolen out of the English Pale; and for that purpose, every one of them keepeth a cunning thief, which he calleth his cater'. Two 'principal gentlemen', Brian Óg MacMahon and Art MacRory MacMahon, who had been indicted for receiving such 'stealths', after 'acknowledging their faults upon their knees before my Lord Deputy, had their pardon granted unto them; so that I believe stolen flesh will not be so sweet to them hereafter'.[86] As events were to demonstrate subsequently, Art MacRory, described as 'an active and desperate fellow',[87] was by no means chastened by the experience. Indeed, it is likely that his feeling of humiliation arising from this incident led him to become involved in a plot in 1607 to seize Dublin Castle, no doubt with a desire to exact personal revenge on Chichester.[88]

During the summer of 1606 there were others in Ulster who clearly lived in fear of viceregal retribution. This was to be reflected by a flurry of activity as the viceroy's entourage made its way into Ulster. Chichester was to learn from Miler Magrath, the Protestant Archbishop of Cashel and foster-brother of Cúchonnacht Maguire,[89] who had been visiting Fermanagh on 'private' business, that the Earl of Tyrconnell and Cúchonnacht had fled the country, taking shipping at Killybegs. By implication, a treasonable complexion had been put on their activities. As it turned out, Tyrconnell and Maguire had not absconded, but Chichester's investigations into the affair convinced him that that had been their intention.[90] Tadhg O'Corkran, a scribe in the temporary employment of Cúchonnacht Maguire, provided the strongest evidence that flight had been planned, describing how Maguire had taken six shirts for the journey.[91] O'Corkran, however, was a servant of the aforementioned Magrath. A sprightly eighty-five-year-old, Magrath was a highly controversial personality, having offended a multitude of people throughout his long life, reputedly living until he was one hundred years of age. Magrath began his chequered career as a Franciscan friar, was appointed Catholic Bishop of Down and Connor, and then converted to Protestantism and was appointed to the see of Clogher, before his final translation to Cashel. The historian Cyril Falls, not normally given to emotive outbursts, described him as a 'drunken reprobate' that neither 'Catholic nor Reformed is entitled to boast of'.[92]

On the surface, there was little that would have endeared Magrath to the Lord Deputy, not least the fact that the archbishop's sons and sons-in-law residing in Cashel were described as 'obstinate recusants'. (The archbishop himself is reputed to have been considering converting back to Catholicism by 1617.)[93] Besides, the fact that Magrath's archiepiscopal cathedral in Cashel was contemporaneously compared to a pigsty would have appalled the pious Lord Deputy.[94] Nevertheless, the fact that Magrath had a foot in both camps, as it were, suited the ever-pragmatic Chichester, who would have appreciated his Catholic contacts in these circumstances. The archbishop having retained the lands of Termon-Magrath in County Fermanagh,[95] his contacts in the north were impressive. Following news of the abortive flight, Magrath took part in the deputy's investigations into the matter, not least by putting heavy pressure on O'Corkran to reveal all that he knew. O'Corkran was undoubtedly a reluctant informant. According to State Paper accounts of his interrogation, he had to be grilled twice by the Lord Deputy and his entourage before he revealed details of the aborted abscondence. The Earl of Tyrconnell was later to allege that O'Corkran had been brought 'secretly into the tent wherein he [Lord Deputy Chichester] slept, where he was bound and tortured with bed-cords, to the end he might charge the earl with something tending to the earl's overthrow and ruin, where he continued for the space of five days'.[96] Despite Tyrconnell's protestations about the manner in which the information was extracted from O'Corkran, the fact remains that he had indeed intended to flee abroad with Maguire. In later investigations into the intended flight, the Earl of Tyrone admitted to the Lord Deputy that the Earl of Tyrconnell and Maguire had been contemplating leaving the realm without formal permission. Tyrone commented on how 'passionate' Tyrconnell felt about his grievances, but added that he, Tyrone, 'dissuaded him from unbefitting courses', encouraging him instead to seek formal licence from the king to leave Ireland.[97] At this stage it is worth bearing in mind that while negotiations for a Spanish annuity for both the earls were at an advanced stage, it had not yet been finalised.[98] Tyrconnell, therefore, feeling vulnerable about his treasonable practices in Ireland, may have had the added incentive of seeking sanctuary abroad where profitable service in the army of the Catholic archduke in Flanders was enticing.[99]

O'Corkran's revelations about the aborted flight during the summer of 1606 convinced Chichester that treason had been practised, the viceroy expressing a particular concern about the communications between the alleged conspirators and expatriate Irishmen serving abroad.[100] Describing Cúchonnacht Maguire as a 'desperate and dangerous young fellow',[101] Chichester placed him under temporary arrest. The Earl of Tyrone later recorded how the Lord Deputy had 'specially very distinctly examined McGouire, and used many persuasions to him, to signify if he might lay any matters to his [Tyrone's] charge'.[102] As the plot thickened, one Farragh MacHugh O'Kelly, who had been arrested and charged with treason in Connacht, offered to 'reveal a present and dangerous plot of treason, to be executed by a great earl of this kingdom'. The Earl of Tyrconnell turned out to be the person in question, though O'Kelly insinuated that the Earl of Tyrone was also involved. Such was the importance attached to O'Kelly's testimony that he was granted a stay of execution because Chichester was so impressed by his credentials as an informant. The deputy described him as a 'notable murderer and a continual practiser of villainy and alterations; which gives the more credit to his informations, making it probable that they [the conspirators] would the sooner reveal their secrets unto him'.[103] Following the actual Flight of the Earls in September 1607, one of the Earl of Tyrconnell's list of grievances which he compiled afterwards was an allegation that O'Kelly 'was to be executed in Galway, whose life was offered unto him if he would accuse the earl, and, because he could not charge him with any crime, he was hanged'.[104] It is typical of the intrigue surrounding the events preceding the Flight of the Earls that, far from being executed, it is possible that O'Kelly was surreptitiously held in custody, with a view to bringing him forward as a witness in any potential treason trial. After he had been transferred to Dublin Castle a formal order was issued for his execution in November 1606, though it was never carried out.[105] In the aftermath of the Flight he was pardoned, having 'proved himself a very honest man in all his former reports and discussions concerning all those effects that have happened since his apprehension and imprisonment'.[106]

Chichester and Davies continued to apply pressure on Irish Catholics in general, and the northern lords in particular, at a time when there were ever-increasing suggestions that such provocation was contributing to the rebellious mood pervading the country. Thus, despite Cúchonnacht Maguire's manifest discontent, the Lord Deputy persisted with his efforts to seek defects in his proprietorial rights. This was demonstrated by a bizarre incident during the viceregal progress into Fermanagh during the summer of 1606. The royal party pitched camp and set up a 'canvas court-house' where the Lord Deputy was attended by judges adorned in 'scarlet robes'.[107] In the course of the proceedings it was learned from local inhabitants that an 'old parchment roll' existed detailing Maguire's rights. It was in the possession of 'one O'Bristan, a chronicler and principal brehon of that country', who lived close to the viceroy's camp. O'Bristan was duly summoned. He was described by Davies as 'so aged and decrepit, as he was scarce able to repair unto us'.[108] (Whether being the worse for drink had anything to do with O'Bristan's indisposition as well is unclear; Fynes Moryson characterised brehons as 'great swillers of

Spanish sack [wine] which the Irish merrily called the King of Spain's Daughter'.)[109] Barely managing to make his way into the viceroy's presence, the doddering old brehon was ordered to produce the parchment. Deeply disturbed by this demand, O'Bristan admitted that while he had once possessed the document in question, it had been burnt by English soldiers during the late war. However, some of the local inhabitants in attendance on the Lord Deputy contradicted him, claiming to have seen it after the war had ended. At this point the Irish Lord Chancellor exerted strong pressure on the feeble old brehon, placing him under oath to tell the truth about the parchment. According to Davies's account of the interview,

> The poor old man, fetching a deep sigh, confessed that he knew where the roll was, but that it was dearer to him than his life; and therefore he would never deliver it out of his hands, unless my Lord Chancellor would take the like oath, that the roll should be restored unto him again. My Lord Chancellor, smiling, gave him his word and his hand that he should have the roll redelivered unto him, if he would suffer us to take a view and a copy thereof. And thereupon the old brehon drew the roll out of his bosom, where he did continually bear it about him.[110]

Humorous as the incident may now seem, the reality was that a deadly serious power struggle was under way. Cúchonnacht Maguire had been on the verge of seeking sanctuary on the continent. The detailed investigations carried out by government officials into his private affairs revealed the hostility of the crown. As a result of his inquiries into the proprietorial rights of freeholders in Cavan, Monaghan and Fermanagh during the summer of 1606, Sir John Davies celebrated the achievements of the viceregal progress by remarking that 'This journey hath cut off three heads of the hydra of the north, namely, McMahown, McGuyre, and O'Relie.'[111] That Cúchonnacht Maguire fled to Europe little less than a year after this humiliating experience is not surprising.

Maguire was not the only person who was antagonised on a systematic basis. The catalogue of provocation offered to the Earl of Tyrconnell was extensive. Tyrconnell was later to complain bitterly about religious persecution, priests being 'daily pursued' by crown officials in his territories. Just as galling for Tyrconnell was the manner in which he alleged that Lord Deputy Chichester had publicly told him that he should 'resolve to go to [the Protestant] church, or else he should be forced to go thereto'. Royal officials, it was claimed, ran amok at times on his territories, and it was impossible to obtain redress for their actions from the Lord Deputy. In one particularly disturbing case, it was alleged that 'one Captain Ellis ravished a young maiden of the age of eleven years, in the earl's country, and caused two soldiers to hold her hands and legs until he had satisfied his lascivious desires'. Although Ellis had been found guilty in his absence by a jury, Tyrconnell asserted that Chichester had pardoned him. The pillaging of the earl's territories even included the theft of casts of hawks, highly prized assets at the court of King James I, where the sport of falconry was avidly pursued. According to Tyrconnell, in order to foster amicable relations with the viceroy, he annually sent Chichester hawks as a goodwill gesture. However, the Lord Deputy requested more than the usual allocation and wrote to Tyrconnell seeking some more. Having only three cast left, Tyrconnell nevertheless sent one of them to the Lord Deputy. Notwithstanding this generous offer, the Sheriff of Donegal had the remaining hawks seized. Tyrconnell, on a visit to Dublin, challenged the Lord Deputy about his hawks, expressing his acute displeasure, saying that he 'found himself more grieved at their loss in that nature than at all the injuries he had before received'. The Lord Deputy's alleged response was far from penitent, replying that 'he cared not a rush for him or his bragging words; warning him withal to look well to himself, in … threatening manner'. As far as the Earl of Tyrconnell was concerned, this was not an idle threat, as he asserted that he had only narrowly escaped assassination on his way to Dublin on a previous occasion. At the abbey of Boyle his lodgings were attacked by over twenty soldiers who attempted to burn the building down. Tyrconnell claimed that in the course of a night-long assault he had been wounded six times. The 'plot' to kill him, he alleged, had been engineered by Sir Oliver Lambert, the Lord Deputy's feared military henchman.[112]

In the early stages of his viceroyalty Chichester was more circumspect in his dealings with the Earl of Tyrone — despite the fact that he entertained an intense loathing of him. To some extent, this resulted from the fact that the Lord Deputy realised that he did not have the political backing in London for engaging in a more aggressive approach. It also reflected the fact that, of the two northern earls, Tyrone was considered a political heavyweight in comparison with Tyrconnell. To some degree too, Chichester's early relations with Tyrone were akin to shadow-boxing, each side testing out how formidable his opponent could be. All this was evidenced by the case brought by Sir John Sidney, who claimed abbey lands in Tyrone's territories. Sidney brought his case to the Lord Deputy, who spent seven days considering it, 'but the earl being so violent on the other side, it was made a matter of state not to displease him at that time'. At Sidney's continued insistence, the Lord Deputy consented to the appointment of a commission to investigate the issue. 'Then the earl, perceiving how it went against him, told the Lord Deputy that he would lose his head ere he (Sidney) should enjoy it quietly.' Despite this, Chichester granted Sidney an injunction to take possession of the lands in question. In the event, Sidney complained that he could not get possession of his castle, and also that in his absence Tyrone had sent his kern (light infantry) to harass Sidney's tenants and seize their goods.[113] The Earl of Tyrone, it was apparent, had no intention of submitting lightly to any infraction on his rights and was quite prepared to stand up to his formidable adversary, Lord Deputy Chichester.

In the course of time Chichester gradually increased the degree of provocation offered to the Earl of Tyrone. When the Mandates campaign was launched initially, northern areas were largely unaffected. As late as the end of 1606 Tyrone responded boldly to the accusation of an 'English heretic' that 'his palace was a monastery of religious, friars and priests; to whom the prince boldly made answer that so it should be till his death, let it please the other or not; that although he laid down his arms, he did not abandon his faith'. Under Tyrone's protection, fourteen friars lived in Dungannon, while Ulster was reputed to be the 'freest from persecution'.[114] But this situation was not to last much longer. The increasingly harsh policy pursued by Chichester is revealed in the case of a priest captured in Ulster who was offered a bishopric as an inducement to conform to the Protestant faith.

> To which he answered, that he would not abandon the Faith for all the bishoprics and goods in the world, and would rather suffer a thousand deaths than do such a thing. Seeing they could not prevail on him, they announced that with balls and blows they would give him the thousand deaths he spoke of: and so they formed themselves in a long file, and charging their guns, made the good priest pass between them and a wall; and as he ran along, they fired their guns at him. Before he got half way he fell down breathless and choked with smoke, though none of the balls struck him, and for three days he could not hear a word.[115]

Imprisoned in a dungeon, the priest was reportedly tied to a post and flogged for two days before having holes bored in his arms and legs in order to be tied up.[116]

That the Earl of Tyrone deeply resented the persecuting policies of the crown government is hardly surprising. Following the Flight of the Earls, Tyrone's list of twenty grievances was headed by his complaint that 'It was by public authority proclaimed in his manor of Dungannon that none should hear mass upon pain of losing his goods and imprisonment.'[117] This measure was particularly galling to Tyrone.[118] In view of his indignant response to the institution of the Mandates policy in Dublin, he was incandescent with rage at this public slight to his reputation as the champion of Catholicism in Ireland; even after the lapse of some time he was still expressing his profound sense of 'great resentment and anger'.[119] Equally intolerable were the persistent and unwelcome attentions of royal officials. As Sean O'Faolain remarked in his celebrated biography of Tyrone,

> Felon-setters, agents provocateurs, spies, petty officials of every kind dogged them [the earls] like shadows. Failing to get any evidence to support the story of a plot, Chichester egged on his men to badger his victims into some indiscretion that would justify him in proclaiming them traitors.[120]

Whereas O'Faolain was entirely correct in so eloquently articulating the degree of provocation offered to the earls, he failed to appreciate a crucial point. The earls had been engaged in treason. To some extent, of course, this culminated from the interminable incitement offered them by Chichester's administration. However, it must also be pointed out that they had been involved in treasonable negotiations for a Spanish annuity since 1604, before Chichester took office.[121]

While the enmity of the crown authorities in Dublin was palpable, Tyrone continued to enjoy a favourable hearing from the king himself. Writing in late August 1606, Sir Thomas Lake, a senior official at court with responsibility for Irish business, wrote to the Earl of Salisbury about the Earl of Tyrone's proprietorial affairs. The point at issue concerned disputed church lands. Lake signified that James was 'now so well informed of those things that he will do little by reference but answer of himself, that men may know it is his own judgment of his affairs that guides his tongue and not infusions from private persons'. Clearly the king was implying that Tyrone was being harassed legally as a subterfuge for the private ambitions of crown officials in Ireland. Acknowledging that legal records in Ireland were 'so ill kept', the king wanted Tyrone to detail his complaints and send an emissary to England to have his concerns aired at length. The earl's case would then be adjudicated by the king and council in London, rather than by referring him to 'the decision of the law merely' in Ireland. Once again James's suspicions of the motivation of crown officials in Ireland is transparent. Even more importantly, the king was worried about the potentially dangerous consequences of provoking Tyrone. Thus Lake commented that as James 'would not maintain Tyrone in any encroaching upon his subjects as were not fit, so he would wish all occasion to be taken from him of just complaint, considering what a dependency the Irish have on him and how ticklish their disposition is towards the state, and he an instrument apt to make innovation'.[122]

The tone of royal appeasement was marked. Writing in November 1606, Sir John Davies, the Irish Attorney General, noted that royal lands in Tyrone's hands had not been repossessed for reasons of state.[123] But while the king's message to the Irish administration had been received and ostensibly acted upon, the crown authorities in Ireland only paid lip-service to it. In almost the same breath in which he acknowledged the political expediency prevailing upon the king, Davies revealed that he had uncovered a major flaw in Tyrone's claims to 'O'Cahan's country', a large area covering most of present-day County Londonderry. Clearly the Attorney General could barely contain his excitement. The event that occasioned his outburst was a report that Tyrone 'had in a violent manner taken a great distress of cattle from O'Cahan, who hath married his [Tyrone's] bastard daughter'.[124] Davies's reference to the illegitimacy of Tyrone's daughter was not merely employed in the strictly legal sense of the term, but was intended as a deliberate insult to Tyrone, such was his hostility to the earl. That Tyrone resorted to force to assert his rights in relation to O'Cahan was a measure of his increasing frustration, displaying a fraying edge of his normally phlegmatic temperament. The pressures exerted by a hostile crown administration in Dublin were beginning to take their toll, and Tyrone's personal relations with the leading royal officials were becoming ever more strained. He particularly disliked the 'irreverent' manner of Attorney General Davies, whom he described as 'a man more fit to be a stage player than a counsel'.[125] And Tyrone was not the only one who found Davies repugnant. The Attorney General's personal appearance and antagonistic demeanour has been the subject of much comment. Davies was noted for his corpulence, 'pock-marked face, awkward carriage, and clumsy gait' and his tempestuous personality.[126] While such comments are far from complimentary, they pale in comparison with a contemporary English caricature which described how Davies 'goes waddling with his arse out behind him as though he were about to make everyone that he meets a wall to piss against ... he never walks but he carries a cloakbag behind him, his arse sticks out so far'.[127] Davies, not a sensitive type, was hardly the ideal government official for handling matters relating to Tyrone as James I desired.

The manner in which a succession of senior crown officials supported O'Cahan's case against the Earl of Tyrone was no accident. There was little personal sympathy for O'Cahan, who was generally considered as an individual displaying marked character deficiencies, a drunkard, a man who could be manipulated but not trusted. Indeed, at one point, during exchanges between O'Cahan and the Protestant Bishop of Derry, the bishop signalled his contempt for the Irish chieftain when he remarked that 'I will not trust you; for I know that one bottle of aquavitae [whiskey] will draw you from me to the earl.'[128] Rather, strategic considerations were paramount. The military capability of O'Cahan's country was of primary importance. It was reputed to be able to sustain an armed force of 400 foot and 140 horse and 'by reason of the neighbourhood of Scotland, heretofore best able to be supplied with necessary means for the continuance of a war'.[129] English military veterans of the Nine Years War reputed O'Cahan's men as their toughest opponents, having 'put them oftener to their defence and fight than any enemy they had to do withal, not suffering them to cut a bough to build a cabin without blows'. Indeed, Tyrone was to admit that O'Cahan's defection during the summer of 1602 had 'undone him, and that as long as he had his country behind him, he little cared for anything they could do to him before'.[130] The additional attraction for the Dublin government of O'Cahan's lawsuit against Tyrone was that it had taken on the character of a test case. Many other individuals were reported to be watching the case with interest 'who will, according to the success of this business, endeavour to procure their freedoms'.[131]

It was against this background of mounting challenges to Tyrone's proprietorial position, and in particular the targeting of O'Cahan, that George Montgomery, the newly appointed Protestant Bishop of Derry, Clogher and Raphoe, and a member of the Irish Privy Council, arrived in Ulster before the end of 1606. Montgomery was to acquire an avaricious reputation not only with Tyrone but also notably among fellow crown officials when the plantation of Ulster was being planned in the years 1608–10.[132] Having delayed coming to Ireland for some two years after his appointment,[133] Bishop Montgomery lost no time in asserting his proprietorial claims when he finally arrived, soon becoming embroiled in heated exchanges with his northern neighbour. On meeting him in Dungannon, Tyrone berated the bishop: 'My lord, you have two or three bishoprics, and yet you are not content with them, but seek the lands of my earldom.' The reply was just as acerbic. 'My Lord,' responded Montgomery, 'your earldom is swollen so big with the lands of the church that it will burst if it be not vented.'[134] The vexatious legal proceedings bedevilling Tyrone were about to shift to a higher plane. Montgomery was to play the role of instigator and O'Cahan that of the stooge, as the unfortunate Irish lord was later to realise. Having 'bade the Devil take all English men, and as many as put their trust in them' when he was double-crossed by the English at the end of the war in 1603,[135] O'Cahan had succumbed to the cajolery of crown officials once again. Events were to show that before long he would have reason to curse himself once again as he was to be duped a second time, though not without having played a key role in bringing about the Flight of the Earls in September 1607.

4

THE 'PASSION' OF TYRONE

Harassed by royal officials seeking flaws in his land grants, incensed by the persecuting zeal of the government, distraught by news that the Lord Deputy was scouring the land for potential witnesses that could be used to entrap him on allegations of treason, and agitated by persistent rumours that an Ulster presidency was on the verge of being instituted with Chichester installed as the royal governor of the north — such was the lot of the Earl of Tyrone by the end of the summer of 1606. In the circumstances, it is significant that Tyrone had not been reduced to desperation, to seeking sanctuary abroad with Tyrconnell and Maguire. Despite Kinsale and the suppression of his rebellion, Tyrone had clearly not resigned himself to abandoning his native land. He was widely renowned as a man of great personal courage, and his behaviour between Kinsale and the Flight demonstrated that he had lost none of his pluck. Tyrone's stoicism in the face of mounting adversity had been forged in the white heat of decades of crises and conflicts. It is clear, therefore, that his decision a year later to flee from Ireland with Tyrconnell and other compatriots was not taken lightly. Tyrone underwent a type of 'passion' as he contemplated his position before making his fateful decision, conscious that he had been betrayed, though he was unaware who it was that played the role of Judas Iscariot.[1] Thus the emergence of a well-placed crown informer, so often a feature of Irish history, proved to be the key to the events which unfolded. As it turned out, the Flight of the Earls, an extraordinarily important event in Irish history, was to occur in highly unusual, even bizarre circumstances. The informer, the mentally unstable Sir Christopher St Lawrence, having incriminated the earls, steadfastly refused in private conversations with crown officials to testify in public against them, preferring death to such a prospect. Therefore, in seeking to understand the reasons for the Flight of the Earls, we should bear it in mind that the event need never have taken place at all.

Tyrone, in spite of his tribulations, clung to hopes of salvation, not least because the aggressive disposition of the royal authorities in Dublin could not

have contrasted more with the salving inclinations of the London administration, a policy dictated in no small measure by the king himself, the com-
pulsively fretful James I. Significantly, it was made clear by the king before the
end of 1606 that Tyrone's fate in his ongoing proprietorial disputes was not to
be decided by a hostile administration in Dublin and it was by no means going
to be dictated by strict legal precedents, a major blow to the pervasive 'legal
imperialism' then so rampant among royal officials in Dublin.[2] Considerations
of state were clearly signified as superseding the law. Indeed, as if to reinforce
this point, the king recalled Tyrone's visit to London in 1603 when just such
politic considerations had dictated the decision on the issue of church lands
in the north and 'what the purpose was of tolerating them in his [Tyrone's]
hands for a time, to make exchange afterwards for lands lying near ports and
forts for his [the king's] service'.[3] Robert Cecil, Earl of Salisbury, dutiful
servant that he was, duly implemented the wishes of his royal master.[4] The
English Privy Council, over which the diminutive earl loomed large,[5] subsequently sent a letter to the authorities in Dublin which encapsulated the king's
desires, noting in particular that Tyrone should be 'relieved whenever it can be
done without injustice to others, by summary course that he might find the
effect of His Majesty's favour'. Interestingly, though, it was also signified that the
king was prepared to retreat somewhat from his 1603 position in the matter of
church lands, the claims of the Earls of Tyrone and Tyrconnell to abbey lands
being dismissed, 'as if such encroachments made in times of trouble could
extinguish His Majesty's interest'.[6] The arrival of George Montgomery, the
acquisitive new Protestant Bishop of Derry, Raphoe and Clogher during the
summer of 1606 served to intensify pressure on the earls with respect to
church lands.[7] Neither had Sir John Davies given up hope of finding flaws in
the land grants of the northern earls. He had, after all, utilised the summer
tour of Cavan, Monaghan and Fermanagh to undertake a snooping exercise in
relation to the possessions of the Earl of Tyrone as well. Officially he had been
investigating the proprietorial rights of freeholders among the MacMahons
of Monaghan, the Maguires of Fermanagh and the O'Reillys of Cavan. On
reflection, Davies argued that there were similar grounds for maintaining the
rights of freeholders on Tyrone's territories. If these claims were upheld, he
believed, the 'greatness of this earl will be moderate enough', and, that being
the case, Tyrone 'would not presume any more to write to the king (as lately
he did) not to make a President in Ulster for his sake only as if there were no
other lord in Ulster but himself'.[8]

For the time being, however, there was little prospect that the designs of
Chichester and Davies to cut the overmighty subjects of the north down to size
would find favour in London. The king and his advisers at court remained distinctly predisposed to treat the northern earls sensitively, a position that they
retained in spite of all the dramatic allegations of rumoured abscondings
and plots which had come to light in Ulster during the summer of 1606.
Responding to news of the aborted flight of the Earl of Tyrconnell, as well as

the insinuations that the northern earls were up to their necks in treasonable activities, the king chose not to work up a lather on either count. The English Privy Council wrote to the Lord Deputy accordingly. 'Considering that many of the better sort of that nation (being nursed up in rebellion) are apt to be discontented, and in particular quarrels are ready to accuse one another', the Dublin authorities were instructed to be 'more cold' in calling any of the accused Irish lords 'in question'. Specifically, the constant interchange of correspondence with the Irish exiles in the Netherlands was dismissed as of little account, 'as liberty had been given them for their sons and friends to serve the King of Spain'. The London administration was concerned more by the excessive zeal of the Lord Deputy and Council, rather than being impressed by their vigilance in unearthing supposed treasonable practices. Unwilling to take any chances, though, the English Privy Council conceded that the northern forts should step up their security measures. What is more, if 'certain proof' was obtained that anyone had actually been involved in treason, then it was left to Chichester's 'discretion to make sure of their persons'. Overall, however, the tone of the missive suggested that the London authorities believed that their Dublin counterparts had created a storm in a teacup and that the Lord Deputy's room for manoeuvre was constricted. To his disappointment, the viceroy was formally instructed to inform those who had been implicated in treasonable activities that although they had been accused, 'the king is unwilling to doubt their loyalty as long as he shall find any reason to esteem them'.[9]

Chichester, it comes as no surprise, caught the general tenor of his instructions to temper the conspiratorial mania gripping the Dublin administration, although he could not resist describing the Ulstermen as the most 'variable and discontented' in Ireland. He did, however, appreciate — indeed had anticipated — the advice of the London authorities to secure the northern garrisons, arranging for the supply of victuals, a sensible precaution in case rebels laid siege to isolated military units. As for his ongoing inquiries into the allegations of treasonable conspiracies, his information suggested that they had originated at about the time of the Gunpowder Plot, November 1605, but that 'failing of the success which was expected, their purpose [treasonable intention]... sleeps yet within them and will undoubtedly awake upon the first occasion that shall present itself'.[10] While the London authorities were inclined to think that Chichester was overreacting to events, it transpired at a later stage that the Lord Deputy's assessment of the situation at this time was accurate. When Sir Christopher St Lawrence emerged as the key government witness in the late spring of 1607, he testified that the conspiracy had indeed originated at the time of the Gunpowder Plot and suggested that religion was the primary motivating factor for the conspirators. The instigation of the design, therefore, coincided with the application of the anti-Catholic Mandates policy in Dublin. Religious grievance provided the overarching discontent motivating the conspirators, even if private resentments consolidated the resolve of many of those involved.

The opening weeks of 1607 witnessed a resumption of the delicate fencing between the Lord Deputy and the Earl of Tyrone. Availing of a visit to Dublin made by Tyrone at this time, but attempting to be careful not to arouse suspicions in the wary earl that he too was under suspicion, Chichester informed him about the allegations that Tyrconnell and Cúchonnacht Maguire had intended to flee from Ireland in the previous spring. The viceroy adroitly put Tyrone on the spot by telling him that the king was convinced that they would have confided in him. Tyrone's reply was effusive, if disingenuous: 'It is true the king knows me well, and I protest I would reveal anything that should concern the good of his service.' He acknowledged that Tyrconnell and Maguire were exceedingly discontented, 'grounded upon their poverty, being greatly indebted'. Tyrconnell, he claimed, was so 'passionate' about his predicament that he had indeed contemplated leaving the country. Tyrone, however, according to his own highly suspect version of events, prevailed on him not to resort to 'unbefitting courses'. In other words, rather than condoning his plan to depart from the country without licence, Tyrone claimed that he had encouraged his ally to seek formal consent from the royal authorities, approval which had previously been granted to many of his compatriots who had requested permission to seek military service abroad. Tyrone, for his part, took advantage of his encounter with the viceroy to raise some of his own concerns. The earl claimed that he was aware of accusations that he had capitalised on his powers of martial law to settle old scores with people who had served the English during the recent war. Tyrone was appalled that he had been so traduced, insisting that he had hanged none but 'lewd and dishonest persons who had worthily deserved it'. (The fact that they had served Elizabeth in the last war was obviously coincidental.) Besides, Tyrone was 'grieved' that his estate was being so 'strictly searched', specifically mentioning the troubling claims of Donal O'Cahan, as well as those of Archbishop Henry Ussher of Armagh and Bishop Montgomery of Derry, Raphoe and Clogher.[11]

During these supposedly frank discussions between the viceroy and the earl neither party had been entirely candid. Chichester, contrary to his instructions, had not informed Tyrone of the full extent of the allegations of treason that had been made during the previous summer, or that he, Tyrone, had been implicated. The earl, for his part, had also been economical with the truth. At this very time, as we have seen, emissaries of the two northern earls were about to conclude a 'treasonable contract' with Spain in return for substantial annuities, which would have ensured a solution to their financial problems — particularly those of Tyrconnell, who by this stage was virtually bankrupt. In these circumstances, Tyrone was hardly likely to reveal a matter of such immense concern to the king as he had affirmed that he would. In the end Chichester, in his attempt to probe the earl for information, had succeeded only in making him suspicious. No sooner had the wary Tyrone returned to Dungannon than he resorted to his customary policy of enlisting royal support, by penning a letter to King James in which he complained that there was a conspiracy to 'overthrow' him.[12]

Events in Dublin and elsewhere ensured that the embers of conspiracy in Ireland continued to smoulder, intense anger having been stoked up once again by renewed outbursts of persecution in Dublin and the Pale at the end of 1606 and early 1607.[13] Government intelligence reports in early 1607 detailed a putative plan by the Irish regiment in Flanders led by Tyrone's son, Henry O'Neill, in concert with Sir Christopher St Lawrence, to 'answer some attempt against Ireland'.[14] These allegations were treated much more seriously than the plethora of similar rumours because George St Lawrence, a former ensign to Sir Christopher St Lawrence in the royal army,[15] had been arrested on charges of plotting to seize Dublin Castle. George St Lawrence confessed to his involvement in the conspiracy, signifying that he had been anticipating foreign assistance, and identified one MacMahon, an Ulsterman as his co-conspirator.[16] This turned out to be Art MacMahon whom the Lord Deputy had humiliated during his summer tour of Monaghan in 1606.[17] The recurrent featuring of Sir Christopher St Lawrence in these transactions, a man who was to be a central figure in events leading up to the Flight, was a source of particular concern to the authorities in Dublin. St Lawrence had valiantly served the royal cause during the Nine Years War, and the alienation of such an experienced officer from the crown was naturally treated as a matter of considerable regret. Perhaps even more worrying for Chichester and his colleagues was St Lawrence's adventurous spirit, tinged with a degree of recklessness, especially as he had become such a 'discontented and unstaid man'.[18] St Lawrence's reputation as a dashing, daring, if at times unpredictable, officer was legendary among his contemporaries. His role in Essex's attempted *coup d'état* in 1601 typified his courageous, albeit irrational, spirit. It was a measure of St Lawrence's audacity that he had volunteered at that time to assassinate several leading courtiers, among whom was Sir Robert Cecil, the English Secretary of State.[19] Ironically, Cecil was to play a pivotal role at the time of the Flight in liaison with his erstwhile prospective assassin, St Lawrence.

Unlike Essex, St Lawrence survived the affair, returning to Ireland where he served the crown with distinction. The important point for Chichester in 1607 was that St Lawrence was exactly the type of enterprising military officer who displayed the audacity and pugnacity required to undertake a dangerous operation. Indeed, it was no surprise that Chichester had endeavoured to prevent St Lawrence from seeking Spanish service in the first place, finally relenting to his solicitations during the summer of 1606 when no other means offered themselves of satiating the maverick adventurer's ambitions. The royal policy of financial retrenchment had witnessed the army in Ireland being reduced to an emaciated force of less than 900 infantry and a couple of hundred horse, the skeletal garrison being so shabbily liveried that Chichester claimed that they were an object of ridicule.[20] The prevailing financial exigencies had conspired to deprive many experienced officers of a means of living in army service, let alone any reward for their endeavours during the Nine Years War, something that embittered these veterans — and the Lord Deputy, for that matter.[21] Their anticipation of a plantation in Ulster at the conclusion of the Nine Years War had been dashed, fuelling an already intense antipathy towards the northern earls that impacted on the situation in the pre-Flight era as Tyrone and his allies complained of abrasive treatment from the disillusioned, prejudiced military caste. Chichester was later to claim that St Lawrence's disenchantment originated from such disappointed ambitions, only in his case the discontent was compounded by a report that St Lawrence, supposedly a Protestant, had attended mass before his departure for the Low Countries.[22] It thus appears quite possible that to St Lawrence's frustrated personal aspirations was added a sense of disillusionment with the campaign of persecution against Catholics that had been waged in parts of Ireland since the closing months of 1605. Interestingly in this respect, St Lawrence's father, Lord Howth, had co-signed a letter from the nobility of the Pale objecting to the anti-Catholic Mandates policy in December 1605.[23] Alternatively, and not uncharacteristically, the notoriously unstable St Lawrence's flirtation with Catholicism may have been a career move designed to pave the way for securing employment in the Irish regiment in the service of the Catholic archduke in Flanders.

Chichester, having been loath to grant St Lawrence a licence to depart directly for the Low Countries, held out one last hope that his departure might be prevented somehow. He was sent to England to receive formal approval for his enlistment in foreign service, if that proved to be necessary. The Lord Deputy wrote a letter of recommendation on his behalf to the Earl of Salisbury, 'whereby he [St Lawrence] may be supported at home, or receive some countenance in his endeavours where he goes'. Given St Lawrence's critical role as the government informer who revealed the details of the plot that culminated with the Flight of the Earls, the fact that he visited Salisbury *en route* to the Low Countries might suggest that he was a government agent from the start, essentially an *agent provocateur*. However, according to his own testimony, he decided not to reveal what he knew when he visited court on his way to Flanders because he was uncertain about the international dimension to the plot, i.e. whether the conspiracy had any support among the large Irish military community in Spanish Flanders.[24] The sequence of events tends to support St Lawrence's version. Otherwise it would surely be stretching credulity too far to suggest that St Lawrence paid a private visit to Salisbury, a man whom he had once threatened to assassinate, admitted to his involvement in yet another treasonable conspiracy, was forgiven once again for having such an infelicitous predisposition for launching *coups d'état*, and was promptly hired as a government agent — unless, of course, one is expected to believe that the Machiavellian tendencies of the Secretary of State got the better of him. What appears more likely, as events later transpired, is that Salisbury, unaware as yet of St Lawrence's participation in a major plot, though concerned about the conspiratorial mania prevailing in Ireland, offered him some prospect of financial reward if he uncovered evidence in the Low Countries that a conspiracy was being hatched between malcontents in Ireland and Irish *émigrés* on the continent.

George St Lawrence's admission of treason was a concrete indication that a festering mood of revolt prevailed in Ireland and that the mounting fears of imminent rebellion which gripped the royal authorities in Dublin had not proceeded from unwarrantable suspicions. That the Dublin administration was being unnecessarily alarmist does not stand to reason. Far from being the nervous type, Sir Arthur Chichester was a doughty military campaigner who could be relied upon in such dangerous circumstances. Precisely why the Dublin government was so concerned about the prospect of revolt and why its London counterpart was so apparently dismissive is readily explicable. Chichester was perfectly aware that the sustained, indeed intensified, application of the Mandates policy in the Pale, parts of Connacht and in Munster was likely to generate conspiracy, although it was a risk that he was prepared to take in his endeavour to eradicate Catholicism once and for all in Ireland. The Lord Deputy was determined to extirpate the menace of religiously inspired rebellion for good. Sensitive, however, to the less than wholehearted support which had been received for this ambitious, if perilous, religious policy from London, Chichester had played down the severity of the penal measures being applied. Correspondence dispatched to England effectively kept even Salisbury in the dark about the true scale of the anti-Catholic measures. The Secretary of State was famous for his spy network at this time, his discovery of the Gunpowder Plot in 1605 being the most celebrated instance of this.[25] However, it appears that his agents were not plentiful in Ireland at this time, not least because he was relying on Chichester to be his eyes and ears in the western kingdom. If Salisbury had been fully aware of developments in the Mandates campaign, he would have been horrified by the risks the Lord Deputy and his officials were prepared to run, not least by Chichester's personal conduct in Drogheda in the early months of 1607 and the even more fanatical conduct of Sir Henry Brouncker, the Lord President of Munster.

The Mandates policy had been in relative abeyance since the summer of 1606 following a decision by the London authorities to review the legal basis of the proceedings. Emboldened by the subsequent findings of the judiciary in England that the Mandates mechanism withstood legal scrutiny (though the London authorities did not consider this as giving the green light for an all-out campaign of persecution), the Lord Deputy travelled to Drogheda in order to superintend personally the penal proceedings in this important Pale town. The prospect of his arrival clearly terrified its Catholic inhabitants, particularly the more prominent, many of whom fled in anticipation of his descent. Alert to this tactic, Chichester promulgated a proclamation ordering them to return. A charge of what effectively amounted to *lèse-majesté*, disrespecting the king's representative, would therefore be added to the dreaded prospect of persecution. The proclamation, not surprisingly, produced the desired result from the Lord Deputy's viewpoint, not least because the recusants had always maintained that they owed temporal loyalty to the king and thereby to his viceroy. The sanitised government version of subsequent events in Drogheda recounted that ten of the town's twelve aldermen had chosen to conform, the other two having been fined and imprisoned. Twenty other chief burgesses also reportedly chose to conform, while some two hundred citizens in all attended Protestant services in the town.[26] Affording brief details of the success of the policy, without dwelling on the methods employed, was typical of the manner in which the royal authorities in Ireland understated the controversial nature of their actions. Catholic reports of the events that had unfolded in Drogheda, by contrast, leave little doubt that the proceedings had been highly confrontational and that tremendous bitterness was unleashed as a result. Persecution was so severe, it was claimed, that no Catholics could traverse the streets,

> but presently they should be apprehended and brought before the Lord Deputy and Council, to be examined of what religion they were. If their answer was that they were Catholics, then they were demanded if they would go to church. If they answer that they would not, then were they presently sent to the jailer to be kept in prison; they were kept so close for half a year, that nobody was let go towards them but those that carried them their meat.[27]

The Lord Deputy himself, allegedly, played an active role in enforcing these extreme measures. He was accused of repeatedly accosting prominent recusants on the streets of Drogheda and demanding their attendance at Protestant services. In one instance, a Mr Barnewall, who was challenged in this manner, accompanied the Lord Deputy to the church door in accordance with his temporal duty to the king's representative, but would go no further. At this, Chichester

> told him, blandly at first, and then savagely, to go in, and seeing he could not prevail on him, struck him a cruel blow on the head with his stick. Then the macebearer attacked him so savagely that he fell to the ground like a dead man, and the viceroy had him dragged into church, where he lay insensible and gasping all the time of the sermon, and no one dared to approach him. Some of his friends afterwards took him home, where he gave his blessed soul to God in two hours.[28]

The contrast between the government and Catholic versions about the methods employed at Drogheda could not have been clearer, though they both agree on the outcome. A Catholic priest writing at the time admitted that the 'inhabitants of Drogheda, a populous town, and hitherto so tenacious to the faith, all went to the Protestant churches last Lent — hardly a dozen of them remained away'.[29]

There is no independent version of these events to confirm or refute the allegations made about Chichester's personal conduct in Drogheda at this time. That being acknowledged, the suggestion that the Lord Deputy would resort to crude physical violence in this manner to achieve his aim of converting Irish Catholics to Protestantism is perfectly credible. The man who had ruthlessly slaughtered women and children during the Nine Years War and had played a key role in reducing many others to starvation would not have baulked at employing physical intimidation or worse. But for the restraining counsels of the London administration, Chichester would have resorted to a policy of widespread executions to bludgeon the Catholic population into submission, with priests particular targets in this respect. He made little secret of the 'best course' of dealing with priests who disobeyed the proclamation banishing them from Ireland — 'hang them by martial law'.[30] The whole point of 'winning' the wars of religion was that the victor's faith should emerge triumphant. This early modern era was a brutal time when Catholic (e.g. the Spanish Inquisition) and Protestant leaders alike throughout much of Europe were prepared to resort to barbarous tactics to ensure religious conformity. However, Chichester was sensitive to the fact that coercing Catholics into attending Protestant services was but the first stage of his crusade to convert the Irish to Protestantism. The Lord Deputy, a religious zealot, was convinced that in the long run the Irish population would thank him for his short, sharp, shock approach. Once attendance had been enforced, the Irish would become allured by the superior qualities of the Protestant faith.

If Chichester furtively employed draconian penal measures against the Catholic population of Dublin and the Pale, the even more fanatical Sir Henry Brouncker, President of Munster, was less circumspect, imposing fines totalling over £7,000, imprisoning large numbers of prominent citizens, and removing Catholics from municipal office on a systematic basis.[31] In Waterford during 1606 five mayors were deposed from office in rapid succession.[32] By the end of 1606 Munster Catholics were reported by a priest to be generally remaining defiant: 'Through the grace of God, very few of our people have shown any weakness: in the city of Waterford only one; in Cork, the mayor ... in Clonmel one; in Limerick two; and in Kinsale and Kilmallock, very few.'[33] But the pressure was mounting. The activities of Brouncker's troops ultimately provoked a prominent Limerick gentleman, John Burke, into trying to raise a rebellion.[34] While mass was being celebrated at his castle a party of soldiers arrived, setting fire to houses in the vicinity of the castle.

> After a little, the gentleman [John Burke] resolved to make a sally with his people, having first recommended himself to the Lord. Taking the chalice in his left hand, under his cloak, and putting the ara [altar stone] between his shoulders, inside his shirt, and the other ornaments about his person, he thus, with his sword in hand, broke through the ranks and camp of his enemies. He killed some, and wounded others, escaping (with his servants) with only a lance-thrust between the shoulders, which broke the ara without injuring him; and he was more sorry for the loss of the ara than if they had half killed him.[35]

Apprehended soon afterwards, Burke was tried and executed for treason, Sir Henry Brouncker taking great satisfaction from the fact that Burke's call to arms had fallen on deaf ears.[36] However, given Brouncker's iron-fisted reputation, it is not surprising that Burke's appeal went unanswered. Such was the extent to which Brouncker cultivated a demonic reputation among Catholics in Munster that it provoked the Catholic Archbishop of Cashel to conclude that 'He lived among us like another emissary of Antichrist, for three years and a half, and it was his boast that his health improved the more the maledictions of the Catholics were heaped upon him.'[37] At a later stage it was reported with relish in Catholic circles that Brouncker's activities did not have the intended salubrious effect, precipitating quite the opposite result instead when he died in early June 1607, 'raving and eating his flesh from his arms, lamenting his rigour against recusants'. While a friend of Brouncker denied this allegation, he confirmed the claim that the Munster President had died an agonising death following a six-week period of illness beginning with

> the stone, which in great extremity afflicting, he endured as patiently as the sharpness of the disease would give leave to the most patient man alive; having after three weeks voided the stone, then was he pained with a melancholic wind in his side … then with a great headache and swelling in his face.[38]

Whatever perverse delight Catholics took from the manner of Brouncker's passing, the fact remained that the repressive measures employed by the Lord President and Chichester had gravely rattled them. In large measure the crown authorities had been successful in stifling expressions of opposition. Sir Patrick Barnewall, the man who had organised the Palesmen's petition against the Mandates policy in late 1605, had been committed to prison, eventually being transferred to the Tower of London.[39] Clearly, however, the Catholic population of Ireland, and ironically the Old English Catholics in particular, had cause to regret the completion of the English conquest. In the circumstances, it is likely that Chichester's policy of persecution provoked elements in Old English society into contemplating a military alliance with the northern earls, as government informers indicated. Not surprisingly, documentary evidence to prove how widespread disaffection had become has not survived. For obvious reasons, conspirators were unlikely to commit their treasonable intentions to paper. Indeed, it has been well remarked of the Butler revolt of 1569 that many of the details 'are unrecorded, an irritating testimony to the ability of each of the parties involved to keep a secret'.[40] However, the absence of a profusion of documentary evidence should not result in the degree of resentment entertained by the Old English being underestimated. As it was, apart from Sir Christopher St Lawrence, the youthful Baron of Delvin was a particularly high-profile member of the Old English community who can be categorically proved to have been involved.

In the light of the fact that the London authorities remained largely in the dark about the full extent of penal proceedings, the upper hand remained with the crown officials in Ireland, though the mood of recusant discontent was being ratcheted up to dangerous levels. For its part, the Dublin government continued to provoke the northern earls. In such circumstances, it is no surprise that conspiratorial machinations were afoot at various levels and among different elements of Catholic society in Ireland. It would have been even more surprising if there had not been rumblings of revolt. Private grievances added to the potent cocktail of discontent. For example, reports reached the Lord Deputy in early March 1607 that a 'petty' rebellion had occurred in Tyrconnell, originating in a power struggle involving the earl. Chichester duly authorised the earl to suppress it.[41] Then, somewhat duplicitously, and against all previous pronouncements that the rule of English law would prevail in Ireland and that the 'old way' of settling grievances by force would not be tolerated, the deputy proceeded to think better of eliminating the rebels. Instead, when the revolt was suppressed, he recommended that the surviving leaders might be 'preserved ... to sway the greatness of others in those parts' (a thinly veiled reference to the Earl of Tyrconnell), an expedient of which the king and the English Privy Council wholeheartedly approved.[42] The northern earls and the discontented Catholics of the Pale and elsewhere were not the only ones plotting nefarious practices. And it was not just the Earl of Tyrconnell, perceived to be the weaker of the northern earls, who was to find himself the target of renewed surreptitious activities on the part of crown officials, but the Earl of Tyrone too.

The manner in which Donal Ballagh O'Cahan was manipulated by crown officials to undermine the position of the Earl of Tyrone was quite extraordinary. ('Ballagh', meaning freckled, was O'Cahan's nickname;[43] the Gaelic Irish needed little excuse, according to Fynes Moryson, for bestowing such soubriquets, 'from the colour of their hair, from lameness, stuttering, diseases or villainous inclinations'.)[44] A breach between O'Cahan and the Earl of Tyrone was cultivated flagrantly, not least by the Protestant Bishop of Clogher, Derry and Raphoe, George Montgomery. Significantly, in the light of the manner in which O'Cahan was later to be hoodwinked once again by crown officials, when he first agreed to be a party to the campaign to prise O'Cahan's country from the control of his 'landlord', the Earl of Tyrone, he made it plain at the outset that 'if he might be freed [from Tyrone] ... then his country should not be divided as MacMahon's country [County Monaghan] was, of which he had some fear'.[45] In other words, O'Cahan was willing to subvert Tyrone's position, but not at the expense of his own. He was not prepared to recognise the claims of rivals either. For the time being the Dublin administration was more concerned to exploit O'Cahan's potential for undermining Tyrone's position than quibble with him about the basis for his support. And there were no limits to which crown officials were prepared to go to prise wider the breach between O'Cahan and Tyrone, his father-in-law. According to Montgomery, by March

1607 O'Cahan was determined to leave Tyrone's daughter, from whom he had separated, 'having a former wife lawfully married unto him', but was worried that the earl would physically seize back the substantial dowry.[46]

Whatever about O'Cahan's misgivings about leaving Tyrone's daughter, Bishop Montgomery relieved him of a personal decision by charging him 'by order of law' to take back his first wife.[47] The employment of clinical legal principles in this case was a poor camouflage for the naked political and personal ambitions of crown officials. But at least some form of legal propriety was observed. The same could not be said of O'Cahan's petition to have Sir John Davies, the Attorney General of the crown administration, appointed to act as his counsel in his lawsuit against the Earl of Tyrone, a petition that the Dublin administration granted.[48] Acknowledged as an 'illiterate',[49] O'Cahan was to have the services of Davies, a man of considerable contemporary repute in legal circles. There was something profoundly unethical about a situation in which the crown authorities in Dublin attempted to sit in judgment in a dispute between two private individuals while its primary legal adviser acted as counsel for one of the contending parties. Not only that, but O'Cahan was lent money by the cash-strapped crown administration in Dublin to pursue his legal case.[50] And if there was any doubt where the sympathies of the Dublin administration lay in the dispute, it may be dispelled by the fact that Donal O'Cahan was knighted by Lord Deputy Chichester two days after his case was considered at a grand meeting of the Irish Privy Council in late June 1607, the Lord Deputy being attended by fourteen members of the Council.[51] What was ostensibly a private legal dispute had effectively been turned into a state trial, with Tyrone in the dock, with the Attorney General as the prosecuting lawyer, and with the plaintiff as the primary crown witness. By any standard, the Earl of Tyrone would have been entitled to feel that he was not going to get a fair hearing and that the outcome of the legal dispute had been decided in the corridors of Dublin Castle between the prosecutor and the so-called 'judges' in the Irish administration. Tyrone, however, defiantly confronted this co-ordinated campaign to undermine his position, quite rightly accusing Bishop Montgomery of inciting people into taking legal action against him. Once more he made his appeal directly to the king,[52] who had thus far proved to be the one source of comfort throughout all the legal tribulations which had dogged him as persistently as Mountjoy's forces had once done on the field of battle.

There can be little doubt that the pressures were mounting on the northern lords. This was reflected in Cúchonnacht Maguire's successful bid to flee the country, turning up at Brussels by the beginning of June 1607.[53] Maguire cited persecution as his motivating factor for absconding, alleging that Chichester would have forced him to attend Protestant services otherwise.[54] As for Tyrone, it was evident that he was finally losing patience with the manner in which O'Cahan's case was being exploited by the crown authorities in Ireland. When the two litigants, Tyrone and O'Cahan, appeared before the Lord Deputy and

Council at a preliminary hearing in May 1607, the earl lost his temper, 'snatching a paper out of O'Cahan's hand, and rending it' in front of the Lord Deputy.[55] In so doing, the earl demonstrated considerable fortitude once more, directly challenging the fiery Chichester to his face. The deputy's response was illuminating: 'much against my nature, and not without dislike of some of my associates', Tyrone was only mildly reproved.[56] But for highly secret intelligence that he had received that there was a major conspiracy afoot which he was unwilling to compromise, there can be little doubt that Chichester would have arrested him. Certainly the deputy acknowledged as much when he recounted that 'severer punishments would better become the honour of the place and his [Tyrone's] chastisement, but understanding these consultations towards innovation I will not cause them untimely to declare themselves'.[57]

What had happened was that less than a week previously an anonymous letter had been found at the door of the council chamber in Dublin Castle which alerted the Lord Deputy to a plot to 'murder or poison' him. The plot was alleged to have the support of Old English and Gaelic Irish Catholics alike. Drogheda, which the deputy was rumoured to be intending to visit once again, was considered an 'apt' place for effecting the deed.[58] Chichester's recent decision to prevent anyone with weapons entering Dublin Castle, the hub of the royal administration, and to increase the guard had ruled out an assassination attempt in the castle.[59] For almost a year the Lord Deputy had been signifying his concern for his personal safety in view of the unsettled state of affairs in the Pale area, eventually appealing for an increased guard for his protection, owing to the profusion of 'traitors, felons, seminaries, priests and Jesuits' and fearing that 'sudden accidents may happen'.[60] As for his reaction to the plot against his life, Chichester remarked that he would normally have paid little heed to the warnings of an anonymous letter, but for the fact that they concurred with the evidence of an informer, known only at this stage as 'A.B.', who had apprised the Earl of Salisbury in England with intelligence that a widespread plot was afoot in Ireland.[61] The existence of 'A.B.' was a closely guarded secret. Certainly at this stage the Lord Deputy was the only person in Ireland who knew of his existence, and only then by these initials.[62] Later correspondence identifies 'A.B.' as Sir Christopher St Lawrence, soon to become Lord Howth.

While these highly sensitive investigations into the alleged plot were ongoing, parallel consideration was being given in London to the proprietorial controversies bedevilling the Earl of Tyrone. Significant in this respect was the contention of Sir John Davies that O'Cahan's lawsuit was but a test case. The considerable territories of Glenconkeyne and Killetragh were similarly targeted.[63] And yet, despite the grand ambitions of the Irish administration, all the indications were that the king continued to be favourably disposed towards the earl. An official at court, Sir Thomas Windebank, recounted in June 1607 that the king had been 'sorry' to hear of Tyrone's complaints that he had raised in his correspondence. However, as the king himself termed it, Tyrone's case was so complex that it would require a 'year's day of probation'. Although he was unable to give a definitive response to Tyrone's grievances, the king's sympathy with the earl was made plain when James issued instructions that Tyrone be 'assured that all His Majesty's goodness has been already graciously begun unto him, so he may not doubt the same shall be continued'.[64] On receipt of these instructions, it must have been galling for Chichester to have to acknowledge that a letter would be written to Tyrone indicating that while it would take James some 'time to consider his requests', he was to be assured of the king's 'favourable consideration'.[65]

This reaffirmation of the king's sympathetic attitude to the Earl of Tyrone took the wind out of the sails of the crown administration in Dublin once again. This was reflected in the proceedings that occurred at the formal hearing into the Tyrone–O'Cahan dispute at the Irish Privy Council at the end of June 1607. Despite acknowledging that they had found that the lands in question did not belong to either Tyrone or O'Cahan, the Lord Deputy and Council felt constrained to add that 'special considerations' prevented them from seeking to enforce their decision without the express approval of the king. The Earl of Tyrone, for his part, emboldened by the king's recent expression of favour, then played what he considered to be a trump card — requesting permission to travel to England to present his case in person to King James. O'Cahan, astounded no doubt by such an unexpected verdict, sought similar permission, though the earl was described as 'chiefly' desirous in this respect, 'relying much, as it seems, on His Majesty's gift'. Significantly, Chichester refused them both permission, citing as a pretext that it was 'in order to spare His Majesty's trouble by their importunities, and to prevent misorders that might happily break out in their countries during their absence'.[66] Evidently Chichester and his colleagues were worried that a visit by Tyrone to court could result in the foiling of their well-laid plans to undermine the earl's proprietorial base. However, as events transpired, Tyrone's inflated confidence was soon to be punctured.

In the middle of July 1607, barely a month after James had signified his favourable disposition towards the Earl of Tyrone, the king suddenly adopted a hostile position. Writing to Chichester, James, against the wishes of his administration in Ireland, summoned Tyrone and O'Cahan to London for the beginning of the Michaelmas term (the end of September). Sir John Davies, who had played such a prominent role in supporting O'Cahan's case against the earl, was also instructed to travel to court to 'guide our judgment'. The general tone of James's remarks was decidedly unsympathetic, even menacing, towards Tyrone. The king intimated that he was prepared to resort to capital punishment if necessary, adding the stern warning that 'If Tyrone means to encroach upon other subjects of little less condition than himself, and to draw them to such a dependency upon him as is inconsistent with the security of the state, I cannot forget what the authority is which God has committed unto me.' What is more, the king made it plain why he wished to summon Tyrone to

England: 'We conceive that we shall sooner and with more authority confirm the earl to our determination in these differences, if the same shall be not according to his desire, as it is likely in some respects to fall out.'[67] Evidently Tyrone faced defeat in his dispute with O'Cahan, as well as on similar issues. So much for Tyrone's complaints requiring a 'year's day of probation' to adjudicate. In one short month James had considered the relevant issues and had come up with his judgment. So why the abrupt change of heart?

Two factors combined to precipitate the king into changing his mind so dramatically. Sir Christopher St Lawrence's revelations had clearly been made known to the king, warning of a planned Catholic revolt in Ireland. This unwelcome intelligence, taken together with the sudden realisation in London government circles during the spring of 1607 of the degree of discontent which had been generated throughout Ireland as a result of the sustained application of the Mandates policy (following a petition from residents in Cork), led the king to fear that an outbreak of rebellion in Ireland was imminent.[68] Previously dismissive of Chichester's repeated warnings that a major conspiracy was afoot, the king now had every reason to be fearful that the deputy had been right all along. The London authorities clearly believed that there was a causal link between the Mandates policy and the treasonable plotting in Ireland. Interestingly, Brouncker rather than Chichester got the blame for stoking up the unrest. The Lord Deputy was instructed to assuage the 'strong discontent of the towns and others now boiling in their hearts' as a result of Brouncker's activities. This was recommended in order that 'the less would be their jealousy if there were any just occasion to lay hold of any persons of mark'.[69] The persons of mark were not named, but by implication consideration was being given to the arrest of Tyrone and Tyrconnell. However, it was far from a foregone conclusion. Despite St Lawrence's testimony and the acknowledgment of widespread disaffection in Ireland, the English Privy Council decided that was it was not 'worthy to draw on the king any sudden action'.[70] Although harbouring grave suspicions about the earls, the Privy Council also had lingering doubts about the reliability of St Lawrence as a witness, and this was the primary reason for the hesitation. Besides, having incriminated Tyrone and Tyrconnell, St Lawrence had steadfastly refused to give testimony against them in open court, protesting that 'he would rather die'. Anyway, according to St Lawrence, both the king and Salisbury had assured him that he would never be called upon to testify.[71]

A maverick, highly unstable figure, St Lawrence was variously described in English correspondence at the time as being 'neither wise nor honest' and behaving in his 'accustomed half-wild' fashion.[72] There was even a suspicion that he was acting as some sort of double agent. What could not be denied, however, was the fact that St Lawrence had excellent connections in Irish society as well as on the continent with people closely linked both to the northern earls and to the Old English. An English spy in the Low Countries reported on the intimate relationship between Henry O'Neill, the Earl of Tyrone's son, and

Sir Christopher St Lawrence. He described them as 'very familiar and inward friends and were oftentimes bedfellows'.[73] (In his absorbing though at times highly tendentious account of the Flight of the Earls, C. P. Meehan disparagingly refers to St Lawrence variously as a 'titled delator' and even more spitefully as a 'recent pervert'.[74] Significantly, Meehan omitted reference to St Lawrence's alleged bedmate, Henry O'Neill.) Such was their affinity that when St Lawrence began his journey back to England and subsequently to Ireland to play the role of informer for the crown against the northern earls and their Old English allies, it was ironic that Henry O'Neill accompanied him seven miles on his journey.[75]

Perhaps surprisingly, in view of his fickle and capricious temperament, St Lawrence's decision to betray the earls was not taken on the spur of the moment after his return from the Low Countries. Evidence shows that he had travelled back and forth to England from the continent at least once after making up his mind and contacting the English government. It is on record that he was imprisoned by one John Somerfield at Gravesend on a debt charge as he made his way to see the Earl of Salisbury in March 1607. Infuriated at his treatment at a time when he was 'employed about the [English] Council's affairs', St Lawrence demanded that his captor, Somerfield, be punished.[76] Before long St Lawrence was released and Somerfield found himself in custody instead.[77] It was Somerfield's misfortune that, while his captive was an individual of highly dubious character, both morally and financially, he had nevertheless been carrying a pass from the English ambassador in Brussels instructing crown officials in England not to hinder him in any way, but rather to assist him by all means possible.[78]

St Lawrence's revelations and conduct were to be pivotal in the events that preceded the Flight of the Earls. He had already made his way back to England during May 1607 when news emerged that his father, Lord Howth, had died and that he had succeeded to the peerage.[79] From the point of view of the Earl of Salisbury, the timing of the elder Lord Howth's passing could not have been more convenient. It meant that his son and heir could return to Ireland in unsuspicious circumstances. Uncertain as to how far he could be trusted, Salisbury instructed Lord Deputy Chichester to interrogate him. The new Lord Howth was also under orders to use his contacts to fathom the progress of the conspiracy in Ireland. Such was the sensitivity of the affair that Salisbury insisted that the Lord Deputy was to be the only member of the crown administration in Ireland who should be aware of his revelations.[80] The Irish Privy Council, though comprised almost exclusively of Protestant Englishmen, mostly newcomers to Ireland, was clearly believed to include secret sympathisers with the Earl of Tyrone. Indeed, such had been the concern that the Irish Privy Council had been riddled with informers during the Nine Years War that a deliberate policy of purging Catholics from its membership was undertaken during the early years of the seventeenth century.[81] Given that Howth was 'so wavering and uncertain', Chichester was unhappy with the burden on his shoulders alone, especially as the 'end may be so full of hazard'. In view of this, he was keen that one other member of Irish Privy Council be permitted to evaluate Howth's evidence, if Howth would agree.[82] Alternatively, as the English Privy Council was to suggest, subterfuge was to be employed. The Lord Deputy was advised to 'place some man of wit and virtue behind some cloth [i.e. a curtain] that he may hear what he says'.[83]

As delicate inquiries continued into Howth's allegations about a major plot, the correspondence of the London government suggests that while acute suspicions were entertained, it was agreed that no action would be taken unless hard evidence was unearthed. Salisbury had instructed Chichester that 'You shall so weigh all circumstances that light or weak proofs, grounded upon reports from second or third hands may not engage His Majesty into any open action against these supposed practices without such proofs as when they should be called in question, might become scandalous to His Majesty's princely justice.'[84] The London government viewed Tyrone's proposed arrival at court as an opportunity to resolve once and for all the earl's proprietorial disputes 'to the end the differences of that kind may be ended altogether ... that His Majesty nor we be troubled therewith all'.[85] However, the fact that orders were given to send Howth back to London at the same time as Tyrone has given rise to allegations that the London government was plotting to have the earl arrested and executed.[86] Such synchronisation certainly lends superficial support to this theory. Notwithstanding this, and in view of Howth's determined resistance to making open accusations, it would seem that this was a precautionary measure, 'whatsoever his [Howth's] evidence may prove', as the English Privy Council remarked at the time.[87] Perhaps Howth's presence in London may well have been intended as a ploy by the crown to lever the earl into acceding to the unfavourable determinations that clearly awaited him in relation to his lawsuits involving O'Cahan and others. What is certain is that Tyrone would have instantly been put on the alert by the manner in which King James overruled the Irish Privy Council by insisting that he travel to court to have his case adjudicated.

Events were rapidly coming to a head during the summer of 1607. Chichester postponed an intended trip to Munster at short notice, travelling north on a snooping exercise instead.[88] The sense of climax is also revealed in a letter from the Earl of Salisbury to Chichester at the beginning of August. Sir Richard Bulkeley, a royal official on the west coast of England, reported that he had received a letter that was to be delivered to Chichester with 'all speed'. As the 'post barks' were then in Ireland, Bulkeley commandeered 'a bark that lay in the haven ... to put to sea that night, and sent your letter by a trusty messenger to be delivered to the deputy's own hands'.[89] As for Chichester himself, he revealed after the Flight that he was on the verge of having the Earl of Tyrconnell arrested and questioned about treasonable activities when news came through that the earls had already fled to the continent.[90] Tyrconnell had been due to visit his pregnant wife at Maynooth.[91] The clock had been ticking down to Tyrone's departure for England, which was at most only a couple of weeks away. However, the English were not the only ones actively engaged in furtive practices. Archduke Albert, the Catholic ruler of Flanders, had received information that the Earl of Tyrone was to be arrested on his arrival in England and that the Earl of Tyrconnell (as Chichester acknowledged) was to be arrested and incarcerated in Ireland. A strong case has been advanced to suggest that the archduke received his information from the Earl of Northampton, a Catholic sympathiser at the court of King James. There is also convincing evidence to suggest that Sir Garrett Moore, a member of the Irish Privy Council, also played a part in tipping Tyrone off.[92]

Whatever about the accuracy of Northampton's report — and it is debatable whether the London government really was on the verge of having Tyrone arrested — it was taken sufficiently seriously by the archduke for him immediately to dispatch a messenger to Ireland to instruct the earls to prepare themselves for the arrival of a ship that would transport them to the continent.[93] Whether or not the government had solid proof of his complicity in treason, the Earl of Tyrone had every reason to believe that he had been compromised. He had, after all, concluded a treasonable contract with the Spanish government whereby he had committed himself to promises of service, including renewing rebellion, in exchange for a substantial retainer, worth 4,000 ducats in the first year, with more to follow in subsequent years. In agreeing to the grant, the Spanish government made it clear in November 1606 that the earls would thereby be 'under obligation' to serve the Spanish king and that in the event of war breaking out again 'they could be of great use'.[94] John Bath, who had captained the ship that transported the earls to the continent and later became an English agent, later offered to 'certify' to the English government 'what pension Tyrone and Tyrconnell had before their departing out of Ireland, which was the greatest motive of their flight, fearing they were discovered'.[95] Ironically, it appears that the first funds from the Spanish annuity that had been secretly granted to the earls during the spring of 1607 were used to hire the ship to convey them into exile. Arrangements to exchange the Spanish crowns for gold were being made by Tyrone's son, Henry O'Neill, during April 1607.[96]

If Tyrone had had any doubts about his predicament, Howth now adopted the role of double agent, putting 'buzzes' in the earl's head warning him that King James 'stood not well affected towards him'.[97] Rumours had also been circulating in Scotland that the earl's treasonable activities had been uncovered and that he had been summoned to England and would 'never come again hither [Ireland]'.[98] As Tyrone had been carrying out negotiations for months for the marriage of his son to the Earl of Argyll's daughter,[99] it is more than likely that he had been apprised of these rumours by contacts in Scotland. Tyrone's spirits were hardly lifted either by renewed reports that Chichester was on the verge of being granted the presidency of Ulster.[100] Besides, a nephew, Brian MacArt, had been arrested on a charge of murder. Despite earnest intercessions by Tyrone to the Lord Deputy to have him released, including a reported bribe of £500, Brian MacArt's death, he alleged, 'right or wrong, was much desired by the Lord Deputy'.[101] The combined effect of these adverse developments was to set off a cacophony of siren voices ringing in the ears of the northern earls, warning them that they stood in mortal danger. That Tyrone was less than his cheerful self in the weeks leading up to the Flight is readily appreciable. Sir John Davies reported on his 'melancholy' and how he had become 'very pensive and passionate; and the friars and priests perceiving it, have wrought nightly upon his passion'.[102] In the end Tyrone signified his fear that 'if he went into England he should either be perpetual prisoner in the Tower, or else lose his head'.[103] Manifestly the decision to seek sanctuary abroad had been an agonising one, though Tyrone felt he had no other choice, not least because he had been unable to build up a military base again. While his resolution to flee from Ireland is understandable, the circumstances in which it occurred suggest that it was a precipitate decision. In the heat of a crisis once again, as happened following the battle of the Ford of the Biscuits in 1594 when the earl paid an impromptu visit to Dublin at a time when he was under acute suspicion, a rush of blood may have clouded Tyrone's judgment. As events following the Flight of the Earls were to demonstrate, he had not been in such imminent danger as he had been led to believe. Even his mortal enemy, Sir Arthur Chichester, was to admit the flimsy nature of the crown case against him. Howth had only incriminated the Earl of Tyrconnell and the Baron of Delvin. As for anyone else, 'he [Howth] has not spoken but by hearsay'.[104] Extraordinarily, given the importance of the Flight in altering the course of Irish history, Tyrone himself need not have fled to the continent for safety. That being acknowledged, the fact is that he did. And having resolved on flight, the manner of its execution had to be negotiated safely. After all, as the Earl of Tyrone remarked, he was under such close surveillance by the 'lurking' Sheriff of County Tyrone, who was spying on him so closely as if to discover 'if he [Tyrone] might have any hole in his coat'.[105]

5

ON A WING AND A PRAYER

The conjunction of events which accompanied Tyrone's summons to England by James I, followed so promptly by the dire warnings about his prospects in London that he had received from his continental friends, marked the decisive point at which the Earl of Tyrone considered that he had no option but to flee. Tyrone made it clear afterwards that it was due to the fact that he was in mortal danger that he resolved to 'make an honourable escape, with his life and liberty only; than by staying ... to lose both life, liberty, living and country'.[1] And Tyrone would not have been the first Gaelic chieftain whose trip to Britain resulted in more than he had originally bargained for. In 1591 Brian O'Rourke, lord of Leitrim, travelled to Scotland to hire mercenaries, only to find himself the subject of extradition proceedings to England which ultimately resulted in his execution at Tyburn. O'Rourke was 'hanged, his members and bowels burned in the fire, his heart taken out, and holden up by the hangman, naming it to be the arch-traitor's heart, and then did he cast the same into the fire, then was his head stricken off and his body quartered'. O'Rourke's grisly fate, it has been well remarked, horrified other Ulster lords and may well have played on Tyrone's mind in the period immediately preceding the Flight.[2] With hindsight, the Lord Deputy and Council noted that close acquaintances of Tyrone observed a distinct change of mood following the earl's receipt of the summons to go to England, when it was observed that he lost 'his former cheerfulness and grew often exceeding pensive'.[3] Tyrone's uncharacteristic sullenness was the product of two factors: a not unnatural despondency with the predicament confronting him, combined with a realisation of the enormity of the task that lay ahead of him in securing safe passage abroad for himself, his family and close allies. In the circumstances, the earl was likely to have appreciated that leaving the country in such a clandestine fashion without 'taking his leave' of the viceroy would have been seized upon by his enemies as tantamount to self-incrimination, an admission of treasonable guilt. Certainly James I lost no time in coming to the conclusion that the Flight had taken place because of the earls' 'malicious disposition to enter into open acts of disloyalty, which being by the vigilancy of our ministers discovered, they out of the guilt of their own conscience, fearing the punishment due to them, have fled'.[4] Just how the Flight was organised at a time when the earl was under such close surveillance is a matter of some interest, not least because Tyrone claimed that he had 'so many eyes watching over him, as he could not drink a full carouse of sack [wine], but the state was advertised thereof, within few hours after'.[5] Nevertheless, Tyrone managed to spirit away a party of some ninety-nine persons (comprising passengers and crew) on a boat which conveyed him from Lough Swilly on 4 September 1607.[6] It is these unfolding events and the subsequent adventures and misadventures of the fugitives until their arrival in Rome that must now be addressed.

Securing a safe passage for the earls and their friends was a matter of considerable urgency, given Tyrone's impending departure for England. In the first instance, some notice of the arrival of a ship from the continent was required. This task was entrusted to one Nicholas Lynch, a servant of the Earl of Tyrconnell. This courier, it later transpired, had arrived in Ireland about a month before the Flight, his errand being to inform Tyrone of the grave danger that he was in and to warn him to make preparations for his evacuation.[7] Meanwhile on the continent, Cúchonnacht Maguire busied himself finding a ship. Maguire leased a French ship to undertake the task, its nationality being important in so far as the French were not suspected of being in league with Irish conspirators. The eighty-ton ship was reportedly armed with sixteen pieces of ordnance and had a complement of sixty soldiers, although great efforts were clearly undertaken to conceal the ship's true mission, it being loaded with a cargo of wines and fishing nets, thereby giving it the impression of being engaged in two normal commercial activities associated with the Irish coast.[8] Maguire travelled to Ulster at great personal risk, 'disguised like a mariner',[9] the perilous nature of his mission being revealed by the fact that the vessel was detained by a Scottish ship before being allowed to proceed.[10] His presence may well have been designed to emphasise the gravity of the situation facing the northern earls and to reaffirm once more the imperative of decampment to the continent. Following the Flight, Maguire was warmly applauded by Peter Lombard, the Catholic Archbishop of Armagh, for his 'dexterity and industry in compassing so worthy a work as to bring out of imminent danger such a noble company'.[11]

Meanwhile, back in Ireland, the earls were confronted with the problem of concealing their true intentions from the legion of professional spies and opportunistic informers who surveyed their every move. The difficulties in making the necessary arrangements were exacerbated by the shortness of time between the arrival of the ominous warning from the continent and the prompt arrival of the ship. The fostering tradition in Gaelic Irish society caused problems for the Earl of Tyrone in rounding up his dispersed children, while the pregnant seventeen-year-old Countess of Tyrconnell was residing with her grandmother, the Dowager Countess of Kildare, at Maynooth.[12] In the event, Tyrconnell, taking with him his infant son Hugh, had to depart without her, having been forewarned by the archduke that Chichester intended to arrest him. His expected arrival at Maynooth to fetch her had been selected by the royal authorities as the optimum moment to pounce, Sir Christopher St Lawrence having tipped off Chichester.[13]

But while the Countess of Tyrconnell had had to be left behind, a sub-plot to the wider machinations was responsible for a subsequent daring bid by friends of the earl to have her spirited out of the country.[14] In order to prevent this, the countess was transported to England.[15] On her arrival at court, she was courteously received, a contemporary describing how 'she kissed His Majesty's hand; and a sweeter face you never saw. Indeed, the king wondered her husband left so fair a face behind him.'[16] The explanation was that the countess's husband's head was on the block, figuratively and almost literally. The Earl of Tyrconnell, for his part, continued with his endeavours to secure his wife's passage to join him. In the meantime he managed to send her some gold pieces to cover her immediate expenses,[17] and several months after the Flight he employed an agent to go to England in a vain attempt to organise her escape to the continent.[18] Fortunately for the Countess of Tyrconnell, she was herself well connected among the highest nobility in Ireland and England. Brigid FitzGerald by her maiden name, the Countess of Tyrconnell was the daughter of the twelfth Earl of Kildare, and the granddaughter of Charles Howard, Earl of Nottingham, Lord High Admiral of England and an important member of the English Privy Council.[19] Not surprisingly, in view of such influential friends, the countess managed to negotiate an annuity of £200 from the English government following the Flight of the Earls.[20]

It is important at this juncture to make a distinction between the two earls. Howth had incriminated Tyrconnell, but he would not indict Tyrone. Consequently, despite the fact that Tyrone was under intense suspicion, the royal authorities in Ireland dared not move to arrest him on the basis of 'reports from second or third hands'.[21] Tyrone, therefore, was more at liberty to move as he pleased. He journeyed south to Slane in August 1607 where he encountered the Lord Deputy. Tyrone's stalling tactics at this time were revealing, particularly with the benefit of hindsight. As Chichester remarked afterwards, Tyrone conducted 'artificial' proceedings with him. Significantly, Tyrone backtracked on his position in regard to the O'Cahan case, virtually apologising to the Lord Deputy for having appealed over his head to his superiors in London. Secondly, the earl signified that 'strictness of time' between the royal summons to England and the proposed date for his actual departure, combined with his 'present poverty', rendered his trip to England highly inconvenient.[22] Playing for time until the ship arrived from the continent, Tyrone was clearly seeking to persuade the Lord Deputy to defer his visit to England. However, news of Maguire's arrival at Lough Swilly made such a postponement immaterial. Instead Tyrone now had to make his final preparations for a hasty departure to Spain.

In the first instance, on Saturday 29 August Tyrone journeyed to Mellifont,[23] the home of his old friend, Sir Garrett Moore, foster-father to one of his sons. While there, Tyrone, 'being in drink', complained to Moore, now a member of the Privy Council in Dublin, that Lord Howth had informed him that the king 'stood not well affected towards him'.[24] The earl collected his son and made his departure, the manner of which provoked considerable speculation about his intentions. The earl's disconsolate demeanour was such that he 'wept abundantly when he took his leave, giving a solemn farewell to every child and every servant in the house, which made them all marvel, because it was not his manner to use such compliments'.[25] Clearly those present sensed that something significant was afoot. On leaving Mellifont on Sunday 30 August, the earl travelled to Dundalk, proceeding on the following day to Dungannon,[26] where he remained for two days — resting, according to the Irish Attorney General, Sir John Davies.[27] More than likely, however, this pause in his otherwise hasty plans for evacuation was occasioned by a feverish search for another son, Conn, who, as it turned out, could not be located in time. Conn, aged six or seven at the time, was with his foster family, who were then engaged in the traditional Irish practice of 'creaghting',[28] a form of transhumance whereby herds of livestock were driven from one area to another in search of grazing pasture. Chichester remarked afterwards that Tyrone had sought out his son 'diligently'.[29] The earl well knew that Conn would more than likely become an English captive, a fate that duly befell him, spending the remainder of his life in custody. Hardly surprisingly in these circumstances, the earl was in a foul mood when he slipped out of Dungannon in the dead of night on Wednesday 2 September, making a headlong rush for Rathmullan,[30] his midnight departure undoubtedly occasioned by a desire to throw off the spies that ever lurked around him. Such was the urgency to reach his embarkation point that, according to Sir John Davies, it was later

> reported that the countess, his wife, being exceedingly weary, slipped down from her horse, and weeping, said she could go no farther; whereupon the earl drew his sword, and swore a great oath that he would kill her in the place, if she would not pass on with him, and put on a more cheerful countenance withal.[31]

Of course, whether this incident happened or not, or occurred in the manner in which Davies recorded it, is open to question, Davies being predisposed not only to exaggeration but even more to a determination to blacken the name of Tyrone — hence his contemptuous comment that the earl's haste to depart had been hindered by his 'impediments, that is, his women and children'.[32] Overall, given the unfortunate circumstances in which the Earl and the Countess of Tyrone were departing the shores of Ireland without their young son, it is very likely that the journey to Lough Swilly was fraught with tension for all concerned. Perhaps, indeed, the countess was playing for more time for her son to be located.

Having apparently escaped the attentions of English agents by his overnight departure, Tyrone once again came under scrutiny as he passed by close to Lough Foyle on Thursday 3 September, the governor of Derry offering dinner to his illustrious visitor. The offer was declined, Tyrone's party pushing on instead to Rathmullan, where they rendezvoused with the Earl of Tyrconnell and others, who were busy procuring food and drink for the journey.[33] While the ship had lain at anchor for eleven days, it was only at the very last moment on Friday 4 September that efforts were made to load it with the necessary provisions for the voyage.[34] Perhaps, no attempt had been made to do so previously in case suspicion was aroused. At any rate, such was the hurried nature of the final preparations for the trip that some cattle belonging to an Englishman, Francis Whyte, were seized and slaughtered for provisions.[35] Then, at the very last minute, there was a final hitch in the plans. According to Tadhg Ó Cianáin, an apologist for the earls, supplies were still being put on the ship after the earls and their associates had boarded. A foraging party that had been sent ashore once again for firewood and water was attacked by some of the local MacSweeneys, being forced to retreat to the ship with their mission only partly accomplished.[36] Whether this mission was as innocent as Ó Cianáin depicted it is a matter of dispute. In the aftermath of the Flight the earls were not only indicted for rustling Whyte's cattle, but were also alleged to have 'traitorously beat and wounded divers of the king's faithful subjects, and robbed and spoiled them … and there committed divers other felonies, robberies, burglaries, and other crimes'.[37] Implicitly, it would appear that some of the MacSweeneys had been on the receiving end of harsh treatment by the earls' followers. Indeed, the Earl of Tyrconnell subsequently recounted several instances of previous disputes with MacSweeneys, including an incident in which one Owen MacSweeney was reputedly reprieved from execution by the royal authorities 'if he would charge the earl with some detestable crime'.[38] At any rate, the conflict that ensued on the shores of Lough Swilly culminated in an undignified departure for the cream of Gaelic society in Ulster. The presence of people ashore waving weapons menacingly rather than bidding them an emotional farewell was an inauspicious start to a traumatic and at times highly perilous journey.

Having failed to take on board adequate supplies, the fugitives considered putting ashore at the island of Arranmore off the coast of County Donegal. An 'exceeding great storm' prevented this, and instead the ship eventually proceeded along the west coast of Ireland as far as Croaghpatrick. At that point, mistakenly fearing the presence of the 'king's fleet' in Galway, the crew plotted a course directly for Corunna in north-west Spain. They need not have had any worries on account of the English navy. Such was its dilapidated state through lack of finances that only one ship was on station in Irish waters at this time, the *Lion's Whelp*, cruising the north-east coast.[39] However, Chichester did issue instructions to royal officials in Connacht to commandeer a well-armed vessel, if one were available, to try to intercept the earls.[40] But the earls' bold plan to travel to the Spanish court was to be frustrated at this initial stage not by enemy action but by fate itself, for thirteen days of 'excessive storm and dangerous bad weather' ensued, reducing them to desperation. In these circumstances, a gold cross belonging to the Earl of Tyrone as well as other holy relics were put in the water trailing after the ship for good luck. Then, much to the surprise of all aboard, two small hawks, merlins, alighted on the ship, a sign at least that they not been driven so far off course into the wide open Atlantic as they feared.[41] The Flight of the Earls was proceeding on a wing and a prayer.

While the religious charms and the presence of the merlins boosted morale on the vessel, not least by proving that they had not been hopelessly blown away from landfall, the persistent bad weather convinced the sailors that they could not proceed to Spain. (Nevertheless, it was later discovered that they had managed to get within eight leagues of Corunna, their projected destination.)[42] Lack of supplies and prolonged bouts of sea-sickness among the passengers forced a change of plan, and a course was charted for the coast of France instead, though there were to be further anxious moments before a landing was safely secured. At one point they were 'obliged to take down their sails by reason of the strength and power of the waves, and to leave the ship to itself to drift over the sea as God should will'. A 'terrible storm' blew their ship past the French coast as far as the 'Flemish Sea', perilously close to England. As the ship attempted to backtrack a second violent storm erupted, forcing them to lower their sails once again. On this occasion the vessel only narrowly avoided being shipwrecked on the 'two islands belonging to the King of England called Jersey and Guernsey'. For a time, therefore, the earls were faced with the prospect of being forced ashore on the Channel Islands, where 'the faces of the inimical, merciless heretics who were before them on the islands would not be as at a meeting of good friends in a foreign land'. After all these dangers and vicissitudes they eventually made landfall at Quilleboeuf at the mouth of the Seine, having been at sea for twenty-one days.[43] It was not before time, with five gallons of beer and less than one barrel of water remaining to share among the ship's complement of ninety-nine.

For some time there has been considerable academic interest in the precise identities of the ninety-nine travellers, and several attempts have been made to compile a list of names. Paul Walsh, the editor of a translation of Tadhg Ó Cianáin's contemporaneous eyewitness account of the Flight, has posited fifty-six individuals from among the associate lords, ladies, children and gentry of the earls.[44] Among these was John O'Punty O'Hagan, the aptly named treasurer of the Earl of Tyrone, his nickname O'Punty being derived from *punt*, the Irish word for 'pound'.[45] After a detailed examination of continental records, a fuller list of over eighty individuals was discovered by Canice Mooney writing in the 1950s, although Mooney acknowledged that by the time this list was drawn up by the officials of the Spanish archduke of the Low Countries some people might either have detached themselves from the earls' entourage since landing in France, while others later joined it.[46] However, even this qualification inadequately accounts for the shortcomings of this list. The inclusion of large numbers of servants is most dubious, given that the spouses of prominent individuals who took flight were not among the ship's complement. In reality, there appears to be little reason for the identities of the entire ninety-nine remaining such a mystery. Contemporary English accounts in the immediate aftermath of the Flight put the figure of those who actually fled with the earls at between thirty and forty (this estimate being provided by the Lord Deputy himself), while the ever-exaggerative Sir John Davies ventured that there were between fifty and sixty.[47] A more considered English record later documents the entire party of fugitives at thirty-seven, including a much smaller number of servants in this instance; according to this account, only six women were on board.[48] The figure of thirty-seven, it should be noted, when added to the crew of sixty soldiers who were said to have been aboard ship when it left Dunkirk,[49] tallies almost exactly with Ó Cianáin's figure of ninety-nine. While the ship's company was not so jampacked with the lords and gentry of Ulster as has been suggested, the fact remains that it nevertheless carried away to exile much of the bloodstock of the premier lines of the O'Neill and O'Donnell families, thereby lending substantial justification to the Four Masters' assertion that this was a

> distinguished crew for one ship; for it is indeed certain that the sea had not supported, and the winds had not wafted from Ireland, in modern times, a party of one ship who would have been more illustrious or noble, in point of genealogy, or more renowned for deeds, valour, prowess, or high achievements than they.[50]

Indeed, it was precisely because of the celebrated individuals involved that international relations in western Europe were thrown into a diplomatic crisis, beginning with the unscheduled arrival of the earls' ship in France on Friday 24 September after twenty days at sea.

The earls' initial experience in France was fraught with awkward complications, their frosty reception by the governor of Quilleboeuf being symptomatic of this. Realising the precarious nature of their position in France (possessing neither a licence from their own monarch for their trip abroad nor a passport from the French government), the earls endeavoured to ingratiate themselves with the local authorities. Accordingly, they invited the governor of the town to dinner, where they entrusted themselves once more to the lucky charms of the 'strange hawks which had been caught at sea', proffering them to the governor as a gift.[51] The meal was a less than convivial affair for either of the parties involved, although it appears to have been devised by the earls in order to humour their guest and to beguile him into facilitating their designs. Dinner, it seems, had hardly been digested when the hiring of boats was arranged for the transportation of the women and children 'by the short route' to Rouen, while the earls and their male companions departed on horseback.[52] However, the governor had not been completely enthralled by the earls and was soon in touch with his superiors elsewhere, as well as dispatching notice to the French king of the fugitive party's wholly unexpected descent. Having first permitted them to depart, the governor then proceeded after them and placed them under a 'kind of arrest', requiring them to attend the Chief Marshal of Normandy.[53] So, having survived a hazardous, incident-packed journey, the earls found themselves once more in jeopardy, not least because the English ambassador to France, Sir George Carew, was seeking an audience with the French monarch in order to obtain their extradition to England as wanted fugitives.[54]

To the considerable relief of the Irish *émigrés*, the attitude of the King of France, Henry IV, could not have been more favourable, not least because the earls made it abundantly plain on their disembarkation that they were the aggrieved party, being forced into exile because of religious persecution.[55] The highly indignant English ambassador was left cooling his heels for three days, without any response to his demands, while Henry went hunting. It has been suggested, indeed, that the French king deliberately cold-shouldered the ambassador until he was 'assured that the lords [earls] were in a place which would be secure for them',[56] i.e. Spanish Flanders. Part of the explanation for Henry's tardy response may be attributed to the fact that he was forced to backtrack on an earlier affirmation to the English ambassador when he mistakenly believed that the earls had landed on the coast of Spain. At that time Henry sanctimoniously suggested that the Spanish king 'did wrong to His Majesty [James I] to receive them', only to find himself open to a similar charge when it subsequently emerged that they had landed in France instead. According to an English account of these proceedings, Henry exonerated himself from any blame on the grounds that a local official, the Duke of Montpensier, 'having already given his word for their safety, the king could not revoke it'.[57] Tadhg Ó Cianáin's description of the earls' cool reception by local officials in Normandy casts doubt on this version of events. Rather, a more convincing explanation for Henry IV's actions emerges in an account of what occurred when an audience was finally granted to the English ambassador. By this time, the earls having already departed from French soil, Henry reputedly remarked that he would not in any case have done 'any injury to noblemen who would be obliged to leave their paternal inheritance because of their faith' and that 'all Catholics were free to go without any interference through the kingdom of France'.[58] Henry was acutely conscious of the baneful effects which persecution, or the attempted assertion of religious dominance by one faith, had wrought in his own country, giving rise to prolonged periods of conflict during the second half of the sixteenth century. What is more, having been forced by political circumstances to convert to Catholicism,[59] the French king undoubtedly realised that it would have been impolitic for domestic reasons to hand over such a famous Catholic 'prince' as the Earl of Tyrone. In any case, little did Tyrone realise that in the French king he had an ardent admirer who styled the earl the 'third soldier of his age, thus implying that he himself was the first and the Conde de Fuentes the second'.[60] Ironically, it was the same French king who afforded Tyrone safe passage through his territories who had years previously knighted Arthur Chichester, Tyrone's arch-enemy, for bravery on a French battlefield.[61]

The gracious manner of Tyrone's treatment by Henry IV greatly enraged the English court, where Tyrone's abscondence had given rise to a state of acute consternation. Uncertain which continental government could be trusted, the English considered it prudent to tone down expressions of discontent with the 'marks of kindness' offered to Tyrone by the French monarch, 'for they do not desire to take offence over an event which may turn out to have a common relation to two such great princes [i.e. the kings of France and Spain].[62] That the Flight had precipitated considerable reverberations in international relations was evident, the conspiratorial fever which had swept Ireland for some years having spread by contagion with Tyrone's physical presence on the continent. The Venetian ambassador in London, Giustinian, provided ample relation of all these affairs. In the first instance, he reported that the Flight resulted in a flurry of activity at the English court. 'Meetings are constantly being held, and they are not satisfied with the steps already taken but are proposing to put a large number of ships in commission', the implication being that a Spanish-sponsored invasion force for Ireland was feared.[63] The affair also impelled the English to take an even greater interest in the ongoing peace negotiations between the Dutch Protestants and the Spanish, with the English contemplating even closer relations with their Dutch neighbours as a counterpoise to what was seen as the menacing designs of an international Catholic conspiracy with Tyrone at its fulcrum.[64] No one was more sensitive to this than the English Secretary of State, the shrewd Lord Salisbury, whose response to an apparently serious crisis in international affairs was both prompt and pugnacious.

Writing to the English ambassador at the Spanish court at the end of October 1607, Salisbury launched into a vitriolic attack on what he believed to be the dastardly activities of the Spanish. The King of Spain, he conceded, may have considered that Tyrone's presence on the continent had presented him with an ace up his sleeve, to be played to Spanish advantage in the event of renewed hostilities with England. But, countered Salisbury, in a broadside as devastating as any the great Elizabethan seadogs had delivered to Spanish fleets in the past, the English ambassador to Spain, Sir Charles Cornwallis, was instructed to blast his Spanish hosts with the affirmation that

> those Irish, without the King of Spain, are poor worms upon earth; and that when the King of Spain shall think it time to begin with Ireland, the king, his master, is more like than ever Queen Elizabeth was to find a wholesomer place of the King of Spain's where he would be loth to hear of the English,

and to show the Spaniards that shall be sent into Ireland as fair a way as they were taught before. In which time the more he [Cornwallis] should speak of the base, insulting, discoursing fugitives, the more proper it will be for him.[65]

Salisbury's sharp references to English intervention in the Spanish Netherlands throughout much of the latter part of the sixteenth century and the expulsion of the Spanish troops that had been forced to depart from Kinsale in 1602 were designed to jar tender nerves in the Spanish pysche.

The London government's demeanour as an aroused English dragon breathed its withering fire concealed the twin realities that the English had neither the means nor the appetite for further hostilities with Spain. Once again the astute Venetian ambassador in London detected the degree of bluff involved with English military preparations which had been set in train following the Flight, noting that the intention to commission a large fleet could not be carried into effect 'so quickly owing to the lack of money, though they desire that the rumour should go abroad; and Lord Salisbury, in the presence of many persons, used words which showed the wish to foster this belief in men's minds'.[66] Apart from financial restrictions, James I was personally not inclined to resort to force if it could be avoided. His aversion to violence, or the prospect of it, was so pronounced that it earned him the unenviable representation by a contemporary as 'the most cowardly man that I ever knew'.[67] To some extent this caricature was borne out when he heard news of the Flight, reportedly becoming 'quite distraught'.[68] Overall, Salisbury's instructions to the English ambassador at the Spanish court must be considered to a large extent as an exercise in sabre-rattling. Equally notable, however, was the caustic language in which the English Secretary of State's opinions were couched, leaving little reason to doubt that the Flight had precipitated a major rupture in relations between England and Spain. Particularly choleric exchanges also occurred during an audience between the English ambassador in Brussels, Sir Thomas Edmonds, and the Spanish archduke following the earls' arrival in Flanders. Not surprisingly, international relations suffered as a result. Edmonds was to complain that he and his wife were subjected to 'unrespectful usage by the best sort, and of daily affronts which have been offered them'.[69] Nor was life any more pleasant at this time for the Baron of Hoboken, the ambassador of the archduke at the court of James I. He also testified to the 'pungent expressions' and 'bitterness' of his exchanges with English government officials over the reception afforded to the earls in Flanders.[70]

But the English reaction to the Flight was not confined to blustering diplomacy. Salisbury also engaged his secret service, a network of agents and would-be assassins. As early as November 1607 two 'agents', at first completely unaware of each other's identity, were simultaneously attempting to inveigle their way into the earls' retinue.[71] Later identified as James Bath and one Travers, the two fell out, with Bath dismissing Travers's attributes as a spy, fuming that 'the Munstermen, of which country Traverse is, are noted to be always as false as the Devil' (arguably ideal credentials for a spy).[72] Bath later managed to gain access to the earls, but was forced to concede that Tyrone and his 'counsellors ... hold all things so secret that there is scarce anything to be known of what he goes about'.[73] For his part, Travers, having been sacked by the English, informed Tyrone that 'he and some others were employed by his lordship [Salisbury] to poison the said earls, which is the cause that Tyrone has taken a straight order that there shall be no access to his kitchen'.[74] Salisbury was later to be disappointed by Bath, 'upon whom his lordship [Salisbury] bestowed so much money', when he failed to travel to Rome with the earls. Bath remained with the Irish at Herrenthals, where he bragged about his correspondence with Salisbury, before being ejected from the town by the governor.[75] Such was the double-dealing conduct of Travers and Bath that either or both may have been suborned into becoming agents of the Earl of Tyrone.

As it was, Salisbury's apoplectic response to the Flight of the Earls and what seemed to him at the time to have been an immensely sinister turn of events on the international stage was wholly unwarranted. The Spanish were indeed sensitive to the degree to which the Flight had distempered international relations, and they were determined to prevent the contagion of suspicion that had been unleashed thereby from spreading. It was for this reason that they moved promptly to consign the earls to quarantine in Rome. The fact was that the Spanish had not solicited the Flight to take place. Indeed, at a time when they were attempting to conclude peace with the rebellious Dutch Protestants, the Flight could not have occurred at a more inopportune moment. True to what was to become established form, the Spanish government, despite casting itself in the role of international Catholic champion, was not prepared to jeopardise its narrower national interests in the pursuit of grand supra-national religious objectives. Financial exhaustion caused in no small measure by decades of warfare dictated that the plight of the 'persecuted' earls could not meet with a determined military response. Frankly, in the short term, the Flight of the Earls proved embarrassing for the Spanish. From a Spanish point of view, the diplomatic furore which had ensued thereafter would have been exacerbated had the earls been permitted to proceed to the Spanish court. In the words of one member of the Spanish Council of State, should 'they [the earls] come here the King of Great Britain would have even greater complaints and the expense and embarrassment caused would also be greater'. Consequently, the Spanish king was advised to have the earls detained in Italy instead.[76] Events were to prove that the Earl of Tyrone, once a major player in the international game of chess, was to be reduced to the status of a pawn.[77] Little did the earls and their entourage realise it at the time, but their celebrated triumphant procession to Rome was actually a trip into an open prison. Even the lavish reception which was to be accorded them in Milan by the Conde de Fuentes had an ulterior motive, the Conde being instructed by the Spanish government to give the earls 'a very good reception when they arrive there [Milan] to detain them on the pretext of awaiting embarkation, to ascertain their claims and their intentions'.[78] Generally the Spanish response to the Flight of the Earls was clinical, even cold. Even when the Spanish government later warmed to the prospect of Tyrone's presence offering them an ace up their sleeve in international relations, as Salisbury had feared, the duplicitous manner in which the Spanish government manipulated Tyrone was to be sustained. Realisation of this only slowly dawned on the fugitives, who remained unconscious of the fact that they were being sold out by their so-called Spanish friends while they were being sumptuously wined and dined by a succession of Spanish grandees on their travels through Europe.

As yet unaware that the Spanish were to betray them, the Irish party had first to undertake the perilous journey from France to Spanish Flanders. From the beginning the earls comported themselves in the manner of pilgrims, depicting themselves as offended innocents persecuted into seeking sanctuary abroad. At Amiens, for instance, they visited a 'gorgeous church' where the head of John the Baptist was on display. The critical point was reached at France's border with Flanders, where they were acutely dismayed when they encountered a large military force, fearing capture by English sympathisers.[79] More pleasurable episodes were experienced as they proceeded deeper into Spanish-controlled territory. At Douai, a principal seat of learning, 'verses and speeches in Latin, Greek and English' were delivered in their honour. The governor of Ath ordered a gun salute, while his counterpart in Nyvel organised musicians and dancers for their entertainment. The high point of what was now turning into a festival procession was reached when they arrived at the court of the archduke of Spanish Flanders at Binche. The major-domo of the archduke came to greet their arrival with 'good coaches and great noblemen'. The stately banquet which followed was described as 'grand and costly enough for a king', served up on such a profusion of gold and silver ware 'that no king or prince in Christendom might be ashamed to have'.[80] It was a measure of his stature that Tyrone was variously styled 'the Great O'Neill' or 'Prince' at the archduke's court.[81] Tyrone's sense of self-esteem was being inflated to dizzy proportions by the day. It was not long before it was punctured and the earl was hurled back to earth with a resounding thud. Having set out for Spain, via Italy, at the end of November 1607 with a retinue of thirty horsemen, the earls were to have their journey cut short by the arrival of a messenger bearing a command that they should return to Louvain to await further instructions.[82]

The earls' determination to complete their journey to Spain, if by a circuitous route,[83] demonstrates convincingly that Tyrone had not intended to abandon his patrimony for ever. On the contrary, despite his advancing years, Tyrone's conduct in embarking on such a difficult journey in the heart of winter with the specific purpose of beseeching the Spanish king to authorise immediate military assistance conveys his resolve from the start to return to Ireland, and urgently at that. As events transpired, his zeal to advance the international 'Catholic' cause was not shared by those whom he considered to be his continental allies. The Spanish authorities in Madrid and Flanders were determined to sidetrack him elsewhere. Neither Spain nor Flanders was considered acceptable. It was not a determination that could be revealed to the earls gently, not least because some senior Spanish officials voiced their objections to this decision.

Unaware of the first instalment of what was to become a consistent pattern of betrayal and fobbing off, the earls were immensely despondent that they had been ordered to suspend their journey to Spain. Little did they realise, moreover, that the archduke of Spanish Flanders had also already determined that they were not be allowed to remain in his territory for fear of offending the English, who had been lobbying vigorously to have them at best extradited or at worst banished to a far-flung destination where they could cause no trouble. Interestingly in this respect, the Spanish ambassador at the court of the archduke strongly disapproved of this 'harsh' determination 'with regard to people who have given such service to God and to Your Majesty [the King of Spain]'.[84] The ambassador was not alone among prominent Spaniards who greatly admired the earls and were appalled at their treatment by high-ranking administrative officials. Such was the earls' celebrated status that while they effectively remained in limbo at Louvain Spanish noblemen in the city were 'accustomed to visit them'.[85] Despite this, the Spanish authorities in Flanders and Madrid had reached the decision effectively to expel the earls from Spanish-controlled territories. However, it was to be some time before the earls were informed of this determination because leading officials were unwilling to undertake the distasteful errand. Neither the Marques de Spinola, the Spanish commander in Flanders, nor the Marques de Guadeleste, the Spanish ambassador at the court of the archduke, were willing to do so. Spinola was described in December 1607 as 'putting off delivering the message' to the earls in the hope that his superiors would have a change of heart on what was described once again as a particularly 'harsh' decision.[86] Despite solicitations on the earls' behalf by such prominent figures, the Spanish government in Madrid persisted in its determination to have the earls sequestered in Rome, at least temporarily. However, having recovered from what they considered to be the potentially disastrous consequences of the earls' arrival on the continent, the Spanish authorities soon signified that the Flight of the Earls was not as baneful as they had first thought. At a substantial step removed (i.e. Rome) the Spanish appreciated that the earls were important figures who could if necessary be exploited in international affairs. Ironically, in the longer run, the Flight of the Earls in some respects actually helped to stabilise international relations, since their availability on the continent would provide the Spanish authorities with useful political leverage. This attitude was explicitly articulated in April 1608 by the Spanish ambassador in Rome, who commented that 'the earls' presence here may act as a deterrent against the persecution of the Catholics in England'.[87]

On learning that their trip to Spain was to be suspended, although unaware that the Madrid authorities had ruled it out completely, the earls put their case for assistance. Convincingly the earls stressed how their war in Ireland had debilitated English efforts to assist Protestant forces in Brittany and the Netherlands. Thousands of English troops and experienced commanders had been consumed by the Irish wars. Critically the earls noted that while they could have concluded 'honourable conditions' with the English during the recent war (1594–1603), they had declined to do so because the Spanish king had persuaded them otherwise. In such circumstances, the earls tweaked Spanish sensibilities to the utmost by claiming, quite justifiably from their viewpoint, that

> By our strength alone, we have kept our lands and our faith for such a long time against foreign nations [that] it would be a cause of astonishment to the whole world that, in the end, because we served such a powerful and Catholic monarch as Your Majesty, we should lose both our lands and our faith.

Besides, the earls stressed the degree of discontent in Ireland that could be tapped to Spanish advantage as a result of religious persecution, the Catholic Old English having been grievously alienated as well.[88]

Clearly taking on board some of the earls' points, the Spanish Council of State conceded that while the earls could have concluded a treaty during the Nine Years War to their 'advantage, they refrained from doing so because of the letters they received from Your Majesty [the King of Spain]'.[89] Nonetheless, it upheld its former decision to have the earls shunted on to Rome for the time being. This option offered the Spanish the best of both worlds. Dispatching the earls to Rome would reassure the English, but at the same time they could yet be of 'great service' in the event of a 'break with the King of England'.[90] Similarly, the Spanish ambassador in London, Don Pedro de Zuniga, at first considered the Flight to have been extremely irritating and the Irish lords to be troublesome, 'ill-disposed people'.[91] Before long, however, such was the protracted unease in London about the Flight that de Zuniga signified a sudden concern in March 1608 for the welfare of the Earl of Tyrone, whom he believed the English wanted to assassinate 'by poison or by any possible means'. In the circumstances, the ambassador urgently recommended that Tyrone be guarded and advised Philip III that it would be

> well that Your Majesty keep him well disposed to your royal service, for to the English he is a bridle. Their fear of him gnaws at their entrails and it will be all the greater if he may go to Rome, for they believe that if Your Majesty should send a hundred men with him to Ireland, all of that kingdom would rise against them.[92]

While the Spanish Council of State had been determined from the very start to rule out the option of the earls coming to Spain, the earls themselves were left in a state of suspense throughout the winter of 1607–8, forlornly awaiting the nod of approval for their trip to Spain which they were never going to get. Instead, in spite of the considerable efforts which were made to entertain them by illustrious sympathisers at Louvain who provided 'musical instruments, dancers and performers',[93] they were forced to idle away their time. The English ambassador in Brussels, Sir Thomas Edmonds, for his part, was delighted that the designs of the earls were being frustrated. Edmonds reported Tyrone's marooning at Louvain, where the earl and his entourage were reported to 'liberally drink sack [wine] instead of usquebaugh [whiskey], for the digesting of their melancholy'.[94] In the circumstances, the degree to which the refugees had become dependent on any hint of encouragement, providential or otherwise, was almost pathetic. The slightest suggestion of divine intervention was grasped at eagerly. Tadhg Ó Cianáin, the contemporary narrator of the earls' travels, attached great importance to the apocalyptic tale of a salmon appearing quite unprecedently almost at the very doors of the earls' palaces at Louvain. According to Ó Cianáin, there was an 'exceedingly small streamlet' between the two palaces where the earls were residing. A servant of the Earl of Tyrconnell was on his way to Tyrone with a message when he saw a 'very large salmon in a small hole in a plank on the stream'. Rather adeptly the messenger drew a weapon and killed it, bringing his prize to Tyrone, where its presence created quite a stir:

> All the nobles of the city who were near them came to see the salmon. They were surprised at his size, and that he was got where he was found. They said they never saw during their lives, and never heard from those who lived before them, that a salmon was ever before got on the river of Louvain, or on that particular branch of it.[95]

Implicitly, the salmon's appearance at Louvain was interpreted as signifying a symbolic message from Ireland, from the great salmon rivers of the Bann and the Foyle which bisected the lands of the two earls. By implication, Ó Cianáin was suggesting that the earls were being beckoned to return to their native lands.

The rumour mill throughout Europe continued to reverberate with suggestions that the Spaniards were surreptitiously intent on aiding the earls. An English spy in the Spanish port of Bayonne was worried about an armada of Spanish ships that was being amassed.[96] It was reported that a friar, 'a tall, handsome man, of a black complexion, and black hair, somewhat long, and to be of the age of thirty or thereabouts', had been entrusted with a special mission to return to Ireland to warn Tyrone's followers to be prepared for his imminent return. A collection among the soldiers of the Irish regiment to finance the friar's trip was viewed ominously by the English.[97] As it was, the prospect of an early return to their native land was non-existent at this particular stage. Far from it, indeed, when they departed from Louvain at the end of

February 1608, it was their intention to travel to Spain via Milan.[98] However, following a dramatic, incident-packed trip to Milan, they were to find themselves frustrated in their intention of continuing on to Spain, and diverted to Rome instead. In more ways than one, it was a roller-coaster journey to Rome via Germany and Switzerland, the physical experiences ranging from traversing ice-packed mountain passes, travelling through valleys and plains, to a somnolent crossing of a tranquil Alpine lake. Emotionally, the journey also had its highs and lows, ranging from grand receptions in Catholic principalities to being reduced to skulking through Protestant territories where the fear of seizure was distinctly palpable in Tadhg Ó Cianáin's narrative of events. In all, the trip could be classified into three categories: part celebratory procession, part pilgrimage, part perilous escapade.[99] On average, for a substantial part of the journey (until an unfortunate accident occurred involving a baggage horse carrying money on a perilous Alpine pass) the earls proceeded at a consistent pace of roughly seven leagues per day, i.e. about twenty-one miles.[100]

The highlight of the early stages of the journey was reached at Lorraine, where the duke received them at Nancy with 'joy and honour'. Coaches and noblemen were dispatched to escort the earls' party, and a grand dinner was held in their honour. Instructions were issued that 'no one should accept gold or silver of them while they should be in the city, but that all their expenses during that time should be borne by the duke'.[101] The Duke of Lorraine's reception of the earls was all the more remarkable in view of the fact that whereas the French king and the archduke of the Netherlands could claim to have been ignorant of the earls' alleged treasonable practices, the Duke of Lorraine had been fully apprised of them by the time the earls arrived in his territory. Sir Thomas Edmonds, the English ambassador at Brussels, had gone to the extent of writing in French to the duke in January 1608, enclosing a copy of James I's proclamation against the earls and stating the English position in no uncertain terms. As a result, Edmonds was confident that the duke would show them no favour. It was therefore with a sense of tremendous shock and horror that Edmonds learned of the earls' gracious reception in Lorraine, attributing it to the 'insinuations' of Tyrone, a past master at winning favour.[102]

Having sampled the hospitality of the Duke of Lorraine, the party then negotiated a succession of German towns, some Catholic, some Protestant. The city of Colmar was considered a 'remarkable' place, adjacent to the 'most beautiful, wide, level, and fruitful plain in the greater part of Christendom'. The spectacle was spoiled somewhat, however, owing to the fact that it was inhabited by 'heretics'.[103] The Swiss city of Basle was the next main stop on their journey, though the travellers promptly departed 'through fear of conspiracy by the heretics' in the city.[104] To the trepidation of passing through such hostile territory was added the misfortune of the minor calamity that befell the earls' party on St Patrick's Day 1608. Having just previously undertaken a memorable journey across a lake against a backdrop of breathtaking Alpine scenery, the *émigrés* undertook the much more hazardous task of threading their way carefully through a snow-bound Alpine pass. They reached a deep glen spanned by what was known as the 'Devil's Bridge'. It was at this point that disaster struck. A pack-horse carrying money plunged into the defile below and was all but swept away in the raging torrent, the sum of £120 being irretrievably lost in the process. The earls' followers managed to haul the unfortunate animal to safety, but protracted searching for the missing money proved in vain.[105] A truly infelicitous St Patrick's Day was experienced by all. The despondency in the migrant troupe only really lifted when they reached Milan, a Spanish dependency, on 23 March.[106] Milan, after all, was intended by the earls to be the staging-post for their later embarkation for the Spanish court. Little did they realise, however, that the waves of international intrigue that had buffeted up in the wake of their Flight had rippled the whole way to Milan.

On their arrival in Milan, almost destitute by this stage, they were accorded all manner of hospitality and marks of respect by the Spanish governor, the Conde de Fuentes. (Their funds had become all but exhausted, despite the fact that they lifted advance rents from their lands prior to the Flight.)[107] Unknown to them, they were the subject of surreptitious attentions of Spanish and English officials alike. The English, for their part, through the activities of spies, were fully apprised of the earls' intentions to use Milan as a staging-post in their quest to travel to Spain. No sooner had the earls arrived in Milan, indeed, than the English ambassador to Venice reported how he had appointed a spy to 'accompany Tirone and his ging [gang] over all Italy'.[108] The Spanish authorities were also conspiring. Anticipating their arrival on Italian soil, whether at Milan or Genoa, the local Spanish officials had been ordered to 'detain them on the pretext of awaiting embarkation' for Spain in order to fathom their intentions.[109] In reality, at all costs, the earls were to be prevented from travelling to Spain. While they were to be treated with 'particular care', they were to be packed off to Rome.[110] When the earls subsequently arrived in Milan, the Conde de Fuentes duly implemented his duplicitous instructions, feasting them 'both to assure them of the generosity and compassion of Your Majesty [Philip III] and to make them amenable to Your Majesty's wishes'.[111] The chronicler Ó Cianáin and the earls were totally unaware that their treatment to 'three full weeks' of such lavish hospitality in Milan was but a smoke-screen for underhand manoeuvrings by the Spanish.[112]

Unaware of the Machiavellian practices attendant on their reception in Milan, the earls revelled in their experience of this grand city, where they were thoroughly indulged. Sir Henry Wotton, the English ambassador to Venice, immediately informed James I that they had arrived 'well armed with arque-buses and pistols, to the no small wonder of the beholders; the governor there having formerly denied entrance into the city with arms of that quality, even to the ambassadors of great princes'.[113] While there, they marvelled at the spectacle of ritual flagellation on Good Friday: 'They saw many hundreds of men in a splendid procession, with lighted waxen torches about them, and their faces covered so that they might not be recognised. They were scourging, smiting and whipping their bodies until the streets and the churches in which they walked were red with blood and gore.'[114] The earls' party were deeply moved by such experiences, while they greatly appreciated the manner in which the Conde de Fuentes had treated them. Ó Cianáin noted how he had been 'kindly and friendly to them at their coming, and he was sad when they left', bestowing expensive gifts of ornamental rapiers and daggers.[115] Perhaps the Conde had warmed to the earls in view of their predicament — Tyrone was an adept in the art of self-ingratiation. Consequently, no undue symbolism may be attached to his choice of presents. However, given the Spanish government's fear that the English were conspiring to have the earls assassinated, Fuentes may well have been offering a subtle hint to the earls to take precautions for their safety. Either way, the presentation of rapiers and daggers to the earls could not have been more apposite, given that the English were contemplating stabbing them in the back quite literally. No sooner had the earls arrived in Italy than a plot was being hatched to dispatch Tyrone to the 'Devil's house' at the hands of an assassin.[116]

Similarly, at this point, the Spanish authorities and the Pope were figuratively engaged in stabbing them in the back as well. This was despite the fact that to the former Tyrone had been a staunch ally, while to the latter he had been a champion of the Catholic faith. As it happened, while the earls were to be treated in a gracious fashion by the Pope in Rome, unknown to them the Spanish ambassador in Rome had noted that the Pope, Paul V, had been dreading their arrival, being 'more timorous in these matters than I would wish him to be'.[117] An English diplomat at the time remarked that Tyrone was unlikely to 'obtain any great relief from the Pope himself, who in his own nature is noted to be extremely miserable'.[118] Nevertheless, the Pope granted Tyrone a monthly allowance of 100 crowns and a sufficient supply of bread and wine for ten persons.[119] And despite the secret misgivings of the Spanish government, it was from Spain that the primary source of the earls' income was to be derived. When the fugitive nobles first arrived in Rome, arrangements were made to pay Tyrone 400 ducats per month, while Tyrconnell was to receive 300 ducats. Afforded this preferential treatment, Tyrone moved quickly to ensure that it would not give rise to bad feelings. He made it clear to the Spanish ambassador in Rome that he did not 'wish Tirconel to know that he, Tiron, is being given more, because they are friends and this advantage would be the cause of great enmity'.[120]

Oblivious to the Pope's apprehension at their imminent arrival, the earls' party picked up momentum on their journey from Milan to Rome, averaging some ten leagues a day, three leagues a day quicker than had been the norm. More clement springtime weather conditions perhaps facilitated this expedition, while the prospect of a hero's reception by the Pope undoubtedly quickened the pulse as well. Shortage of funds more than likely also played a part, the Conde de Fuentes having reported their straitened circumstances by the time of their arrival in Milan,[121] a financial situation that had been exacerbated by the St Patrick's Day fiasco at the Devil's Bridge *en route*. Wotton, the English ambassador in Venice, commented on the 'strange haste' of Tyrone to get to Rome, attributing it to a belief that 'his provision lies low'.[122] The headlong rush abated at the last moment, the final couple of days of their journey to Rome witnessing a decidedly sedate pace of three and two leagues respectively. Despite his parlous financial situation, Tyrone had no intention of entering Rome with unseemly haste.[123] Like the heroes of ancient times, Tyrone craved a triumphant reception in Rome. As a warrior in the cause of the Counter-Reformation, he appears to have considered that he deserved no less. He was not to be disappointed, for the purple carpet was duly rolled out. Fifteen coaches, most of them drawn by six horses, were dispatched by cardinals to provide a ceremonious escort for Tyrone's retinue as it entered Rome and then proceeded to a 'splendid palace' that the Pope had made available to them.[124] Even the English ambassador in Venice, Sir Henry Wotton, had to admit that 'all Italy rings of his reception at Rome'.[125] An English intelligence report also noted how the Countess of Tyrone 'is much commended and admired for her beauty and modesty of behaviour'.[126] Following a period of rest, Paul V received them at three o'clock on the afternoon of 4 May 1608, granting them an audience of one hour. The earls then 'paid a special visit to each of thirty-seven cardinals in succession'.[127] The hectic round of religious and social engagements proceeded apace. On Saturday 18 May Tyrone, displaying remarkable energy for a man of advancing years, led a 'meritorious pilgrimage' to the seven principal churches in Rome.[128] The sturdy old earl may have been fit to stick the pace, but the younger Earl of Tyrconnell was unable to attend vespers celebrated by the Pope on the eve of Pentecost Sunday owing to a 'feverish sickness', an illness that was soon to claim his life.[129]

Tyrone, for his part, was experiencing a different sort of feverishness, a desire to make the most of what he considered to be but a temporary sojourn in Rome. At this stage the earl confidently expected that his return to Ireland was imminent. Had he even contemplated that his residence in Rome would entail any sort of prolonged duration, let alone the eight years that he was destined to remain there, there is little reason to believe that he would have proceeded helter-skelter on such a frenetic round of engagements. It is all the more poignant, therefore, that the precipitate manner in which the earls' party sought to complete their pilgrimage to Rome contributed to a series of untimely deaths among their number caused by the unfamiliar climatic conditions of the Mediterranean world.

Before a succession of personal tragedies engulfed the fugitive party, they enjoyed a series of splendid occasions in Rome. On the Thursday before Trinity Sunday, according to an English account, the canonisation of St Francesca took place. The Pope instructed that Tyrone's party should occupy the most prestigious places at the ceremony. The Pope's niece honoured the Countess of Tyrone by accompanying her by coach to the service, where the countess had pride of place among the ladies present, including the 'Pope's sisters ... the duchesses and other nobility of Rome'.[130] Trinity Sunday witnessed a spectacular fireworks display in the city, the pyrotechnics emitting 'flashes, and flames, and thunderous, fiery, red-flaming showers on high'.[131] To the thrills of such a wondrous extravaganza were added a succession of marks of favour from Pope Paul, perhaps seeking to indulge the earls for his distinct lack of material support for their cause with honorific gestures instead. At any rate, his guests were accorded almost unprecedented distinction on the feast of Corpus Christi, 1608, when the Pope requested that eight of their number carry his canopy on this occasion. The Italians present were greatly surprised, as 'seldom before was any one nation in the world appointed to carry the canopy'.[132] However, as even an English account acknowledged, the 'Italians speak much good and very honourable of these earls'.[133] Over a thousand lighted torches were borne in the procession, which also comprised some twenty-six bishops and archbishops, thirty-six cardinals, as well as an escort of the Swiss guard and two large troops of cavalry. This grandiose display was witnessed by a crowd of some 100,000.[134] In addition to this mark of recognition, the earls enjoyed the added privilege of a series of pilgrimages to famous churches, with the Pope's permission to have 'exhibited to them all the relics of each church to which they would go'. The array of relics was immense, including the hammer used to nail Jesus to the cross, the purple garment that Pilate ordered to be put around him, a portion of his blood, and a splinter from the cross. Among the relics of Christ's disciples was the forefinger that St Thomas had put into his master's wound and a tooth of St Peter. As well as the specially approved access afforded to the earls on these pilgrimages, there was the added bonus that twelve thousand years' 'remission' for sins was granted to those so privileged by the Pope.[135] Little did the earls realise at the time, but occasion would be offered much sooner than anticipated for such indulgences to be cashed in. Certainly the English maintained a lurking presence around the earls, seeking a chance to strike. Wotton, the English ambassador at Venice, recommended putting a bounty on the head of the Earl of Tyrone. Even if Tyrone was not killed, Wotton speculated that the earl 'may walk in the more fear, which will angustiate his counsels and spend them about his own security'.[136] To his great disappointment, however, Wotton reported that one of his spies had returned from Rome in 'great fear ... there is much vigilance and jealousy about him [Tyrone]'.[137]

Fate soon delivered to the English what underhand practices had failed to achieve. In quick succession, fever claimed the lives of the Earl of Tyrconnell, his brother Cathbharr, Tyrone's son Hugh, Baron of Dungannon, as well as Cúchonnacht Maguire, lord of Fermanagh.[138] Maguire, whose role in the events leading up to the Flight was as crucial as that of the two earls, was an individual of manifold qualities whose passing was a major loss to the fugitive party. The Four Masters described him as 'an intelligent, comely, courageous, magnanimous, rapid-marching, adventurous man, endowed with wisdom and personal beauty, and all the other good qualifications'.[139] The manner of Tyrconnell's passing was particularly poignant, the youthful earl having become disillusioned with life in Rome, where he had not been well. Seeking a change of air as well as a holiday, he travelled to Ostia. Here, however, he soon became afflicted by a violent fever, as a result of which he succumbed after eleven days of 'violent sickness and great pain'. He was only thirty-three years old. The Pope ordered a grand funeral, with 'large numbers of lighted waxen torches and sweet, sad, sorrowful singing'.[140] Once again the Four Masters lamented the loss of such an important figure in Gaelic Irish society, a man who was a 'generous, bounteous, munificent, and truly hospitable lord, to whom the patrimony of his ancestors did not seem like anything for his spending and feasting parties; and a man who did not place his mind or affections upon worldly wealth and jewels, but distributed and circulated them among all those who stood in need of them, whether the mighty or the feeble'.[141] Tyrconnell's legendary generosity, it is worth noting, had probably contributed to the enormous debt problems he had been experiencing in Ireland before his departure for the continent.[142] The deaths of Tyrconnell, the Baron of Dungannon and Maguire had a major psychological impact on the remaining Irish contingent in Rome. Certainly Tadhg Ó Cianáin considered that the deaths did not bode well for the future:

> It may well be believed that it was not through good fortune or the best of fate that it happened to Ireland that so many of the choicest of the descendants of Míl Easpáinne died suddenly, one after another, in a foreign and strange land, far removed from their own native soil.[143]

Rome, as it turned out, was to become not only the graveyard of the earls' ambitions, but the final resting place of their mortal remains as well.

6

ROBIN HOOD AND HIS
NOT-SO-MERRY MEN

The Flight of the Earls in 1607 had momentous implications for many others besides the members of the fugitive party who embarked on their storm-tossed, perilous journey. Those who were left behind, particularly in Ulster, found themselves the figurative occupants of a dangerously listing ship as well. But while the earls eventually arrived safely on the continent, their departure and continuing absence was to have a devastating impact on Ulster society in general. Such was the paranoia generated in government circles by the earls' departure that even key crown supporters in the north, including O'Cahan, Niall Garbh O'Donnell and Sir Cahir O'Doherty, soon found themselves enveloped by the buffeting waters unleashed thereby. O'Cahan and Niall Garbh ended up as lifelong captives in the Tower of London, while O'Doherty was even more unfortunate in losing his life as a result of his desperate act of rebellion during the spring of 1608. These dire consequences ensued despite the fact that O'Doherty, in particular, had been making particularly strenuous — and genuine — efforts to assimilate himself within the burgeoning English system. Subsequent developments showed that vast quantities of land were to be appropriated by the crown and designated for colonisation by Protestant settlers. All this occurred despite a proclamation issued by the Dublin government a matter of days after the Flight to 'assure the inhabitants of Tyrone and Tyrconnell that they will not be disturbed in the peaceable possession of their lands'.[1]

The crucial point is that while the crown authorities harboured grave suspicions about the existence of a plot prior to the earls' departure in September 1607, the Flight itself was hailed as proof that the concerns of the viceroy regarding the alleged conspiracy had been vindicated. Far from the rumblings of revolt being considered to have died out following the abscondence of Tyrone and Tyrconnell, the opposite conclusion was drawn. After their arrival on the continent, the earls were suspected by Lord Deputy Chichester, quite rightly as it turned out, of fomenting revolt in Ireland and seeking the backing of foreign powers. What complicated matters — and this is the key to explaining the downfall of O'Cahan and O'Doherty — was the fact that royal officials in Ireland were uncertain as to whom they could trust. Once again the confused situation owed much to the activities of Lord Howth, the double agent, who wrought havoc in Irish society by his conduct. And it was not just the fate of the remaining northern lords that was jeopardised by his activities, but the careers of leading members of the crown administration in Ireland were also threatened with ruin. Lord Chancellor Jones and his close ally, Sir Garrett Moore, a senior member of the Irish Privy Council, and even Lord Deputy Chichester, were to find themselves caught up in the convulsive state of affairs which prevailed for some time following the Flight. They were all to become entangled in Lord Howth's elaborate web of intrigue.

Having compromised the earls by his information, Howth was concerned following the Flight that 'his discovery is made known to his disgrace and dishonour'.[2] It was perhaps to divert suspicion away from him that he spearheaded an audacious plan to secure shipping at Howth to be manned by 'six young and lusty fellows'. The intended complement for this ship was unknown, but it was observed at the time that the old Countess of Kildare and the 'Lady Dowager' of Delvin were then residing at Howth.[3] The Countess of Kildare, it should be noted, was later asked to account for the treasonable practices that had taken place at her residence in Maynooth, where Howth and Delvin had liaised.[4] What is more, there is a lingering suspicion that Howth was seeking to facilitate the flight of the Countess of Tyrconnell, who had been staying at Maynooth when the earls secured their passage at Lough Swilly.[5] Certainly there were several reports at the time that efforts were being made to procure passage for her to the continent.[6] To what extent Howth was plotting to effect the escape of those whom he had incriminated may be open to debate, the fact remains that his duplicitous, or at the very least suspicious, behaviour served to intensify the rampant paranoia gripping the Dublin administration. More detached from the rumour-ridden situation in Dublin, the English Privy Council remarked of Howth's alleged double-agent role (informing on the earls to the crown and then informing the earls of the crown's intentions) that he hoped thereby to save himself from being exposed as the crown informer by 'underhand with a counter-practice' sending the 'chief conspirators away'[7] and thereby appearing as the saviour of the day for both sides. It was a schizophrenic tightrope that anyone in Howth's situation would have found very difficult to walk. What made it virtually impossible for Howth was the fact that he could be categorised as schizophrenic by nature rather than by design.[8] His propensity for erratic behaviour greatly exasperated the leading officials in the crown administration charged with dealing with him. Not knowing whether to trust him entirely following the incident at Howth harbour, they had him committed to custody, first in Ireland and later transferring him to England, where it was soon observed of him that he 'carried himself in his accustomed half-wild fashion'.[9]

Just as perplexing for the Dublin authorities was the fact that they were finding it difficult to counter the perception in Ireland that the earls had been badly treated, that they were forced into exile by unwarrantable pressure, rather than as a result of their own treasonable conduct. This attitude persisted despite the Baron of Delvin's arrest and subsequent confession to treason in early November 1607.[10] Delvin, it might appear to doubters, had been set up in much the same way in which it had been intended to entrap the earls. In these circumstances, Chichester wanted Howth to make a clean breast of his involvement in the affair and of what he knew, 'rather than by this underhand dealing to blemish the judgement of so great a state among that wicked crew in giving them a thought that they overreached by his and their secrecy'.[11] Finding Howth's reluctance in this respect infuriating, the Lord Deputy later quipped sarcastically that an 'open confession' could be 'done without any great blemish to his honour here, where so little shame is taken of being rebels or traitors, that the most part account him unworthy the name of his ancestors that hath not done some notable mischief'.[12] Even the Baron of Delvin's dramatic escape from Dublin Castle has not dispelled the perception that the royal authorities had indeed 'overreached' themselves. C. P. Meehan, often perceptive in his analysis of the circumstances of the Flight, lapsed into one of his occasional nationalistic diatribes when he alleged that Delvin's escape was contrived by Chichester with the connivance of the constable of Dublin Castle as part of an elaborate exercise in deception.[13] That Delvin risked life and limb by clambering down a thirty-five-yard-long rope is not considered, nor is the fact that a bounty was offered to bring him in 'alive or dead'.[14] It is equally worth noting that the constable of Dublin Castle was removed from his post, fined heavily and committed to prison.[15] The episode was so embarrassing to Chichester that he described it in private correspondence to the English Secretary of State as the 'most unpleasing tidings' that he had ever had to relate since taking office.[16] Indeed, the intrepid nature of Delvin's escape excited contemporaneous comparisons with the legendary Sherwood Forest outlaw, Chichester describing him as 'this young Robin Hood'.[17] To compound matters, it was later reported that Lord Howth (ever to the fore where matters of conspiracy, subplots and daring escapades were concerned) had 'advised' Delvin to escape from the castle and had 'taught him how to do it'.[18] Such was the instability in Irish affairs provoked by the Flight of the Earls and its highly uncertain aftermath that many more outlaws soon emerged, some innately hostile to the newly imposed English system of administration, and some who had genuinely fallen foul of events contingent upon the Flight.

It was in the powder-keg atmosphere that prevailed in Ireland after the Flight that even Sir Cahir O'Doherty, a youthful war hero on the side of the crown during the Nine Years War, came under acute suspicion of disloyalty. As a fifteen-year-old boy Cahir O'Doherty had distinguished himself in battle with Sir Henry Docwra, the commander of the English garrison at Derry.[19] Docwra described how Cahir had been 'with me, alighted when I did, kept me company in greatest heat of the fight, behaved himself bravely, and with a great deal of love and affection: so much so, that I recommended him at my next meeting with the Lord Deputy Mountjoy, for the honour of a knighthood, which was accordingly conferred on him'.[20] And yet even Sir Cahir, pejoratively described as the 'queen's O'Doherty',[21] was to find himself reported for treasonable activities by local government officials in the north-west in the aftermath of the Flight, allegedly having gone 'upon his keeping' (in effect raising revolt) with a group of followers and his wife, stationing themselves on Tory Island. O'Doherty was appalled that he had been so traduced by crown officials who, he claimed, had entirely misconstrued a wood-cutting expedition which he had undertaken at Canmoyre Wood, near Kilmacrenan in Donegal. The action of Sir George Paulet, the governor of Derry, in attempting to seize his castle at Burt, where his wife was then in residence, particularly enraged him. Given that the local crown authorities had effectively engaged in military action against him, O'Doherty considered it prudent to take military pre-cautions for his safety before he hastily addressed a written defence of his conduct to the Lord Deputy, followed by his prompt arrival in Dublin to seek the Lord Deputy's personal intervention in resolving the matter.[22]

Overall, O'Doherty's demeanour was not suggestive of a rebellious tempera-ment. Indeed, his wife's presence at Burt Castle when Paulet arrived to seize it betrayed the inaccuracy of the original report that she had departed for Tory Island with her husband. What had happened was that the conspiratorial mania sweeping the central government in Dublin, and in particular the obsessive notion that rebellion was looming, had permeated to local officials, who had even greater reason to be sensitive to the prospect of a renewed conflagration, many of them occupying exposed positions with little more than 'scarecrow' forces at their disposal in hostile territory. Owing to severe financial stringency that culminated from the Nine Years War, the royal garrison nominally numbered only 880 infantry from 1606. Following the Flight, the infantry garrison doubled within a matter of months.[23] However, the quality and equipment of the reinforcements demonstrated that the English govern-ment was scraping the barrel when it came to undertaking military preparations at this time. Two hundred men who arrived from Workington after the Flight 'were without arms and clothes, and an object of derision to the Irish'. Thirty were sent back by Chichester because they were unfit to serve.[24] Many more of the reinforcements who subsequently arrived were sent back before long as well. Indeed, a controversy soon arose because so many troops were being rejected by the commanders in Ireland. The Lord Deputy felt obliged to come to the defence of his officers, claiming that a further twenty men might have been sent back to England, describing them as 'old persons or otherwise disabled and insufficient, and who, for mere debility of body, will be soon con-sumed here without any other adversary'.[25] (The fact that James I had resorted to raising a company of foot from the jails of northern England as well as from among groups of wanted outlaws a matter of months before the Flight of the

Earls also testified to the difficulty of enlisting troops for Irish service. The Commissioners for Northumberland were instructed in May 1607 to 'select 100 men from any of the outlaws of Riddesdale and Tynedale, except the ringleaders, taking from prison those accused of lighter crimes and to enlist them for the king's service in Ireland'.)[26] Clearly there was little stomach in England for renewed conflict in Ireland. Consequently, even with the arrival of additional troops, it is clear that a sense of vulnerability pervaded the crown administration. Regional officials such as Paulet, therefore, had every reason to feel exposed.

In these difficult circumstances, O'Doherty had the misfortune of not only contending with a paranoiac situation in the wake of the Flight but also of coping with a particularly fractious individual such as Paulet. As the historian Richard Bagwell noted, Paulet was 'soon at daggers drawn' following his assumption of the Derry command, not only with local Irish chiefs but the local Protestant bishop as well.[27] Significantly, Lord Deputy Chichester admitted in February 1607 that Paulet's arrival at Derry had been an 'ill exchange … many dissensions have arisen since he came thither'.[28] Disillusioned by his paltry reward for his services during the Nine Years War, and appalled by Mountjoy's 'extreme leaning' towards Tyrone in its aftermath, Sir Henry Docwra had sold up his lands and military command at Derry to Paulet.[29] Had the complaisant Docwra remained at Derry, there can be little doubt that events in the north subsequent to the Flight of the Earls would have taken on a very different complexion. In the first instance, O'Doherty would not have been provoked into resorting to rebellion. Nor would the Ulster plantation have been as extensive as it was following the suppression of the revolt. In Docwra's retiring from Irish service there was to be a poetic injustice. He had consistently sought 'fair play' for the co-operative Irish, such as O'Doherty, Niall Garbh O'Donnell and O'Cahan, and his disgust that this had not materialised and his subsequent departure resulted in a train of events that left the Ulster Irish in general immeasurably worse off. As a direct result of O'Doherty's rebellion, the Ulster plantation was greatly extended in scope at the expense of the indigenous populace of the north.

Thus it was that Paulet, and not Docwra, was in command at Derry in 1607. In any other circumstances, Chichester would more than likely have considered that O'Doherty's word and deed conveyed innocence rather than revealing guilt. However, it was to be the youthful chieftain's misfortune to arrive in Dublin to justify his conduct a matter of days after Delvin had made his audacious escape from Dublin Castle, inclining the Lord Deputy to 'mistrust many in whose care and honesty I could before that time have reposed my life and safety'.[30] Clearly O'Doherty fell into this category. Having at first found it hard to 'give firm credit' to the allegations which had been made against O'Doherty on account of his 'outward carriage heretofore', Chichester dramatically changed his mind in the wake of Delvin's escape, suddenly finding it difficult to believe that O'Doherty was 'free from ill-meaning'.[31] Indisposed to gratify

O'Doherty's petition to declare him innocent, the Lord Deputy instead slapped a massive 'recognisance' of £1,000, with two sureties of 500 marks each, on the Inishowen lord, forbidding him to leave the country without licence, before releasing him.[32] Subsequent experience demonstrated just how unhappy O'Doherty proved to be with his peremptory treatment in Dublin. As fate would have it, in his next clash with the irascible Sir George Paulet, he chose to resort to traditional Irish methods, raising revolt, rather than seeking English justice. In the meantime he redoubled his efforts to assimilate with the English system, acting as foreman of a jury in Donegal that indicted the Earl of Tyrconnell for treason in January 1608.[33] He also began lobbying to be appointed to the household of the Prince of Wales.[34] It was a measure of the distrust rampant in Irish society that O'Doherty, such a prominent ally of the crown, was now struggling to remain on good terms with the royal authorities.

Sir Donal O'Cahan, who had proved so instrumental in the crown's campaign to undermine the Earl of Tyrone's territorial claims, was soon to find himself in a similar predicament. Marks of favour, such as the knighthood conferred upon him, and offers of 'legal aid' in which he had received the assistance of no less a person than Sir John Davies, the Irish Attorney General, were no longer the order of the day. Within months of the Flight, Chichester was to describe the man he had so recently knighted as 'a barbarous unworthy man'.[35] His services now surplus to requirements, O'Cahan found himself cast aside. O'Cahan's fate in 1607, it is worth stressing, strikingly recalled the Lord Deputy's view of him at the time of his submission to the crown in 1602. Chichester stated then that 'It will be profitable to temporise with him until the greatest work be done, after which these petty lords will be dealt withal at pleasure.'[36] Having exploited O'Cahan to undermine Tyrone's position, following the Flight the Dublin government was no longer interested in asserting the proprietorial rights of major indigenous freeholders claiming substantial tracts of land; instead official thinking was turning towards a plantation of some sort by Protestant colonists. O'Cahan's personal claim to own 'O'Cahan's country', much of present-day County Londonderry, was no longer tolerable. In his turn, he was to be cast in the mould of an overmighty subject with grandiose ambitions. Ironically, it was to be the Protestant Bishop of Derry, George Montgomery, O'Cahan's mentor in his earlier disputes with Tyrone, who led the assault on O'Cahan's proprietorial claims. In particular, Sir Donal was incensed that Montgomery was 'demanding great quantities of lands within his country'.[37] Too late, therefore, was O'Cahan to realise that he had been duped into becoming a stooge when he took such an avid part in the plot to undermine Tyrone. It was not a fate he accepted with equanimity. Seething with resentment, he refused, pointedly, to take part in the indictment of the Earl of Tyrone in January 1608, at a time when the royal authorities noted that, while he himself had 'not as yet done any violent act', it was suspected that his brother was playing 'Robin Hood' with his connivance.[38] Chichester, it is worth noting, was no Sheriff of Nottingham in any other respect than having a ruthless streak. The Lord Deputy was a military leader of the highest calibre. Bungling was not one of his characteristics. The Robin Hoods of his era and their merry men did not cock a hoop at him for long.

So far as O'Cahan's conduct was concerned, at another time his understandable petulance might have been interpreted as just that, and overlooked. This was not how such behaviour was interpreted by the crown authorities in the aftermath of the Flight, Bishop Montgomery leading the accusations that Sir Donal was manifesting rebellious tendencies.[39] What exacerbated matters for O'Cahan were the treasonable allegations levelled against him by his brother, Shane Carragh.[40] Fraternal jealousy, indeed ambition, appears to have motivated Shane Carragh into betraying his brother, though the fact that Shane Carragh himself later became an outlaw undermined the original allegations that he had made against Sir Donal, as Chichester admitted.[41] Sir Donal, as fate would have it, was to find himself the subject of precisely the same pressures that had beset the Earl of Tyrone in the period before his departure, when an avaricious Bishop Montgomery and a disgruntled kinsman proved willing to do the crown's dirty work. It is doubtful whether O'Cahan was conscious of the irony. What is certain, however, is that he did not appreciate his precarious position.

Quite simply, however justified Sir Donal may have been in his view that he had been double-crossed in his proprietorial aspirations, and outraged that he had been unjustifiably accused, he failed to appreciate his vulnerability in the wake of the Flight of the Earls. Mistakenly entertaining notions of self-importance that the royal authorities were no longer prepared to tolerate, O'Cahan queered his pitch with Lord Deputy Chichester by his unco-operative behaviour with local crown officials. When he was later summoned to Dublin by the Lord Deputy to explain his conduct and refused, he endangered his position still further. Determined not to brook such insolence, Chichester immediately ordered military dispositions to be put in place to force O'Cahan to back down and come to Dublin.[42] Even then, Sir Donal was not to be easily chastened, Chichester describing him at the time as a man of 'bold spirit'. Such was O'Cahan's mettle that he volunteered to be 'restrained' in prison until he could disprove the allegations that had been made against him or 'better excuse himself'.[43] Such an offer proved too tempting for the royal authorities to resist. Besides, reasons of state were soon to be offered as a pretext for keeping O'Cahan in prison, culminating in his lifelong confinement in the Tower of London. When the plantation of Ulster was later implemented, it is unlikely that O'Cahan's treatment had been forgotten by the so-called 'deserving' Irish who had little reason to be happy with their own allocations. As one who had played such a crucial role on the crown's behalf in the run-up to the Flight, no man would appear to have been more 'deserving' of crown patronage than O'Cahan. The significant point is that questioning the legitimacy of crown policy could have disastrous consequences, a factor which undoubtedly contributed to some extent to the passive response of the Ulster Irish to the subsequent plantation.

Overall, far from the crisis situation having abated with the Flight of the Earls so far as the royal authorities in England and Ireland were concerned, the event itself, in conjunction with the behaviour of Howth and Delvin's subsequent confession and escape, provided conclusive proof that the grave suspicions which had been entertained before the Flight had been justified. The English ambassador in Spain reported on the clandestine plotting in progress both in Ireland and on the continent during the spring of 1608. One Patrick Grant, a Waterford merchant, had been sent to the earls with letters informing them 'that most of the gentlemen of the country and many of the towns would either publicly or secretly give them assistance at their return'. The earls were told only to bring money, 'for the country would yield so many bodies as the English forces sent thither by the king should be but a breakfast'. Plans were being laid to send six experienced officers in disguise from the continent at Michaelmas, the season for herring fishing in the Irish Sea. Secret transport, it was also suggested, was to be made available at the same time to convey the earls back home, using French shipping carrying wine. Michaelmas, the harvest season, was believed to be the 'fittest in regard of the corn in the barns, and the good case that the cows and other cattle of the country be in'. In Ireland supplies would be stored in the house of the daughter of the Bishop of Cashel (i.e. Archbishop Magrath), while 'of all the towns in Ireland, the greatest confidence is in Galway'.[44] Thus, despite the fact that English ambassadors on the continent had been issuing threats about the dire consequences that would ensue for Spain in the event of Philip III providing military assistance for the fugitives, an intense suspicion remained in royal circles in England and Ireland that Tyrone could be returned to his homeland with the clandestine support of foreign allies. It was for this reason that although the royal authorities in England were encountering great financial hardships in making ends meet, costly military preparations continued to be undertaken to secure the western kingdom. In the financial year subsequent to the Flight of the Earls (which encompassed O'Doherty's short-lived rebellion) some £100,000 was spent on Ireland, resulting in 'not a penny left' in the English treasury. The Earl of Salisbury, it was reported, was 'tearing his hair out in despair' at the expenses incurred.[45] It was a measure of the English crown's anxiety to relieve the immediate financial burden that it was decided to introduce the infamous 'impositions' in England.[46] The 'impositions' were taxes raised on the basis of crown prerogative rather than with parliamentary consent. Speaking in the 1610 parliament in England, the Earl of Salisbury attempted to justify these extra-parliamentary taxes: 'The cause of them was the wars in Ireland, for this kingdom being in great fear, nay in assuredness of the wars there, it was no time to call a parliament to relieve the present occasion.'[47]

As it happened, Salisbury's defence of the impositions cut little ice in the English parliament. The furore over the impositions was to prove a crucial factor in poisoning the relationships between the Stuart monarchs and their parliaments, not least by featuring prominently in the English parliament's rejection of Salisbury's 'Great Contract', an ambitious scheme which had been designed to set crown finances on an even keel once and for all.[48] Desperate to raise funds to cover the expenses that had been incurred in Ireland, James was persuaded to resort to another controversial expedient, the creation of a new hereditary title known as a 'baronet'. Baronetcies could be purchased for an annual sum of £1,000 over three years, this being the amount required to sustain a band of thirty soldiers in Ireland.[49] Events associated with the Flight of the Earls, therefore, were to have profound ramifications for the body politic of England, playing at least some small part in the sequence of events leading up to the English Civil War.

As for the king himself, at the time of the earls' departure the cautious sovereign was particularly upset by the Flight and its potentially dangerous consequences. James was famous for his predilection for the chase, with the result that administrative affairs in England were often left unattended, much to the exasperation of the king's ministers. In his handling of the aftermath of the Flight, however, James was nothing if not the model sovereign. By early December 1607, while the crisis was at its height and developments were awaited anxiously, troops were dispatched to Ireland and the royal fleet was in the process of being hurriedly refitted. All precautions having been taken in hand, James departed for the chase. His Privy Council in London, though, according to the Venetian ambassador in London, was left specific instructions to keep him 'duly informed of all that is going on'.[50] And for James I to allow himself to be disturbed on his hunting expeditions testified to the seriousness with which he viewed the affair.

Chichester's problems, meanwhile, persisted. He was flabbergasted by the capricious conduct of Lord Howth, and perturbed as to whether in fact he was still engaged in treasonable practices. Besides, the Lord Deputy was faced with the added difficulty of preventing Howth's exposure as the informer. In the end he decided that he could not possibly release Howth 'without giving a palpable feeling to all suspicious and understanding men that he is the discoverer of the treason of which there is already some mistrust'.[51] As for Delvin, every effort was being made to secure his capture. Such was the consternation with which news of his escape was received in royal circles in Dublin, that the Lord Deputy was attended by as many as eighteen Privy Counsellors (rather than the usual average of between five and eight) — a measure of the seriousness of the situation — when he issued a proclamation banning people from 'receiving or harbouring' Delvin and promising a reward for his 'apprehension'.[52] Chichester's primary concern was that although the youthful baron was initially supported by a small group of forty men, there was a danger that he would act as a magnet to draw together 'loose and idle men', Ireland being 'full of that sort', who would congregate with any leader prepared to 'make a head for rebellion'.[53] Such concerns induced the Lord Deputy to respond favourably to a letter written to him by Delvin shortly after his escape in which he sought pardon for his indiscretions, claiming that 'his fault [was] only in thought, and not in act'.[54] Delvin, not surprisingly, was anxious to play down the degree of his involvement in the treasonable intrigue. However, it was later reported that he had not simply been tinkering with the idea of revolt but actively engaged in planning it over a sustained period. Delvin and Howth, it was to be revealed, had grown into 'such great familiarity and had so many meetings under colour of hunting, so that all good subjects began to suspect that they had some ill intention'.[55]

Chichester's response was not entirely unfavourable to Delvin's request to be pardoned, despite his 'double crime', i.e. treason and escaping. Ever the pragmatist, and describing the offer of protection as a 'course too much sought and used in this country', the Lord Deputy nevertheless offered terms to the fugitive lord whereby if he turned himself in within five days, then the matter would be reserved for the king's decision.[56] Believing that he had a stronger hand to play, Delvin declined the general offer, standing 'stiffly for a protection' instead.[57] His predicament worsened, however, when Chichester became aware that Delvin had been more deeply involved in treasonable practices than had previously been believed. During a visit that Delvin had undertaken to England in connection with a proprietorial dispute he had had to be physically restrained by a close associate from assassinating there and then the English Secretary of State, the Earl of Salisbury. According to Chichester, when Salisbury rejected his solicitations, Delvin became 'so discontented … that he went to a gentleman of his acquaintance then present … and told him thereof, protesting that he would forthwith take away his Lordship's [Salisbury's] life, whatsoever became of him'.[58] It was later confirmed that the source of this information was Delvin's brother-in-law, Luke Plunkett.[59] In the light of this revelation, Chichester signified that he was glad that Delvin had not availed of the opportunity to cast himself at the mercy of the king.[60] Determined to bring Delvin to his knees, the Lord Deputy deployed a further 200 troops in his pursuit. Before long, indeed, Chichester reported how his military dispositions had reduced Delvin to utter desperation. A foraging party sent out by Delvin was ambushed. Devoid of supplies, the youthful baron was forced to dissolve his company of followers, taking to the countryside himself with but 'one gentleman of his own name and a poor slave for his guide'.[61] His position had become so dire that he was mockingly depicted as lurking like 'a woodkern [Gaelic Irish outlaw] in a mantle and trouses',[62] quite a come-down for a member of the Old English nobility. This Irish 'Robin Hood' and his merry men had little reason for being cheerful.

Though he was as yet unaware of it, there was evidence that Delvin was not in an utterly forlorn situation. The English Privy Council responded to his escape (uninformed at this stage of the new allegations concerning Delvin's flirtation with the notion of murdering Salisbury) by signifying that in view of the reinforcements sent to Ireland it would be 'not only dishonourable but dangerous if the state should stoop to protections or conditional submissions'. His only prospect of salvation lay in throwing himself unconditionally upon the king's clemency. Critically, though, it was King James's 'inward purpose to be merciful to him'. Once again the London administration opted for appeasement. They explained their decision by acknowledging that they were not 'ignorant that he [Delvin] is well allied; by his mother a Geraldine, by his father a Nugent, by himself allied with the Plunkets', his father-in-law being the Baron of Killeen.[63] Essentially the London authorities were acutely sensitive to the curdling of relations with the Old English nobility that could result from Delvin's execution. That Delvin had been seduced into becoming involved with the conspiracies of the Earls of Tyrone and Tyrconnell was bad enough; there was little point in alienating other leading figures in Old English society if it could be avoided.

In marked contrast, there was less reason to be sensitive to vulnerable members of the Earl of Tyrone's extended family who had remained behind following the Flight. In the first instance, the Flight of the Earls effectively sealed the fate of Brian MacArt O'Neill, Tyrone's nephew. He was already in custody on a charge of murder, and the earl had failed in his endeavour to bribe the Lord Deputy into securing his release before the Flight. To some extent Tyrone's solicitations in this respect proved the key to Brian MacArt's undoing. Fynes Moryson commented on what he termed the earl's 'tyranny by craft', recollecting that the 'famous traitor Hugh, late Earl of Tyrone, used in his cups to brag that by one trick he had destroyed many faithful servants to the state, namely by causing them underhand to be brought in question for their life, and then earnestly entreating the Lord Deputy and the judges to pardon them, who never failed to execute them whose pardon he craved'.[64] Certainly Chichester suspected that despite the earl's 'nearness in blood and other entire obligations' to Brian MacArt, Tyrone was not without 'a jealousy of him'.[65] Either way, close ally or rival of the Earl of Tyrone, the Lord Deputy was determined to get rid of Brian MacArt. The charge against him was dropped to manslaughter, though capital punishment would still nevertheless result from conviction. The viceroy claimed that MacArt was so popular that his transportation from Newry to Armagh for trial could not be risked 'for fear of rescue'. He was sent for trial to the King's Bench in Dublin instead.[66] What Chichester was not prepared to admit was that no jury in Armagh would have convicted him, whereas a guilty verdict in Dublin was a foregone conclusion, such was the manner in which the due processes of the law could be manipulated at this time. Described as the 'last man that submitted himself in the end of the war … he is besides so gracious and popular that after the decease of the earl it is credibly thought he will attempt to restore the name of O'Neill again'.[67] And for the Irish administration led by Chichester this was sufficient to secure his death warrant. His subsequent execution was a source of great satisfaction to Sir John Davies, who affirmed that 'the hand of justice has cut him off, which is a notable example to all the kingdom'.[68]

There was also the question of how to deal with Conn O'Neill, the Earl of Tyrone's young son who had been left behind. As a security precaution he was immediately committed to custody, at first at the hands of Sir Toby Caulfield at Charlemont, though this was to be the beginning of a lifelong detention in English custody. The key to Conn's treatment lay in Chichester's affirmed delight that Tyrone had chosen to flee with so many of his family circle. As far as the deputy was concerned, the Flight was far 'better for the king and commonwealth than if he were in the Tower of London, for by this course he has carried his children and kinsmen with him who were in remainder in the estate of his country, and I think unacquainted with his treasons before their departure, when by this all will clearly be in His Majesty's [possession]'.[69] However, the deputy had exaggerated on two counts. In the first instance, experience was to prove that the spectre of Tyrone's return, raised so often in forthcoming years, made him the deputy's recurring nightmare, his bogey-man. In the second place, the scenario that Chichester had painted was not as rosy as he had suggested. There were loose ends in the O'Neill family circle remaining in Ireland that needed to be tied up (placed in fetters being perhaps a more appropriate description). Apart from Conn O'Neill, there was the earl's brother, Sir Cormac O'Neill, who had also not taken part in the Flight, by choice rather than by accident in his case. Sir Cormac claimed after the earl's departure that he had not enjoyed particularly fraternal relations with his brother since the end of the Nine Years War in 1603. Indeed, it is quite clear that he had been unaware of Tyrone's treasonable conduct. He was reported to have accompanied Tyrone to within five miles of Derry, at which point he learned of the resolution to take flight. Evidently Sir Cormac wanted no part in the escapade, although it was later held against him that he had not warned the local crown authorities about what was to take place. In the absence of advance warning of the event, the Baron of Dungannon had been able to travel uninhibited to Derry to buy 'bread and other necessaries' that were in short supply for the trip. However, what especially concerned the authorities in Dublin was that Sir Cormac was the 'only man now left in this kingdom who is in reversion of the earldom'.[70] Hoping to utilise the Flight of the Earls to embark on a plantation in Ulster, Sir Cormac's legitimate claim to the earldom provided the proverbial fly in the ointment. It was perhaps this unpalatable prospect that inclined the ever-inventive Sir John Davies to conjure up the fanciful notion that Sir Cormac's request to have *custodiam* of the earldom had been prearranged with the earl with a view to forestalling the crown's intentions to dispose of the lands by plantation.[71]

The reality appears to have been much more mundane. Sir Cormac, after all, had demonstrated his unwillingness to be associated with the Flight by refusing to take part in it when offered the opportunity. What is more, he clearly did not enjoy the earl's confidence, only learning so late in the day that the Flight was about to take place. In the circumstances, that the earl and Sir Cormac had contrived such an understanding as Davies alleged seems highly improbable. In Sir Cormac's so-called confession after the Flight the only titbit of additional information that he could provide was that the message which Tyrone had received from the continent had been delivered in a hollowed-out 'cudgel' (a shillelagh). In vain did the naïve Sir Cormac offer to become an informant on his release, promising to 'get good intelligence of his brother's intentions', even suggesting that he would communicate with the fugitive earls 'in Irish and acquaint the Lord Deputy and state with his letters and answers from time to time'.[72] Far from being a confederate in Tyrone's scheming, the sentiments expressed in Sir Cormac's 'confession' testify rather more to fraternal rivalry than collaboration. It seems clear that Sir Cormac viewed the Flight as an opportunity for staking his own claims, little realising his vulnerability; this attitude was typical of many of his contemporaries, Gaelic chieftains beguiled by the prospect of every cloud having a silver lining. That Sir Cormac's conduct did not merit the lifelong captivity to which he was to be subjected was intimated at the time by the opinion of Sir Oliver St John, a senior figure in the Dublin administration. Sir Cormac, he affirmed, 'besides the opinion of his house [i.e. the O'Neills], has little in him to make him dangerous'.[73] In other words, complicity in treason was not the issue that determined Sir Cormac's fate. Rather, he was to be damned for his name at a time when the crown authorities were determined to eradicate the many-headed 'hydra' of the leading O'Neill family in Ulster. The Flight having lopped off so many of the figurative heads of the O'Neill hydra, the crown authorities had resolved to complete the task of decapitation.

Throughout the closing months of 1607 and into the spring of 1608, the sense of crisis gripping the government in Ireland remained conspicuous, a mood which prevailed on both sides of the Irish Sea. Contrary to the belief that once the 'initial shock of the flight had worn off, the government in London began to take less account of the seriousness of the situation than did Chichester and his associates in Dublin',[74] the London authorities remained every bit as concerned as their counterparts in Dublin. While the Venetian ambassador in London noted that the worries of the king had subsided somewhat during the early months of 1608, plans went ahead for the raising of special funds to deal with the emergency.[75] Indeed, at the end of March 1608 the ambassador was still referring to the '*current* crisis of Irish affairs'.[76] Diplomatic relations in Europe continued to suffer. The Earl of Salisbury, it was reported, had used 'very sharp language' to the archduke's ambassador, complaining about the reception afforded the earls. Once again the Venetian ambassador had got to the nub of the issue. Despite the fact that the archduke of the Netherlands and the Spanish government in Madrid had been striving to 'remove suspicion from the minds of the English, they will never succeed in doing so until the English see Tyrone entirely cast off by them' — a prophetic statement in the light of subsequent experience.[77] Strapped for cash, James I had resolved on raising a loan of a 'million of gold. ...The object for which this money is required, though not specifically stated, is for Ireland, where matters, though quiet, are still a cause for suspicion, especially as the peace in Flanders will leave Spain the freer.'[78] Such was the prevailing sense of consternation that military provisions were being made in England in direct response to the

Flight as late as May 1608 (by which time the new crisis of O'Doherty's revolt had erupted, serving to accentuate the consternation of the London government even more).[79] The authorities in London and Dublin continued to display sensitivities to the possibility that sedition and conspiracy were still rife and to harbour acute suspicions as a result. And they were entirely justified in so doing. Some Catholic priests were undoubtedly doing their best to inflame matters in Ireland, exactly as Chichester alleged.

According to the Lord Deputy, it was 'no marvel' that the Irish were so 'inconstant and wavering; they are so abused by their priests … who daily secretly … keep them in ill humour and appetite until the return of the fugitives, whereof they assure them; which causes them to think of nothing else but preparations of arms, and in the meantime to pursue that privately in their houses and loughs, which are seminaries of Catilines [i.e. revolutionary conspirators]'.[80] During the spring of 1608 Chichester reported that 'twelve apostles from the Pope' had arrived in Ireland, each appointed to one or other of the Old English towns 'to stir them to rebellion'. Tyrone, they assured their flocks, would return before the end of September with 'powerful succours'.[81] Reacting to the activities of the 'twelve apostles', Chichester gave vent to his frustration that 'Common law does not warrant the drawing of the sword against them, yet it is necessary to offend or transgress against the law in some things in order to maintain justice in great matters or in the whole.'[82] Charges that priests kept the pot boiling on Tyrone's behalf were to be sustained until the earl's death in 1616. While there was some truth in this, since priests were in the vanguard of a Counter-Reformation cause which at times had a military as well as a strictly religious dimension, the fact was that the Lord Deputy tarred all Catholic clerics with the same brush, itching to destroy them all by 'fire and sword' if only King James would grant him free rein.[83] While not all priests were engaged in treasonable practices, there can be little doubt that the Catholic clergy played a critical role throughout the years 1607–16 in perpetuating the expectation that Tyrone's return was imminent. Bardic poetry of the period epitomised the aspirations of the earl's supporters, who never lost hope that he would one day return. Tyrone was portrayed as the 'liberator' or cast in the 'messianic role of Moses'.[84] And yet, until the plantation of Ulster ultimately materialised to the detriment of the indigenous populace of the north in 1610 (much to Chichester's disappointment), the situation remained fluid. Whether such hankering after the fugitive lords would have been sustained had the plantation allocations been more generous to the Ulster Irish is open to question. Many, like the earl's brother Sir Cormac, may well have been tempted to forswear loyalty to the exiled Tyrone if they had been given a substantial stake in the new settlement. Certainly there is evidence in the early period after the Flight that an opportunity existed for driving a wedge between the earls and many of their supporters.

The instance of Henry Hovendon, a former secretary to Tyrone who accompanied him on the Flight, illustrates the point that loyalties were not set in stone. Such was the secrecy in which the decision to take flight was shrouded that many of those who accompanied the earls to the continent had either not been informed of what was taking place until a very late stage in the enterprise, in some cases not until they had actually boarded the ship. Thus Hovendon alleged that he was 'innocent ... of partaking in any of Tyrone's councils' and that there were many other gentlemen in a similar position to himself who were greatly discontented.[85] Having anticipated a warm welcome, generous hospitality and the prospect of liberal 'entertainment' from the Spanish, Hovendon and others were disillusioned by their future prospects on the continent when it became clear that the Spanish had not encouraged the earls to seek refuge abroad. In the cold light of reality, financial concerns greatly worried many of those in the earls' retinue. That Hovendon had been frozen out from Tyrone's inner councils, being 'nothing so much trusted by Tyrone as heretofore', obviously played a part too in his disillusionment.[86] However, Hovendon's general sentiments were shared by many in the Irish regiment in Flanders, who would have welcomed a reconciliation with the English at this stage.[87] An English spy in Tyrone's camp encapsulated the prevailing mood among even the earls' closest followers when he commented that 'All those that are come with them [the earls] have, for the most part, a thousand times wished themselves safe back again.'[88]

The key issue at this time was that the expatriate Irish on the continent were unsure of the degree to which their ambitions would be satisfied as a result of the earls' perceived influence with the Spanish authorities. Ducats talked. At first, according to the English ambassador in Brussels, such were the 'favourable entertainments' accorded Tyrone on his initial arrival in the Spanish Netherlands that 'it put him [Tyrone] into a pride that great matters would have been done for his re-establishment'. When the earls' trip to Spain was so dramatically aborted in November 1607, it not only 'checked his [Tyrone's] hopes' but provided a sharp jolt to the aspirations of his companions at a time when there were rumours that the Irish regiment was to be disbanded.[89] The long years of conflict between the Protestant Dutch and the Spanish were drawing to a conclusion. The opportunity was not lost on Lord Deputy Chichester, that often astute observer of the Gaelic Irish mindset. Responding to the intelligence reports of disgruntlement in the Irish regiment, Chichester hatched an ingenious plan to lure its most prominent officers from their attachment to the earls by offering them a stake in the proposed Ulster settlement. His policy of enticement included a suggestion that 'they might be induced by entertainment or gifts of land, with some reasonable help to stock and manure it, he [Chichester] is of the opinion that they will soon be withdrawn' from foreign service.[90] The fact that this ambitious project was not taken on board by the London authorities, circumstances changing when rebellion flared once more in Ulster in 1608, should not lessen its historical importance. Had Chichester's advice been implemented, both in this respect and in seeking to grant substantial lands to the indigenous Irish who remained in Ulster, then the legacy of bitterness ultimately bequeathed by the Ulster plantation may well have been avoided to some considerable degree. As it happened, it was the Earl of Tyrone who managed to secure patronage for his followers on the continent. The English ambassador at Brussels noted that a new company was 'purposely erected in the Irish regiment for the disposing of those soldiers who came over in the ship with Tyrone'.[91] Chichester himself acknowledged that the regiment had been on the point of breaking up 'if the fugitive earls had not come amongst them, and dealt with the archduke for their stay and better usage'.[92] Not only that, but it is also arguable that the continued survival of the Irish regiment in subsequent years, particularly following the signing of a truce between the Dutch and the Spanish in 1609,[93] owed much to Tyrone's military potential to the Spanish in the event of renewed hostilities with England. As a result, the livelihoods of the soldiers serving in the Irish regiment came to depend on the Earl of Tyrone.

Intelligence reports of menacing Spanish military preparations reinforced the sense of beleaguerment afflicting the crown authorities in England and Ireland. Despite Salisbury's braggadocio in dismissing apprehensiveness about Spanish intentions, lingering suspicions remained in London and Dublin that the Spaniards would at some point seek to exploit Tyrone's potential as a diversionary ploy. Certainly Spanish government documents made it plain throughout the period of Tyrone's exile that they would be prepared to return the earl to Ireland forthwith in the event of renewed hostilities erupting between England and Spain.[94] The Anglo-Spanish war had petered out in 1604 through sheer exhaustion on both sides, not least financial. However, the searing religious, economic and national antipathies that had fuelled the hostilities could not be expected to evaporate overnight. Such prejudices could just as easily have reignited conflict. Consequently, when intelligence reports suggested that a new armada of as many as one hundred ships was being prepared by the Spanish in the early months of 1608, the worst was feared — that it was destined for Ireland.[95] An Irish pilot of one of the Spanish men-of-war was reported to have commented that 'before long it would be seen that Tyrone would do something'. An Irish merchant quizzed on the matter 'made no answer, but put his finger into his mouth and bit his nail; and in the end told him that before it were long there would be something done, which men little dreamed of now'.[96] That these rumours emanated from Irish sources perhaps indicated that they resulted from flights of fancy. On the other hand, that such speculation existed in Spanish naval bases may not be all that surprising. Elements in the Spanish military may still have harboured aspirations to bring war to the doorstep of the enemy that had frustrated the ambitions of so many of their predecessors.

Regardless of the actuality of Tyrone's imminent return, the prospect that he could come back was sufficient to impact on royal policy in Ireland. Religious persecution of Irish Catholics, which had played such a part in fomenting the conspiracies that precipitated the Flight, was abruptly suspended in the wake of the departure of the earls. The Venetian ambassador in London reported that King James and his advisers were endeavouring to 'hold the Irish by clemency rather than by force, and show themselves very indulgent, especially on the point of the Catholic religion'.[97] Whether such belated 'clemency' would have been sufficient to hold the Irish in the event of Tyrone's arrival back in Ireland is highly questionable. So worried were the London and Dublin authorities about the potentially disastrous consequences of the earls' return that they were to offer a reconciliation with the Baron of Delvin on terms which they had not previously been prepared to consider. In February 1608 Chichester acknowledged Salisbury's 'noble disposition in forgiving Delvin' for his alleged impulsion to assassinate him. The deputy, indeed, in 'private manner' put out feelers to acquaintances of Delvin at this time, informing them of Salisbury's 'disposition' in the matter. Chichester, against his natural inclinations, was now prepared to promise Delvin his life in return for his submission. Such were the dangers attendant on the possible return of the earls that not only was it feared that Ulster and other parts of Ireland would rise in their support but that 'this young Robin Hood [Delvin] will have many in the Pale that will aid and assist him in open action, and more in secret — a class more dangerous than the known rebel'.[98]

Conscious of the growing strength of his hand, though at the same time playing a risky game in view of the fact that Chichester had troops and spies scouring the countryside, Delvin held out for even more advantageous terms. Delvin let his conditions be known via an intermediary, Ralph Miles. Delvin did not personally meet Miles, but sent an envoy who would not 'open himself until he (Miles) had passed his oath that he would not discover him, or the time or place of their conference'. In an elaborate ploy to ensure that none of his accomplices should be exposed to danger, Delvin's proxy delivered a letter to Miles containing Delvin's demands, mostly written by a scribe on Delvin's behalf. Miles was then instructed to familiarise himself sufficiently well with the contents of the letter before the missive was torn up, in case 'the hand should be known'. In what amounted to an audacious attempt to secure maximum advantage, and to ensure that he would not be double-crossed, Delvin noted that the promise of his life would be of little avail if he were to end up a life-long captive, citing the case of Florence MacCarthy, from Munster, who he claimed was 'imprisoned in the Tower [of London] upon suspicion only, after he had his pardon'. Not content with assuring his own life and liberty, Delvin insisted that all his accomplices who had 'relieved' him since his escape should likewise be pardoned. Delvin concluded by signifying his regret about his 'unfortunate fall ... inveighing against those that entrapped him'.[99] The youthful baron did not specifically mention any names in this respect, but his subsequent demeanour towards Lord Howth made plain his belief that he himself had been the victim (to some extent disingenuously) of entrapment at the hands of his erstwhile comrade.

It was partly as a result of Delvin's subsequent overt hostility towards Howth that the 'discoverer' of the earls' treason was finally exposed, though the hare-brained Howth contrived to draw suspicion on himself in this regard, ultimately going so far as to admit brazenly in public his role in the affair. Symptomatic of his erratic behaviour in this regard was the fact that, on the one hand, within a matter of days after the Flight had occurred, Howth signified how aggrieved he was by 'those men's departure, thinking his discovery was made known to his disgrace'. Almost in the same breath, however, he lobbied for the command of a troop of horse both for himself and Delvin when the garrison was strengthened in the wake of the Flight, Chichester remarking that Howth expected 'great rewards for this discovery'.[100] Such an overt mark of patronage, if granted, however, would have done more than anything to confirm suspicions about the identity of the 'traitor' — as was implicitly acknowledged in June 1608 when Howth was finally granted command of a company of 150 infantry, 'having raised to himself many adversaries for doing the king service'.[101] Significantly, this appointment coincided with a rash of rumours that Howth had indeed been the 'traitor'.[102]

It was when Delvin took advantage of the renewed outbreak of hostilities in Ulster in April 1608 to secure his own submission that the finger of suspicion started to be firmly pointed at Howth.[103] On taking custody of the former outlaw in May 1608, Chichester noted that Delvin 'will not to this day confess anything against Howth, albeit he does mistrust him to be the discoverer and would not willingly come near him or discourse with him at his being here'.[104] Before long, Howth was to find himself ostracised by Delvin, with the Lord Deputy noting that 'many here are of Delvin's mind'.[105] Such was the degree of suspicion entertained about Howth that it was claimed that he was in danger of being murdered; Howth himself became so obsessed by this possibility that he even 'mistrust[ed] his best friends'.[106] Eventually, unable to bear the cold-shouldering any longer, he revealed his entire role in the affair: Chichester recorded that the 'Lord of Howth has by his own tongue declared that he is the discoverer of the treason, and that the king has given him a reward for the same, of which and divers other passages in that business, both there and here, it is said he spares not to speak'.[107] The Lord Deputy was appalled by Howth's conduct in this regard, referring to him as this 'intemperate lord'.[108] However, Howth's exposure as the 'discoverer' of the treason was to have a sting in its tail. Perhaps unwilling to shoulder the entire opprobrium for the affair, Howth caused a scandal in the Irish administration when he levelled the accusation that Sir Garrett Moore, a confidant of the Lord Deputy, had financially assisted Cúchonnacht Maguire's departure from Ireland some months before the events of September 1607 and had then later connived at the Flight of the Earls itself.[109]

Howth's testimony which had proved so beneficial to the crown authorities, in so far as it had flushed out the earls, rebounded on senior officials in Dublin when he indicted Moore as a party to the Flight of the Earls. Furthermore, Howth subsequently broadened the scope of his accusations to include lurid allegations against Thomas Jones, Protestant Archbishop of Dublin and Lord Chancellor of Ireland (whose son had married a daughter of Sir Garrett Moore).[110] Indeed, in what turned out to be a running feud that lasted for over four years,[111] several nephews of the Lord Deputy were to be implicated in a killing connected with the bitter dispute by Lord Howth.[112] Having compromised the earls then, Howth's bizarre conduct caused chaos in the very highest echelons of the Irish administration as well. His intention seems to have been to bring about the downfall not only of Sir Garrett Moore, but also of Moore's in-law, Lord Chancellor Jones, and even Moore's close personal friend, the Lord Deputy of Ireland. So far as the Flight of the Earls was concerned, however, Howth's assertion that Moore had prior knowledge of Tyrone's intentions to flee implicitly raises the fascinating possibility that Moore had apprised Chichester of Tyrone's resolution and that the Lord Deputy thereby also connived at the Flight. After all, the Lord Deputy quizzed Moore about the substance of the exchanges that had taken place at Mellifont the day after Tyrone left Moore's residence on his way to Lough Swilly. The charge that Chichester turned a blind eye to the Flight cannot be dismissed lightly. Having made such serious allegations against Sir Garrett Moore, is the 'half-wild' Howth to be believed in this instance or not, when experience in the period leading up to the Flight of the Earls had demonstrated the folly of being dismissive of his testimony in its entirety?

As with the evidence that he had furnished before the Flight, there remains a difficulty in disentangling elements of truth from the complex web of deceit and innuendo which characterised Howth's charges against Moore and his illustrious associates. In other words, what value may be attached to the accusations of such an unstable figure, a man under threat of assassination, a social outcast, as a consequence of his 'betrayal' not only of the Earls of Tyrone and Tyrconnell but his close friend, the Baron of Delvin? It was typical of Howth, and the web of intrigue and duplicity that surrounded him, that his testimony in this affair was tinged by bizarre allegations — some of which, quite remarkably, turned out to be accurate! Besides accusing Moore of conniving at the Flight, Howth furnished grotesque details about the personal conduct of Sir Garrett Moore and Lord Chancellor Jones. These centred on the behaviour of the 'conjuror and raiser of spirits', Mr Aston, a former chaplain to Sir Garrett Moore. Aston was allegedly employed on behalf of Lord Chancellor Jones, Archbishop of Dublin, to practise witchcraft with a purpose to uncovering the whereabouts of £60 that had been stolen from his trunk during the summer of 1608 — an allegation utterly refuted by Jones.[113] For such a senior figure in the Established Church to have employed a necromancer in this fashion was a damning accusation. When Aston was examined on this charge, the deviant minister confessed to the Lord Deputy that he had indeed practised sorcery to unmask the identity of the mysterious thief, alleging that the culprit had in fact been Lady Jones, wife of the Lord Chancellor.[114] Such was the sensitivity of the affair that the identity of the suspect was communicated by the Lord Deputy to the Earl of Salisbury in code.[115] Clearly, Chichester did not want to upset Jones.

The important point to bear in mind in this scandal, however, was that Sir Garrett Moore had sacked Aston as his chaplain some time earlier.[116] Thus it is quite possible that Aston was simply avenging himself on Moore, and that Lord Howth exploited this situation in an attempt to ruin his adversaries in the Irish administration. Whatever about the politics of the situation, the problem that confronted Moore and Jones in refuting Aston's allegations was that it was indisputable that Aston, though undoubtedly a man of objectionable personal conduct, had nevertheless served as Moore's chaplain and had actually been recommended for the position by Jones in his capacity as Archbishop of Dublin.[117] That Moore sorely regretted having employed Aston was made clear in his refutation of Howth's insinuations regarding the cleric. Sir Garrett pulled no punches in his condemnation of Aston's practices as a sorcerer whose activities, he claimed, resulted in his wife and children 'loathing … their home for a time'. Deeply embittered thereby, Moore launched a scathing attack on other aspects of Aston's personal conduct when he not only accused him of being a bigamist but depicted him as 'a common whorehunter' besides. Moore's bitterness at the can of worms opened up by Howth was manifest, not least because as a result of Howth's testimony the Lord Deputy judged it expedient to impose a massive bond of £9,000 on his friend and confine him to his residence while the allegations against him in relation to the Flight of the Earls were investigated.[118] Clearly Chichester was anxious to be seen to accord Howth's allegations due seriousness. Nonetheless, in an impassioned defence of Moore, the Lord Deputy exculpated his old friend from any blame in so far as the accusations regarding the Flight of the Earls were concerned. According to the Lord Deputy, if he had had any reason to 'suspect him [Moore] guilty of any treason [he] would rather be his executioner than his excuser'.[119] Similarly, Lord Chancellor Jones came to Moore's defence, affirming that he would never have permitted his son to have married Moore's daughter unless he had been assured that Sir Garrett 'carries a loyal and dutiful heart towards the king, and a zealous mind to further all his services'.[120]

Having come to the defence of Moore, however, the Lord Deputy was hard pressed to explain Moore's conduct, and indeed his own, in the days immediately preceding the Flight. According to Chichester's recollection of events following Tyrone's departure from Mellifont, he recalled that he had questioned Moore about Tyrone's 'mode of departure' early on the following morning. Acutely concerned by the fact that the earl had taken his 'little son', who had been fostered by the Moores, Chichester immediately dispatched Sir Toby Caulfield to Tyrone to muster all available forces in the area to counter what seemed to be such a menacing development. However, owing to the successful policy of confiscating weapons after the war, so that Tyrone was known to be 'altogether without arms and munition', the deputy explained that he was not greatly concerned that a major insurrection was imminent, never suspecting his 'flight beyond seas'. It was on this occasion that

Chichester signified that Tyrone's abscondence was 'far better for the king and commonwealth than if he were in the Tower of London', especially since he had taken most of his family with him to whom the earl's lands might otherwise have reverted.[121] Sir John Davies had also celebrated news of the Flight, describing it as an auspicious event 'wherein the countenance and majesty of the law and civil government hath banished Tyrone out of Ireland, which the best army in Europe and the expense of two million of sterling pounds did not bring to pass'.[122] The comments of Chichester and Davies give rise to a degree of suspicion that the Lord Deputy and his officials had been badgering the earls into fleeing from Ireland as Sean O'Faolain suggested.[123] Indeed, as the controversy over the circumstances of the Flight rumbled on Chichester responded to the allegations made by the earls that he had exerted pressure on them in the period preceding the Flight. As far as he was concerned, he declared, he cared 'not if he had scared them [from] hence, for worse members there could not be in a Christian commonwealth'.[124] The aborted flight of Tyrconnell in the spring of 1606, followed by Cúchonnacht Maguire's escape during the late spring of 1607, would have indicated that the leading Gaelic lords of Ulster were betraying vulnerability and that seeking refuge abroad was being contemplated seriously. If the Lord Deputy had been engaged in a clandestine policy of goading the earls into fleeing abroad, the role of Sir Garrett Moore in respect of the Earl of Tyrone would have been pivotal. Howth's allegations against Moore, therefore, may not have been as entirely absurd as they might otherwise seem.

As the fosterer of one of Tyrone's young sons, Moore was a confidant of the earl. As a close friend of the Lord Deputy too, Moore and his Janus-like tendencies could well have served Chichester's ends. Thus it is quite possible that Moore could have collaborated in Maguire's escape in the late spring of 1607. The fact that Captain Richard Tyrrell lent credence to Howth's allegations against Sir Garret Moore, averring that Lady Moore had given Maguire £30 'at the time of his going',[125] is significant in this respect. Even more crucially, in the aftermath of his flight the Earl of Tyrone claimed that he had been forewarned by 'intimate friends of theirs on the king's very council' that dire consequences would ensue from his proposed visit to London.[126] Micheline Kerney Walsh has suggested that the source of this warning was the pro-Catholic Earl of Northampton, a senior member of the Privy Council in England, and that the message was passed on to Tyrone via friends on the continent.[127] However, Tyrone's employment of the terms 'friends' (in the plural) and 'intimate' opens up the possibility that Sir Garrett Moore, described by Chichester as 'a prime counsellor',[128] looms large in the frame as one of those who played a role in raising the earls' apprehensions to such a degree that they made their fateful decision to seek sanctuary abroad. At most the Lord Deputy was prepared to admit that Moore's conversation with Tyrone 'did rather hasten his flight out of the kingdom by delivering unto him unnecessary speeches and reports, than that the other [Moore] winked at his departure'.[129]

Circumstantial evidence also induces suspicion of Chichester's ostensible disbelief at the Flight. In this context, it is worth recalling the rapid dispatch of Sir Toby Caulfield to his post at Charlemont in the heart of Ulster with instructions to be on full alert following Tyrone's departure from Mellifont, as well as the Earl of Tyrone's allegations that he had been so closely spied upon that he 'might have any hole in his coat'. In the aftermath of the Flight Chichester claimed that he had 'ever good watch and espial upon' the earls.[130] And yet the earls managed to evade such intense surveillance by a ruse as elementary as a midnight departure. The standard reaction of Dublin government officials had been to portray the Flight as an unsolicited 'accident'.[131] Depicting the Flight as a completely unforeseen event raises questions about the sincerity of such remarks, not least when Lord Deputy Chichester signified that he could never have contemplated that Tyrone would resort to such a 'disloyal and shallow intention as this', i.e. a sudden departure from the country.[132] The tongue-in-cheek nature of this comment is revealed by the fact that the viceroy had been persistently reiterating grave suspicions about Tyrone's questionable loyalty for several years previously. The undisguised euphoria in Dublin government circles that greeted the Flight is also interesting in this respect. Ireland, they believed, had reached a crossroads. The 'tyrannical' lords of Ulster had conveniently, if with a little help from their enemies, absented themselves, and Chichester was intent on filling the vacuum by giving a broadly based group of Ulstermen a stake in any new settlement. In the battle for the hearts and minds of the Ulster populace, it was a race against time. As the deputy quite rightly suspected, Tyrone was making determined efforts from the very start to secure foreign military support for his return. Much depended, therefore, on whether or not the Lord Deputy could deliver on his promises of fair treatment for the Ulster Irish. The outbreak of O'Doherty's rebellion in April 1608 precipitated a train of events whereby the Lord Deputy lost control of the plantation process and more punitive confiscatory policies were resorted to instead. In the end, as events turned out, the Ulster Irish, far from rejecting their former lords, continued to cast them in the messianic role of liberators who would one day deliver them from the yoke of foreign domination.

7

REBELLION

Before the initial crisis caused by the Flight of the Earls had a chance to subside Ulster was to be convulsed by yet more turbulence when the lord of Inishowen, Sir Cahir O'Doherty, launched his rebellion in Derry in April 1608. This event demonstrated the manner in which the Flight of the Earls continued to destabilise Irish society. The youthful O'Doherty, who had made more strenuous efforts to assimilate with the ascendant English system than any other indigenous Ulster lord, ultimately found himself forced to resort to arms and throw in his lot with the cause of the fugitive earls. Once more Irish affairs had international implications as the English authorities anxiously awaited the outcome of events, fearing that Tyrone might manage to exploit the situation in his homeland in such a way as to persuade friendly continental powers to provide him with military assistance. While O'Doherty's rebellion was to prove short-lived, the response of Philip III demonstrates that the Spanish king was at least prepared to consider this possibility. Such was the concern in London about the implications of the rising that some thought was given to effecting a rapprochement with the exiled earls. Had the rebellion lasted longer and proved more damaging to crown interests, there was also the prospect that Chichester would have been recalled from his post as Lord Deputy. Although Chichester managed to retain his position because of the prompt and effective manner with which he dealt with the rising, he lost influence with the London authorities as far as the plantation process in Ulster was concerned. The alleged tyranny of the traditional Gaelic lords in Ulster was not to be eradicated but supplanted when the indigenous populace generally received miserly allocations in the plantation and the opportunity created by royal policy for bringing about a reconciliation in the province was effectively stifled.

Despite his treatment over the Canmoyre Wood episode, O'Doherty persisted with his efforts to curry favour with the crown. Having served in the closing days of 1607 as foreman of the jury at Lifford, consisting of thirteen Irishmen and ten Englishmen, which indicted the Earl of Tyrconnell for treason,[1] the Inishowen lord embarked on an ingenious scheme to lock himself securely into the English system and insulate himself once and for all from the gratuitous hostility of crown officials. During the early months of 1608 he launched an ambitious project to become a member of the Prince of Wales's household. To this end he dispatched his 'solicitor', Henry Quinn, a Dublin merchant, to London. Quinn's brother Walter was 'in attendance on the prince in his court'. Henry Quinn carried several letters with him to London, including one from the Protestant Bishop of Derry, George Montgomery, perhaps indicating that Montgomery was writing a letter of recommendation to the prince on Sir Cahir's behalf.[2] At the very least, O'Doherty clearly enjoyed cordial relations with Montgomery. Indeed, it is possible that the bishop himself had devised this radical tactic. What is more, it is likely that Montgomery sympathised with O'Doherty's predicament in the harassment to which he had been subjected by Paulet, having himself suffered grave insult at the hands of the gruff governor of Derry. Overall, the youthful lord of Inishowen's conduct conveyed a willingness to be reconciled with the crown authorities rather than to distance himself from them.

Evidence suggests that O'Doherty's strategy was in the process of reaping dividends. Walter Quinn, for instance, wrote to assure him that he would do everything in his power to promote his suit at the court of the Prince of Wales. O'Doherty was advised not only to travel to London in order to advance his cause in person, but to send the prince a present of some hawks, a highly effective sweetener at a time when hunting was such a favourite royal pastime.[3] O'Doherty, very astutely, had also enlisted the support of the principal lord of north Antrim, Sir Randal MacDonnell, his 'loving friend', who was attending court at that time in his attempt to insulate himself from hostile crown officials in Ireland.[4] MacDonnell, a Scot by ancestry, had skilfully ingratiated himself with James I[5] and was therefore considered to be a conduit to the king's favour. MacDonnell's success in exercising leverage with the king to resist the pressures of a hostile royal administration in Dublin was all the more remarkable considering that Lord Deputy Chichester had pursued a personal vendetta against him that was even more venomous than that which he had harboured against the Earl of Tyrone. The longstanding feud resulted from Sir Randal's beheading of the viceroy's brother, Sir John Chichester, during the Nine Years War.[6] Despite Sir Arthur Chichester's searing hatred, Sir Randal MacDonnell was later to be elevated to the title of Earl of Antrim and to have the last laugh at the expense of his old adversaries the Chichesters. Years later, on visiting the tomb of Sir John Chichester in St Nicholas's Church in Carrickfergus, with a sculpture showing an image of Sir John (head included), Sir Randal quipped: 'How the de'il came he to get his heid again? — for I was sure I had ance ta'en it frae him.'[7] O'Doherty's tactics in pursuing his interests through the agency of influential friends soon secured a victory in a protracted proprietorial dispute over the island of Inch. The English Privy Council issued a letter on 18 April 1608 signifying their decision in O'Doherty's favour in the matter.[8]

This day was to be a fateful one not only for O'Doherty but for the course of Irish history in general, for it was the very day on which O'Doherty, oblivious to his striking success at the English court, launched a very different type of strike in Ireland instead, assaulting the English garrison at Derry.

When O'Doherty launched his attack on the tiny settlement of Derry on 18 April 1608, it was characterised in royal circles in Dublin as part of the ongoing conspiracy that the earls were believed to have been fomenting. Voicing his frustration that 'such perfidious accidents as this have ever been as natural here, once every six or seven years, as showers are in April',[9] Chichester blamed the sudden revolt on the circulation of false reports that eight strange ships had arrived on nearby coasts. The deputy claimed that these rumours had been 'devised on by some turbulent and seditious brains, who have given an untimely fear unto this treason, which should not have been acted but after assurance of the fugitives' landing'.[10] The real reason for O'Doherty's revolt was much more mundane, emanating from private grievances for which Chichester was to some extent responsible. That O'Doherty resorted to declaring his attachment to the earls as his clarion call was merely an act of desperation.

The attack on Derry culminated from O'Doherty's ever-growing conviction that he would not get justice from the English. The trigger for the rebellion resulted from yet another incident involving Sir George Paulet, O'Doherty's *bête noir*. In early April 1608 the Inishowen lord was in Derry on business. In the course of the proceedings O'Doherty and Paulet became involved in a heated exchange. According to the Four Masters,

> Great dissensions and strife arose between the governor of Derry, Sir George Pawlett, and O'Doherty. ... The governor not only offered him insult and abuse by word, but also inflicted chastisement on his body; so that he [O'Doherty] would rather have suffered death than live to brook such insult and dishonour, or defer or delay to take revenge for it; and he was filled with anger and fury, so that he nearly ran to distraction and madness. What he did was to consult with his friends how he should take revenge for the insult which was inflicted upon him.[11]

O'Doherty's instigators were not named, but there is a *prima facie* case that Sir Niall Garbh O'Donnell, a powerful figure in Donegal, played an instrumental role in encouraging O'Doherty to take action. It appears, however, that Niall Garbh was acting as a double agent, affecting to be O'Doherty's friend on the one hand while bartering his co-operation with the crown authorities on the other, soliciting a grant of O'Doherty's lands in return for collaboration. Significantly, when O'Doherty was originally suspected of treason at the time of the Canmoyre Wood incident, Niall Garbh had been promised Inishowen in return for bringing O'Doherty to submission.[12] Manifestly, or so it appeared at the time, Niall Garbh had much to gain should O'Doherty actually embark on a treasonable course of action.

If Sir Niall Garbh's role cannot be categorically proved,[13] there is no doubt that O'Doherty's foster-father, Feidhlimidh Riabhach Mac Dhaibhéid, convinced him that he had no option but to rebel. Shortly before the attack on Derry O'Doherty had been instructed by Chichester to hand over Mac Dhaibhéid to the local English authorities to answer charges that had been made against him. That he should be expected to turn in such a close ally was interpreted by O'Doherty as yet another sign of the Lord Deputy's hostility towards him personally. It was 'with tears in his eyes' that O'Doherty approached several English officers beseeching advice on how to regain the Lord Deputy's favour. On being advised that delivering up his foster-father would assist this process, O'Doherty reluctantly obliged, though it clearly pained him greatly to do so, etching another bitter wound on his psyche.[14] Ironically, O'Doherty's representations on his behalf may well have resulted in Feidhlimidh Riabhach Mac Dhaibhéid's subsequent release in time to take part in the rebellion.

Significantly, it was not just a matter that O'Doherty felt aggrieved at the treatment that had been meted out to Feidhlimidh Riabhach. According to Henry Dillon, the English Attorney General of Ulster,[15] Feidhlimidh Riabhach had been provoked into rebellion by the pettifogging behaviour of the newly appointed justices of assize, the great majority of them Englishmen, who had been baiting him for several years, not least by making 'many referments of his causes to such persons as maligned him'.[16] Evidently Dillon believed that the clinical application of English legal strictures, so novel to the Ulster Irish in the wake of the petering out of hostilities in 1603, had proved counterproductive in the case of Mac Dhaibhéid, a leading figure in Donegal society who had otherwise shown himself well disposed to the crown. In Dillon's view, Feidhlimidh Riabhach had been exasperated by the activities of the itinerant judges, 'so that by this proceeding the fellow was impoverished and made desperate, and for revenge drew Sir Cahir to this rebellion'.[17] Sir Henry Docwra was even more forthright in condemning the crown officials who unjustifiably provoked Feidhlimidh Riabhach. He bitterly regretted the deaths of the Mac Dhaibhéids in the subsequent rebellion, describing them as

> all men of very good parts, and deserved a better countenance, at least from the state, than my credit was able to procure them, which, if they had had, and those courses foreborne that Phelime Reaugh was vexed withal, by particular persons, upon no sufficient ground of reason that I am witness to, their lives had perhaps been preserved to this day, and a better opinion conceived of us in general than is by the rest of that natiŏn. Let no man censure me amiss for this kind of saying, for I hold it a sin to conceal a truth where I am interested and have occasion to speak it.[18]

Overall, it is clear that O'Doherty's rebellion was provoked by an accumulation of injustices at the hands of crown officials in Dublin and locally, as well as personal insults. The Inishowen chieftain's conversation with his acquaintance

Captain Hart, constable of Culmore Fort, on the evening before the attack was launched on Derry lends credence to the contention that his decision to take drastic action originated from private grievances. O'Doherty harked back to the incident at Canmoyre Wood the previous autumn, insisting he had been misrepresented by local crown officials when they accused him of launching a revolt at that time. Consequently, having been 'so hotly pursued' by Paulet, he declared that he would now 'play the enemy whom they [the English] would not admit for a friend'.[19] At a later stage Chichester signified his personal regret about the manner in which the Canmoyre Wood episode had been mishandled, not least by himself implicitly, acknowledging that 'all men believed he [O'Doherty] had been wronged'.[20] Events in Derry during the initial attack reinforce the impression that the rebellion was entirely avoidable. As few as six or seven on each side were killed in the course of the assault.[21] Evidently the assailants were discriminate in whom they attacked. The Lord Deputy signified as much when he reported that

> When Sir Cahir O'Doherty had killed him [Paulet] and the subsheriff, and understood for certain that the Recorder and one Coatmore were not to be had there (whom he likewise hated) he said he had as much of his desires as he could effect for the present and so forbore the slaughter of the people.[22]

Among those taken prisoner were Bishop Montgomery's wife and sister.[23] Soon afterwards some of the prisoners were released, O'Doherty proclaiming that 'it was not blood that he sought for'.[24]

The nature of the attack on Derry also supports the contention that the resolution to embark on a revolt had been an impromptu rather than a premeditated decision, so poorly armed were the assailants — even if the strategy employed was ingenious. On the evening before the assault on the tiny colony of English at Derry, O'Doherty invited his friend Captain Hart, constable of Culmore Fort, and his wife to dinner at Buncrana. Following the meal O'Doherty revealed his plan to take military action against his enemies. Hart, described as his 'gossip',[25] was not considered as belonging to this category. O'Doherty asked him to betray Culmore Fort, which Hart resolutely refused to do, despite being threatened with death. At this point in the proceedings O'Doherty prevailed on Captain Hart's wife, who, fearing for her husband's safety, agreed to take part in a clever ruse to deliver Culmore Fort into O'Doherty's hands. She returned to the fort in affected distress that her husband had fallen from his horse and had broken his leg. The warders of the fort immediately rushed out to the rescue, only to find that they had been lured into an ambush, and the fort was thereupon captured by the rebels.[26] Culmore's seizure was critical to O'Doherty's plan to attack Derry, as he was desperately short of weapons. In fact, even after securing the royal arsenal at Culmore, not all of his band of about one hundred men who took part in the assault on Derry were armed, a testimony once again to the success of the government's disarmament policy in the aftermath of the Nine Years War. This was manifested in the ensuing hostilities when a certain Lieutenant Gordon, who 'issued forth naked upon the rampart', killed two rebels, only to be hit on the forehead with a stone and rendered 'somewhat amazed' thereby. He was then overcome and met his death not far from the 'bogside' area of Derry, the scene of another famous battle involving stone-throwers almost four centuries later.[27]

Lacking sufficient arms and men, O'Doherty depended on the element of surprise for success, launching his attack at two o'clock in the morning.[28] Paulet's superiors in Dublin were appalled on learning of the fall of Derry, given the fact that there were about a hundred soldiers and another hundred male inhabitants who could have been mustered to its defence.[29] It was not as if concern for the welfare of Derry postdated the rebellion, or in other words that castigating Paulet for his poor defensive arrangements was a convenient way of self-exculpation for the authorities in Dublin and London. Several times in the aftermath of the Flight of the Earls concern was expressed for the security of Derry. Following a tour of inspection of Irish fortifications under-taken by Sir Josias Bodley as a security precaution in the wake of the Flight, the English Privy Council signified their disquiet about the decaying state of the settlement at Derry.[30] Chichester responded at the beginning of April 1608, a matter of weeks before the rebellion, expressing his own concern for the welfare of Derry, not least because of 'dissensions between Sir George Powlett and the bishop, captains, and principal inhabitants, the poor infant city daily consumes and wears away'.[31] Most damning of all for Paulet was the fact that Sir Richard Hansard, the English commander at Lifford, had notified Paulet of suspicious activities in the region several days before the assault on Derry.[32] In view of the feebleness of the resistance put up by the garrison, Paulet was to become the victim of posthumous character assassination by the incensed authorities in London and Dublin. The English Privy Council noted that had 'not the rebels taken away his [Paulet's] life, it could not in justice have been left him by the state'.[33] The martinet Chichester was even more scathing. He attributed the disaster at Derry to Paulet's failure to take the simplest of mili-tary precautions, posting a nightly watch.[34] Given the military weakness of his enemies, perhaps the arrogant governor of Derry was imbued with a false sense of security. That Paulet's personal defects contributed to the catastrophic out-come of events is patently clear. According to Chichester, Paulet was such a detestable individual, 'so odious to the soldiers [the English garrison] and to the rest of the inhabitants of the town besides, that they would have done him a mischief in the tumult, if he had escaped the rebels and come in amongst them'.[35] As it happened, according to one account, it was Feidhlimidh Riabhach Mac Dhaibhéid who wreaked his personal revenge on the governor of the city, breaking open the doors of his residence and pursuing Paulet, who made a desperate bid to escape in the dark, only to be killed shortly afterwards.[36]

Elsewhere in Derry O'Doherty attacked the 'lower sconce', beginning significantly at the residence of one Mr Harrison, the under-sheriff, one of the newly appointed English officials in Ulster. It was a reflection of the manner in which English local government officials had been badgering him and his close associates that when O'Doherty called at Harrison's door he mockingly notified the under-sheriff that 'he had a writ for him to serve presently'. Instantly realising his predicament, Harrison was reported to have rushed out of his house with a pistol in one hand and his sword in the other, shooting a 'kern [rebel], whom O'Doghirty readily had thrust between himself and the danger' as a human shield.[37] Having seized the 'infant city' of Derry, O'Doherty then torched it, all eighty-five houses.[38] Bishop Montgomery's library, containing some 2,000 books, was also set on fire, despite the fact that the bishop offered a £100 ransom for their safe-keeping.[39] In the circumstances, the burning of the books was probably not an act of mindless, wanton destruction. Rather, it is likely that they were consigned to the flames owing to their perceived 'heretical' content. For their role in the sack of Derry, the Mac Dhaibhéid clan were afterwards known by their Protestant neighbours as the 'Burn-Derrys'.[40] The Inishowen lord followed up his striking successes at Culmore and Derry with an ingeniously simple plot to seize Doe Castle. A 'cowherd of the place' was reputedly persuaded by a friar into raising a false alarm that a number of wolves were attacking the cattle. Falling for the ruse, five of the six warders of the castle dashed out to rescue the livestock, only to meet their deaths at the hands of the rebels, the castle then falling into O'Doherty's hands. Basking in the euphoria of victory, O'Doherty's force soon swelled to 500 men. By contrast, the tiny number of British colonists in Ulster at the time panicked on hearing news of the rebellion. Some Scots who had set up home in Strabane burnt their residences before making for the relative security of the English garrison at Lifford.[41]

What had started out as a rebellion emanating from essentially private grievances was beginning to snowball, not least because O'Doherty jumped on the fugitive earls' bandwagon, declaring that 'all he has done is in zeal for the Catholic cause'.[42] While it is difficult to ascribe strategy to the actions of a man who had embarked so spontaneously on revolt, O'Doherty's conduct and statements hint that his actions were not quite so rash. His previously ambitious scheme to ingratiate himself with the crown authorities by seeking to become a member of the Prince of Wales's household, combined with his stunning successes at Culmore, Derry and Doe, demonstrated that the youthful chieftain of Inishowen and his advisers manifested a considerable degree of cunning. Having been provoked into rebellion, it is arguable that O'Doherty pursued two interlinked approaches to realising his objective, either of which would have secured his position. Having been sparing in whom he had killed at Derry, he seems to have been hopeful that the crown authorities would placate him rather than risk costly hostilities, particularly as the English were so sensitive to the prospect of the earls' return. Alternatively, if this failed to materialise, given the prevalence of reports that the exiled earls were on the point of returning, O'Doherty perhaps hoped to hold out until help arrived from the continent. According to the testimony of Feidhlimidh Riabhach, O'Doherty had been given to understand that the earls would return with aid by the end of September 1608.[43] Consequently, latching on to the 'Catholic cause' was his best method of generating popular support for his rising.

Early indications suggested that O'Doherty was managing to win over key elements in Ulster society to his side. Not only did the O'Gallaghers, fosterers of the Earl of Tyrconnell, participate, but the spread of the rebellion to south Armagh was also ominous for the crown authorities. Eoghy Óg O'Hanlon, O'Doherty's brother-in-law, embarked on hostilities near Newry. More significantly, Eoghy Óg was Tyrone's nephew,[44] a fact which was regarded by the Venetian ambassador in London as adding gravity to the situation.[45] As events turned out, Eoghy lived up to his name (*Eochaidh*: horseman, cavalier), proving an elusive enemy to the English.[46] All in all, the situation was deeply depressing for Lord Deputy Chichester. Following the outbreak of the revolt he launched a vitriolic attack on the recurring problems caused by 'under-officers', an implicit reference to the dereliction of duty on the part successively of the constable of Dublin Castle, who had permitted Delvin's escape, as well as the provocative activities of Paulet. In the circumstances, Chichester expressed a desire to be allowed to relinquish his position as Lord Deputy when the rebellion had been suppressed.[47] While the Lord Deputy had no qualms about publicly blaming others for the disastrous state of affairs, it is possible that the tendering of his resignation proceeded just as much from private reservations about the manner in which he had mishandled O'Doherty at the time of the Canmoyre Wood incident and the perception that he could be held culpable as a result. What is certain is that Chichester's position was in jeopardy as a result of O'Doherty's revolt. Rumours circulated in England and Ireland that he was about to be replaced. Significantly, in one instance it was reported that James I had become 'persuaded that the mistaken conduct of the present viceroy has much to do with these events'.[48]

Chichester's determination to suppress the revolt before relinquishing his post was the key to the developments that unfolded, not least because his reputation was at stake. In contrast to the typical experience of the sixteenth century, when outbreaks of rebellion were often appeased by timorous or ill-equipped viceroys, O'Doherty was unfortunate in encountering a Lord Deputy as courageous as Chichester, an experienced soldier who compensated for apparent military vulnerability by resolute action with whatever forces he had available. For Chichester, the best means of defence was attack, despite the fact that the entire English garrison in Ireland comprised no more than 1,700 infantry.[49] To some extent he was fortunate in being able to facilitate a prompt response by utilising some 400 troops already stationed in northern regions of Ireland in preparation for an operation that was being planned against rebellious elements in the Scottish Isles.[50] In total, a body of some 800 or 900 men was dispatched to encounter O'Doherty,[51] a force described at the time by Sir Josias Bodley, a military expert, as a 'small diminutive of an army'.[52] Five hundred Ulstermen were also to be raised to take part in the campaign, Chichester justifying this tactic on practical grounds, 'to engage so many able men who would otherwise be stirring against them and would confirm the rebels'.[53] The royal commanders were instructed to engage in a 'thick and short' military campaign, implying that the deputy's penchant for resorting to all necessary ruthlessness was to be employed.[54] Instinctively Chichester himself was 'very desirous to have gone down into the north … to make a speedy and gross prosecution of these rebels, before the fugitives should return or they should receive further comforts or assistance from them'. On reflection, he opted to take stock of the general security situation in Ireland and awaited instructions from England.[55] Meanwhile he busied himself with preparations for the field, ordering a general hosting in the Pale for 24 May.[56]

Responding to events in Ireland, the authorities in London noted the 'gravity' of the situation, the rebellion having 'greatly disturbed the king and the government'.[57] The Privy Council promptly authorised Chichester to launch his campaign in the north, noting that 'speedy success will divert any foreign forces, if any such be destined for the rebels'.[58] That profound suspicions were entertained in London about the possibility of Tyrone exploiting the rebellion with foreign assistance was revealed by a prominent figure in court circles in London, Sir Ralph Winwood, who noted in the wake of the rebellion that 'If all advertisements be true, there is a purpose to assist Tyrone not only in Spain but likewise in Italy.'[59] Overall, so far as the English were concerned, bringing a speedy conclusion to the rebellion was critical, forestalling any attempt by the exiled earls to capitalise on it. Early modern communications were so cumbersome, however, that there was to be a suspension of many weeks between the outbreak of the revolt and the news percolating as far as Rome. Even if the earls were contemplating returning as a result, a period of at least several months would have been likely to have elapsed.

Such was the purposefulness of the deputy's response to the rising that it goes some way to explaining why the rebel forces congregated to no more than 1,000 at their peak.[60] To some extent also, this was attributable to the general scarcity of arms in the hands of the indigenous population of Ulster as a consequence of the 1605 disarmament proclamation. Perhaps most important of all for the earls' sympathisers, though, was the fact that many in Ulster were awaiting firm news of the widely expected return of the fugitive earls before rising out in rebellion themselves. As Lord Deputy Chichester remarked, 'It may be taken as certain that every mother's son of them will go into rebellion if any foreign assistance … or but some of the principal fugitives shall arrive.'[61] While news of the return of the earls was anxiously awaited on both sides, O'Doherty led a force of some 400 on a foray deep into the heart of Ulster.[62] Chichester commented on O'Doherty's tactic of ranging from 'place to place' as a ploy to keep the 'vulgar sort in expectation of the return of the fugitives'.[63]

Interestingly in this respect, the rebel chieftain was careful not to ravage the lands of the Earl of Tyrone, but conducted himself 'so warily that he burnt not Dungannon as he threatened nor took the prey of the country but to restore all again, except a few beeves'.[64] Evidently O'Doherty was conscious that a returning Earl of Tyrone would be less than amused by the sack of Dungannon. By contrast, the rebels had no such qualms about wreaking destruction on the lands of crown allies. Thus Sir Henry Óg O'Neill's settlement at Kinard was attacked. The town was burnt and Henry Óg was killed. Even more disturbing for the crown authorities was the fact that Eoghy Óg's contingent had swollen to 300 and was expected to make a rendezvous with his brother-in-law. More comforting for the deputy, though, was the expectation that O'Doherty's forces would 'spoil' the country and that 'these grasshoppers will be consumed for their excesses next winter'.[65] Chichester was clearly contemplating resorting once again to the type of starvation policy that had been employed to finally bring the Earl of Tyrone to terms at the end of the Nine Years War. As for O'Doherty, he swept so far south as to threaten the Pale, a tactic which the Lord Deputy considered was designed to draw crown forces back from the north.[66] Chichester, extremely hostile to the Old English Catholics, was unimpressed by this strategy and unconcerned about any potential damage inflicted on the Pale, in spite of the fact that the maintenance of order and civility in this region was a traditional preoccupation of viceroys. Consequently, he persisted with the campaign in the north. Instead it was O'Doherty who was to find his freedom of manoeuvre restricted as his ancestral lands, including his primary residence at Buncrana, suffered an onslaught from crown forces. Sir Thomas Ridgeway, who took part in the northern expedition, noted how the army 'could not abstain from burning it [Buncrana] as well from anger as for example's sake'.[67]

Even more galling for O'Doherty was the fact that he was too late in returning to his patrimony to prevent his wife from falling into enemy hands. She had taken refuge in Burt Castle with her infant son. The remaining prisoners from the capture of Derry were also lodged there, including Bishop Montgomery's wife. In O'Doherty's absence, Burt Castle was besieged and ultimately surrendered. On arriving at Burt, the royal forces encountered a belligerent response from its defenders, who declared that they held the castle for O'Doherty and the King of Spain, 'adding withal that they had but a life, which they owed to God, and would rather pay it there than fall into their [English] hands, where they would be used like dogs'. Lady O'Doherty and her advisers then attempted to negotiate, seeking to protract the deliberations until Sir Cahir returned to raise the siege. Unwilling to offer terms to the rebels, the English commander discharged a cannon at the walls. Undeterred at first, the rebels responded spiritedly by threatening to put Bishop Montgomery's wife in any breach in the castle walls. However, if they felt this was their trump card, they were mistaken. The English countered by declaring that the 'king's honour was a fairer mark and to be handled more tenderly … than any woman in the world'. The opportunity of seizing the wife and son of the rebel chieftain evidently outweighed concerns for the wife of a Protestant bishop. Consequently, several more volleys were then discharged at the castle, soon achieving the desired response of surrender. The only condition sought by the besieged was one night's grace in the 'hope that Sir Cahir would with a swift march come to the raising of the siege and rescuing of his lady'.[68]

And Sir Cahir was returning, but not swiftly enough. Finding his troops disheartened by the setback at Burt Castle, O'Doherty reportedly came under pressure from his men 'to do something against the king's forces, or there vowed to leave him'.[69] Smarting from the setback of the seizure of his family, the rebel leader within a matter of days decided to confront the small crown army at Kilmacrenan, a few miles west of Letterkenny. Writing to the O'Gallaghers of Loughveagh, O'Doherty declared that no man should 'imagine we are any weaker' for having lost Burt. Far from it, such was the rebel chieftain's confidence at the time that he declared that 'Now that we have given them over [i.e. having defeated English forces at Derry], we make no reckoning of them.'[70] Vengefulness mixed with bravado was a potent cocktail, a combination that may have had a bearing on the disastrous outcome of events at the battlefield of Kilmacrenan a few days later. The rebel chieftain, it is reasonable to assume, was hell-bent on defeating the government's forces in the area with a view to securing the release of his wife and son. Ideally his strategy for long-term survival, while awaiting the arrival of aid from the earls on the continent, lay in traditional Gaelic hit-and-run practices. The unexpected turn of events at Burt Castle put paid to this. At any rate, O'Doherty took to the field at Kilmacrenan at the head of a force of up to 1,000 men.[71] Hostilities occurred on ground well chosen by the youthful chieftain, 'the ways being impossible for [English] horse to serve upon them [the rebels]'.[72]

According to a contemporary propagandist English account, the battle that took place was ferocious, both sides engaging each other with gusto:

> The music of war struck upon both sides, to give encouragement to those that wanted no spurs to prick them forward. Bravely was the onset given, and as bravely answered: you would have thought that thunder had been only upon earth, the guns did speak so loud, and with such dreadful voices: yea, swords meeting with swords threw abroad such sparkles of fire, that the field seemed to be all made of flames.

The fighting was reputed to have raged, according to this version of events, for many hours, in the course of which 'arms and legs flew up into the air',[73] before the crown forces eventually won the day. This account, while obviously highly exaggerated in its description of events, demonstrates clearly that the English were ecstatic that victory had been wrapped up so promptly against O'Doherty at a time when yet another prolonged rebellion had been feared. A less dramatic version of the battle recorded that a 'hot skirmish' raged for half an hour before a most unexpected development occurred.[74] The rebel chieftain was hit 'by a happy shot which smote him on the head'.[75] After being shot, O'Doherty was reputed to have fallen prostrate to the ground, 'his hand ly[ing] directly under his cheek (his head leaning upon it)'.[76] Feidhlimidh Riabhach Mac Dhaibhéid made a spirited attempt to rescue the youthful chieftain's body before being driven off.[77]

Such was the inaccuracy of early modern weaponry that the bullet that hit O'Doherty was undoubtedly a fortuitous one. However, that the lord of Inishowen should have found himself the principal mark aimed at by English musketeers would not have been at all surprising, since a reward of £500 had been placed on his head, a sum that was duly paid out of the 'preys and booties taken from the rebels'.[78] An undignified scramble then ensued to secure O'Doherty's head and the reward that went with it.

Who killed Sir Cahir O'Doherty is a mystery that has intrigued historians over the years. One version suggests that O'Doherty was killed by one of his own men who could not resist the temptation of gaining the reward.[79] A much more lurid and dramatic account of Sir Cahir's death attributes it to private revenge. The wife and children of a Scottish colonist, Sandy Ramsay, were reportedly slaughtered by O'Doherty's marauding troops. For days on end Ramsay waited, stalking the rebel chieftain. His patience was finally rewarded, and he shot O'Doherty in the forehead. O'Doherty's men fled the scene, and Ramsay severed the dead chieftain's head from his body, wrapped it in his plaid, and then set off for Dublin to claim the reward. However, there is a twist in the tale. Availing of the hospitality of one Terence Gallagher, Ramsay stopped off for the night. He fell asleep, using the plaid containing Sir Cahir's head as a pillow. Waking first in the morning, Gallagher noticed blood oozing from his guest's pillow. Slitting a hole in the tartan plaid, Gallagher recognised O'Doherty's face. Realising that it was worth a fortune, Gallagher promptly filched O'Doherty's head from the sleeping Ramsay and set off to claim the reward.[80] That there is scarcely a grain of truth in this account of O'Doherty's death testifies to the confusion that has existed over the centuries about the precise circumstances of the event. The reality was that neither Ramsay nor Gallagher ever laid a hand on O'Doherty's head. English troops recovered it from the battlefield at Kilmacrenan, and the head was delivered to Dublin by Rice Coatmore, the English government official who had been lucky enough not to have lost his own head at Derry at the outbreak of the rebellion when O'Doherty came looking for him.[81] English treasury accounts demonstrate that a rank-and-file English soldier, John Trendor, claimed and received the bounty.[82]

What is not in doubt is the fact that O'Doherty's death demoralised his men and that they retreated in disorder from the field. The corpse having fallen into English hands, the decision was then taken to dismember it in the manner appropriate for a traitor (from an English point of view). For salutary effect, O'Doherty's quarters were to be put on display in Derry as 'signs', and his head was to be brought to Dublin, where it was later put on display at

Newgate.[83] There was a punctilious determination on the part of the authorities to ensure that the proprieties of English justice were observed and an exemplary lesson offered to all potential rebels. To this end, great efforts were made to capture rebels alive in order to put them on trial for treason. In one instance, a provost marshal, who had the legal power to inflict summary execution, was recompensed instead for holding twenty-six rebels in custody for twenty-seven days before they were executed at Lifford.[84] Spared hanging at the provost marshal's halter, the captives perhaps never imagined that an even more ghastly fate awaited them. There were special reasons why the provost marshal was rewarded. Chichester's administration had opted for formal treason trials, since the sentence of hanging, drawing and quartering was not permitted under martial law. 'The spectacle of this horrid form of death, which was new to them' was resorted to for maximum impact on the people of Ulster.[85] Among the first to suffer this fate was Shane Carragh O'Cahan, brother of Sir Donal. Condemned to death as a traitor, and on the gallows, Shane Carragh was given religious instruction to prepare himself for his imminent demise by a monk who had himself been involved in O'Doherty's rebellion. However, the monk had abjured his Catholic faith in order to be spared a similar fate. As a result, Shane Carragh was appalled to hear

> the monk give instructions contrary to that form of religion which he knew the monk had professed in former times; he thrust him away from him and said that he deserved hanging for revolting from the Pope's religion: and so cast himself from the gallows and was hanged.[86]

Chichester described the manner of Shane Carragh's execution as a 'kind of death seldom or never seen in these parts of Ulster before this time, and seems to terrify them more than that of hanging by martial law'.[87] However, on reflection, it was a source of bewilderment to the Lord Deputy how the Irish reacted even to the prospect of hanging, drawing and quartering, describing them as 'generally so stupid by nature, or so tough or disposed by their priests, that they show no remorse of conscience, or fear of death'.[88]

There was even greater celebration among English ranks at the capture of Feidhlimidh Riabhach Mac Dhaibhéid. Having been found isolated in a wood by a company of troops, he was only eventually taken into custody after being severely wounded in the chest by a pike, and even then had to be 'beaten down before he could be taken'. The marshal of the army took 'great care for his curing or keeping him alive for his trial'. Spared death in order to be executed, Feidhlimidh Riabhach and twenty others were to be 'tried and executed as traitors'.[89] As a result, Lifford was to be the scene of a macabre spectacle as the rebels were ceremoniously subjected to the penalty for treason, hanging, drawing and quartering. The grotesque nature of the punishment was meant for ostentatious effect. The convicted traitors were first dragged around the streets tied to horses. After that they were hanged. They were then disembowelled, had

their bodies cut in quarters and their heads put on display.[90] In view of the precarious state of Feidhlimidh Riabhach's health, it is uncertain how much of this
gruesome ritual he endured before finally succumbing. Described as the 'firebrand of the rebellion',[91] he was regarded as O'Doherty's principal lieutenant,
and it is likely that it was his head that a contemporary pamphlet depicted
impaled above Newgate in Dublin along with O'Doherty's in its aftermath.[92]

O'Doherty's 'happy' demise, from the point of view of the authorities
in London, was an unexpected godsend. James and his advisers were still reeling
from the military expenses which had been incurred by the precautions neces-
sitated in the aftermath of the Flight of the Earls.[93] Following the outbreak of the
revolt, the Venetian ambassador noted that the 'affairs of Ireland occupy the sole
attention of the king and his council'.[94] Problems were being experienced in
raising troops to send to Ireland because of the difficulty of 'persuading troops
to fight in that country where they are sure of suffering for no profit'.[95] Had the
youthful chieftain chosen the more traditional Irish policy of evasion, there was
every likelihood that even a limited form of rebellion could have been sustained
for quite some time. Delvin, after all, had evaded capture for over six months
despite being relentlessly pursued. Indeed, many of O'Doherty's followers held
out for over a year before the government resorted to the compromise measure
of transporting them abroad. Thus the London government was extremely
apprehensive that the rebellion would result in massive expenditure. Such had
been the trepidation in London on news of the rebellion that consideration was
given for a time to pardoning the fugitive earls.[96] Had Chichester not remained
so stoical in the face of the challenge, ordering his meagre forces to engage the
enemy, the ramifications of O'Doherty's rebellion could have been very different: the earls could have been invited to return, and Ulster would not have been
colonised by Protestants in the manner that it subsequently was. O'Doherty's fortuitous death changed all that. There was jubilation in London when O'Doherty
was killed, his death redounding to the Lord Deputy's credit. A contemporary
English pamphlet boasted that 'as O'Dougherty was speedy in the execution of
his mischief, the Lord Deputy made as quick a dispatch for the prosecution of
revenge'.[97] Far from being replaced, as had been seriously contemplated,
Chichester was showered with praise for the expeditious manner in which he
had stamped out a menacing revolt. It was a measure of the gratitude of King
James I that the Lord Deputy was rewarded with a grant of virtually the entire
peninsula of Inishowen.[98] By contrast, news of O'Doherty's defeat and death was
greeted with dismay among the expatriate Irish communities abroad, not least
in the retinue of the Earl of Tyrone. But a period of time was to elapse between
O'Doherty's death and news of it reaching the continent; and in the interval
between the first reports of the outbreak of the rising and the subsequent arrival
in Europe of confirmation that it had been suppressed, several interesting
developments occurred.

As with the situation which prevailed in the aftermath of the Flight of the
Earls, the eruption of O'Doherty's revolt poisoned international relations

once more. English suspicions that it had been fomented by Spain, or could be exploited by the Spanish, inclined James and his advisers seriously to contemplate sabotaging the peace negotiations between the Dutch and the Spanish. The Earl of Salisbury, for instance, made it abundantly plain where he believed the fault for the rising lay. Reports of the lavish manner in which the Spanish authorities at Milan had entertained the earls on their journey to Rome had been particularly damaging, 'whereby the minds of the ill-affected Irish, who brag of nothing more than of great succours and support which Tyrone is to receive from Spain and the archduke, are made insolent and drawn into such inconsiderate attempts as that of O'Doherty's is'.[99] That the hindering of the negotiations was a serious option in London was made clear by the Venetian ambassador, though the English were worried in case they were suspected of having 'upset the truce'.[100] The London authorities were thus faced with a dilemma. Sabotaging the peace negotiations between the Dutch and the Spanish might go some way to ensuring that the Spanish were tied down militarily and diplomatically, thereby inclining them to steer clear of making commitments either to the exiled earls or the rebels in Ireland. On the other hand, should the Spanish suspect English machinations in this regard, there was a danger that they could prove counterproductive. In other words, the Spanish could be provoked into exploiting the situation in Ireland in revenge. Either way, a complex diplomatic scenario prevailed on the continent in the wake of the Flight of the Earls and O'Doherty's revolt. What was certain was that the rebellion bolstered Tyrone's claims that Ireland was a powder-keg waiting to explode on his return.[101] And yet it was a measure of the fluidity of the situation which pertained in the aftermath of the Flight that the Earl of Tyrone, before the arrival of the news of O'Doherty's revolt, was leaving his options open for a rapprochement with the London authorities. Tyrone was described in an English intelligence report as using 'all reverent talk and dutiful respect towards His Majesty [James I], and so that it may seem that he doth not only honour him as his prince but love him as his sovereign, lauding greatly his many virtues, and excusing what any man may seem to mislike'.[102] Hitherto a master of *realpolitik*, Tyrone obviously had begun to sense that diplomatic considerations were precluding the prospect of immediate Spanish military assistance and that it would be advisable to pursue an alternative approach, utilising Spanish leverage to secure the best possible deal. O'Doherty's revolt changed everything, and for a time Tyrone's star was in the ascendant once more. On the international stage he was no longer a pawn, but a prince who had his own pawns to play — in this case the rebels in Ireland.

C. P. Meehan, in his absorbing account of the 'fate and fortunes' of the earls, objected vigorously to the manner in which the earls had been 'stigmatised as his [O'Doherty's] abettors and setters-on'.[103] Tempted at times to indulge in a hagiographical rendition of Tyrone's career at the expense of everybody else, Meehan was determined to dispel the 'delusive halo' that Irish nationalist posterity bequeathed on O'Doherty. Instead the youthful lord of Inishowen was execrated for having been foreman of the jury that had found the Earl of Tyrconnell guilty of treason following the Flight. Such was the nature of Meehan's invective against O'Doherty that he even suggested that O'Doherty's fate was richly deserved: 'Little did he [O'Doherty] think that the retributive justice of heaven was to overtake him …'[104] There was no appreciation of O'Doherty's vulnerability in the wake of the allegations which had been made against him at the time of the Canmoyre Wood incident. Besides, when dynastic considerations inclined O'Doherty and his foster-family, the Mac Dhaibhéids, into 'deserting' Tyrone's cause during the Nine Years War, the boy chieftain of Inishowen was engaging in the type of parochial, arguably 'selfish', politics of which Tyrone himself had become such a masterly exponent in his own rise to power. Indeed, Tyrone's response to the rebellion in 1608 demonstrates conclusively that no hard feelings were entertained about O'Doherty's earlier desertion. The revolt was simply seen as an opportunity to be exploited, even if its timing had not been orchestrated by the expatriate earls.

Far from disowning O'Doherty, the fugitive earls described the rebels as 'our vassals' and immediately launched a propaganda offensive designed to win financial and military assistance from the Spanish and papal authorities for their return to Ireland where they would assume their rightful position at the head of the revolt.[105] Pent-up frustration with Spanish prevarication concerning their position featured strongly in several letters written after news of O'Doherty's revolt had arrived in Rome. Not inclined to understate their position, the earls affirmed to Philip III that Catholic discontent in Ireland was so profound that the Old English Catholics would 'open all the ports to Spanish help' and that 'within a few days Ireland would belong to Your Majesty'. Conscious of the diplomatic concerns swirling around them, the earls argued that returning them to Ireland would trump England's diplomatic and military ace in relation to the Low Countries and that 'the English and Dutch would be held in check'.[106] (At the very least, the earls were correct in their conclusion that their flight and the subsequent rebellion in Ireland had altered the stakes on the international scene in Spain's favour. The English were reported in June 1608 to be 'more determined than ever to avoid mixing in anything that could cause annoyance to Spain', especially in regard to the Dutch. In a general comment on the situation, the Venetian ambassador in London noted that 'In truth for some time past they [the English] have treated the Spanish with much more respect than heretofore.')[107] Attempting to exert the greatest possible leverage on the Spanish, the earls engaged in what was tantamount to religious and emotional blackmail. Should 'reasons of state' not prevail on the Spanish king,

> We humbly beg that Your Majesty be moved by Christian feelings to defend the Irish nation so that its people may not lose the Catholic faith which they have professed and upheld for thirteen hundred years. If now, through lack of help from a Christian prince, the Irish should lose this faith, they [the

earls] may well call God and his saints to witness that it was not because their courage failed them. … Perhaps others may be called upon to answer to God for having failed to help them when it was easy to do so, either openly or in secret.[108]

There was a growing recognition, indeed, among the earls and their Irish associates on the continent that persuading the Spanish to aid them in a clandestine fashion was likely to be a more profitable avenue of approach.

The English ambassador in Spanish Flanders, Sir Thomas Edmonds, relayed intelligence reports that the Irish *émigré* community was only requesting financial assistance from the Spanish which would then be expended to make appropriate preparations. The implication was that by a variety of subterfuges Spanish military assistance would materialise — without it being apparent. As for the earls, it had been determined by their supporters in Flanders to advise them to convey themselves and their entourage in small groups back to Ireland via Germany and Scotland. Just as importantly, while permission would be sought to transport the Irish regiment *en masse* back to Ireland, the alternative of having the regiment discharged 'under colour of the truce or peace (then pending between Spain and Holland)' and procuring its transportation in small numbers was also broached. Edmonds signified that he was sceptical that the Spanish would countenance these machinations.[109] Nonetheless, the English ambassador at the Spanish court, Sir Charles Cornwallis, reported that large numbers of the 'vagabonding Irish' had converged on the port of Corunna (a key Spanish port which had been used as a base from which many expeditions had been planned against the English in the sixteenth century). Cornwallis attributed this to a growing, if, in his view at the time, misplaced, feeling among the Irish that military assistance was being planned for Ireland.[110] Significantly in this regard, following news that O'Doherty's rebellion had been suppressed, it was reported that the Irish had been 'lately roused and ferreted' out of Corunna.[111] Circumstantial evidence suggests then that the Spanish authorities were contemplating providing some form of military assistance for the earls and the rebels in Ireland. Indeed, Cornwallis later acknowledged that had O'Doherty managed to sustain his rebellion for a longer period 'some underhand help in money and munition would have been sent them'.[112] Meanwhile in Ireland suspicions were aroused by the activities of an unidentified ship flying English colours which had been observed surveying the ports of Baltimore and Cork in Munster in June 1608. The Lord President of Munster concluded that the ship had been 'sent to see what state we are in, and finding she would not be free amongst so many English, will hover about the coast until they have taken notice of all our preparations and strength'.[113] At about the same time Henry IV of France indicated that he had learned that the Spanish were planning to send seven warships to Ireland.[114]

And yet, on the face of it, initial Spanish reaction to news of the rebellion suggested that they were decidedly unsympathetic to sending military aid — at least as far as the Spanish Council was concerned. With Spain suffering from financial exhaustion, Philip III's advisers rejected outright any consideration of helping the earls in the situation that prevailed in the aftermath of the rebellion.[115] Previous experience, though, had demonstrated that the Spanish Council was amenable to persuasion on behalf of the earls. When the earls first attempted to negotiate Spanish financial assistance in the years following the Nine Years War, the Council was also initially indisposed to accede to their request. In the end the Spanish Council conceded the grant of an annuity, but not without securing commitments by the earls to renew rebellion in the event of new hostilities with the English. This 'treasonable contract' certainly broke the spirit, if not the letter, of the Anglo-Spanish treaty of 1604. Even more importantly, Philip III was personally inclined to take the issue of assisting the Irish rebel cause much more seriously than his council.

Responding to the 'troubled state of England' in the wake of the outbreak of the O'Doherty rebellion, Philip III remarked that it was 'clear that any effort made now to re-establish the holy faith in those parts would have a favourable chance of success and would be most pleasing in the eyes of God'. In his view, the best means of providing that help would be through the intercession of the Pope. The Spanish ambassador in Rome, consequently, was instructed to 'incite' the Pope to recover Ireland. The ambassador was ordered to 'advise me [Philip III] immediately of everything you do and of how the Pope receives all this'.[116] Writing a short time later in response to a further recommendation from the Spanish ambassador in England that the O'Doherty rebellion should be exploited, Philip III annotated the letter: 'Write to the Pope on this matter and await his reply. When it comes we shall see what may be done.'[117] The evidence suggests, therefore, that the Spanish king was contemplating a joint effort with the Pope. Exploiting the papal flag of convenience, Philip III tinkered with sponsoring some form of military help for the earls at this important juncture. It is interesting in this regard that the Spanish had previously packed the earls off to Rome to circumvent accusations of collusion with the fugitives, while at the same time secretly providing them with financial assistance. Philip III's train of thought in 1608 indicates he was considering a policy of military assistance by proxy, through the provision of indirect financial aid.

Spanish intentions at this critical period, however, can only remain a matter of speculation. The fact was that O'Doherty's sudden, unexpected death put paid to Tyrone's ambition to return to Ireland at this time. (The Earl of Tyrconnell's death at almost the same time, 28 July 1608, can only have increased Tyrone's despondency.)[118] It was with ill-disguised relish that news of O'Doherty's death was relayed by the authorities in London to the English ambassador in Venice, when it was remarked that 'It will bring him [the ambassador] good contentment to hear that the fugitive earls will find their party in the dust.' Of particular satisfaction was the fact that the collapse of the rebellion would 'pull down their [the earls'] insolency and discredit them with those states whom they have possessed with the fame of these men's [rebels'] greatness, to make themselves so much the higher by comparison'.[119] Tyrone's credibility in seeking to enlist Spanish military assistance subsequently may well have suffered from the fact that the rebellion had turned out to be so short-lived. Yet his reaction to the rebellion is in itself instructive. At a time when the implications of the revolt in Ireland remained uncertain, when English vulnerability had induced overtures of pardons for the earls, Tyrone was not interested. Instead all his correspondence indicates that he sought to exploit the O'Doherty revolt to enlist Spanish support for military intervention.[120]

Not surprisingly, after the failure of the rebellion, Tyrone, ever the pragmatist, attempted to resurrect the option of a pardon.[121] Political circumstances dictated that at the time he met with a cold response from the English authorities, who, thunderstruck by the Flight and the subsequent rebellion, resolved on the precipitate policy of saturating Ulster with Protestants. However, such was the uncertain state of affairs that persisted in Ireland that the option of pardon was not to be altogether ruled out by the English. The reality, therefore, was that despite having his designs frustrated, Tyrone remained a figure to be reckoned with and that the threat of foreign support continued to be taken seriously in London. Work proceeded apace on major fortifications that had already been begun in the wake of the Flight of the Earls in Galway, Limerick, Castlepark (near Kinsale), Haulbowline (near Cork) and Duncannon (near Waterford).[122] The strategic situation of these forts in the south of the country betrayed the very real concern that Tyrone could yet succeed in soliciting foreign support, despite confident affirmations at times by the London government to the contrary.[123] As it was, the crown authorities in Whitehall and Dublin appreciated that they had had an extremely lucky escape. The rising could easily have been sustained on its own steam for a much longer period. How much worse the situation could have been had Tyrone returned can only be imagined. Indeed, the prospect of Tyrone's return to claim his lost territories was the recurring nightmare that haunted the crown authorities. It was in an attempt to lay this spectre to rest once and for all that the plantation of Ulster was treated as a matter of absolute priority and increased in scope quite dramatically. Filling the vacuum in Ulster left by the departed earls was now considered more important than ever by the government in London. A thoroughgoing colonisation of the north by Protestants was considered the most effective means of frustrating Tyrone's return. In these circumstances, Chichester's attempts to wean the indigenous populace of Ulster from their attachment to Tyrone were largely abandoned, as impediments to the plantation were to be swept away, the ends justifying the means. Unfortunately, as subsequent history has demonstrated, the ends did not justify the means, the lingering bitterness among the indigenous Catholic population of Ulster about the raw deal they received at the time of the plantation doing much to poison subsequent history, and the 'Ulster question' remaining a thorny issue to the present day.

8

Plantation and transportation

Sir Cahir O'Doherty's head had no sooner been impaled on a spike
above Newgate in Dublin than Sir Arthur Chichester was making plans
to survey the lands of the northern fugitives with a view to having them
planted. The Lord Deputy had continued his advance into the north
despite news arriving that Sir Cahir had been killed. A senior official in the Irish
administration, Sir Thomas Ridgeway, set out post-haste after Chichester with
a 'commission' empowering him to undertake the formalities of the plantation
process.[1] It was the Lord Deputy's intention to survey the lands of the 'traitors'
(those of O'Doherty now included), while at the same time undertaking
mopping-up operations against dispersed groups of rebels in Ulster. In the
period between the formulation of the scheme for the Ulster plantation during
the summer of 1608 and its implementation during the summer of 1610
Chichester engaged in a clinical exercise of ridding Ulster of alleged traitors,
rebels, outlaws and potential malefactors, most of whom fell into the category
of unemployed 'swordsmen', a relic of the wars of Gaelic Ireland. With typical
military efficiency, the Lord Deputy orchestrated a series of bitter internal
feuds leading to killings among the rebels themselves, show-trials of captured
rebels and leading suspects, as well as the transportation of shiploads of
malcontents to Sweden. For the Lord Deputy, though, such brutal treatment
was no more than these transgressors deserved. By contrast, he persisted with
his policy of attempting to seek a generous allocation of lands to the Gaelic
Irish of Ulster who remained peaceful. Plotting treason was to be demonstrably
shown as a futile and unprofitable expedient, while obedience to English laws
would be shown to reap dividends. In the deputy's view, giving a stake in the
plantation to sufficient numbers of the indigenous populace would soon
reduce the hankering cacophony after the departed earls to a whimper. That
an air of expectancy pervaded the Ulster Irish concerning the prospective land
settlement was revealed by the remark of the Attorney General, Sir John
Davies, in August 1609 that Ulster was 'exceeding peaceable and quiet now.
They all stand upon their good behaviour now, for all expect some portion of

land.'[2] Had an equitable allocation of lands been offered the Ulster Irish, as the deputy intended, Tyrone's star in Ulster may well have faded. As it was, the Lord Deputy's advice was not followed in several important respects, not least when the Ulster Irish were apportioned a paltry share of the plantation lands.

Having ordered Marshal Wingfield to conduct a 'thick and short' campaign against O'Doherty, the Lord Deputy himself resorted to ruthless measures to flush out the remaining bands of rebels who had fled into hiding in different parts of the Ulster countryside. On Chichester's approach into Donegal, a large party of some 240 rebels dispersed, a group of sixty taking refuge on Tory Island. While some of them managed to avail of severe weather conditions to elude the crown forces, those who remained trapped on the island were reduced to desperate acts of murder among themselves in order to survive. Sir Mulmory MacSweeney, constable of Tory, offered to deliver up his castle on terms. This was contemptuously dismissed, MacSweeney being ordered to deliver instead the heads of his garrison in return for pardon. What then unfolded was a series of macabre events in which MacSweeney succeeded first in killing some of his own men and then pursuing others to craggy rocks. Not content with this, the English commander ordered the constable to produce their heads within two hours on pain of death. And so the grisly work proceeded. When several men managed to evade Sir Mulmory, making it to English lines, where they made desperate pleas of 'service', they were cast back again into the hands of the constable to be hanged. Being led to the place of execution, one of the captured prisoners produced a concealed 'scian', or knife, and stabbed Sir Mulmory in the heart, before cutting him 'in pieces'.[3] Having inaugurated this type of internecine strife as the price of survival, the Lord Deputy later formalised the policy in an official proclamation containing a grotesque enticement clause which stated that those availing of the proclamation would not only be pardoned but would receive the goods of any of their former comrades whom they managed to deliver up to the crown authorities 'dead or alive'.[4] Sir John Davies reported on the efficacy of the deputy's policy with great enthusiasm in August 1608, describing how it had 'taken effect beyond expectation among this viperous generation of rebels, who are become like the armed men of Cadmus, who sprang up from the teeth of a serpent sown in the earth, but presently fought and utterly destroyed one another'.[5]

Such gloating that the rebel problem would be resolved by fratricidal blood-letting, however, turned out to be premature. The ingenuity of the Lord Deputy was to be matched by the resilience of many of the remaining rebels, a substantial number of whom had sought refuge in parts of Armagh and Down. The mountainous terrain of south Armagh, homeland of Eoghy Óg O'Hanlon, offered particularly good shelter for fugitives. What is more, traditional Gaelic cultural styles of dressing and hairstyle offered additional camouflage, impeding efforts to track down the rebels. Fynes Moryson, former secretary to Lord Mountjoy in Ireland, noted the difficulties involved. Moryson frowned upon the Gaelic Irish practice of nourishing of long hair (vulgarly called glibs) which hangs down to the shoulders, hiding the face, so as a malefactor may easily escape with his face covered therewith, or by colouring his hair, and much more by cutting it off, may so alter his countenance as those of his acquaintance shall not know him. ... Also they wear ... mantles instead of cloaks, which mantles are as a cabin for an outlaw in the woods, a bed for a rebel, and a cloak for a thief, and being worn over the head and ears, and hanging down to the heels, a notorious villain lapped in them may pass any town or company without being known.[6]

By a variety of subterfuges, exploitation of favourable geographical terrain and fleetness of foot, many rebels had managed to survive.

The limits of his Machiavellian policy of inducing self-destruction among his enemies having been reached, and substantial numbers of rebels still remaining at large, the ever-resourceful Chichester resorted to an alternative strategy in order to reach his goal of flushing them out. If the rebels could not be induced to betray one another in return for pardon, then the communities considered to be offering them shelter would be coerced into doing so instead. To this end, it was announced in February 1609 that a fine of 1,000 marks had been imposed on several northern counties. Some of the money had already been levied, with the prospect that the rest would be duly raised. As a result, declared Chichester, the 'principal rebels are grown to great necessities and misery'. That the policy was beginning to have the desired effect was revealed by a petition signed by residents from County Armagh which suggested that the best way to resolve the protracted problem was either to pardon the remaining rebels or permit them to go abroad.[7]

By implication, service in the army of a Catholic monarch was the desired destination of any prospective transportation scheme. At first the reaction of the Lord Deputy was dismissive. In particular, he declared that several prominent rebels, including Eoghy Óg O'Hanlon, would neither be pardoned nor permitted to depart the realm.[8] By the summer of 1609, however, the persistent rebel menace in the north had induced the Lord Deputy to consent to a scheme of transportation. Eventually, if extremely reluctantly, he even agreed to Eoghy Óg's inclusion. Critically, however, he was not prepared to permit the rebels to join the menacing Irish regiment in Flanders, Protestant Sweden being the chosen destination instead. (The new colony in Florida had previously crossed Chichester's mind as a suitable destination for the transportees.)[9] The first shipload of 240 men was being organised by early July.[10] Chichester was clearly concerned that opting for Flanders as a destination could boomerang on the crown authorities in the event of the Irish regiment being employed in any foreign-aided invasion by the Earl of Tyrone.

Before the end of the summer of 1609 a more ambitious scheme to ship another thousand men to Sweden, all dressed 'after the English fashion', had been contrived. Initially it was intended that the majority of this complement would be drawn from Munster and Connacht, the earlier contingent that had already departed having comprised men from Ulster and Leinster. In implementing this project, Chichester employed tactics which once again demonstrated his uncanny grasp of human nature in the pursuit of achievement of policy. In order to promote the success of the scheme, he recommended 'the most factious and stirring men to take the charge and command of the soldiers to be levied, who will soonest gather idlers together, and there will be a good riddance of them all when they are gone'.[11] On the surface, initially, the levies were 'volunteering', i.e. they were not being coerced into foreign service. In practice, however, transportation was considered by the 'volunteers' as the lesser of two evils, in view of the devious and deadly strategems which the Lord Deputy had been so recently employing in his endeavours to stamp out the last vestiges of rebellion in Ireland. Foreign service in the army of Protestant Sweden was not greatly relished by the transportees. Those from Ulster in particular had an additional reason for their reluctance: they were convinced that the entire project was a 'device of his [Chichester's] to send them out of the way [so] that they might not assist the fugitives who, as they presumed, and so much the rather for his advising and urging them to be gone, were to return this summer'.[12] This was probably nearer the mark than the Lord Deputy would have cared to admit. And it was not only Chichester who was worried about the nightmare prospect of Tyrone's return. Lord Salisbury, the English Secretary of State, also acknowledged the necessity for precautionary measures to be taken as a matter of urgency during the summer of 1609. In his view — and he was not predisposed to alarmism — even if Tyrone only managed to return with a handful of his own followers, the consequences could still be disastrous.[13] Despite the failure of the O'Doherty rebellion, the situation in Ireland remained a source of grave concern to the government in London. A rumour circulating in London that Tyrone was on the point of returning to Ireland resulted in King James cutting short his 'progress', that is, from one hunt to another. Such was James's predilection for the chase that he did not take such an action lightly.[14]

From the point of view of the royal authorities, therefore, it was imperative that the ambitious scheme to transport the additional one thousand swordsmen should be undertaken as a matter of urgency. The entire operation, however, as it turned out, was bedevilled by a series of hitches. Even the arrival of three ships at Derry and one at Carlingford by early October 1609 had not gone according to plan, a storm having scattered the vessels.[15] This was to be the least of the problems that occurred. Reporting from Coleraine at the time, Sir Thomas Phillips noted that many of the prospective levies had gone into hiding, 'for they are very fearful' of going to Sweden.[16] It was perhaps to encourage those reluctant to go that Chichester consented to the transportation of Eoghy Óg and his 'wicked crew'.[17] As a further inducement, the judges of assize in Ulster during their summer tour had executed only a handful of malefactors, reserving the majority for transportation instead,[18] clearly in the hope that acquaintances of the spared prisoners would accompany them to Sweden. Despite all these ploys, the Lord Deputy reported that the original expectation that the transportation scheme would proceed favourably had been disrupted, 'certain furies and firebrands of sedition' having deterred many who were previously disposed to take part.[19] The dissemination of rumours by priests that it was intended to throw the conscripts overboard at sea proved particularly disquieting.[20] Just as effective was the argument by Catholic priests that it was unlawful to fight for a 'heretic', the Protestant King of Sweden, against the Catholic monarch of Poland.[21] The extraordinary influence of the Catholic clergy at this time was acknowledged by the Lord Deputy when he remarked that 'There is not one, from the murderer of his brother to him that steals a goat, but believes in them [priests].'[22]

That desperation was permeating the royal authorities concerning the transportation scheme was evidenced by the fact that while it had been portrayed at the start as a 'voluntary' exercise,[23] this had given way to compulsion. Sir Oliver St John, a senior figure in the Dublin government, praised the project for offering a 'possibility to compel those that live idly and unprofitably here to be transported into foreign countries, and will cause those who remain behind to learn to labour in order to free themselves from such a just punishment'.[24] The mask of official policy was slipping, as became even more obvious with the Lord Deputy's acknowledgement that 900 of the levies were Ulstermen,[25] contrasting with his earlier stated intention that the majority would originate from Munster and Connacht. The transportation scheme was in reality designed to rid Ulster of undesirables, and the pretence of 'volunteering' had been abandoned, banishment by press-ganging now being more the order of the day. Once more it was the Lord Deputy's awesome military reputation which managed to salvage the scheme, as he himself took charge of the ship which was to depart from Carlingford carrying Eoghy Óg and his companions. Chichester reported that he personally put on board, 'full sore against their wills', some of the 'notablest outlaws upon all the borders'. However, by the time 160 of the ship's projected complement of 300 had been put aboard, disaster struck, at least from the point of view of those in charge. The transportees having, it seems, been plied with drink with a view to numbing them into reconciling themselves to their fate, the alcohol had the alternative effect of inflaming emotions. A mutiny unexpectedly erupted on the ship, and the inebriated transportees seized the crew and 'stowed them under hatches'. They then slipped the ship's cables and made a bid to elude the crown forces which had converged on the area from the garrisons at Carlingford, Newry, Greencastle and Dundalk. A contrary wind frustrated their endeavour. Through the prompt utilisation of shipping in the area, the mutiny was brought under control within twenty-four hours, and the Lord Deputy summarily ordered the execution of half a dozen of the 'principal mutineers' in retribution.[26] It must be presumed that Eoghy Óg had not yet boarded the ship with his band of fifty kinsmen and followers,[27] as there is little doubt that the Lord Deputy would have gratefully exploited the opportunity to order his execution. The mutiny having been quelled, the Carlingford ship was set on its way with the Lord Deputy's prophetic words ringing in its wake. Chichester expressed his fear that 'at their coming thither [Sweden] they will run to the adverse side and thereby discover the perfidy of their nation'.[28]

Before any of the ships managed to get anywhere near Sweden the 'perfidy' of the transportees was to become manifest to the royal authorities. By the end of November 1609 serious problems occurred when several of the ships *en route* to Sweden were forced into the River Thames by a storm. 'There the men were landed to refresh themselves in Kent, and could not be gotten on board again, but spread all over the country.'[29] At roughly the same time a further ship had been forced to take shelter at Newcastle.[30] The disaster-prone tendencies of the transportation scheme were a source of considerable exasperation in government circles in London, not least because by the time the escapees had been rounded up it was too late to contemplate completing the journey. The prospect of having to provide winter quarters was unpalatable, not least from the point of view of expense. Indeed, such was the degree of annoyance caused that a covert plan was devised at court to convey the transportees 'by stealth' to the service of the Marquis of Brandenburg instead.[31] Russia, even Virginia, were also proposed as alternative destinations.[32] The general impression, therefore, was that the crown authorities were intent on dispatching the levies as far away as possible in order to prevent their returning to Ireland.

The highly eventful transportation of the Carlingford levies was also interrupted by poor weather, forcing the ship into Newcastle. Captain Lichfield, who had been seized by the mutineers at Carlingford, reported to Salisbury the latest misadventures to befall him at the end of December 1609. Describing the transportees as 'these most wicked and ungodly creatures', the much-harassed captain reported that some of his charges had managed to escape. He pinned most of the blame for this disastrous turn of events on Hugh Boy O'Neill. (Hugh Boy was the son of Sir Turlough MacHenry, an erstwhile ally of the crown and, as Tyrone's half-brother, the most senior O'Neill remaining at liberty in Ulster following the Flight.)[33] Symptomatic of Lichfield's unabating tale of misfortune was the fact that by the time he had concluded his letter he was forced to write a postscript: 'The same Hugh Boy is now himself run from them, for whither he is gone or about what business they know not.'[34] Lichfield, other sources make clear, had not revealed the full extent of the misfortune that had befallen him. Correspondence among the records of the Scottish Privy Council dated several days previously shows that large numbers had escaped, many of whom had made their way to Edinburgh. The Scottish authorities took instant measures to deal with the situation. Scottish mariners in the western ports were forbidden to convey the absconding transportees back to Ireland, while a proclamation was promulgated in Edinburgh to the effect that the fugitive Irish were ordered on 'pain of death' to turn themselves over to the English captains who had been charged with their transportation.[35] The sequence of events suggests that Hugh Boy O'Neill had remained with the ship until he had induced a large number to escape, before finally absconding himself. Even when the fugitive passengers, or as many of them as could be located, had been reassembled on board, the journey to Sweden was to be blighted by a further unanticipated misadventure. It was to be as late as early February 1610 before the ship sailed under a 'fair wind' for Sweden, previous departure having been prevented by the fact that the ship had become icebound on the River Tyne.[36]

Remarkably perhaps, in view of the chaotic nature of the 1609 transportation scheme, the English Privy Council persisted with the strategy. In order to facilitate the impending plantation of Ulster, a further 600 men were to be dispatched during the summer of 1610. This time the chosen route was via the west coast of Scotland. Once again the ship that departed from Carlingford was beset by problems. During a storm the ship 'was cast upon the Isle of Man, in extreme danger of drowning there, after she had spent her masts, with all her sails she had; but in the end, she was, by good fortune, relieved by a Scottishman, who espied her in that distress and guided her into a port of Scotland, where the captain hired another ship and is departed in good trim'.[37] In the event, Lord Deputy Chichester was to claim credit for having transported a total of 6,000 'to the wars in Sweden'.[38] While records of further voyages do not feature in the State Papers of the period, this may well be attributed to the fact that the subsequent passages were less newsworthy, perhaps less problematic, than the pioneering voyages. In one respect, however, Chichester had not been mistaken. Many of the original transportees deserted their new Swedish masters, exactly as the Lord Deputy had anticipated. This may well have been due to the influence exerted by several Catholic priests, who were alleged to have set out after the levies, dressed as soldiers, with the intention of encouraging them to defect from service in Protestant Sweden.[39]

Within a short period of time after arriving in Sweden substantial numbers of the exiled Irish managed to desert their new Swedish masters. It was the Earl of Tyrone who related their adventures in 1613. Seven companies engaged in a daring escapade when they deserted to the side of the Catholic Polish during a battle. Two other companies which the Swedish army had retained in garrison were reportedly executed in reprisal, including 'nephews and close relatives' of Tyrone. Having served the Polish king for three years before being demobilised, many of the soldiers came to Rome to solicit the earl's assistance, 'for they feel that he has an obligation towards them'. The earl acknowledged this as being 'true, for in his cause they were exiled'.[40] There was little that Tyrone could do for them in Rome. 'Like another race of gypsies,' as Tyrone poignantly described them, 'they now wander through the world, lost …'[41] Ultimately many of them ended up in service with the Irish regiment in Flanders.[42] As to the fate of the subsequent consignments of Irish conscripts, there are few details. Among the little that has come to light were allegations that the English had 'scuttled the ships in which they were embarked'.[43] Whether any ships had been deliberately sunk is very doubtful, as there is evidence that Irish soldiers continued to be sent to Sweden until the early 1630s, when the Swedish king Gustavus Adolphus finally resolved never again to accept Irish levies. Their military capabilities were never in doubt, for they established a reputation as fine fighting men in Sweden.[44] Rather, the Swedes considered them untrustworthy.[45] This strongly suggests that further desertions to Catholic powers took place.

Overall, the government's persistence with the transportation policy, despite the attendant problems, is a testimony to the importance with which it was regarded. It also indicates the degree to which it was believed that a serious threat remained to the Ulster plantation. Transfusing the life-blood of Ulster's manhood into Sweden was to have several benefits as far as the English authorities was concerned. In the first instance, as Sir John Davies put it, 'If the empty veins of Ulster were once filled with good British blood ... the whole body of this commonwealth [Ireland] would quickly recover perfection of health.'[46] What is more, it was considered as a priority to get rid of the 'swordsmen', who were believed to be a 'fifth column' waiting to strike on news of Tyrone's return. Their removal became an even more pressing concern to Lord Deputy Chichester when the plantation allocations ended up proving so unfavourable to the so-called 'deserving' Irish.[47] In view of the ruthlessness of the Lord Deputy's transportation policy, it is not surprising that the Ulster plantation encountered such a relatively 'passive' response from the disgruntled natives, the potential penalty for any overt displays of hostility being so severe.

Such was the determination of the royal authorities to smooth the path for the plantation process that promises made before the Flight of the Earls were cynically abjured. Chieftains loyal to the crown, such as Connor Roe Maguire in County Fermanagh, who had previously been courted by crown officials as counterweights to the Gaelic lords regarded with suspicion before the Flight, found themselves being treated with much the same disdain and hostility as the fugitive lords themselves. Writing in 1610, Chichester depicted Connor Roe as just another troublesome and overmighty subject and advocated reneging on a promise previously made to him that he should be granted three baronies. The Lord Deputy stated his opinion that, 'a more prudent course being now in hand', he 'sees not that the king is bound in honour to make so barbarous and unworthy a man greater than his neighbours, but rather in true construction of state to suppress him; for all his actions declare an ill mind, and sure he will do much harm to the plantation if he be made so great'. Chichester recommended Connor Roe receive one barony rather than three and considered this 'rather too much than too little for him'.[48] Eventually granted a single barony, though the bitter pill of losing huge swathes of land was sweetened by an annuity of £200,[49] Connor Roe did not do 'much harm' to the plantation. But his grandson, Lord Maguire, did, playing a leading part in the conspiracy of 1641 to overthrow the plantation.[50] Of the 40,000 Protestant colonists in Ulster in 1641, 12,000 were to die in the hostilities which resulted from the 1641 rebellion, many of them massacred in cold blood.[51] It is not stretching things too far to suggest that a lingering bitterness at Chichester's decision to repudiate the promises made to his grandfather had a part to play in Lord Maguire's actions in 1641.

Even the much-trumpeted policy of disseminating English legal practices as a source of allurement to the indigenous populace was to be compromised. This was demonstrated by the show-trials of Sir Niall Garbh O'Donnell and Sir Donal O'Cahan on treason charges. Sir Niall Garbh O'Donnell was arrested on a charge of being complicit in Sir Cahir O'Doherty's rebellion, while Sir Donal O'Cahan was incriminated by his relative and rival, Shane Carragh O'Cahan. Shane Carragh's subsequent involvement in the O'Doherty revolt, it has been well observed, 'tended to cancel the propriety if not the probity of his [Shane Carragh's] earlier information' regarding Sir Donal.[52] Such was the flimsy nature of the case against O'Cahan that the Lord Deputy contemplated releasing him in June 1608, 'for the accusation made against him will not hang him in this kingdom'.[53] While the charge against O'Cahan was of questionable validity, the weight of evidence against Sir Niall Garbh O'Donnell indicated that he did have a case to answer. As the deputy noted, 'The crimes with which each of them is charged are foul, but more probable against Sir Neale than the other.'[54] Of greatest import in the case against Niall Garbh was the attitude of Lady O'Doherty towards him when they encountered each other in the dying days of the revolt. A senior royal official commented upon the 'ferocious invectives of the Lady O'Doherty against Sir Niall Garbh O'Donnell, for the persuading of her husband to his treacherous revolt'.[55] Of the other witnesses who testified against Sir Niall Garbh, the most notable was Finola O'Donnell, the formidable 'Iníon Dubh', mother of the Earl of Tyrconnell.[56] However, there may well have been dynastic reasons for Iníon Dubh's willingness to give evidence against Niall Garbh, as he had long been a rival of the Earl of Tyrconnell. Indeed, Niall Garbh's aspirations were clearly revealed when he bartered for a grant of O'Doherty's lands in return for joining in the war against him.[57] Such grandiose ambitions did not accord with the prevailing crown policy 'that Ulster will never be reduced to the form of good government until the principal heads are cut off'.[58] Lord Deputy Chichester was absolutely determined to eradicate the menace of the overmighty subject in Ulster. Niall Garbh therefore, in his view, was guilty, if not of treason, then of overweening ambition — and this despite the fact that as recently as March 1607 he had been severely wounded in action against rebels in Tyrconnell.[59] How to proceed against Niall Garbh and O'Cahan was a matter of some puzzlement for the crown authorities in Ireland. However, a sense of urgency that something should be done was apparent from Chichester's report in early 1609 that the pair had been 'by accident discovered' attempting to make their escape from Dublin Castle.[60] In March of the same year Niall Garbh almost pulled it off again when he was found in possession of a rope of sufficient length to make good his escape.[61] The deputy's determination to press ahead speedily with the indictment against the two suspects was to have the desired effect, and preparations were well under way for proceeding with their trials by May 1609. The Irish Attorney General, Sir John Davies, sanguinely predicted a guilty verdict.[62] Such confidence, however, was to prove misplaced.

The trial of Sir Niall Garbh O'Donnell turned out to be an extraordinary affair. When it seemed likely that he would be found not guilty, the jury was confined for several days without sustenance in order to secure the desired guilty verdict. With the passage of time, and despite the blatant intimidation, the prospect of a guilty verdict receded further. Rather than risk the 'dangerous' prospect of an acquittal, Sir John Davies contrived to nullify the proceedings by withdrawing the indictment, 'pretending that he [Davies] had more evidence to give for the king, but that he found the jury so weak with long fasting that they were not able to attend that service and deliberate thereupon so long time as was fit, and therefore in commiserations of their faintings, and for reasons concerning His Majesty's service, he desired that the jury might be dismissed'. Davies put the ultimate blame for the débâcle on a prejudiced jury. It was as a result of the collapse of this trial that plans for prosecuting O'Cahan were shelved.[63] If Niall Garbh could not be convicted, there was virtually no chance that O'Cahan would be. Not to be outdone in the blame game, Niall Garbh himself levelled charges of jury-packing against the crown in relation to his trial, claiming that the jury consisted of 'those that were at deadly suit' with him.[64] While refusing to concede this point, even Sir John Davies acknowledged Niall Garbh's objections to the Irish jury chosen as 'too base and mean to be his triers', preferring instead a jury of English knights. Davies would have 'gladly' acceded to this request.[65] However, legal proprieties dictated that Niall Garbh should be tried by a jury of his peers from County Donegal. Davies's concern for such legal niceties was commendably scrupulous — until, that is, the 'not guilty' verdict seemed likely, at which point all concern for due legal process went by the wayside and the trial was wound up for patently spurious reasons. Interestingly, within a short period thereafter, four members of a northern jury were prosecuted in the prerogative Court of Castle Chamber in Dublin for failing to convict alleged traitors 'contrary to the clear evidence'. They were each fined the massive sum of £100 and sentenced to be pilloried, as well as to losing one of their ears.[66] The message was brutally clear. Failure to deliver the required verdicts could have serious repercussions. However, it was too late to have any effect on the fate of Niall Garbh and O'Cahan.

The collapse of the trial of Niall Garbh confronted the royal authorities with a dilemma. Strict legal practice implied that Niall Garbh and O'Cahan should be released. (Indeed, of Niall Garbh's son and his brothers who were also in custody, the deputy remarked that 'no criminal offence can be justly laid to their charge', though he was to describe Niall Garbh's son as the 'wickedest boy he [Chichester] ever dealt with in all his life'.)[67] However, as both Niall Garbh and O'Cahan were claimants to vast tracts of land that the crown had set aside for the plantation of British colonists, it was considered imperative in royal circles that the two lords should be taken out of circulation for good.

Whether the appropriate legalities were observed in the process or not was immaterial. Reasons of state, as the crown's motives could be euphemistically described, prevailed. In O'Cahan's case, for instance, by the time Niall Garbh's trial had taken place, representatives of the London companies who ultimately undertook the plantation of the 'infant city' of Derry and 'O'Cahan's country' were on the verge of undertaking a fact-finding mission.[68] The presumption in royal circles was that Sir Donal should be regarded as guilty as charged rather than innocent until proven guilty. In other words, while O'Cahan was waiting to be tried his lands could be subjected to the process of colonisation. From the point of view of the crown, disposing somehow of these troublesome captives was the priority, not least because they were persistently attempting to escape from prison. Commenting in July 1609 about the recurring escape attempts, Chichester predicted that unless all of them, including Tyrone's son Conn, were removed to England out of harm's way, it would 'breed an infallible mischief, which in wisdom ought now to be prevented'.[69] By the end of the month the Lord Deputy had his reply. King James ordered that Niall Garbh and O'Cahan should be transferred to custody in England,[70] where they were to remain in detention in the Tower of London for the rest of their lives, dying in 1626 and 1627 respectively.[71] No such order, however, was received in relation to the other prisoners. Experience was to prove that the Lord Deputy's prediction was well founded, as the intention to liberate Conn O'Neill from custody was to be a central element of the 'Ulster Conspiracy' of 1615.

The 'principal' inhabitants of Counties Cavan and Fermanagh were similarly to find themselves on the receiving-end of English legal chicanery in the aftermath of the Flight. Thus the 'freeholder' policy which had been championed since the end of the war as a means of procuring a more equitable distribution of land in Ulster was abruptly abandoned, at a time when agreements were so tantalisingly close to being finalised in the two counties. Before the departure of the northern earls prominent residents of these counties were being encouraged by the crown authorities in Ireland to establish rights in English law as freeholders.[72] The intention was to weaken the proprietorial positions of the principal Irish lords in Cavan and Fermanagh. Writing in 1606, Sir John Davies was able to remark enthusiastically upon the fact that 'the number of freeholders was exceedingly great' in County Fermanagh.[73] In this connection, he noted that only two freeholders from Fermanagh had been killed during the Nine Years War, and explained this by commenting that Fermanagh men 'are reputed the worst swordsmen of the north, being rather inclined to be scholars, or husbandmen, than to be kern, or men of action'.[74] Whereas in 1606 freeholders had been springing up like daisies all over the place, with 200 alone being identified by the crown authorities in County Monaghan,[75] after the Flight they had virtually become an endangered species. Following the departure of the northern lords, the Lord Deputy was suddenly to be found commenting disapprovingly on the number of those claiming to be 'accounted freeholders' in Cavan and Fermanagh.[76] This untoward development was a fate not taken lightly by those who were to find themselves double-crossed. Significantly in this respect, when the plantation of Ulster was eventually implemented in 1610, the indigenous residents in County Cavan were to be its bitterest opponents, and this despite the fact that Chichester inaugurated the plantation process there 'by reason the people there are more understanding and pliable to reason than in the remoter parts, and because there is more land to dispose towards the contentment of the natives in that county than in any of the rest'.[77] The Lord Deputy's sense of benevolence clearly did not permeate to the people. Thus it was that Chichester encountered the 'passion' of the population in County Cavan who were 'ill contented, being grieved to leave their possessions to strangers'. In the end the deputy only prevailed when he so mixed 'threats with entreaty' that the inhabitants could have been left in little doubt that a heavy penalty would be paid for further recalcitrance.[78] Given the manifest discontent, it was no coincidence either that the Gaelic Irish in Cavan continued to mount legal challenges to the plantation in 1612, resulting in prolonged legal proceedings.[79] Such was the degree of disenchantment in County Cavan that King James expressed his concern in 1612 that conspiratorial activities were afoot in the county, armaments reportedly being prepared in the vicinity of Belturbet.[80]

Whereas Chichester had decided to sacrifice the 'freeholder' element among the indigenous population in Ulster, he had not abandoned his view that a substantial stake in the settlement should be parcelled out in smaller lots to the native inhabitants in the various localities as a means of weaning them away from loyalty to the exiled earls. This was a marked reversal of the far more punitive plantation policy which he had briefly advocated in the immediate aftermath of the O'Doherty rebellion.[81] Following the outbreak of the revolt, the Lord Deputy affirmed that the 'forfeiture of his [O'Doherty's] country, with the extirpation of the ungrateful inhabitants will recompense all their harms'.[82] As for the population on the estates of the fugitive earls, he advocated banishing them 'beyond the rivers of Lough Erne, Blackwater and the Bann'.[83] Such comments were typical of Chichester's often iron-handed approach. However, the Lord Deputy was a consummate pragmatist. Grand plantation schemes were one thing, the ability to implement them was quite another. Thus, on reflection, he retreated from his retributive approach, reverting to his policy of seeking to employ the plantation as a means of reconciling the predominant part of the populace of Ulster to English rule. As he remarked of this opportunity, 'We are now all of us become builders and planters here, and not wasters and destroyers as in our younger years, and would gladly rest in quiet if our ill neighbours will permit us, and that makes us the more studious to prevent their revolt and to settle peace and quiet among them.'[84]

For some time Chichester continued to enjoy his position as the 'oracle' guiding the plantation.[85] In fact he had been so determined to retain control of the planning process that he attempted to prevent other crown officials in Ireland from exerting any influence on the projected settlement. Sir Geoffrey

Fenton, the Irish Secretary of State, was to complain about the manner in which Sir Oliver Lambert, the deputy's henchman, had 'out of a strange and insolent presumption' attempted to impede the delivery of a letter that Fenton had sent to the London government.[86] That Chichester's advice continued to inform the general tenor of crown policy in relation to the plantation of Ulster was reflected by the observations of the Venetian ambassador in London in October 1608 when he remarked that the English had 'resolved to confiscate Tyrone's property and that of the other rebels. Part will go to the king to cover the expenses he has been put to, and part will be given to other Irish to secure their hostility to Tyrone and the rebels, and thus they hope to put an end to the movement.'[87] To some extent, therefore, Chichester's intention to offer the inhabitants generous treatment as a device to neuter the lurking menace of Tyrone was still being indulged in London government circles. Increasingly, however, it seemed that only lip-service was being paid to this strategy. While O'Doherty's rebellion had only temporarily altered the Lord Deputy's perception of the plantation, the revolt resulted in a decisive shift in attitude in London. The treasonable intrigues of the northern earls were perhaps only to be expected, but the treachery of Sir Cahir O'Doherty, the 'queen's O'Doherty', struck a particularly bitter chord in English society. A contemporary English observer remarked of the event: 'As the serpent never stings more deadly than when he bites without hissing, so an enemy never intends more deep mischief and villainy than when he shadows his purposes under the show and pretence of friendship and amity.'[88] Of the Irish wars the same correspondent bewailed: 'How many hundreds of thousands of our English nation have been drowned in their own blood.' The Irish were caricatured as beyond redemption: 'Murder and massacres and uproars are to them as music and banquets: blood as the most delicate cups of wine.' The writer's bitterness was encapsulated in his opprobrious remark: 'Thou [Ireland] hast deserved to be called not one of the daughters of Britannia, but to be rejected as a bastard.'[89]

O'Doherty's rebellion, therefore, persuaded the London government to adopt a radically different attitude, abandoning Chichester's relatively minimalist plantation approach. Once more the Venetian ambassador in London captured the changing mood. The king and his advisers were 'thinking of nothing else than of how to cover themselves out of the property of the rebels for the cost they have been put to'.[90] This emphasis on the military contingencies that had been resorted to in the wake of the Flight and O'Doherty's rebellion is an indication that immediate financial considerations were to dictate the evolving plantation strategy. It was for this reason that a spectacularly ambitious, if utterly unrealistic, policy was devised which anticipated the colonisation of almost 250,000 acres and the transplantation of some 5,000 British families to the new colony in Ulster.[91] Among the sponsors of these grandiose plans was Sir John Davies, who entertained high hopes of its success.[92] King James, who had uncharacteristically applied himself feverishly to the task of planning the Ulster plantation, was just as optimistic. Appreciative of the enormous practical difficulties that would be encountered, Sir Arthur Chichester, that highly experienced military logistician, had a more sober view of the scale of the proposed plantation project, recommending that the long-term welfare of the new colony would be best ensured if it were sponsored by a parliamentary 'subsidy or two'. In his view, it would be money well spent in that it would ultimately 'save many a subsidy in forty years'.[93] The London government, though, had an alternative plan for providing the cornerstone of the settlement. This centred on enticing the wealthy London companies to become involved.

O'Cahan's 'fruitful country',[94] comprising a substantial portion of what was contemporaneously termed County Coleraine by the English, bordered on either side by the rich salmon-fishing rivers of the Bann and the Foyle, was chosen as the apple to entice the Londoners into the proverbial garden of Eden.[95] The importance of the Londoners to the success of the entire project was emphasised by the English Privy Council in August 1609 when it remarked upon 'what good use their example will be to draw on others'. Consequently, every effort was to be made to ensure that the fact-finding mission by a delegation of London agents travelling to Ireland during the late summer of that year should be as trouble-free as possible. The Lord Deputy was 'anxiously' urged to select 'discreet persons to conduct and accompany them, who shall be able to control whatever discouraging reports may be made to them out of ignorance or malice'. However, it was made plain that the 'conductors' were to do more than filter malicious influences on the agents; they were required in addition to provide a highly embellished view of the prospective plantation lands, being instructed to 'take care to lead them [the London agents] by the best ways and to lodge them in their travel where they may, if possible, receive English entertainment in Englishmen's houses'.[96]

The Lord Deputy went to great pains to ensure that the Londoners' trip went as smoothly, and as profitably, as possible. He procured them 'raw hides, tallow, salmon, herrings, eels, pipe staves, beef, and the like at *easy prices*' [author's italics]. Iron ore was also provided, while it was also planned to procure samples of lead and copper.[97] Every muscle was being strained by the royal authorities in Ireland to persuade the Londoners to persevere in their intention to become involved with the plantation. Throughout the entire time of their visitation no stone was left unturned to ensure that the trip was a resounding success. The only hitch which might have deterred the Londoners on their tour of the prospective plantation lands occurred when one of the agents fell sick. Such was the degree of concern engendered by this turn of events that the Lord Deputy, no less, and his viceregal entourage, were on hand to 'comfort him and to retain him lest this accident should discourage his fellow citizens'.[98] Rarely can a prospective investor in Ireland have received such illustrious attention. Having tempted the London agents with all manner of prospective riches and pampered the unfortunate member of the delegation who had fallen ill, the royal authorities in Ireland were in self-congratulatory mood when the agents departed for home. Quite by chance, as a result of a 'tempest', their ship sought shelter in Carlingford Lough at the end of October 1609. As fate would have it, this coincided with the mutiny of the conscripts destined for Sweden, who, in a drunken outbreak of violence, had seized control of their ship. Indeed, the Londoners' vessel, 'not without some danger', took part in the operation to quell the mutiny, leaving the Lord Deputy on tenterhooks that this wholly unexpected turn of events might incline the Londoners to have second thoughts about embarking on their projected enterprise.[99] As it happened, the Londoners persevered with the foundation of the city of Derry and the plantation of County Coleraine, soon to be respectively renamed Londonderry and County Londonderry in honour of their sponsors. Whether or not second thoughts had been entertained is unclear. The tantalising prospect of reaping lavish dividends had obviously proved too alluring. However, subsequent experience in the early decades of the seventeenth century resulted in the London companies having some cause to regret their decision, for in 1635 they were fined the colossal sum of £70,000 by the Court of Star Chamber in London for failing to abide by the contractual obligations of their plantation commitments, and in particular for not clearing the Gaelic Irish off the plantation estates.[100]

While the king and his advisers rejoiced at successfully involving the London companies in the Ulster plantation, it was proving much more difficult to attract other private investors. The onerous conditions imposed on the British undertakers (the new owners charged with responsibility for implementing the plantation) were so demanding as to deter many prospective planters. There were three standard categories of estate allocated: small (1,000 acres), medium (1,500 acres) and large (2,000 acres). Within three years twenty-four British males had to be settled per thousand acres on the estates of the English and Scots. Large estates were to have a castle and a bawn (a stone defensive wall) erected, medium ones were expected to have a large brick house and a bawn, while only a bawn was required on the small estates. All bawns, it is worth noting, were to be built within a month, 'an impossibly short time' in the view of a modern historian. Undertakers were also obliged to build houses for their tenants close to the fortifications.[101] While the Gaelic Irish were permitted on the estates of the servitors (almost all of whom were soldiers), they were to be cleared off the estates of the English and Scottish civilian grantees and transplanted to other parts of Ulster, as the 'basic principle of the scheme was segregation'.[102] All in all, such were the demands imposed on the undertakers that it was noted by an observer in London in September 1609 that the plantation had been 'suspended owing to the numerous obligations imposed upon the colonists, to build Protestant churches, schools and block-houses'.[103] The failure to proceed with the plantation during the summer of 1609 was also attributed by the Protestant Archbishop of Armagh to the 'common report in England, and a strong expectation in Ireland, that the Earl of Tyrone or his sons will draw certain forces into Ulster this summer, which is no small discouragement of the plantation'.[104] Lord Deputy Chichester also commented on the manner in which the earl's rumoured homecoming had 'somewhat cooled men's affections to the Ulster plantation'.[105]

That Tyrone was motivated by an increased sense of urgency to effect his return to Ireland there can be little doubt, not least from the point of view of his private affairs. The increased Spanish pension of 500 ducats (gold pieces) a month was considered grossly inadequate by the earl.[106] The Venetian ambassador in Rome reported during the summer of 1609 that the 'Earl of Tyrone is living here in poverty on the small provision His Holiness gives him. He has applied to his Catholic Majesty [the King of Spain] for some pecuniary assistance.'[107] The report of the ambassador suggests that the Spanish had managed to maintain the subterfuge of using the Pope as a proxy for providing Tyrone's annuity. The reality was that the English knew about the Spanish financial support for the earls almost as soon as it was granted following their arrival in Rome in the spring of 1608. A highly indignant Sir Charles Cornwallis, English ambassador to Spain, reported in July 1608 that the earls had been granted 1,000 crowns a month — despite the fact that the Spanish Secretary of State had given him categoric assurances in April of that year that 'there was intended no receipt, countenance or comfort to any of that condition' (i.e. the fugitive earls).[108]

The Venetian ambassador was entirely correct, on the other hand, in depicting the earl as dissatisfied with the allowance that he had been granted. His correspondence during his years in exile abounds with references to his acute chagrin in this regard.[109] Part of the problem resulted from the fact that Tyrone's household had become a refuge for many of his followers, on whom, the Countess of Tyrone affirmed, the earl 'spent more of his grant than in ostentation or on his own comfort'.[110] Tyrone's financial embarrassment, therefore, cannot simply be put down purely to the paucity of his Spanish allowance. As far as the Spanish were concerned, it was the best they could do for their distinguished 'guest'. Philip III responded to one of Tyrone's periodic complaints by pointing out that Irishmen currently in the service of the Spanish, as well as those who had been awarded 'pensions', were costing his exchequer 150,000 ducats a year, a very substantial sum at a time when the Spanish were experiencing serious financial insolvency.[111] Rather, the financial implications of his decision to seek sanctuary abroad were hitting home on the exiled earl. Tyrone had been an enormously wealthy man in Ireland — yet another reason which supports the contention that his Flight had been a far from voluntary abandonment of his customary way of life. During the three years after the Flight the crown authorities had managed to raise over £8,000 from his estates.[112] Quite apart from financial considerations, Tyrone's concerns for his health in the unaccustomed climate of Italy was also a crucial factor underpinning his desire to return home. Despite the arguments of some who would portray his sojourn in Rome as a voluntary experience characterised by an indulgence in the pleasures of life, in particular his increasing fondness for Italian wine, in actual fact Tyrone was acutely worried about his health. Too many of his relatives and friends had passed away prematurely. Writing in 1609, Tyrone signified his concern that he would not live much longer and his determination to relocate 'anywhere else rather than here in Rome where I can only bury my bones with those of the other Irish who have died here'.[113]

The paranoia generated in England by the reports that Tyrone was ever more determined to return to his homeland to reclaim his patrimony from the Protestant colonists undoubtedly damped enthusiasm for the plantation. The prevalence of these rumours bears testimony to the success of the Earl of Tyrone's propagandists, mostly Catholic clergy, in maintaining the prospect of his imminent return. The power of perception in these circumstances should not be underestimated. The spectre of the earl's return was sufficiently menacing to deter prospective colonists. As it was, there was little prospect that Tyrone would secure Spanish military assistance at this time. The best that he could reasonably hope for were the good offices of the Spanish king and his officials to secure a rapprochement with King James before the plantation was implemented. As the Spanish ambassador in Rome reported in June 1609, Tyrone believed that 'it is of the utmost importance to conclude these negotiations as soon as possible for the King [of England] is distributing the lands of the country among the heretics and, once they are rooted there, it will be difficult to remove them'.[114] Tyrone's diplomatic offensive to secure Spanish intervention moved up a gear when his eldest surviving son, Henry O'Neill, colonel of the Irish regiment in the Spanish Netherlands, travelled to the Spanish court with a glowing reference from Archduke Albert (governor of the Spanish Netherlands), who paid tribute to the 'valour' and distinction of his four years of service with the Irish regiment.[115] Henry had come to Spain to attend to the 'business matters of the Earl of Tyrone'.[116] His presence in the country may have been sanctioned by the Spanish authorities as legitimate at a time when overtures were being made to secure a reconciliation between the Earl of Tyrone and the English king. However, Henry's trip to Spain also lent credence to the rumours that were being disseminated of Tyrone's imminent return at the head of an armed force, serving to bring Irish affairs even more to the forefront of international diplomatic concerns. The departure of a fleet of twelve ships containing Irish and Spanish troops with two or three priests on board each ship was the subject of speculation in the early autumn of 1609 by observers sympathetic to the English cause. The fleet was reckoned to be 'equipped by the Pope rather than by any other prince and ... that on arrival in Spain the Pope will take the soldiers and ships into his service. It may be that the Earl of Tyrone intends some exploit.'[117] A report was even conjured up that the Pope had conferred the title 'King of Ireland' on Tyrone.

In response, King James and his advisers assumed an ostensible air of bravado. Seeking some form of solace from the unhappy situation confronting him, James I remarked to the Venetian ambassador that 'the earl [Tyrone] is an old man of sixty-five, and could not live much longer'. (Part of Tyrone's mystique centres on inaccurate contemporary assessments of his date of birth; he was, in fact, only fifty-nine years old in 1609,[118] a man of advanced years nonetheless by contemporary standards.) Despite the dismissiveness of the English king, the ambassador reported that troops were being transferred from Holland to Ireland.[119] Provision of victuals for the Irish garrison, a sure sign that potential trouble was considered seriously, was also taken in hand during the summer months of 1609.[120] But with the passing of the summer season, the optimum time of the year for military operations, the prospect of Tyrone's return with an invasion force receded yet again. Now that the immediate threat had been lifted, planning for the implementation of the plantation in the following summer proceeded apace.

With the likelihood of Tyrone returning having been postponed once again, the pressing concern of the existing residents on the prospective plantation lands in Ulster centred on their allocations under the new settlement. This was the subject that preoccupied both those who had hoped all along either openly or secretly to profit by the earls' departure and those who hankered after their return but whose immediate priority was to survive. Reporting from Dungannon at the end of August 1609, Sir John Davies joyously remarked on the air of expectancy permeating the indigenous populace in regard to the plantation that had led to 'exceeding ... quiet' in the north.[121] Anticipation there may have been in some quarters, but the quiescence referred to by Davies was also attributable in large measure to the concurrent transportation scheme to Sweden. Nevertheless, Chichester had argued that the plantation offered a material means of weaning supporters away from the Earl of Tyrone. By the time the plantation was implemented, though, Chichester had lost his battle to secure at least half the plantation lands for the native population, less than a quarter being ultimately allocated to them.[122] Besides, many who were allocated lands in the settlement were to find that they were to be transplanted to other areas, a prospect that appalled them. Petrified by the O'Doherty rebellion, King James had been won round to a scheme that theoretically offered the prospect of extirpating the menace of a northern revolt for ever. Ulster was to be the subject of a policy of wholesale settlement by Protestants. Sir John Davies, a key strategist influencing the plantation scheme, had argued that the fate which had befallen the Munster plantation in having been so rapidly uprooted during the Nine Years War would also recur in the Ulster project if 'the number of civil persons who are to be planted do not exceed the number of the natives, who will quickly overgrow them as weeds overgrow the good corn'.[123]

Infamous for his administrative indolence, in a fit of uncharacteristic industry James I launched himself into the plantation with a zeal that has been described as 'missionary'.[124] It was symptomatic of the importance James attached to the enterprise that the English Privy Council reported to Chichester in early 1609 that King James had 'lately attended two meetings' of the council to discuss the issue.[125] Such was the determination of the king to ensure a successful plantation project that not only were the interests of the natives to be sacrificed but those of the servitor class as well, the serried ranks of officers who had seen active service during the Nine Years War. The servitors were considered insufficiently wealthy to be allocated a preponderant share of the plantation lands. Chichester, the champion of servitor interests, subsequently embarked on a series of other plantations, notably in Wexford, with a view to compensating the servitors for their disappointment in Ulster.[126]

However, it was the reaction of the Gaelic Irish to their pitiful allocation that was decisive in ensuring that yearning for Tyrone's return was not only maintained but increased. As the modern historian Aidan Clarke has noted of the plantation allocation, 'Few of the favoured Irish received grants of the land which they actually occupied; none received as much as they believed themselves entitled to. They had every reason to remain resentful and unreconciled, and their discontent merged with that of the majority, who had received nothing, to generate a hostility that endangered the success of the project.'[127] There can be little doubt that the Ulster Irish had considerable reason to feel justifiably aggrieved by the treatment meted out to them by the legal officials of the crown since the end of the Nine Years War in 1603. In the years before the Flight of the Earls Sir John Davies had insisted that the Earl of Tyrone did not own vast tracts of land to which he laid claim, arguing instead that they belonged to freeholders. But if that was in fact the case, then there was no legal basis for the confiscation of the vast bulk of the lands at the time of the Ulster plantation. What happened, of course, was that Davies, the legal mastermind of the plantation, whom Tyrone had characterised as a 'stage player', had changed the script. After the Flight Davies drastically revised his opinion: the Earl of Tyrone, it now transpired, had indeed personally owned all the land he had once claimed.[128]

Just how incensed the indigenous inhabitants were with the plantation allocation was evidenced by a report in 1610 from Sir Toby Caulfield, a prominent army commander based at Charlemont, in the heart of the north. He articulated the sentiments of the Ulster Irish on hearing news of their prospective allocations as the so-called 'deserving' Irish. Among their number, for example, was Sir Turlough MacHenry O'Neill, a member of a delegation that had lately returned from London.[129] He had been given an estate of some 9,900 acres, the largest single grant to a native Irishman in the plantation allocation.[130] The size of Sir Turlough's grant reflected his position as the most senior O'Neill remaining in Ulster. And yet Sir Turlough clearly felt he had been harshly treated, since he had received only half the barony of the Fews in County Armagh when he considered that he was entitled to it all.[131] To make matters worse, from a personal viewpoint, one of three sons reputed to be 'swordsmen' had been banished to Sweden.[132] The delegation which returned from London reported that many in Ulster would be forced to become outlaws 'out of necessity, no other means being left them to keep a being in this world than to live as long as they can by scrambling'. Caulfield interpreted their strategy as being to frustrate the plantation and play for time until the Earl of Tyrone managed to return. An appeal was made to the English authorities suggesting that the transplantation of native proprietors from their lands should be delayed until the next spring, arguing it would be a 'great cruelty' to remove them from their houses with winter approaching and without the harvest reaped. Besides the practical considerations, Caulfield attributed their request to their conviction that by the spring of 1611, 'if ever Tyrone can or will come, he will wait for no longer time, since delays and further deferring cannot be less prejudice to him than the utter ruin and extirpation of his dearest friends'. Overall, the Ulster Irish were incensed by their treatment, believing that 'if this course had been taken with them in war time, it had some colour of justice; but they having been pardoned and their lands given them … they conclude it to be the greatest cruelty that was ever inflicted upon any people'.[133] Not only had the Act of Oblivion of 1604 confirming indemnity for past offences been itself consigned to oblivion, but the grand promise in the proclamation of September 1607 following the Flight, guaranteeing that the inhabitants of the north 'will not be disturbed in the peaceable possession of their lands', was also manifestly revealed to be a deception.[134] Consequently, in Caulfield's opinion, 'there is not a more discontented people in Christendom'.[135] As a substantial beneficiary of the plantation, Caulfield had nothing to gain by overstating the profound discontent of the indigenous populace with their fate in the plantation. Rather, alarmed by the justifiable degree of hostility, he was genuinely concerned about the security of the plantation, urging the authorities to make the necessary military provisions to defend the Protestant settlers.[136] It is perhaps an indication of the great number of the old Ulster elite who were disappointed not to receive land grants that whereas 200 freeholders had been identified by crown officials in County Monaghan alone in 1606, only 280 Gaelic Irishmen received land grants in the plantation of Ulster, covering six counties.[137] Disinheritance, dislocation and the disjunction of traditional religious, cultural and socio-economic customs all ensued in the wake of the settlement project. In the circumstances, it is little wonder that the colonisation of the north has bequeathed a legacy of such enduring bitterness in Irish history.

Following the implementation of the plantation during the summer of 1610, and the paltry share which he believed had been allocated to the natives, it was a rueful Lord Deputy who noted that residents from Counties Tyrone, Armagh and Coleraine had in large measure turned out for the plantation commissioners in English clothing and had promised to live in 'townreeds', thereby ending the traditional Gaelic Irish custom of 'creaghting' (transhumance), following herds of cattle to fresh pastures. Far from being fairly treated in the redistribution of property, the despondent residents complained bitterly that they could not even live as tenants on their traditional lands.[138] And it was the issue of transplantation that upset many of the natives as much as the expropriation itself. Commenting on the transplantation controversy, Sir John Davies, one of the principal architects of the plantation, considered the transplantation scheme a benign affair, citing historical precedents ranging back to classical times. In his opinion, 'This transplantation of natives is made by His Majesty rather like a father than like a lord or monarch. The Romans transplanted whole nations out of Germany into France. The Spaniards lately removed all the Moors out of Granada ...'[139] Instead of complaining, Davies argued, the Irish should have the sense to realise their good fortune. But, however 'benign' their fate in comparison with historical precedent, it did little to diminish the burning resentment of the native inhabitants of Ulster. That their dislocation was relatively limited geographically was not considered a source of comfort. Indeed, Chichester noted that the priority of many of the Ulster Irish was to become 'tenants to any man, rather than be removed from the place of their birth and education'. It was, however, the Lord Deputy's belief that this was regarded by them as no more than a temporary expedient, since they secretly harboured an aspiration 'at one time or other to find an opportunity to cut their landlords' throats'.[140] Despite the affirmation that segregation was based on the principle of separating the wheat from the tares, such was the sluggish start made to the plantation process by many of the undertakers that the royal authorities tolerated the Gaelic Irish remaining on estates from which they should have been cleared, not only for the forthcoming harvest of 1610 but in many areas, in clear breach of the plantation scheme, for subsequent years as well.

The relative failure to implement the transplantation aspect of the Ulster settlement reduced the prospect of a violent response to the plantation. 'Continual fear of constraint' into the service of the King of Sweden also served to intimidate the native populace.[141] As for the crown authorities, a pragmatic decision to suspend religious persecution in Ireland while the plantation took root played a part in reducing tensions. News of the untimely death of Colonel Henry O'Neill at the Spanish court in the late summer of 1610, at the age of twenty-three,[142] combined with (exaggerated) reports of the blindness of the earl himself, which Chichester did his utmost to publicise,[143] eroded speculation about the likelihood of Tyrone's return. The Lord Deputy reported in December 1610 that news of these developments had led to Ulstermen descending on Dublin in droves to 'accept of that little portion of land which heretofore they so much scorned'.[144] The despondency of the fugitive earl in Rome and his supporters in Ireland plumbed a new depth. To make matters worse, Lord Deputy Chichester, Tyrone's arch-enemy, had allocated himself 1,320 acres in Dungannon under the auspices of the Ulster plantation.[145] Choosing Dungannon was entirely deliberate, as he fully appreciated the 'name and opinion held of it by the people of that country'.[146] In essence, Chichester was taunting the exiled Earl of Tyrone with a provocative message. To the victor had gone the spoils.

9

'FOR THEY WOULD HAVE BARABBAS'

The late summer of 1610 witnessed the implementation of the plantation of Ulster and the apparent dashing of Tyrone's hopes of frustrating the designs of the crown authorities in this respect. An energetic start by the Londoners in their plantation of Coleraine augured well for the future of the colonisation project. Commenting on the feverish industry that he witnessed at the construction of Coleraine, Sir John Davies compared it to the building of Carthage in Virgil's *Aeneid*, where everything was a 'ferment of activity'.[1] The only apparent blot on the horizon for the settlers was the oversight of the planners in failing to anticipate the practical difficulty of removing the indigenous populace from the plantation lands before enough settlers had arrived not only to begin erecting buildings but also to ensure that sufficient food supplies were available for surviving the first winter. The decision to permit the local inhabitants to remain on the estates of the English and Scots colonists during the first harvest season and subsequent winter alleviated the problem in the short term. However, the immediate prospects for the plantation as a whole were not good. Persistent reports that Tyrone was on the verge of returning damaged confidence. Political circumstances in Ireland itself also contrived to create a hostile environment for the settlement project. Having suspended penal policies since the Flight of the Earls, the royal authorities in Ireland set the pot boiling once more when a new phase of anti-Catholic practices was embarked upon. On this occasion, in the absence of the northern earls, the Protestant authorities extended their penal activities throughout the entire province of Ulster, where Andrew Knox, the Protestant Bishop of Raphoe, earned the unenviable reputation of having 'out-Heroded Chichester'.[2] Against this backdrop, the craving for the return of the Earl of Tyrone was to reach new heights.

Before long the logistical problems of implementing the plantation of Ulster according to the terms and conditions laid down by the plantation strategists in London became apparent. It was a striking testimony to the difficulties that were arising that King James issued a proclamation in April 1611 ordering the British undertakers to 'repair' to Ulster before May 1611.[3] Almost one year of the three allocated for the fulfilment of the plantation conditions had already passed, and clearly there had been no stampede of British settlers to Ulster. Having availed of the convenience of having the Ulster Irish on their estates during the first year, the undertakers were reluctant to dispense with their services. As Sir John Davies pointed out in May 1611, 'whereas it was doubted that the natives … would not have been transplanted but with some difficulty, it has fallen out contrary to their expectation, that they are more willing to leave the British undertakers' lands, than the British undertakers are to leave them',[4] i.e. do without the Gaelic Irish as tenants. The sluggish performance of the undertakers vindicated Chichester's belief that the enlarged plantation scheme was misconceived. Such undertakers as had arrived, he believed, 'are not the men who must perform the business; for to displant the natives, who are a warlike people, out of the greatest part of six whole counties, is not a work for private men who seek a present profit'.[5] Enlisting private finances to underpin the plantation was a key aim of the project at a time when royal finances were in an embarrassed state. However, as Chichester implied, such a strategy invited profiteering that could jeopardise rather than advance public policy.

Having invested so much time in the plantation project, and having entertained such high hopes of its success, King James I was appalled by the reported shortcomings in its implementation, though he was reluctant to take Chichester's word for this at face value. After all, in the debate about plantation strategy, the king had adopted crucial policy decisions that were at variance with the advice of his Irish viceroy.[6] The king suspected that Chichester's disparaging attitude was occasioned by nothing more than sour grapes. In order to acquire a clearer picture of the situation in Ireland in general, but in Ulster in particular, a special commissioner, Sir George Carew, was dispatched to Ireland during the summer of 1611. Noting the reports of 'great slackness' in the Ulster plantation, Carew was instructed to devote his primary attention to reviewing the settlement in Ulster.[7] To the king's dismay, Carew's report on the plantation of Ulster was just as depressing as the viceroy's accounts.[8] The scarcity of British undertakers and tenants on the ground in Ulster by the late spring of 1611 was so manifest that for the second successive year the Lord Deputy predicted that the settlement of the British undertakers' lands could only survive if the Gaelic Irish were permitted to remain to work the land. Reluctantly the royal authorities in London conceded on this point for one more year only.[9] But even with this extension, the lethargic approach of such undertakers as took the trouble to travel to Ulster during the summer of 1611 offered little prospect that the issue of transplanting the indigenous population from the lands of the British settlers would be resolved by the following summer. Chichester reported that the 'king's intention of bringing colonies out of Great Britain does not go so far forward as is to be wished. Most of those who have come over hither, come to look upon their portions and see how they can like them, and so return back again, rather than with an intention to adventure their persons or substance in the plantation.'[10]

While the onerous stipulations of the Ulster plantation were sufficient to induce a certain amount of trepidation about what lay in store for the Protestant undertakers and their tenants, it is also apparent that the lingering uncertainty concerning the aspirations of the Earl of Tyrone contributed to the stupor afflicting the plantation project. As long as Tyrone's intentions remained a matter of considerable speculation, so too, it seemed, did the plantation hang in suspended animation. Every year since the Flight in 1607, summer after summer, rumours abounded that Tyrone was on the verge of returning. And 1611 was no different. An English spy in Madrid reported that there was a plan afoot for the earl to come 'disguised' to the court of Spain. News of this projected plan having leaked, it was reportedly abandoned. In its place an alternative strategem was supposedly hatched. Tyrone, it was suggested, was seeking instead to induce the 'potentates' of Italy to undertake the 'conquest' of Ireland.[11] Whether Tyrone actually intended any of this is uncertain. Such desperate, even fanciful, machinations were to be increasingly symptomatic of the rumour-mongering associated with the earl's latter years in exile. Most of them were divorced from any genuine prospect of realisation. Nevertheless, Tyrone's persistent efforts to accomplish his return to Ireland by a reconciliation with King James I or by some more dramatic means had an important bearing on events in Ireland. A cloud of uncertainty was to hang over the Ulster plantation that was proving almost impossible to dispel while Tyrone lived. Indeed, when an international crisis erupted between England and Spain in 1612, followed by tumultuous events in Ireland at the time of the convening of the Irish parliament in May 1613, King James and his advisers were once again to demonstrate that a reconciliation with the Earl of Tyrone was not completely out of the question. The obvious implications of such a development for the British settlers were profound. Against this background, it was no surprise that the undertakers were proving so reluctant to adventure their lives and money.

The suspension of penal proceedings against Catholics while the Ulster plantation took root had given rise to misplaced expectations of a 'great toleration' of the Catholic religion in Ireland.[12] Speculation about the prospects for an official toleration was intense. The prayers of Irish Catholics appeared to have been answered when John Franckton, the royal printer in Dublin, published a declaration of 'toleration for religion without controlment'. For his part in hoodwinking Franckton in this respect, one Symon Paulee was to pay a heavy price. Prosecuted in the Lord Deputy's prerogative Court of Castle Chamber, he was sentenced to an indefinite term of imprisonment, but only after he was 'committed to the grate of Dublin Castle … then whipped from the Castle Bridge to the Newgate, and set on the pillory with his ears nailed and a paper on his head, where he is publicly to acknowledge his offence'.[13] Chafing at the bit to re-engage in a determined campaign to convert the Catholic population of Ireland to Protestantism by a mixture of the 'sword and word',[14]

Lord Deputy Chichester was infuriated by any suggestion that toleration of the Catholic religion would even be contemplated. Focusing on the role of the Catholic clergy as an 'enemy to this state', the viceroy offered the opinion that they 'cannot otherwise be expulsed but with fire and sword'.[15] Still smarting from his 'Mandates' experience of 1605–7, when King James's practical support for a thoroughgoing penal policy was to fall far short of his rhetoric on the issue, Chichester was reluctant to proceed further in religious affairs. 'If I should use the sword in these times of peace,' he declared, 'it would be accounted too severe a course.'[16] Experiencing once again one of his occasional paroxysms of Protestant zeal, King James appointed a firebrand Scotsman, Andrew Knox, as bishop of the northern diocese of Raphoe, with a remit to report on methods of eradicating popery in Ireland. The Lord Deputy's perennial enthusiasm for anti-Catholic campaigning was soon rekindled and before long was burning once again with its customary ferocity.[17] Writing in November 1611 to the English Secretary of State, the Earl of Salisbury, the Lord Deputy urged him to sanction a renewed campaign of persecution in Ireland, arguing that the crown authorities had nothing to lose, as 'daily reports and apparent testimony that the fugitives and priests abroad and discontented at home, study and practise nothing more than to raise commotions here'. Faced with such a volatile situation anyhow, 'dealing severely in reducing them to the true service of God can add but very little' to the discontent which was so pervasive in Irish society.[18]

While not unbridled, support in London for a robust approach to dealing with the Catholic question in Ireland became more evident. A new proclamation banishing Catholic priests was issued in 1611, giving rise to the practice of priest-hunting. The sense of tension and bitterness that ensued is revealed by a Catholic account from the period: 'The priests are all on their guard, and none of them dares to go out of the house by day lest he might be recognised, and no place is secure for them, there are so many nets and snares laid for them by their enemies, whose maddening thirst no liquor can satiate but the blood of the priests of Christ.'[19] Meanwhile a penal code of sorts was applied to the Catholic laity. The Catholic nobility, landed gentry and wealthier members of society bore the brunt once more — in keeping with Chichester's hierarchical approach to tackling religious recalcitrance. In his view, it was axiomatic that if the will of the leaders of Catholic society were broken, then the spirit of the masses would be demoralised.

Instead of employing the old 'Mandates' device, Chichester relied on the administration of the Oath of Supremacy (recognising the English monarch rather than the Pope as head of the church) as a penal broad sword. There were serious penalties for failing to subscribe to this oath. Catholic wardships (the care of minors) were no longer granted to the Catholic nobility and landed gentry. Catholic lawyers were debarred from practising in royal courts, while Catholic civic officials were disqualified from serving as mayors, sheriffs and bailiffs. Extant records show that towns as far apart as Galway, Limerick,

Youghal and Kilkenny were all affected.[20] Indeed, such was the sustained manner of proceedings in Limerick during the years 1611–14 that the period has been referred to as 'the wars of the mayors'.[21] This policy of exclusion from municipal positions combined with a term of imprisonment, it was later acknowledged by the English Privy Council, was 'for terror and example unto others'.[22] Though not used extensively, the ecclesiastical censure of excommunication was also employed against those considered to be particularly contumacious individuals. Ostensibly it seems rather absurd that Catholics were to be excommunicated from a Protestant church to which they did not belong. The official government line, though, was that the Act of Uniformity, 1560, resulted in everyone in Ireland being regarded as technically a member of the Protestant Established Church of Ireland. Social ostracism, the principal practical penalty of the sentence of excommunication, was rendered ineffectual in a largely Catholic Ireland for an offence that was deemed honourable, but failure to observe Protestant religious practices leading to excommunication could have serious consequences in church courts where fines and terms of imprisonment could be meted out.[23] Certainly two sheriffs of the city of Dublin were to feel the brunt of such ecclesiastical censure, finding themselves locked up by order of the Protestant Archbishop of Dublin in the latter part of 1612.[24] Contemporary Catholic accounts suggest that the practice of imposing ecclesiastical penalties was much more widespread than the extant church records indicate. 'Great numbers' of Catholics were reported to have been imprisoned, while the punitive aspect of the penalties inflicted extended even to those dying under such censure, being 'denied Christian burial and thrown into holes dug in the highways'.[25]

Penal practices employed against the lower echelons of Catholic society centred mainly on the application of the Act of Uniformity whereby a one-shilling fine was imposed for failure to attend the services of the Established Church. Assize judges riding their circuits biannually played a key role in enforcing this law throughout the country. Catholics were to complain at the time about 'our sweating stoop under the yoke of the aforesaid statute'.[26] Catholic jurors who attempted to subvert the application of the Act of Uniformity by refusing to convict defendants found themselves prosecuted in the Court of Castle Chamber, where some individuals were fined the massive sum of £200.[27] In addition, financial exactions were levied for the repair of Protestant churches,[28] and there was also the imposition of tithes.[29]

A novel departure in the 'new and furious persecution' that began in 1611 was the manner in which it was extended throughout Ulster in the absence of the northern earls.[30] In County Monaghan alone £500 yearly was raised from recusancy fines.[31] Even more remarkably, it was alleged that fines totalling £8,000 were imposed in County Cavan during 1615.[32] Moreover, unlike the experience during the 'Mandates' campaign of 1605–7, when the civil administrators were the primary functionaries in spearheading the anti-Catholic policy, senior churchmen in the north played a much more prominent role from

1611. Brutus Babington, the new Protestant Bishop of Derry, emphasised his determination to 'bring this rude and uncivilised people to some good conformity'. And he lost no time in setting about his task, remarking that although he could not claim 'as sometime Caesar did, *Veni, vidi, vici*, yet he blesses God he may boldly say, that in so short time, he has prevailed more for the reformation of the better part of his charge, than any of his predecessors have in many years'.[33] Equally rigorous in his methods was the 'swaggering' Bishop Knox of Raphoe, known at the time as the 'governor of the redshanks'.[34] It is hardly surprising that these northern Protestant bishops earned a notorious reputation among Catholics in Ulster. It was a measure of the hostility they generated by their activities that King James I himself acknowledged that seven ministers whom Knox had brought over from Scotland were 'hated by the Irish'. Fearing that their lives were in danger in the unfortified dwelling on Lough Swilly where they resided, the king ordered the deployment of a troop of twenty-five cavalry to protect them, as well as the raising of fifteen additional soldiers.[35] Contemporary Catholic sources detail the excesses reputedly committed by Knox and Babington and the intense loathing with which they were viewed by the Gaelic Irish of Ulster. Having instituted a 'bloody persecution', the two bishops paid a joint visit to a 'little church' near Coleraine where a statue of the Virgin Mary was on display. Knox ordered its seizure. When his men refused to obey the order, he carried it out of the church himself and brought it to Coleraine,

> where he caused a great fire to be made in the midst of the town, and had the image cast therein, which remaining a long time in the fire, till the fire was near spent, and taking no hurt, it was taken up out of the fire, and a new fire made, whereunto the said image was cast again, which, notwithstanding, took no great hurt by the said fire; and being admired of many, the said Knox, fearing farther notice should be taken thereof, sent for a carpenter, and caused him to bore several great holes into several parts of the image, whereunto he also caused a company of small dry sticks to be thrust with powder and tar, which being kindled, the image took fire and was burned.[36]

While they succeeded in destroying the statue, reports that the two prelates suffered almost instantaneous divine retribution for their conduct were received with considerable delight in Catholic circles. Babington, described as being in 'perfect health', succumbed to a fatal seizure, while Knox was rumoured to have drowned shortly afterwards *en route* to Scotland.[37] While the reports of Knox's demise turned out to be wishful thinking, English records confirm that Babington's death was sudden, 'being well at 7 o'clock evening and dead at 8'.[38]

Overall, the renewed campaign of persecution throughout Ireland generated waves of discontent. The prospect of even tougher anti-Catholic laws being passed in the Irish parliament that was soon to convene heightened the general sense of unease and apprehension. In the words of a Catholic commentator, 'What keeps everyone in a state of suspense is the fear of the approaching parliament … in which the heretics intend to vomit out all their poison, and infect with it the purity of our holy religion.'[39] While there may not have been a legislative penal code in existence in Ireland at the time, a practical one had effectively been put in place. Confronted in 1611 by further religious repression, Irish Catholics, Old English and Gaelic alike, began to look to the Earl of Tyrone, with the assistance of the King of Spain and the Pope, for liberation. Learning from the 'Mandates' experience of 1605–7, when the opposition of isolated elements of the Old English had been suppressed relatively easily by the crown authorities, Catholics began to react in a different way to the new campaign of persecution launched in 1611. A newly politicised, mobilised Catholic 'people' was becoming increasingly active from this time. Part of this process involved a 'great meeting' in Ireland in 1611 attended by senior Catholic clergy and 'many other persons of virtue and learning' which decided to form a 'league' to 'free themselves from subjugation to the tyrannical heretics'. William Meade, a prominent Old English expatriate, was delegated to secure Spanish military support and the leadership of the Earl of Tyrone. Evidence shows that Meade subsequently travelled to Rome to liaise with Tyrone in this matter.[40] Meade's involvement in the affair demonstrates that it must be taken seriously as a measure of Old English disenchantment with their treatment and a growing tendency to look to the Earl of Tyrone to champion the Catholic cause in Ireland.

William Meade had been the ringleader of the recusant revolt in Cork in 1603. Although he had on that occasion been charged with treason, the English authorities had anticipated grave difficulties in securing a conviction anywhere in County Cork, 'so great is his popularity there. … So great indeed is the general interest in all the people of this land … in the religion he professeth.'[41] When he was eventually brought to trial, sympathisers on the jury refused to convict him. Having narrowly escaped with his life, Meade journeyed to the Spanish court in 1603, where he was acclaimed as a representative of Irish Catholics. Meade's influence prevailed in Munster, despite living in exile. Describing him as the 'reprobate recorder' of Cork, the English Lord President of Munster, Lord Danvers, noted in 1608 that he was 'the oracle that leads the towns of this province'.[42] The persistence of Meade's influence was such that English State Papers include advice on non-compliance with the Act of Uniformity which he tendered to the residents of Munster. Meade urged compliance with the royal authorities on all secular matters. However, when it came to matters of conscience, Catholics were implored to take a united stand in opposition to the crown's anti-Catholic measures at the sessions where charges of recusancy were prosecuted. Meade advised that 'all principal persons with the rest of the town and country be present that one may comfort and animate another'.[43] While Meade entertained 'great esteem' for the Earl of Tyrone for his martial qualities, such Old English as Meade purported to represent had no intention of installing the earl as their king in the event of the English authorities being overthrown. In such an eventuality, the crown of Ireland would be offered to Spain.[44] Meade's liaison with the Spanish authorities and the Earl of Tyrone lends credence to two important developments. As a result of her exhaustive study of the Spanish archives, Micheline Kerney Walsh has shown that the experience of persecution was reorientating the Catholic Old English away from their traditional affiliation with the English crown towards the Spanish monarchy instead, to the extent that offering the Irish crown to Spain was 'acceptable to many'.[45] Perhaps even more importantly, persecution was driving the Old English to seeking common cause with the Gaelic Irish, and the Earl of Tyrone in particular. Unfolding events in Ireland during the years 1612–13, in the run-up to the meeting of the Irish parliament, reinforced this realignment in Old English attitudes.

Growing worries in London about an international Catholic conspiracy provided Lord Deputy Chichester with the opportunity he had been longing for to take resolute action against priests in Ireland. It was a measure of his pathological hatred of the Catholic clergy that he variously referred to them as 'locusts', 'caterpillars' and even 'corsairs'.[46] This latter reference was occasioned by a comparison with the swarms of pirates plaguing Irish coasts at the time. In Chichester's view, however, 'this kind of pirates and sea thieves is much inferior for malice and dangerous effects to another sort [of corsair] which infests this land and sea',[47] namely priests. Owing to the decrepit state of the English navy as a result of financial difficulties prevailing in the aftermath of the Nine Years War and the Anglo-Spanish war, the Lord Deputy had access to pitifully inadequate shipping to deal with the menace at sea. At certain times, indeed, when there were only one or two vessels of the English navy on patrol in Irish coastal waters, there was a powerful fleet of up sixteen pirate ships.[48] By contrast, circumstances had afforded Chichester an opportunity to take resolute action against the ecclesiastical 'corsairs' he so despised. In a high-profile test case, an aged bishop and a priest were tried in Dublin in January 1612. Conor O'Devany, the octogenarian bishop of the northern diocese of Down and Connor, and Patrick O'Loughran, formerly a chaplain to the Earl or Countess of Tyrone, were put on trial on trumped-up charges of treason.[49] Such evidence as there was to implicate the two men was circumstantial, and guilt by association with the Earl of Tyrone appears to have been their main offence. Not that Chichester would have been unduly concerned by the legalities of the affair. He was determined to eradicate the influence of the Catholic clergy either by inducing apostasy, or by banishment or execution.

Bishop O'Devany was arrested in May 1611 in Ulster, and O'Loughran was seized a short time later in Cork. The case against O'Devany was particularly contrived. One aspect of his indictment related to his alleged involvement in the Nine Years War — on which point the bishop reminded his accusers of the Act of Oblivion of 1604 which was supposed to have pardoned all those involved.[50] It was also alleged that O'Devany had afforded the Earl of Tyrone 'counsel and material aid' at the time of the Flight of the Earls, an accusation that the bishop rebutted by offering to 'produce many witnesses who would attest that he was in a far distant part of the kingdom at the time of this flight'.[51] For O'Loughran's part, the fact that he had once been a chaplain in Tyrone's household 'lent some colour' to the charges which had been made against him.[52] It is at least possible, though far from certain, that O'Loughran was on a mission to stir up sedition in Ireland at Tyrone's behest, as the viceroy had often accused priests of doing. However, as the Lord Deputy had himself admitted a year previously of those alleged to be the 'messengers' of Tyrone, 'death itself will not make them reveal what they carry'.[53] If O'Loughran was engaged in such activities, he clearly fitted Chichester's stereotype as a man preferring death to disclosure. Despite months of bad treatment in prison, O'Loughran did not confess to anything that implicated the Earl of Tyrone. Far from admitting culpability in treason, at the point of being executed he declared to the assembled multitudes that 'the only crime they found in him was the exercise of his functions among the faithful'.[54] In the interim, between the arrests and the executions, it seems that the royal authorities were more interested in inducing the conversion of the two clerics to Protestantism rather than in establishing their guilt of any offence. They were offered all manner of inducements to abandon their faith, entirely consistent with Chichester's 'carrot-and-stick' religious policy. Promising allurements of material welfare or status, such as 'the offer of bishoprics and benefices', was his preferred option of securing religious conformity.[55] It was only when the two clerics refused the sweeteners that the Lord Deputy proceeded to impose the ultimate sanction of capital punishment. While Chichester's record in Ireland affords ample testimony to sustain his blood-curdling reputation among Irish Catholics, he would have preferred in these instances to have avoided bloodshed. He would have considered the enforced 'conversion' of O'Devany and O'Loughran as a major coup in his campaign to undermine the recalcitrance of Irish Catholics. Clearly this was an eventuality feared by prominent figures in Catholic society, who accordingly exhorted the prisoners to 'remain constant'.[56] O'Devany and O'Loughran did not disappoint their supporters, but the penalty for their steadfastness was to be gruesome. Chichester went ahead with their trial for treason, securing a guilty verdict, and opting for showpiece executions in Dublin as a means of 'terrorising' the Catholic clergy and laity alike.[57] The staunch demeanour of the doomed clerics put paid to these aspirations, generating in turn an impassioned response from the vast crowds which turned up to witness the executions.

Transported to the scene of his execution in a horse-drawn vehicle, Bishop O'Devany had the temerity to observe that 'he went much more comfortably to death than his Master, our Lord Jesus Christ, who had to walk on foot and bear the weight of His cross'.[58] As the cart proceeded along the streets, the crowds became ever more hysterical. A Jesuit priest recorded the scenes as the two clerics were being brought to the scaffold:

Along the road by which they went there was a multitude of people of all degrees, such as was never seen at such a spectacle before; and the Catholics, despising the danger, cast themselves upon their knees to ask the bishop's blessing, which he gave them to satisfy their devotion, and the blows and kicks of the heretics were not sufficient to deter them.[59]

It is common to find that Catholic and Protestant versions of controversial events are so different as to defy mutual recognition. However, in this case, the account of the Jesuit priest was largely corroborated by Barnaby Rich, the rabidly puritan chronicler of Irish affairs. The bishop, he records, was followed by 'troops of citizens', men and women, 'not of the inferior sort alone, but of the better, and amongst the women, of the best men's wives within the city of Dublin'. Along the way, Rich further observed, the throngs sustained 'such a screeching, such a howling and such a hallowing, as if Saint Patrick himself had been going to the gallows'.[60] Raising of the 'hubbub', as it was known, was a traditional practice at times of distress. Fynes Moryson described it as a 'doleful outcry which they take from one another's mouth till they put the whole town in tumult'.[61]

Significantly, while the bishop was being transported to the scene of his execution by means of hanging, drawing and quartering, two Protestant ministers implored him to abandon his faith. O'Devany was challenged by one of them to 'announce to the people that you suffer this penalty solely for the crime of high treason', to whom the bishop replied: 'Defile not your own soul by falsehood, for you yourself conveyed the message to me that my life would be saved if I would consent to exchange my faith for Protestantism.'[62] After this emphatic and spirited rejoinder O'Devany was brought to the scaffold and thrown off, precipitating an enormous clamour from the crowd, followed by deathly silence. According to the Jesuit's account, they 'took him down very soon, and from the cheerfulness of his countenance, they thought he was still alive; then they cut off his head, opened his body, and burned his bowels, and cut him into four quarters'.[63] Hysteria before the bishop's execution gave way to pandemonium afterwards. Barnaby Rich noted that

Happy was she that could get but her hankerchief dipped in the blood of the traitor. And the body being once dissevered into four quarters, they left neither finger nor toe, but they cut them off and carried them away. And to show their Catholic zeal, they tore his garments into tatters, and some others that could only get no holy monuments that pertained to his person, with their knives they shaved off chips from the hallowed gallows.[64]

In the mêlée the bishop's head was spirited away by his supporters and could not be located despite the fact that a £40 reward was offered.[65] All this while the frail figure of Father O'Loughran had been standing by the scaffold as a witness of the bloody spectacle. Bishop O'Devany, fearing that O'Loughran 'might be seized with horror and dismay at the sight of the tortures about to be inflicted upon his own body in his presence', asked the executioner to put O'Loughran to death first. 'The priest said that he need not be in dread on his account, and that he would follow him without fear, and remarked that it was not meet an honourable bishop should be without a priest to attend him.'[66] On being summoned to his own execution, O'Loughran, living up to his word, 'commenced to exhort the people', though he was 'immediately stopped and put on the scaffold to his great joy'.[67] Such remains of the bodies that had not been stolen away by the crowds were buried by the authorities, only to be disinterred the following night by twelve young Catholics.[68]

Clearly the fact that the two clerics were sentenced to death for their supposed treasonable association with the Earl of Tyrone did little to assuage the intense anger of the Old English in Dublin, who were outraged by the executions. Far from quelling manifestations of solidarity with the fugitive earl, the executions appear to have had precisely the opposite effect, as is indicated by the openly distraught demeanour of the 'infinite number of people' in attendance.[69] The persecution of the Catholic laity and clergy since the ending of the war appeared to be entering a new phase of ferocity. In the circumstances, it would not be going too far to suggest that the Old English had increasing cause to regret that they had not thrown in their lot with the Earl of Tyrone during the Nine Years War. That William Meade was collaborating with Tyrone on behalf of a substantial proportion of the Old English is entirely possible. What is certain is that the sympathies of the large crowds for O'Devany and O'Loughran was so profound that they were instantly reputed as martyrs and 'adored for saints' following their executions. The Lord Deputy, for his part, was not in the least intimidated nor deflected from his intention of suppressing Catholicism in Ireland. Reacting to the affirmation that O'Devany and O'Loughran were venerated as martyrs and saints, Chichester is reported to have remarked that if the 'people venerate them as such ... I will soon give them plenty like them'.[70] Sanctioning such high-profile executions in Dublin was typical of the Lord Deputy's confrontational approach in religious affairs, a man who was prepared to bring to bear the full ruthlessness of his military background. He compared the Irish 'unto nettles that bite and sting if they be played withal or lightly touched, and being otherwise handled have no such effect'.[71] He was determined to grasp the nettle of recusancy once and for all.

Fortunately, from the point of view of Irish Catholics, while King James was at times inclined to boast about leaving no stone unturned in his endeavour to Protestantise the Irish, he more typically shied away from the prospect of conflict resulting from an overly aggressive approach. On hearing the reports of the scenes at the executions, the king moved promptly to restrain his over-zealous deputy, impressing upon him that he could only 'forward anything that may tend to the advancement of religion so far forth as it give not occasion to make any disturbance among the people'.[72] As it turned out, as a result of the king's moderating counsels, the executions of O'Devany and O'Loughran, it has been well remarked, represented a defining moment in the history of Catholicism (and for that matter for the future prospects of Protestantism) in Ireland. 'This large-scale public profession of the Catholic faith in the very capital itself irrevocably committed the Old English community to Counter-Reformation Catholicism.'[73] Repression, especially when conducted in half-measure, often proves counterproductive. How much different the story might have been had the Lord Deputy been supported by his monarch can only be surmised. Chichester, the gritty Elizabethan crusader, had fought against 'heretics' for much of his adult life on the continent, in the New World and, latterly, in Ireland. For him, pressing home the advantage of Protestantism in Ireland in the wake of the conquest was to witness the object of his crusading zeal achieved. That the Lord Deputy would have been prepared to proliferate the number of Irish martyrs should not be doubted. Having slaughtered defenceless men, women and children in his ruthless prosecution of the Nine Years War, Chichester would not have baulked at advancing the cause of his beloved Protestantism at the point of a sword, or the gibbet for that matter. His penchant for 'thick and short' military campaigns would undoubtedly have been transferred to the sphere of religious policy.

Meanwhile, marooned in Rome, Tyrone was experiencing enormous frustration that he could not return to Ireland to lead a revolt against the English 'heretics' at a time when passions were running so high in his homeland. With the Spanish government remaining unwilling to sanction an invasion, the ageing earl was becoming ever more desperate. It was in these circumstances that he countenanced a tentative plot to launch a piratical expedition from the coast of Flanders, without Spanish approval, involving troops from the Irish regiment, with orders to 'take the spoil of English and Hollanders; to receive into protection all pirates which are abroad, and to join with them; and when they should be able to make 4,000 or 5,000 men, to land in some part of Ireland most convenient for their purpose upon the sea-coast, and to fortify, and there to employ certain principal men of each province to begin a tumult; and their shipping to be dispatched to sea again to follow their former course'.[74] Experience had proved that large pirate fleets had been able to base themselves with relative impunity on southern coasts of Ireland for months at a time.[75] And there had been a scare in September 1611 when a pirate fleet was reported to have left Irish shores bound for Italy, with an implicit suggestion that the Earl of Tyrone had a hand in this development.[76] Generally, however, at this time the English were dismissive of Tyrone's covert schemes and transactions, ridiculing them as delusionary. Such lulls in English suspicions gave rise to a degree of smugness. Typical of this attitude was a contemporary report which noted that the earl 'whilst he is his own man, is always much reserved', seeking a negotiated return to Ireland. 'But when he is *vino plenus et ira* [drunk and angry], as he is commonly once a night, and therein is *veritas* [truth], he doth then declare his resolute purpose to die in Ireland, and both he and his company do usually in that mood dispose of governments and provinces, and make new commonwealths'.[77]

Gathering events in Ireland and on the continent, however, once again persuaded the English to reconsider their contemptuous attitude as the Earl of Tyrone was once more propelled into the limelight of international affairs. Applauded by the Spanish ambassador in Rome as a 'great nobleman' manifesting exemplary 'Christianity',[78] Tyrone suddenly found his stock rising once more in the eyes of the Spanish, a recommendation passing the Spanish Council of State in October 1612 that a jewel worth 500 crowns be granted to him.[79] Not long afterwards the Spanish authorities in the Low Countries fêted the earl's son at his confirmation, bestowing on him a chain worth 100 crowns and organising a banquet in his honour.[80] That the Spanish were concurrently enduring their most turbulent phase of relations with the English since the end of the Anglo-Spanish war in 1604 was hardly coincidental. The situation was deteriorating so rapidly that by early 1613 the London government was expecting renewed war. Mercantile issues and colonial interests in the New World, this time focusing on Virginia, the old rivalries that had done so much to provoke and sustain the prolonged Anglo-Spanish conflict of the late sixteenth century, were once more causing problems.[81] At the height of the crisis four men-of-war were dispatched to patrol Irish coasts at a time when the English navy was suffering from dilapidation in the aftermath of the wars with Spain and in Ireland.[82] As sabre-rattling between the English and Spanish increased in intensity, the London authorities let it be known that the entire navy would be fitted out to counter the threat and that the militia would be mobilised throughout England in the face of an amassing 'Spanish Armada' reputed to be even bigger than that of 1588.[83] By March 1613, with the crisis in Anglo-Spanish relations still festering dangerously, beacons 'had been prepared all round the coast [of England] to be lighted should an Armada appear'.[84]

And it was not just an armada descending on England that was feared, but the nightmare scenario of Tyrone being transported back to Ireland. Gone, all of a sudden, was the derisory attitude towards the old earl. Once again the blind mists of panic descended on the English government in London at the prospect of Tyrone returning to Ireland. No longer were the English inclined to dismiss any strategy that the earl might employ. An Irish merchant's intention to ship wines from Naples was considered as a subterfuge for transporting munitions. No option was dismissed. Two previous expeditions to assist the Catholic cause in Ireland during the sixteenth century, it was recalled, had been dispatched directly from Italy with papal approval. Thus rumours that Tyrone intended to travel back to Flanders by land were considered to be a possible diversionary tactic to conceal his true intention of taking shipping from Italy. And the ex-patriate Irish, it was affirmed, in their new found confidence 'do not desire the assistance of strangers, whom experience shows to be unfit for the service of that country, only they require to have writings from Rome and dollars from Spain'.[85] Tyrone's hopes had once again been rekindled, while the dying embers of English suspicions had once again been fanned into an inferno. Even the Spanish, normally wishing to discourage Tyrone's aspirations to return to Ireland at the head of an invasion force, had warmed to the prospect.

Against the background of the sudden eruption of the international crisis, it comes as little surprise that the Spanish were just as suddenly courting the earl's views not only on the prospects of securing a decisive military success against the English in Ireland but also on the possibility of a rising in Scotland as well. So far as Scotland was concerned, Tyrone suggested that rebellious sentiment was brewing there and that the 'warlike' Scots were anxious to be 'free of the tyranny in which they live' and would be prepared to owe allegiance to the Spanish monarch. Interestingly, Tyrone cited William Meade as the prime source of this information. Having some months previously returned from Scotland, Meade had reportedly been asked by the 'most powerful Scottish chiefs' to secure Spanish help.[86] (In 1614, as events turned out, rebellion did indeed break out in the western isles of Scotland.)[87] As for Ireland, the really significant development was the complete *volte-face* in Spanish policy. Up to the international crisis which erupted in 1612 the Spanish had consistently cold-shouldered Tyrone's requests for assistance to invade Ireland. Presented now with what seemed a heaven-sent opportunity, Tyrone prepared a detailed response. In the first instance, he identified English military weaknesses in Ireland: the army was badly paid, and there were maritime ports where there were some fortresses 'which at present are like sentries who are ill-armed and without sufficient supplies'. He was careful to recommend, however, that any action undertaken in Ireland should be swift and decisive, as these fortresses could be supplied quickly. His advice, therefore, was informed by realism rather than by self-delusionary assumptions that the task would be easily achievable. As for the mood of Irish Catholics, he remarked that the 'principal cities and towns' were experiencing 'unceasing and increasingly severe persecution from the heretics'. Advocating the invasion of Ireland, Tyrone noted that 'it is a common saying among the English themselves that whosoever wishes to conquer England must begin with Ireland'. In order to demonstrate that his proposal was not self-motivated, the earl frankly advised the Spanish that the 'proper manner' of dealing with the English once and for all was to go straight for the jugular by invading England itself. Whether an invasion of Ireland or England was chosen, and despite his advancing years, Tyrone offered to 'risk' his life furthering either, 'for I have no greater wish in the world than to spend the few years of life which are left to me in matters which concern the exaltation of the Holy Catholic Faith and the advancement of the kingdoms and honour of the Catholic King [of Spain]'.[88]

Tyrone, therefore, was a feisty old character whose commitment to the 'Catholic' cause was not only sustained but was burgeoning, despite years of disheartening disappointment at being confined in his open prison, Rome. Equally, as his rhetoric makes clear, he was becoming ever more wedded to the cause of Catholicism, a factor induced in part, no doubt, by his sumptuously pious surroundings in the Eternal City, as well as by his own advancing years, when a man's past life tends to loom into larger focus as he contemplates his approaching end. The earl may have had a fondness for tippling which English commentators at the time mocked. However, he was far from the dipsomaniac of contemporary English invention, who, if not actually blind, was blind drunk as often as not, a miserable creature wallowing in self-pity and living in a 'Walter Mitty' world in which delusions of conspiracy and great campaigns haunted his befuddled mind. That the old earl remained a force to be reckoned with was clearly revealed in the welter of alarmist reports circulating in English administrative circles regarding the prospects of a Spanish-sponsored invasion of Ireland during the international crisis of the latter part of 1612 and the early months of 1613.[89] Preparations had been put in hand in England and Scotland to dispatch 7,000 or 8,000 infantry to Ireland 'at a moment's notice'.[90] In one particularly telling diplomatic communication, the English ambassador at Brussels reported in December 1612 that 'At this present there is a confederacy between the Pope and the King of Spain (as soon as there shall happen any disgust between Your Majesty and him) to send six thousand men into the realm of Ireland.'[91] And there were to be no prizes for guessing who would lead it. In the circumstances, the English authorities strained every sinew to frustrate the designs of the Spanish and the expatriate Irish. In the latter respect, a senior official in London suggested that 'jealousy' should be contrived between the Old English and the Gaelic Irish in the Irish regiment in Flanders. The English ambassador in Brussels was advised to 'nourish a difference between the ancient Irish, such as O'Neale, Odonnell and Thomond … and those descended from English races, though degenerate into Irish, as Ormond, Kildare, Desmond, Clanricard, whose ancestors … were planted there by English kings'.[92]

Within this rancorous atmosphere of the prevailing poisonous relations between England and Spain, events in Ireland in the run-up to the convening of parliament sustained Tyrone's aspirations of returning to lead a revolt of 'Catholic' Ireland. The royal authorities there were engaged in what constituted a 'political revolution' in the country,[93] whereby the predominance of the Catholic Old English was to be subverted by the means of a parliament 'packed' with Protestants. To this end, forty new boroughs were incorporated, eighteen of them in Ulster, each of which could send two M.P.s to parliament.[94] The strategy owed much to the prospective urbanisation of Ulster that was one of the principal aims of the plantation. However, by 1613, as with the plantation itself, the prospect for the erection of towns was bleak. Some undertakers had yet to lay a brick in fulfilment of their plantation commitments. With the exception of Coleraine and Derry, the proposed establishment of a network of towns in Ulster had made negligible progress. Most of the new boroughs in Ulster, it has been well remarked, were 'little more than sites on which it was hoped that strong British settlements would arise'.[95] It was little wonder, therefore, that Irish Catholics viewed the policy of incorporation apprehensively. Five Catholic lords from the Pale articulated the fear of Irish Catholics in general in November 1612 when they wrote to King James noting:

> A fearful suspicion, that the project of erecting so many corporations in places that constantly pass the rank of the poor villages in the poorest country of Christendom, do tend to nought else at this time, but by the voices of a few selected for that purpose, under the name of burgesses, extreme penal laws should be imposed upon your subjects.[96]

To allay the fears of Irish Catholics in this respect, the five Catholic lords urged the king to withdraw any intended penal legislation. Should penal laws be proceeded with, James I was left in little doubt of the potential consequences. Anti-Catholic legislation, it was made clear, would 'suffer the secret, home [i.e. in Ireland], evil-affected subjects (of whom we wish there were none) to be transported with hope and expectation of the effects, which a general discontent might in time produce'.[97] The implied threat was not lost on Protestants in Ireland, who noted that the Catholic lords had 'darkly intimated, under colour of representing the perils depending upon the parliament, the danger of revolt'.[98]

By May 1613 sectarian tensions had risen to such a pitch that serious religious strife threatened to break out in Dublin and elsewhere. Once again, in another menacing letter, signed this time by a total of twelve Catholic lords, the warning was repeated to the king about the dangers of 'disorders', as there were numerous 'evil-affected' in Ireland. In the circumstances, there was a prospect that 'the rebellious and discontented of this nation abroad' might take advantage of the situation to 'labour some underhand relief from any prince or estate abroad'.[99] The spectre of Tyrone's return to take advantage of the turbulent political climate in Ireland had loomed into ever larger focus. What is more, as the Catholic lords implicitly made clear, should Tyrone manage to effect his return, he would be met with a wave of support from the Catholic Old English as much as the Gaelic Irish. The reasons for the volatile situation in Ireland may be accounted for by two factors: continued government provocation in the realm of religious policy, combined with an ever-growing Catholic political mobilisation in resistance to it.

Lord Deputy Chichester, in contravention of the king's explicit advice to temper his religious policy, exercised a degree of autonomy that his viceregal position and the problems of early seventeenth-century communications afforded him, to increase pressure once again on leading members of Catholic society in Ireland. In the process, however, he managed to provoke the Old English into engaging in open acts of defiance against the king. Critical in this respect was the tendering of the Oath of Supremacy to municipal officials as a condition for holding civic office. The Oath of Supremacy recognised the king as head of the church. Catholics, of course, considered the king to be their temporal leader, the Pope being their spiritual leader. Such sophistry did not impress James I, who was acutely sensitive of his royal position and was unwilling to suffer any derogation of it. He was incensed by the blatant refusal of so many Catholic magistrates throughout Ireland to take the oath and signified his displeasure in this regard to the Lord Deputy in September 1612. Reflecting on his lenient attitude to the Munster towns in the wake of the 'recusant revolt' of 1603, James observed that it was 'found by experience that the easy and gentle hand which he has hitherto borne towards them has wrought no other effect but the abasing of his regal authority amongst them'. James clearly considered persistent refusal to acknowledge his regal position at the head of the church as a case of *lèse-majesté*, and the hardening of the king's attitude towards the Old English was signified when he announced that the repeated election of officials who refused to take the Oath of Supremacy would result in the forfeiture of municipal 'liberties' (privileges accorded to towns).[100] Chichester had tendered the Oath of Supremacy on religious grounds, as a means of persecution. By refusing to take the Oath of Supremacy, the Old English had played into the deputy's hands, as the king took offence at their recalcitrance on a political basis.

Utilising procedures that afforded him a legal cloak for his persecuting zeal, Lord Deputy Chichester intensified his anti-Catholic campaign in the weeks leading up to the convening of parliament. Less than a fortnight before parliament was due to assemble, the Lord Deputy's Court of Castle Chamber convicted two recusant juries for refusing to indict fellow-Catholics for failure to attend Protestant services. According to statutory law, it was an offence not to be present at Protestant service. Catholic juries who failed to convict in these circumstances were therefore leaving themselves open to 'justifiable' legal punishment. And the Lord Deputy, seeking to confront Catholic recalcitrance head on, did not pull his punches. All the jurors appearing in Castle Chamber at this time were heavily fined and imprisoned. Three jurors were singled out for particularly stringent punishment, being fined the massive sum of £200 apiece.[101] Such severity was not lost on the assembling Catholic M.P.s, many of whom arrived in Dublin in aggressive mood at the head of well-armed troops. This engendered Protestant apprehensions that they intended to 'effect their designs by force'.[102] Tempestuous events in many parts of the country during the elections to the legislature contributed to the mood of latent violence that so manifestly pervaded the country. Again Dublin was to be the scene of some of the most 'hurly-burly' events. Protestants alleged that a 'great tumult and mutiny' occurred in the Tholsel where the election was taking place, during which Catholics physically ejected Protestants from the proceedings. In the end the mayor had to enlist the Lord Deputy's assistance to quell the disorder that resulted from recusant objections to the election procedures, several aldermen and other leading recusants being imprisoned in consequence.[103] Elsewhere in the country the manner in which crown officials interfered in the due electoral process enraged Catholics. Sir Oliver Lambert, a leading Privy Counsellor and senior army officer, who enjoyed an awesome reputation in Ireland second only to Lord Deputy Chichester, was reputed to have resorted to outrageous tactics to ensure that he was personally elected in Cavan. Not only did he allegedly imprison one of the Catholic candidates, but an armed guard with 'burning matches' was stationed outside the courthouse where the election was to take place, physically preventing anyone of whom they disapproved from voting. One voter who managed to make it past the armed guard and had the temerity to vote for the Catholic candidates was then apparently assaulted by Lambert, Catholics alleging that he suffered a serious head injury. Indeed, not content with the vicious assault, Lambert then put his hand on his dagger and would have stabbed the man but for the fact that a fellow-officer intervened.[104] That an altercation had occurred in Cavan was confirmed by a government inquiry into the disturbances at the elections, though the seriousness of it was played down: Lambert was merely said to have struck one George Brady 'with a little walking-stick ... but his [Brady's] head was not broken'.[105]

The violence and disorder that accompanied the elections spilled over into the opening session of the Irish House of Commons, where the first order of business was the election of a Speaker. This offered the Catholic M.P.s their first opportunity to register their objections to the manner in which so many new boroughs had been created with the deliberate objective of subverting the Catholic majority in the lower house. The policy of choosing Dublin Castle as the location of the parliament was justified on security grounds by the royal administration in Ireland. The Catholic M.P.s, for their part, objected to the choice of the Castle, complaining about the 'powder and ammunitions which evermore had been placed in a room within the castle', thereby implying that they feared a Protestant version of the Gunpowder Plot.[106] The presence of an armed guard of 100 troops who searched the assembling M.P.s aggravated the mood of simmering belligerence. Worried that the recusant M.P.s, together with the defeated recusant candidates from the contentious elections, were intent on occupying the Commons chamber, the Lord Deputy took the unusual step of issuing a proclamation ordering all elected M.P.s to present themselves before him. On their so doing, the martinet Lord Deputy carefully inspected the assembled group, taking a 'view of every particular person appearing'. Having completed his scrutiny of the M.P.s, he promptly promulgated a proclamation to the effect that 'none should presume to come into the house of the Commons but such as were returned as aforesaid'.[107] Chichester's record of employing Castle Chamber to punish offenders against the royal prerogative could have left few in doubt that flagrant defiance of the deputy's proclamation would have had dire consequences. However, if the deputy's tactic frustrated an audacious bid by the recusants to occupy the Commons chamber, it did not deter them from resorting to a similarly dramatic demonstration of their profound displeasure at the rigged nature of many of the elections and the incorporation process. If the Commons chamber could not be occupied, then the Speaker's chair could, as the highly irregular events that subsequently unfolded were to demonstrate.

When the proceedings began in the Commons, it very quickly became apparent that the recusant M.P.s had drawn a battle-line on the issue of the election to the Speakership.[108] The eerie hush at the start of the proceedings as everyone sat quietly for some time waiting on someone to 'first break silence' belied the tempestuous events that were on the point of erupting. Sir Thomas Ridgeway, a senior member of the royal administration in Dublin, then rose and broke the strained silence, proposing the Attorney General, Sir John Davies, as Speaker of the House. In response, Sir James Gough 'stepped out of his place disorderly into the middle of the house' and launched into his speech. Quiescence had soon given way to an increasingly bear-pit atmosphere. Immediately the Protestant M.P.s barracked Gough to return to his seat. Gough then raised Catholic objections to those Protestant M.P.s who had been unduly elected, arguing that these matters should be resolved before the matter of choosing a Speaker could be proceeded with. At this point Gough was berated by Protestant M.P.s for not having spoken on the matter to hand, i.e. the election of a Speaker. Gough then nominated Sir John Everard, a former senior judge who had been removed from the judiciary because of his recusancy.[109] Undeterred by the rebuke offered previously to Gough, several other prominent Catholic M.P.s returned to the thrust of the recusant contention that the matter of electoral malpractice should be dealt with first. The fact that a parliament had not been held in Ireland since 1586 may well have contributed to the procedural wrangling, as a grasp of parliamentary conventions had become uncertain. Certainly Sir Oliver St John, another senior member of the crown administration in Dublin, believed so. He declared on the basis of his more recent experience in English parliaments that precedent dictated that a Speaker should be elected in the first instance and that the issue of election returns should be dealt with subsequently in committee. St John was, of course, conveniently overlooking the fact that the 'packing' of the parliament with Protestants would have a decisive bearing on the result of the election to the Speakership (Protestants held only a thirty-two-seat majority).[110] Seeking to bring the issue to a head, St John appealed to the assembled members to observe parliamentary etiquette:

> Gentlemen, the use of parliaments is to decide controversies by questions, and questions by numbering of voices, and for the trial thereof I know by experience that they that are of the affirmative part are to go out of the house to be numbered and to leave those that are of the negative part to be numbered within the house.

What followed was not only far from gentlemanly conduct, but departed markedly from parliamentary decorum.

Following St John's appeal for a division, the Protestant M.P.s filed out of the chamber in conventional fashion in order to be counted. Two senior Catholic M.P.s, Sir Christopher Plunkett and Sir Christopher Nugent, were requested to validate the counting of those who had left the chamber in support of St John's motion. This they resolutely refused to do, nor would they take part in enumerating the recusants who remained in the chamber. When Sir Thomas Ridgeway and Sir Richard Wingfield, two senior members of the crown administration, returned to the chamber and offered to count those opposing the motion, the Catholic M.P.s immediately rose from their seats and 'gathered themselves into a clump to the end they might not be numbered'. Unconventional behaviour soon gave way to the truly bizarre, and finally to pandemonium. This sequence rapidly unfolded after Ridgeway and Wingfield had left the chamber for a second time. The door to the Commons chamber was immediately closed behind them. At almost the same instant cries went up from within the Commons: 'An Everard! 'An Everard!' To the amazement of Ridgeway and Wingfield, who promptly returned to the chamber, Sir John Everard was sitting in the Speaker's chair, while his colleagues were hailing his assumption of the position. Astounded by this turn of events, the Protestants reacted by enumerating their M.P.s in a 'loud voice' as they re-entered the chamber. Responding to the recusant tactic of foiling a count of the Catholic M.P.s, the Protestants declared on the basis of simple mathematical computation that Sir John Davies was the rightfully elected Speaker, i.e. that the entire complement of M.P.s was 232, that there were six absentees (four Protestant and two Catholic), and that 127 had declared for Davies.

Despite the best endeavours of the Protestant M.P.s to persuade Everard to vacate the Speaker's chair, he 'sat still and refused to come out'. Everard was then told that the Protestants would 'be enforced to pluck him out' unless he voluntarily removed himself. Everard still refused to move. Then, in one of the finer points of parliamentary order, the Protestants decided to deposit Sir John Davies on Everard's lap, in an attempt to supersede Everard's supposed authority. However, this was easier said than done. Davies being a distinctly corpulent individual, it took Ridgeway, Wingfield and 'divers knights and gentlemen of the best quality' to hoist him on top of Everard. Ironically, while English parliamentary tradition normally witnessed the Speaker being ceremonially dragged to the Speaker's chair on his election, the converse happened in this situation, with Everard being unceremoniously hauled from the chair. Versions of the events that subsequently unfolded as Everard was removed widely diverge, depending on the source, Protestant or Catholic. What is not in doubt is that some Protestant M.P.s decided to put an end to the absurdity of Davies perching on Everard's knee by physically removing the latter from the Speaker's chair, while Catholic M.P.s just as vigorously attempted to prevent his ejection. In the rucking and mauling that resulted, the amount of force employed by the Protestant M.P.s is the point at issue. According to a Protestant version, not even Everard's hat had been disturbed in the process.[111] Catholics, by contrast, alleged that Everard had been ejected in a 'great rage' by Protestant M.P.s, including Privy Counsellors, who 'cast him to the ground and bruised him, tore his gown and used many a threat towards him'.[112] Thwarted in their attempt to assert their 'constitutional' right to elect a legitimate Speaker, the recusants then resorted to a mass walk-out, inaugurating what was to become a time-honoured policy of abstentionism in Irish political history. By walking out of the Commons, the recusants displayed the contempt with which they viewed the proceedings. However, there were to be further burlesque scenes before they could realise this objective. As the Catholic M.P.s attempted to leave the chamber, they found that the Protestants had locked the doors, so that they were 'kept prisoners for the space of an hour or better'.[113] That an observer recorded that 'many words of hate' had been exchanged during the parliamentary deliberations was perhaps the most telling commentary on what had occurred.[114]

While the crown authorities were anticipating some form of dramatic stunt, protest or outright aggressive action by the recusant M.P.s, there can be little doubt that they were stunned by the events which took place. The subsequent abstentionism of the Catholic members of the House of Lords accentuated the sense of crisis gripping parliament and country. Even the normally garrulous Sir John Davies seemed nonplussed by what had transpired, lost for apposite words. Instead, in the wake of the tumultuous circumstances of his 'election' as Speaker of the Irish parliament, Davies proceeded with his carefully researched, if incongruously inappropriate, acceptance speech. Impressively laced with classical and biblical references it may have been, but it was absolutely divorced from reality by the time it was delivered to a half empty House of Commons. Nevertheless, like a true 'stage' player as the Earl of Tyrone had depicted him, Davies stuck to his lines, persevering with his affirmation that 'God hath blessed the whole island with an universal peace and obedience, together with plenty, civility, and other felicities, more than ever it enjoyed, in any former age.'[115] The reality of events suggested otherwise. Disobedience was the order of the day, precisely because the recusants refused to obey the crown dictats to attend Protestant services. Indeed, such was their determination to subvert crown policy in this regard that it was to be some sixteen months before the Catholic members of both Houses of Parliament were persuaded to abandon their policy of abstention from the Irish parliament.

It was a measure of the bellicose nature of the exchanges that had unfolded in the Irish parliament that when twelve Catholic lords wrote to the king expressing in strong terms their acute disquiet at what had happened, Irish Protestants were to construe their remarks once more as intimating 'a menace of rebellion'.[116] A government report on the parliamentary controversy singled out Lords Trimleston and Slane as 'busy and violent'.[117] That a potentially explosive situation permeated Dublin is manifest. One crown official claimed that 'Had the parliament been held not in the Castle but in the town, they [the recusants] might have broken in, and they would all have fallen to cutting of throats.'[118] Indeed, it is evident that a belligerent mood prevailed in the city for some time following the acrimonious proceedings in the Commons, with more than a suggestion that Catholics in the city were on the brink of a revolt. A particularly combustible incident occurred as the Lord Deputy was being escorted on his return from church by the dignitaries assembled in Dublin at the time. Two Catholic lords 'contended for precedence' in the viceroy's train in what Protestants considered an arranged signal for launching a *coup d'état.* When two of the followers of the quarrelling Catholic lords 'drew their swords, close by the Ld Dep. ... he himself called the guard. At least 500 swords were drawn, everyone fearing there had been a massacre intended by the papists.'[119] Such was the seriousness with which this episode was viewed by Protestants that it highlighted their fear that an Irish version of the 1572 St Bartholomew's Day massacre of Protestants in Paris had been on the verge of being perpetrated.[120] So concerned were the crown authorities that the Lord Deputy was said to have resorted to dramatic measures to deter revolt. Chichester, it was alleged, had placed 'store of cannon on the churches, intimating first to the conspirators that if they made any insurrection ... houses and families should be razed to the ground'.[121]

The power struggle in Ireland proceeded apace following the recusant withdrawal from parliament. In response, Lord Deputy Chichester moved rapidly to suspend all sailings for a number of days while he prepared a report on the affair for the king. The recusants, however, had moved even more expeditiously, managing to transport a delegation of four representatives to England before the Lord Deputy's interdiction on shipping came into effect. It was a measure of the organised character of recusant politics at this time that the delegation carried with them a letter signed by 155 'nobles, gentlemen and burghers', men described in a report circulating in Spanish government circles as 'those who were most opposed to the Earl of Tiron during the war [Nine Years War] and who now publicly express their grief at having opposed him'.[122] The realignment of the Old English was similarly observed by a Protestant Englishman who remarked that these 'paragons of obedience to the Kings of England were now found to be possessed with other spirits'.[123] Appealing to the monarchs of England for redress of grievances was a classic ploy of the descendants of the Anglo-Normans in Ireland. However, in this instance the fact that the Old English had not relied solely on constitutional methods of redress, but were seen on reflection to have resorted to an obstructionist strategy mingled with the menace of physical force, was later to prove their undoing.

The intensity of Catholic anger at the way the crown authorities in Ireland had been so provocatively treating them, including the sustained application of a panoply of penal measures and then the charade of rigged elections, showed no sign of abating. The Lord Deputy, for his part, was endeavouring by every means possible to coax or coerce them into attending the parliament, thereby legitimising the proceedings. In an effort to exert maximum pressure on the recusant M.P.s and lords to return to parliament, Chichester let it be known that only the bill recognising the king would be proceeded with.[124] Each Catholic lord had 'an express messenger purposely sent unto them' in this respect.[125] This proved of no avail, as the recusants signified their determination to refrain from taking part in parliament until their grievances had been raised with the king. The fact that Catholics in the House of Lords concurrently abstained from the upper chamber demonstrates that whether or not the policy of abstentionism was a premeditated one, it was one in which the Catholic members of the Lords and Commons were united until they agreed by common consent to end it in October 1614. In the intervening period the recusants mounted a determined and prolonged campaign to discredit the crown administration in Dublin. Traditionally the Old English had appealed over the heads of Lords Deputy in Ireland to have unpopular policies reversed, and this case was to be no different.[126] In pursuit of this objective, a second, much bigger, recusant delegation prepared to travel to court during the summer of 1613. Before they departed for London, though, yet another incident occurred which betrayed the simmering violent undercurrent of political affairs in Ireland. An abrasive clash occurred between a senior recusant representative, Thomas Luttrell, and the Lord Deputy. Luttrell claimed that during this altercation Chichester threatened to kill him. The Lord Deputy rejected the accusation in his recollection of events, though he admitted that the exchanges had been ill-tempered. According to Chichester, some of Luttrell's comments were

> uttered with such frowns and bitterness that I could not but tell him that he was a paltry unworthy companion, and were it not for the place I held did refrain me, I would not do him the honour to strike him with my sword, but he should have felt the weight of my fist, and the rather for he spake it to provoke and despite me. ... Then I bid him be gone, and advised him not to tell me so when I was a private man nor to speak it among the king's captains and men of war; if he did, some would fall foul of him and from their fingers I could not protect him. And so manifest how far I was from killing him or doing him wrong, I required some captains and others whom I found apt to call him to account for his words, to forbear him, which they did, and shall do whilst I have any power over them.[127]

Perhaps thankful to get on their way to London, the recusant delegation that departed from Ireland was made up almost exclusively of Old English Catholics. However, the delegation was to lobby vigorously in support of Gaelic Irish candidates (mostly from Ulster) who had lost elections in controversial circumstances. Increasing indications of a coalescence of interest between Old English and Gaelic Irish Catholics was capitalised upon by Lord Deputy Chichester, who noted that the recusant delegation was

> content to admit into the house of parliament to make laws, some of the principal actors in that rebellion [the Nine Years War], and are offended that they cannot expulse the king's honest subjects to draw in more of that wicked crew. ... For they would have Barabbas and exclude Jesus.[128]

Interestingly, Chichester included in the 'wicked crew' complement such prominent Ulster landowners as Sir Turlough MacHenry O'Neill (9,900 acres), Connor Roe Maguire (5,980 acres), Turlough MacArt O'Neill (3,330 acres) and Henry MacShane O'Neill (1,500 acres).[129] These were among the principal Gaelic Irish 'beneficiaries' of the Ulster plantation, the so-called 'deserving' Irish. However, the Lord Deputy's derogatory remarks leave little doubt about the degree of hostility which he entertained towards them.

For years Chichester had showered the king and London administration with a torrent of tirades that Irish Catholics in general, and not just the Gaelic Irish in particular, were not to be trusted. The solidarity that had been displayed between the largely Old English recusant delegation and the defeated Gaelic Irish candidates in the elections was a godsend for the Lord Deputy. It enabled him to depict the Earl of Tyrone's wartime associates and their Old English allies as the baying mob supporting Barabbas, i.e. Tyrone. But it was a dangerous game. While political capital was undoubtedly to be made in convincing the king and his advisers of the untrustworthiness of all Irish Catholics — and the need for a determined anti-Catholic line — the concomitant dangers of propelling the Old English and Gaelic Irish Catholics in Ireland into a united political, and possibly military, pan-Catholic front should not be underestimated. Significantly in this respect, while the much more politically sophisticated Old English dominated the recusant delegation that travelled to court, a major fund-raising drive, described as the 'first Catholic rent on record',[130] was organised by Catholic clergy in Ireland to provide financial support for the delegation. In one notable instance, Tyrlogh McCrodyn, a Franciscan friar, lobbied a crowd of about a thousand strong in the 'county of Londonderry' who presented him with '60 cows and oxen, 100 sheep at the least: the poorer sort gave 12d each' (the equivalent of the fine for recusancy). Such fund-raising was widespread: 'there is nobody in the country of the Irishry, but has given somewhat according to their abilities'.[131] McCrodyn also preached to a large crowd in Tyrone, eliciting impassioned responses from several of the congregation. One Neale McTirlaugh remarked of the crown policy of persecution that 'We will rather go into rebellion, and be eaten with dogs and cats, rather than go to the English service, to hear the Devil's words.'[132] A gathering in Fermanagh was even more interesting in so far as it linked the collections for the Old English delegation going to England with assurances about Tyrone's prospective return. The crowd were exhorted to be of 'good courage, for that [Tyrone] was coming at the head of 18,000 men, sent by the King of Spain, and that, according to a prophecy in a book at Rome, England had only two years more to rule in Ireland'.[133] A government investigation into the issue concluded that 'a general levy of money was made throughout the realm whereunto the popish subjects did willingly condescend'.[134] In an attempt to frustrate this recusant tactic, the government issued a proclamation forbidding such collections.[135]

Politicised and mobilised across wide areas of the country, Irish Catholics of divergent cultural and ethnic backgrounds were becoming unified to an unprecedented degree. As ever, Lord Deputy Chichester was typically phlegmatic in the face of this alliance. However, it was not an attitude shared by his superiors in London, who were to be so concerned about developments in Ireland that serious consideration was soon to be given to effecting a rapprochement with the Earl of Tyrone, with obvious implications for what had so far proved to be a largely still-born plantation of Ulster. Indeed, the most critical juncture had been reached in Tyrone's quest to return to Ireland, either by means of a reconciliation with London or by more forceful means. The eruption of the Anglo-Spanish international crisis in late 1612 and the early months of 1613, followed so soon afterwards by political turbulence in Ireland, combined to offer the most serious prospect that Tyrone would return to Ireland one way or the other. Besides, the ageing earl became increasingly determined to return to his homeland with or without the indulgence of the King of England, with or without Spanish military assistance — preferring 'death with sword in hand'.[136]

10

THE SWORD PASSES ON

The ramifications of the Anglo-Spanish crisis of 1612–13 and the volatile political situation in Ireland that resulted from the convening of the Irish parliament redounded to the advantage of the Earl of Tyrone, offering him a strong hand once more in international diplomacy, at least temporarily. Advancing in years, the elderly earl was offered a reconciliation by the English crown following the turmoil at the opening of the Irish parliament. Petrified by developments in Ireland, a timorous King James engaged in negotiations with the earl's representatives. In these exchanges Tyrone made it clear that he was not prepared to sacrifice his own followers in Ireland, nor to relinquish his request for toleration of Catholicism — preconditions which ultimately damaged his personal chances of being restored to favour peaceably. Nevertheless, he was adamant that he would not accept a rapprochement unless his imprisoned 'vassals' were released. By implication, he was bartering for the freedom of his brother Sir Cormac O'Neill, Sir Niall Garbh O'Donnell and, remarkably as it may seem, Sir Donal O'Cahan. Rather than abandon them, it was signified on his behalf in negotiations with the English that he 'would rather choose to live and die in exile' than allow the 'honour' of his 'house' to 'fall into disrepute'.[1] Thus ensued the final years of Tyrone's life, 1613–16, a period of even more profound emotional turmoil for the old earl as the prospect for salvation — a return to his patrimony — beckoned as a mirage before his failing eyesight only to recede the closer he seemed to get to it. By late 1615, less than a year before his death, a crown informant revealed that Tyrone was 'in health and lived in plenty; and yet wished himself in Ireland again'.[2] From landing on the continent in 1607 until his dying day, Tyrone's conduct manifested that his Flight had never been intended as a one-way trip.

At the time of the recusant delegation to England in the summer of 1613 it was not apparent how the London authorities would react. At first there were rumours at court that the Lord Deputy had been guilty of serious misconduct.[3] In a ploy to discredit Chichester, the recusant delegation broadened the scope of the attack against his administration by alleging that it was riddled with corruption. The activities of troops serving in the Pale area featured highly in the list of grievances, with accusations that money and supplies were being extorted from the local population. At worst, troops forcibly seized supplies not only for themselves but also 'for other soldiers absent, which the country call blackmen, because they are not seen'.[4] Clearly taken aback in particular by the recusant delegation's representation of the dramatic developments that had taken place during the parliamentary session, the king promptly moved to mollify them with a gracious reception.[5] Reports emanating from recusant as well as crown circles in Ireland confirmed that violent altercations had occurred. They were deemed sufficiently serious to prompt the Earl of Northampton, King James's most senior minister at the time, to refer to the 'storm of Ireland'.[6] So worried had the London authorities become that prompt measures were undertaken to make naval and military forces available to deal with the crisis that had erupted.[7] Indeed, it was a sign of the gravity of the situation that the Presidents of Munster and Connacht, quasi-military officials, were ordered to their posts in Ireland.[8] The last time this had happened was in the period immediately following the Flight of the Earls in 1607. On the surface, however, King James attempted to exude an air of dismissiveness about the whole affair. Remarking in the presence of foreign dignitaries that he knew that Spain had 'a hand' in the Irish disturbances, James 'smiled as he spoke', assuring his listeners that he could reinforce his Irish garrison 'in a very few hours'. James then mocked his Spanish adversaries for employing the advice of the Earl of Tyrone, 'jestingly' remarking that the Spanish were reduced to employing the services of Tyrone, a 'captain of eighty years or little less'.[9] (Tyrone was actually sixty-three years old at this time.) Despite the uncharacteristic bravado of King James, whose personal cowardice was legendary, the reality was that James soon reverted to character, revealing an actutely nervous disposition. A spectral figure the Earl of Tyrone may have been, but he haunted King James even in his waking hours. This was manifested by the fact that while the poisonous political crisis in Ireland festered, King James, far from being unperturbed by the threat posed by the Earl of Tyrone, initiated a serious overture to the exiled earl suggesting a reconciliation. For a time the future of the Ulster plantation hung in the balance.

The king's willingness to reconsider his position in relation to the plantation of Ulster culminated to some extent from his extreme dissatisfaction with the manner in which the colony was making such sluggish progress. Even the jewel in the crown of the settlement process, the Londoners' plantation, was failing to sparkle. In late 1612 King James notified Chichester that he had learned of the 'general backwardness' of the plantation, and that while the Londoners 'pretend to great expenditure … there is little outward appearance'. Extremely disappointed, James ordered his viceroy to institute a survey of the plantation, expressly affirming that he was not to 'care or fear to please … or displease any of our subjects, English or Scots, of what quality soever'.[10] That the Londoners were the target for such explicit royal criticism resulted from the fact that the king had been informed that they were more concerned with exploiting their new lands for commercial profiteering. Far from industriously proceeding with their plantation commitments, they had 'committed great havoc in the woods of Glanconcane and Killetra' for the purpose of converting the timber into pipestaves for export.[11] With the plantation making such poor progress, therefore, contemplating aborting it in order to secure a rapprochement with the Earl of Tyrone was not inconceivable. Such was the contractual nature of the undertakers' obligations under the terms of the Ulster plantation that the king had little reason to consider that he might be reneging on his part of the deal. Rather, the undertakers were quite clearly failing to deliver on their side of the bargain with just one year left of their allotted three years for fulfilling their plantation commitments.

Even before the political crises on the continent and in Ireland in 1612–13, the Earl of Tyrone had been regularly petitioning the London authorities about the possibility of a reconciliation. With the passage of time he had come to accept that the prospects of Spanish military assistance were slim. As a result, Tyrone attempted to cash in his nuisance value as his primary bargaining chip in an attempt to barter a deal with the King of England. Reasonably confident that the Spanish would not risk hostilities by helping Tyrone, and entertaining aspirations that the Ulster plantation would neuter the menace of a northern revolt for ever, the London authorities initially proved impervious to Tyrone's overtures.[12] Then, out of the blue, Tyrone revealed in correspondence in July 1613 that King James himself had suddenly taken 'the first steps ... towards an offer of reconciliation'. At the time Tyrone considered it an act of providence, God having proferred the 'remedy' to ending his years in exile.[13] The reality was rather different. As yet the Earl of Tyrone was oblivious to the events that had unfolded so favourably for him in Ireland. The London authorities, by contrast, were only too painfully aware of what was going on. Correspondence suggests that news had arrived in London by the end of May 1613.[14] Within a fortnight, in great secrecy, an English agent had approached an intermediary to the earl, Hugh MacCaughwell, Guardian of the Franciscan College of St Anthony, Louvain, 'begging' Tyrone to state his terms for a reconciliation. The go-between produced a letter concerning the affair from Robert Carr, Viscount Rochester, principal favourite at the court of King James, to demonstrate the *bona fides* of the English government in the matter. Tyrone was assured that King James would grant him either his 'own lands, or the equivalent, or even better lands'. Indeed, so keen was James for a prompt reconciliation that Tyrone was urged by the English representative to seize the 'opportunity, and the time is now or never'. The decision, Tyrone was assured, would not go before the English Privy Council but would be taken by James himself. Besides the English envoy, no one apart from Rochester knew of this development. Significantly, given the urgency of the situation in Ireland, Tyrone was informed that this was a 'take it or leave it' offer which was open for forty days, and that the offer would be invalidated if the Spanish authorities were apprised of it.[15]

Taken aback, and delighted by King James's sudden change of heart, Tyrone was much too cagey to be hustled into a reconciliation with the English without the Spanish acting as guarantors. Immediately, therefore, Tyrone informed the Spanish about King James's offer. In a detailed memorandum addressed to the Spanish authorities he outlined his position in response to this development. First and foremost, he acknowledged that there were potentially fatal risks involved, should his repatriation be agreed with the English. Tyrone realised that he could be duped and that being 'taken to the block' was a distinct possibility. Notwithstanding this, the rapidly ageing earl was becoming ever more desperate to reclaim his patrimony, fearing that if he died in exile, the English would never regrant the lands to his family. Gambling on a reconciliation, Tyrone argued, while not an ideal scenario, represented the most practical means of attaining his objective. The passage of years had impressed upon him that the likelihood of Spanish military intervention, unless there was a marked 'change of circumstances', was remote. And Tyrone had arrived at his decision despite the fact that circumstances in Ireland had never been more propitious (though it is unclear whether he was aware of the parliamentary furore at the time of writing). Irish Catholics had 'never been so united and so strongly in league for a rising against the heretics with any help, no matter how small'. Tweaking every sinew of Spanish pride, Tyrone let it be known that if the Spanish would not provide him with military assistance to reclaim his lands at the point of a sword, then a negotiated reconciliation was his only alternative. Failure to exploit the conducive circumstances in Ireland to assert the rights of Catholics by force of arms, he was adamant, should not be left at his door. He was not to blame.[16] By implication, the Spanish were.

The existence of the English offer to Tyrone was reaffirmed by the Spanish ambassador in Brussels, the Marques de Guadaleste, in September 1613. He reported that the English had repeated their offer, noting that the parliamentary disturbances in Ireland had added urgency to the matter. In actual fact the crisis in Ireland had been directly responsible for the initial offer. What is certain is that King James was serious — despite the fact that on the surface the English were anxious to play down the affair. When the first rumours of the possibility of a reconciliation emerged, it was believed that the covert negotiations had been facilitated through the agency of Prince Henry, King James's eldest son. Following the premature death of the young prince in November 1612, the Earl of Tyrone was said to have 'mourned for his death', believing that Prince Henry had facilitated the apparent breakthrough. By the time the rumours had become more generally current in the summer of 1613, however, English officials were keen to dismiss any suggestion that a rapprochement was even being contemplated.[17] That such an eventuality was being genuinely entertained could not be revealed as official policy; otherwise the planters in Ulster would be discouraged. The reality may have been, of course, that rumours of a reconciliation had been current in England, thus accentuating the undertakers' unwillingness to fulfil their obligations.

Informed by Tyrone of King James's offer, the Spanish Council of State deliberated upon it. The general consensus within the Council was one of extreme reluctance to sanction a deal with the English, as there was a fear that the Earl of Tyrone was being lured into a trap. To some extent too, the Spanish had more selfish reasons for frustrating a rapprochement. Tyrone, it was pointed out at the meeting, 'could be of great importance in the event of the King of England's death'.[18] The temptation of some members of the Spanish Council to manipulate Tyrone rather than assist him was once again evident. This is not a charge that could be levelled at Philip III, who appears to have been conscious of Spain's indebtedness to the old earl. Responding to a communication from the Earl of Tyrone in the spring of 1613 which urged him to lend military assistance to the oppressed Catholics of Ireland, the Spanish king informed his ambassador in Rome that 'I shall give due consideration to this matter and I shall see what may be done for them in view of present circumstances.'[19] In particular, Philip III was keen to know the intentions of the Pope in this regard. The impression remains that the Spanish king was a good deal more willing than his advisers that Tyrone should be assisted militarily to return to Ireland. However, he wanted the Pope to be seen as Tyrone's patron and banker, though the possibility of secret financial assistance by the Spanish could not be ruled out. In an intriguing reference to an Irish suitor in Flanders in 1611, Philip III had indicated that an allowance was to be paid from the 'secret expenses of army funds'.[20] Money could just as surreptitiously have been channelled to support a military expedition by Tyrone. At any rate, Philip III disregarded the advice of his Council of State when he wished Tyrone well in relation to his negotiations with the English, though he also cautioned him regarding the risk involved.[21] From Tyrone's point of view, the dangers were greatly outweighed by the potential benefits, not least from the tactical and strategic points of view. The earl had not lost his knack for engaging in Machiavellian practices himself, as soon became apparent.

In order to facilitate his negotiations with the King of England, Tyrone requested permission to return to Flanders.[22] Given the shortcomings of communications in the early seventeenth century, when letters could take months to go backwards and forwards between London and Rome, Tyrone's request seemed perfectly reasonable. Returning to Flanders, what is more, offered the earl further options should the negotiations break down. Acknowledging that this was a possibility, he requested that William Meade should accompany him, describing the Old English expatriate as being of 'great importance' to his plans.[23] Meade's presence is crucial in appreciating Tyrone's tactics. He was clearly contemplating using Flanders as a springboard for a last desperate bid to return to Ireland — perhaps even without the approval of Spain. Certainly the English ambassador in Brussels signalled his concern about such a scenario.[24] Should this have materialised, Meade's presence on the expedition would have been vital as a means of winning Old English support. From Tyrone's point of view, getting to Flanders was fundamental to his plans, whether the reconciliation worked out or not. The earl's mood of desperation was revealed by his declaration that he 'did not wish the world to believe that he does not persevere unto death in what he has undertaken'.[25]

Rumours of Tyrone's impending return, which had been current at various times since his departure, once more reached a crescendo in the aftermath of the fall-out from the fractious proceedings in the Irish parliament. That Tyrone's star was increasingly in the ascendant was recognised resentfully by Viscount Rochester, the royal favourite of James I, who in October 1613 described the earl's demands in his negotiations as 'high and arrogant'.[26] Despite this, the parleying was not terminated. Significantly in this respect, the Spanish ambassador at Brussels revealed the sincerity of the English overtures when he remarked on the 'great efforts' which had been made on behalf of James I.[27] Just as importantly, the chief negotiator on the English side concurred that the 'business' of Tyrone was a 'matter of great consideration', adding that the king wanted to take more time to consider it.[28] This was not merely a matter of playing for time, although there was undoubtedly an element of a delaying tactic while the English assessed the situation both in Ireland and on the international scene. There were weighty considerations that James had to bear in mind should he accede to Tyrone's demands. Effectively the Ulster plantation would have had to be aborted — not an option that James would lightly adopt in view of his previous personal attachment to the project, even if the progress of the settlement had so far been disappointing.

Such was the menacing nature of developments in Ireland and abroad that the prospects for a reconciliation remained very much on the cards throughout the latter part of 1613 and early 1614. So sensitive had the situation become that one of the highlights of the courtly social calendar in England, the Christmas masque, composed by the dramatist Ben Jonson, was considered as potentially destabilising. The London court gossip John Chamberlain noted in January 1614 how the 'masque is repeated, though it is ill-timed, being in mimicry of the Irish, and likely to exasperate them'.[29] Such was the degree of alarm in London that Sir Ralph Winwood, a highly influential figure in London court circles, signified in the House of Commons that 'Ireland is not a thorn in our foot but a lance in our side', describing how the 'memory of the last war [the Nine Years War, 1594–1603] is yet bleeding fresh'.[30] The same commentator remarked that the affairs of Ireland had never stood in 'more desperate terms'. The prospect of foreign invasion, and a concomitant internal revolt involving the Old English as well as the Gaelic Irish, was considered sufficiently serious to induce the London government to sanction further finance for the erection of costly 'citadels' in Cork and Waterford, Old English heartlands.[31] The emphasis on these locations reinforced the impression that the London authorities were gravely alarmed that an invasion of Ireland would enjoy widespread domestic support. However, while the volcano of resentment in Ireland had rumbled, it had not belched out in revolt. And this was to prove decisive. Had even a limited rebellion occurred at this time, the likelihood is that the financial ramifications of a costly revolt could well have led to a prompt capitulation to the demands of the Earl of Tyrone. As it was, the prospects for a widespread revolt, involving a combination between the Catholic Old English and the Gaelic Irish, depended on Tyrone's ability to deliver on his return to Ireland. And yet it was highly uncertain that the earl could deliver on this vital matter.

But it was not all doom and gloom for the crown authorities in Ireland, even if caution prevailed. As the Spanish ambassador in Brussels had already suspected by February 1614, James I and his advisers were contemplating abandoning their intention to effect a reconciliation with Tyrone because they believed that they could 'overcome the troubles' in Ireland.[32] The principal reason for this new-found confidence originated in discussions between James I and the Old English Catholic delegates during the winter of 1613–14, when the king appears to have made an informal promise to tolerate Catholicism in Ireland. This had the effect of calming, at least temporarily, fears of an imminent revolt. What James I had not bargained for, however, was the behaviour of the Catholic delegates after they returned to Ireland in early 1614 and announced publicly that religious toleration had been granted. Sir James Gough, a leading Catholic spokesman, had been particularly vociferous in this respect. The zealously Protestant Lord Deputy Chichester was appalled by Gough's conduct and resorted to a typically robust course of action to counteract the impression that toleration had been secured. In a lighter moment amidst the ongoing crisis, Chichester communicated with an acquaintance in County Cork that

> Your neighbour James Goagh's extravagant carriage and discourses declare that his brains are not well in temper: his report did affright the ladies at Youghall, but his commitment here hath somewhat revived them and qualified the heat of those that entertained an opinion that the free exercise of their religion would accompany his report.[33]

Embarrassed that his private understanding had been aired in public, James I backed away from the position that he had taken, reaffirming his support for Chichester. However, the Old English were left with the impression that they had driven a wedge between the crown and the Lord Deputy. And while that prospect remained, it was a wedge that also diminished any immediate prospect of a revolt involving the Old English and Tyrone's supporters in Ireland.

The demeanour of Gough and his associates in disseminating the reports that religious toleration had been granted rebounded on Irish Catholics. Appalled by such indiscretion, James reacted angrily. It was one thing that James did not personally favour persecution and that he had acted at times to temper the more extreme impulses of his ministers. It was another matter entirely for the king to dare publicly to come out in favour of toleration. England had, after all, only recently come through a nerve-racking war with Spain in which its very survival as a Protestant nation had been at stake. The Gunpowder Plot of 1605 had also demonstrated that a Catholic menace also existed within the state. A public acceptance of Catholicism in Ireland would have caused an outcry in England. It is this background which explains why James, having mollycoddled the recusant delegates who had come to England in the wake of the collapse of the parliament, later summoned them back into his presence in order to berate them. Old English relations with the crown were to be severely damaged further as a result of acrimonious exchanges that had occurred between Sir William Talbot and the king. Talbot was challenged to reject the Jesuitical doctrine of Father Suarez that excommunicated monarchs could be deposed. For refusing to condemn Suarez, Talbot was tried in Star Chamber in London during February 1614. The punishment meted out to him was draconian: he was incarcerated in the Tower and fined the massive sum of £10,000.[34] Within a matter of weeks the entire recusant delegation was summoned to a public audience with the king during which James rejected virtually outright the complaints that had been raised by the recusants in 1613. Such was the degree of royal displeasure that James denounced their conduct, branding them 'half subjects'.[35]

Reeling from the wrath of James I, the recusant delegates were initially somewhat cowed. Summoning up courage once more, however, the recusants delivered a 'humble petition' to the king that questioned James's adjudication of their complaints.[36] Far from it being considered a 'humble' petition, the king was gravely insulted. Once more the recusants were ushered into his presence. In the course of the deliberations the delegates were reported to have uttered such 'unsavoury' language that an indignant James had a number of them thrown instantly into prison.[37] It was a measure of the distrust which had been generated by these developments that directions were issued to lords lieutenant of maritime counties on the west coast of England in May 1614 to hold in readiness at a 'day's warning' almost 2,000 troops, 'not knowing how soon His Majesty may be pleased to make use of their service'.[38] Royal suspicions were so intense at this time that a hostage scheme was devised whereby the sons of selected Old English leaders were to be brought over to England, an expedient later described by the Privy Council in London as 'so necessary for the future safety of that kingdom'.[39] (Significantly, of the nine children chosen by the king, six were near relatives of Old English Catholic lords who had signed what Protestants considered to be a seditious letter at the height of the parliamentary crisis in 1613.)[40] By June 1614 James had agreed to a wide-ranging package of extra-parliamentary anti-Catholic measures for Ireland, undoubtedly a further illustration of his disillusionment with the Old English.[41] Events that transpired in London marked an important departure in Old English relations with the crown. During the second half of the sixteenth century the ancestors of the Old English had exercised political leverage with the monarch to undermine previous royal governors of Ireland with whom relations had broken down. What was different in 1614 was that the breach had also occurred with the sovereign as well.

Overall, the developments between February and May 1614 reinforce the impression that had Tyrone managed to return to Ireland, the Old English constituency would have been receptive to his overtures. Certainly expectations had been greatly raised in Ulster once more. One Owen Maguire of Augher, County Tyrone, described as a yeoman, was put on trial for sedition on the basis that he 'he would kill Emanuell Ley, and throw his head out of the window of his own castle, for that the Earl of Tyrone should come with the King of Spain his forces, and come to Mounaghan, Dundalk, Drogheda, and Dublin, and that the Earl of Tyrone should be king in Ireland, and would kill all the Scots and Englishmen in the kingdom'.[42] It was perhaps in recognition of the dangerous drift that events were taking that James and his advisers decided during the summer of 1614 to retreat from their hardline position in relation to the Old English. It was in an effort to take the sting out of the bitterness of the exchanges with the Old English that James I resorted to a *volte-face* in policy, conceding some of the points that had been raised in the 'humble petition' and withdrawing the anti-Catholic measures that had been proposed for the Irish parliament. Investigations into electoral malpractice resulted in the Protestant majority in the Commons being reduced to only eight.[43]

Part of the explanation for this turn of events may be attributed to financial expediency. After all, James I was anxious for a financial subsidy from the Irish parliament, and to ensure this he needed to bring the Old English policy of abstentionism to a conclusion. James's concurrent decision to discontinue his negotiations with Tyrone should also be seen as an important factor influencing the king's sudden change of mind regarding the Old English. During July 1614 James broke off his contacts with the Earl of Tyrone for the restoration of his lands 'because that would disjoint the whole course which His Majesty hath been so careful to settle in that country'.[44] Clearly James had been under no illusions that the plantation of Ulster would have had to be sacrificed as the price of his reconciliation with Tyrone. Having decided to dash Tyrone's prospects of a negotiated return to his homeland, James would have been aware that the earl would have been incensed into redoubling his efforts to return to Ireland to retrieve his lands by force. Mollifying the Old English to some extent, therefore, was important in this scenario. There was also an additional attraction for the government in facilitating a resumption of the Irish parliament. One of the first proposed bills provided for the attainder of the Earls of Tyrone and Tyrconnell. Securing Old English support for this bill would disconcert the aspirations of the Earl of Tyrone that their support could be relied upon should he manage to return to Ireland. This was a classic example of the application of 'divide and rule' tactics. However, as a matter of precaution, the Archbishop of Canterbury reported in July 1614 that military contingencies remained a high priority, funds having been available to pay the Irish garrison 'to a farthing to midsummer last'.[45] Meanwhile on the continent the 'garboils' involving rival Catholic and Protestant powers in the duchy of Cleves, an area of strategic interest to the Spanish, indicated that international affairs were far from on an even keel. Indeed, it has been remarked that on two occasions involving crises in Cleves in 1610 and 1614 war between England and Spain was 'only narrowly avoided'.[46] Spanish 'aggression' in Cleves in 1614 resulted in the London government giving orders for a 'general muster', while the fleet was to be prepared for service, since the possibility of a direct attack on England 'or upon some other part of His Majesty's dominions' was not ruled out.[47]

Having had the enticing prospect of a reconciliation dashed, the Earl of Tyrone did indeed become ever more desperate to accomplish his return. Robert Lombard, an informant for the English with access to the earl's household and who boasted a senior cardinal among his confidants, noted how the 'old man every night hereupon sleeps with his sword naked by his bedside, and believes that he and his doubt not to have a day yet at home: howsoever, there are lets and obstacles many in the way'.[48] (Fear of assassination may also have contributed to this peculiar habit, though the manner in which the earl often went to bed under the influence of drink meant that this was a somewhat hazardous routine.) And nothing short of repatriation could console him. Even the imaginative efforts of the Spanish ambassador in Rome to lay on 'sports and cheer' for his amusement could not dissipate the earl's 'melancholy'.[49] Advancing in age and infirmity, the earl once more petitioned the Spanish for military aid before the end of 1614. Rather than holding out for a full-scale invasion force, Tyrone asked for only four or five ships, the Irish regiment from Flanders and some artillery. In other words, he was only requesting that the expatriate Irish themselves be given back-up support in challenging English domination in Ireland. Should even that limited scale of assistance be denied, Tyrone signified that he would rather return to Ireland with a hundred men and 'expose himself to any danger rather than remain in Rome'.[50] Tyrone's sentiments convey the feelings of a man who believed himself to be at death's door. He anticipated (rightly as it turned out) that he had not long to live, preferring to die in battle than rot in Rome. The English, it appears, were similarly convinced. Thus during 1614 the Earl of Tyrone was advised to take extra security precautions to counteract an assassination plot; he was visited privately by a cardinal who warned him 'that he should do well to look warily to himself, news being come that England employs many abroad to offend him in all and worse manners'.[51]

When the overtures for a negotiated return were terminated by James I, the Earl of Tyrone was left with little option but to seek to return to Ireland to try to claim his lands by force. The passage of the bill of attainder was duly carried unanimously in the Irish parliament.[52] That the Catholic M.P.s, Gaelic Irish and Old English alike, voted for the attainder could be interpreted as indicating that Tyrone's claims of widespread support in Ireland were unfounded.

Alternatively, given the manner in which the recusants had been involved in bruising encounters with the crown, refusing to sanction Tyrone's attainder would have left them open to charges of countenancing treason. Besides, the attainder was but a piece of paper that would have been rendered meaningless in the event of the earl's return. After all, both the Act of Oblivion of 1604 and the proclamation supposedly reassuring the inhabitants of Ulster immediately after the Flight of the Earls in 1607, having been so blatantly dishonoured, demonstrated that they were not worth the paper they were written on. Abrupt policy reversals were not uncommon in early seventeenth-century Ireland. Recent experience had demonstrated that the king had seriously contemplated the abandonment of the Ulster plantation, despite the implied contractual nature of his obligations to the undertakers. Faced with the prospects of Tyrone's imminent return and a costly military campaign, an already uncommitted royal administration in London could readily have revoked the attainder and abandoned the plantation. In the latter respect it is worth noting that by 1614, a year after the allocated time-span for the completion of the plantation conditions had expired, the plantation was described by a knowledgeable observer as progressing 'slowly forward, the buildings not half performed'.[53] Given the hostile environment encountered in Ulster by the colonists, this is not at all surprising. The persistent threat of Tyrone's return hung over the plantation like the sword of Damocles. His supporters longed to strike at the planters. One Dermot Óg MacDoun was prosecuted for openly declaring in late 1614 that 'he had two swords, and that he did hope to have good use for them before Christmas, for the Pope of Rome would send over O'Neale, the Earl of Tyrone, as a king to govern this kingdom with great authority as he had in former times'.[54] And the threat was not just figurative nor confined to verbal menace. Violence against the colonists was so prevalent in Ulster that it gave rise to the contemporary depiction of Protestant settlers undertaking their building work 'with the sword in one hand and the axe in the other', workmen on the Londonderry settlement refusing to work by themselves in the woods.[55] While a full-scale assault had not been launched on the Protestant colonists, the lurking menace of woodkern, or outlaws, was a perennial one from the start.[56] 'For although there be no apparent enemy, nor any visible main force, yet the woodkern and many other (who now have put on the smiling countenance of contentment) do threaten every hour, if opportunity of time and place doth serve, to burn and steal whatsoever.'[57]

Overall, despite the concessions that had been offered to the Old English to secure a resumption of parliament, the atmosphere in Ireland remained fraught with tension. Indeed, it was a measure of the persistent concern of the London authorities that Tyrone's return remained a distinct possibility that they agreed in September 1614 to the costly provision of four months' supply of victuals for the garrison in Ireland,[58] always a reliable barometer that the pressure was rising in Ireland, that trouble was anticipated. Providing the garrison with a winter's supplies reduced the dangers attendant on foraging expeditions where isolated troops would be exposed to attack. What is more, following the collapse of the Addled Parliament in England,[59] at a time of particularly acute financial embarrassment on the part of the crown, it was an indication of how serious the situation was considered that this expedient was approved by the king. The continued application of penal measures by Lord Deputy Chichester's administration once again kept discontent simmering. Before the parliamentary session ended in October 1614 the recusant M.P.s, after behaving so compliantly, once again fired a broadside across the bows of the crown authorities when they delivered a petition seeking an end to penal practices. This renewed outbreak of recalcitrance added to the uneasiness of royal officials.[60] The clear impression remains that an underlying friction had pervaded the 1614 session of the Irish parliament. The conduct of the Catholic M.P.s suggests that they had been keeping their powder dry. Wasting it on trying to prevent the attainder of the Earl of Tyrone, which was going to pass in any case owing to the Protestant majority in the Commons, would have been a poor tactical move, leaving them open to accusations of disloyalty. That a treasonable construction was placed on their petition for an end to penal practices demonstrates the degree to which their loyalty remained questionable in the eyes of the authorities, despite their acquiescence in the attainder of Tyrone.

The apprehensions of the English authorities were not simply generated by domestic developments in Ireland. As ever, Tyrone remained a pawn on the international chessboard of intrigue. Spanish government documents indicate a continued unwillingness to facilitate his return with military assistance. However, they remained acutely conscious that the old earl provided them with powerful leverage in diplomatic affairs. As a member of the Spanish Council of State remarked in 1614, the continued 'detention of the earl in Rome could be sold dearly to the King of England'.[61] Despite the goodwill of Philip III and other senior Spanish officials, these sentiments revealed once again that some in court circles in Spain remained determined to exploit Tyrone as a prize asset in international relations. English government sources at the time concurred that Tyrone's availability to the Spanish checkmated potential moves in English foreign policy. Responding to renewed rumours in February 1615 that the earl would be permitted to return to a 'neutral' town in the area of the English Channel, the English diplomat Sir Thomas Edmonds speculated that the Spanish were intending to keep him near at hand in a state of constant readiness to return to Ireland in order to 'hold His Majesty [James I] in jealousy of the employing of him with a regiment into Ireland to contain His Majesty from being too forward' in relation to English foreign policy elsewhere.[62] Writing from Venice, Sir Dudley Carleton relayed intelligence reports that Tyrone was intending to base himself in Liège.[63] The reality was that the Spanish were not complicit in encouraging his relocation. Indeed, Spanish government records reveal that they were actively discouraging him from leaving Rome.[64] However, the English were correct in some aspects of their intelligence reports. By early 1615 the earl was indeed seeking to reside in Liège, then an independent principality adjacent to Flanders.[65]

For the entire period following his flight from Ireland Tyrone, it had turned out, had been at the focal point of the cold war that had persisted between the English and the Spanish since the Anglo-Spanish war ended in 1604. Financial and human exhaustion had forced an end to the protracted warfare, and these factors continued to exercise a restraining influence on both sides. But the causes of the Anglo-Spanish conflict of the sixteenth century had not disappeared. Mercantile rivalries and sectarian bitterness remained. Even the negotiations for a marriage between Prince Charles and the Spanish Infanta during 1615 should not be considered as indicating that amicable relations had been established between England and Spain. There was a fine line between the brokering of peace and the instigation of war. This was to be demonstrated in 1623 when Prince Charles travelled incognito to Spain to claim the hand of the Infanta. When Charles returned to England empty-handed, war soon ensued.[66] Just how fragile the Anglo-Spanish peace remained in 1615 may be measured by the reaction of the Archbishop of Canterbury, a senior figure on the English Privy Council, to rumours that the Spaniards were making arrangements for Tyrone's return to Ireland through France. He believed that the Spaniards intended to divert English forces from the Low Countries to Ireland. For his part, however, the archbishop made it abundantly clear that he would not have found such a Spanish ploy to be unwelcome, 'because thereby may be procured a just breach with the Spanish'.[67] As it turned out, the earl's continued 'detention' in Rome, as the Spanish official so candidly termed it, acted as a deterrent which helped to prevent a renewed outbreak of actual fighting between the English and Spanish. Tyrone's availability to the Spanish discouraged the English from pursuing an overtly anti-Spanish foreign policy. The Spanish, for their part, were determined to hold Tyrone in reserve.

While the Spanish manipulated the Earl of Tyrone, developments in Ireland were beyond their control. Despite the ostensibly compliant behaviour of the Catholic M.P.s at the time of his attainder, the common perception remained among the royal authorities in England and Ireland that there was a major plot afoot in Ireland and that Tyrone's return was fundamental to its execution. Andrés Velázquez, a key figure on the Spanish Council of State with responsibility for the secret service, confirmed to his government in July 1615 that reliable sources had informed him that a major conspiracy was being orchestrated in Ireland.[68] The persistent menace of revolt led to increased repression of Irish Catholics by penal measures as James I became ever more convinced that they could not be trusted. And yet, ironically, it was the very existence of these measures in the first place, and their subsequent proliferation, that had to a large extent instigated the initial plotting and later reinforced the discontent of the conspirators. The Spanish authorities, from their detached viewpoint, could appreciate this. It had been for this very reason that the Spanish ambassador in London had been delegated by Philip III during the spring of 1614 to reason with James I that the prudent way to deal with Irish Catholics was to 'treat them well and he [James I] would then experience their devotion and loyalty'. The Spanish ambassador reported with great regret that his 'conversation with this king has had no effect on him'.[69] James had been manoeuvred into a blind alley by the extremism of his Irish viceroy, Sir Arthur Chichester. James's blinkered approach precluded him from recognising what should have been blatantly obvious. The Old English Catholics were genuinely disposed to be loyal to him, but had been persistently alienated by the persecuting tendencies of Chichester since he assumed the mantle of Irish government in 1605.

By the spring of 1615, as Spanish government archives reveal and English intelligence reports confirm, the Earl of Tyrone was engaged in a last desperate attempt to return to his homeland. Described as 'very old' and in 'failing' health, Tyrone had reiterated 'that rather than live in Rome, he would prefer to go to his land with a hundred soldiers and die there in defence of the Catholic faith and of his fatherland'.[70] That rumours of Tyrone's anticipated return had reached fever pitch once more was reflected in the fact that levels of violence had increased dramatically in Ireland. Lord Deputy Chichester observed in March 1615 that he had 'not observed so many cruel murders, robberies and outrages to have been committed in many years preceding as within these six months', indicating, in the deputy's opinion, that there was an expectation of 'invasion from foreign parts ... or of some home insurrection'.[71] Only a few days later the sense of crisis afflicting the crown authorities in Ireland was intensified when Chichester reported that James Meagh, an influential Catholic priest, had landed with the news that Tyrone was preparing to return to reclaim his lost territories and to assert freedom of worship for Irish Catholics.[72] This was not a matter of Chichester's pathological hatred of Catholic priests clouding his judgment. Spanish sources confirm that several emissaries had been sent from Rome to Ireland 'to raise the people through the intermediary of the priests of their nation'.[73] At this time of a rigidly enforced policy of religious persecution, Tyrone, the 'liberator', the Catholic champion, was eagerly anticipated throughout the country.

To the alarm and perturbation of the royal authorities, the inauspicious omens seemed to multiply inexorably. By early April 1615 Sir Ralph Winwood, now the English Secretary of State, was complaining to his ambassador in Flanders that he was receiving daily reports that Irish soldiers who had been serving in the Irish regiment in Flanders had been given passports to return to Ireland. Winwood instructed the ambassador to stop this practice, 'for it is of dangerous consequence, as things stand now in Ireland, to furnish that country with well-trained and disciplined soldiers'.[74] All of a sudden the English policy of seeking to break up the Irish regiment appeared to have rebounded. The dreadful fear occurred to Winwood that Tyrone's supporters had turned the tables on the English government, exploiting the passports policy in order to filter back large numbers of trained troops to await Tyrone's arrival. The affinity of Irish expatriates for their homeland bewildered

Chichester, who remarked on how they displayed a 'natural love ... unto their native soil which carries them back again into it, beyond the common opinion conceived of their better being there [the continent] generally'.[75]

By early April 1615 the belligerent mood prevailing in Ireland was once again palpable. By that time the Lord Deputy had been informed by King James that 'either Tyrone is coming here, or some strange and dangerous plot is in hand'.[76] Within a matter of weeks the so-called Ulster Conspiracy of 1615 had come to light. One of the aims of the 'plotters' was to seize Tyrone's son Conn from captivity in Charlemont, an objective confirmed by a spy in Tyrone's entourage.[77] The Ulster Conspiracy of 1615, often dismissed as a negligible affair, may well have reflected the outline of Tyrone's plans, though the people arrested by the Dublin government may not have been delegated to undertake it on the exiled earl's behalf. Tyrone clearly realised that he would have to organise Conn's escape from custody before he landed in Ireland. Otherwise the government would have taken immediate steps to secure Conn's person, most likely by transferring him to England. However, political enemies of the Lord Deputy within the Dublin administration had serious reservations as to whether a plot existed at all. That the Lord Deputy himself had genuine reason to fear that a new rebellion was on the verge of erupting is beyond doubt. So serious did he consider the situation that army commanders who were M.P.s in the Irish parliament were immediately sent back to their stations. At a time when crown supporters had only a knife-edge majority in parliament and the finance bill was being considered, Chichester was prepared to endanger the passage of a vitally important piece of legislation.[78] The subsequent trouble-free enactment of the bill was described by Sir Thomas Ridgeway, a senior figure in the Dublin administration, as a 'half miracle ... without one public, no or private murmur'.[79] No effort was made by the recusant opposition to exploit the situation to bargain for an end to the penal laws. Sir John Everard did point out, though, that but for the expenses incurred by the application of the penal laws, he would have been in favour of granting the king even more money.[80] The meekness of the recusant position may be explained in part by the supposition that the discovery of the conspiracy had neutered any intention to drive a hard bargain and that the Old English were afraid of finding themselves once more blackened with the same brush of disloyalty as their Gaelic Irish co-religionists. However, as Ridgeway had intimated, and as past experience had shown, the recusants were not noted for a timorous approach to securing their objectives. They had already demonstrated a willingness to take a bold stand not only against the Lord Deputy, but against the king as well. Thus a second scenario presents itself in accounting for Ridgeway's 'half miracle'. The recusants were embroiled in a major plot themselves and were keen not to blow their cover before it could be realised by any overt sign of disloyalty, as their refusal to sanction the finance bill would undoubtedly have been construed. That no attempt was made to barter concessions beggars belief — unless the recusants had a hidden agenda.

Certainly the response of Chichester's administration to the arrests in Ulster strongly suggests that he considered that, far from a conspiracy having been nipped in the bud, the skulduggery of the Ulstermen was only the tip of the iceberg. (In this respect, his investigations mirrored his response to the Flight of the Earls.) The arrested Ulster 'conspirators' were a motley crew, memorably branded by a recent historian as comprising among their complement a 'pirate', a 'dwarf' and a 'one-eared man'.[81] Besides, the copious consumption of alcohol played no small part in inhibiting their designs.[82] Significantly in this respect, the conspirators had planned on going to a tavern in Coleraine to drink all day until the gates of the town were shut. Once the gates had been closed, they intended to open them again and allow their rebel comrades to storm the town.[83] Given the challenged physical condition of the conspirators, it is all the more surprising that Chichester, a highly courageous military officer, was to be so worried. That he had concocted the conspiracy with a view to securing the passage of the finance bill is not unimaginable. The viceroy was more than capable of such a devious ploy, as his enemies in the Dublin administration alleged.[84] But the volume of correspondence detailing Chichester's investigations into the plot went on for some months, long after the finance bill had passed through parliament. What is more, executions of members of isolated rebel bands had been a regular feature of life in Ulster since the plantation. Indeed, provost marshals dispensing summary justice had been employed in various parts of Ireland since 1614, such had been the number of outrages perpetrated.[85] Summary justice, however, was not to be the fate of this particular group of rebels. Investigations into their activities were to be prolonged. The suspects were still being grilled at the end of June 1615 when Chichester sanctioned the employment of the rack as a means of torture for the first time in Irish history.[86] Thus the State Papers contain the incongruously entitled 'Voluntary confession of Cowconnaght O'Kenan upon the rack'.[87] That the Londoners involved in the plantation had had quite a scare was reflected in the fact that an urgent shipment of arms was sent to Coleraine during July 1615. Included in the consignment were 144 swords, 48 pikes and light armour for 94 men.[88]

The captured conspirators confessed to being motivated by discontent with the plantation of Ulster. This being so, the response of King James to the events in the north is all the more extraordinary. Having read the Lord Deputy's report, the king 'immediately called to mind' the orders given to Chichester in 1614 to arrange for the sons of selected noblemen and gentry to be sent to England, 'it being conceived to be a point so necessary for the future safety and quiet of that kingdom'.[89] The Catholic Archbishop of Tuam similarly remarked that the ordering of the eldest heirs of 'the principal gentlemen' was designed 'to hold their fathers in subjection and prevent any rising within the kingdom'.[90] But it was not the scions of the remaining leading Gaelic families in Ulster who were to be targeted in this respect. Rather, it was to be the cream of Old English society who were expected to deliver up hostages for good behaviour. Of the Old English of Leinster, the heirs of Lord Gormanston, Lord Trimleston and the Baron of Delvin were singled out. The Munster nobility were also targeted. Lord Power, then a minor, Lord Courcy's two sons, Lord Barry's grandson, Lord Dunboyne's grandson and Lord Cahir's nephew were all included.[91] This was hardly the response that would have been expected of the administration to what has been represented as an 'Ulster Conspiracy', essentially a Gaelic Irish plot in the north, but was rather a reaction that conveyed a conviction that there existed a widespread Catholic conspiracy throughout Ireland, involving the Old English as well as the Gaelic Irish. Thus, what has become known as the 'Ulster Conspiracy' of 1615 might more accurately be termed the 'Irish Conspiracy' of 1615. Had Tyrone managed to return, there is little reason to doubt that he would have been as widely welcomed by Old English as by Gaelic Irish Catholics. When the Old English and Gaelic Irish ultimately united in rebellion in 1641, the *prospect* of severe repression as a result of an increasingly assertive puritan parliament in England is considered to have been decisive in overcoming the historical animosity that often existed between the Old English and the Gaelic Irish. In 1615 the crown authorities were *actually* pursuing a vigorous campaign of persecution aimed mainly at the Old English.[92] The clear impression remains that Irish Catholics in general were turning to Tyrone, a renowned military leader, for deliverance.

Taking hostages from noble families was to be but one way of applying pressure on leading Catholic families throughout Ireland; incarceration of large numbers of the leading members of the gentry and mercantile classes was to be another. By the time Chichester left office in February 1616 the full extent of government repression was to be revealed. The English Privy Council acknowledged that non-conforming magistrates in the principal cities and towns during 1615 were 'fined and imprisoned, for terror and example unto others'.[93] As a result, by February 1616 more than eighty leading townsmen in Leinster and Munster were still languishing in prison having refused to take the Oath of Supremacy when they were elected to senior municipal positions in the previous September.[94] The severity and timing of the punishments were no accidents. Significantly, Spanish archives reveal that the target date for Tyrone's return to Ireland was the end of September 1615, the very time that new municipal magistrates were to be elected.[95] Beset as he was by English spies, and traitors among his own entourage and his confidants in Spain (including one Sir John Bath, who was suspected of having been a double agent in the service of Spain and England),[96] there was little that the London authorities did not know about Tyrone's intentions. It is this context which explains the English Privy Council's endorsement of 'terror' tactics. Throughout Chichester's tenure of office the English Privy Council had exercised a restraining influence on the persecuting predilection of the Irish viceroy. But now in 1615, with what seemed like the certain prospect of Tyrone's return to Ireland, the Privy Council's remarks indicate that they now wholeheartedly supported Chichester's policy of imprisoning recalcitrant civic officials. It is important to note, however, that in the circumstances of 1615 these incarcerations were sanctioned by London not so much on the grounds of religious policy but as a means of removing leading figures from recusant society before Tyrone's return.

What so concerned the London authorities, and for that matter their Spanish counterparts, was that Tyrone and his Catholic allies in Ireland had resolved to take action with or without Spanish military support. Once again Tyrone was reported to have ordered some of his followers to put to sea in warships as pirates, seize all the shipping they could, and then land on the coast of Ireland. Andrés Velázquez, the member of the Spanish Council with special responsibility for the Spanish secret service, affirmed in June 1615 that a rising was intended 'whether or not they receive open or covert help'.[97] Tyrone's declaration that he was willing to return to Ireland with a handful of men was more than rhetoric, it was his firm intention. And he had nothing to lose. As he remarked so poignantly in May 1615, he was on the 'point of total destruction', death beckoning.[98] Velázquez's contacts had convinced him that a rising was imminent. He explained in July 1615 how he had carried out extensive consultations with Sir John Bath and William Meade. Bath was widely regarded as a spokesman of the Old English Catholics of the Pale, while Meade was the 'oracle' of the Old English of Munster.[99] Velázquez interrogated them 'separately and repeatedly', mainly about Tyrone's claims that Irish Catholics were united in their determination to revolt, but also in order to fathom whether Tyrone's proposed return had 'any personal ulterior motive'. Velázquez was not easily beguiled. His conclusion was that 'I have always found them to agree in saying that their countrymen are calling them and assuring them that if help is not sent to them they will perish miserably at the hands of their enemies, that they are ready to avenge themselves and to die for their country.' At least 8,000 men had indicated their intention to rebel at short notice: 'one day or even one hour' would only be required.[100] Significantly, in view of the traditional rivalries between the Old English and Gaelic Irish, Bath and Meade were careful to explain the reasons why Tyrone was so important to the conspirators' plans. Despite the high regard which Bath and Meade entertained of the earl, there was no question that Tyrone would be made King of Ireland, 'for there are other Catholics who only recognise him as their leader because of his personal talents and the fortunes of war and obey him willingly in wartime but would not recognise him as their lord'.[101]

Sensitive to the reservations within the Old English community concerning his ambitions, Tyrone had devised an elaborate plan to assuage their fears. He requested that between four and six 'experienced and trustworthy' Spaniards should accompany him to whom the captured fortresses could be handed over 'in the name of His Majesty', i.e. the Spanish king. A further one hundred personnel, under the 'guise of foreigners or corsairs', were requested to man Dublin Castle. 'Provided that these are trustworthy persons and provided that they know the French and Italian languages so that no suspicion may attach to them, it will be easy to find a means of bringing them secretly.'[102] The plot had acquired a distinctly cosmopolitan complexion in keeping with the international experiences of Tyrone and his wide circle of expatriate supporters on the continent. That Tyrone sought to camouflage his intentions by exploiting the masquerade of pirates struck Velázquez as ingenious. He considered the subterfuge of using this stratagem to conceal Spanish involvement as 'wonderful cover'.[103] After all, there had been a large-scale pirate presence on Irish coasts since the ending of the Anglo-Spanish war in 1604. Overall, Velázquez was impressed by Tyrone's plans, not least because he believed that Spain had little to lose at little expense. By July 1615, according to Velázquez, Tyrone was scheduled to leave Rome shortly for Genoa in disguise, where he intended to board a ship 'which some Irish merchant friends of his will hold in readiness' while he awaited Philip III's approval for this venture.[104]

That Tyrone's latest, and as it proved, final bid to return to his patrimony should be treated seriously is evidenced by the reaction of the English to his latest manoeuvrings. In June 1615, while Tyrone's plans were being considered, the English ambassador in Spain was observed to become 'excited for the slightest reason, and it is well known how suspicious he is lately with regard to the Irish'.[105] At almost exactly the same time the English Secretary of State, Sir Ralph Winwood, paid a formal visit to the Spanish ambassador in London. Winwood emphasised to the ambassador that intelligence reports had strongly suggested that Tyrone was preparing to return to Flanders imminently and that this was 'a cause of much worry' to James I.[106] In a similar vein, the English ambassador in Brussels was lobbying vigorously to prevent Tyrone's return to Flanders.[107] However, the English were mistaken in believing that Tyrone's actions had the seal of Spanish approval. On the contrary, far from being manipulated by the Spanish in his endeavour to return to Ireland, the opposite was the case. The Spanish were doing everything in their power to prevent him leaving Rome. For his part, the archduke of the Netherlands bluntly informed Philip III that Tyrone's presence in Flanders would be an 'embarrassment'.[108] In April 1615 the Spanish Council of State recommended that the earl be spoken to 'clearly' about the inadvisability of returning to Ireland.[109] In February, and again in July 1615, Tyrone was threatened with the withdrawal of his Spanish annuity should he persist with his plans.[110] The view of the Spanish Council was that they had nothing to gain from Tyrone's return, perhaps fearing that they would be inevitably sucked into a new war with England. Retaining Tyrone as the ace up their sleeves, however, was much more appealing. Tyrone was worth more than his weight in gold. As the Spanish ambassador in London remarked in December 1615, 'They know here the great influence which Your Majesty [Philip III] has in Ireland and this gives them sufficient worry; that we should add to it would carry no advantage.' Besides, Tyrone was described as a person who, despite his ever-advancing years, 'could be of much importance for great purposes'.[111] Throughout his years in exile, therefore, the Spanish authorities were consistent in resisting appeals for providing military assistance to the repressed Irish Catholics. Equally apparently, there is little doubt that Tyrone would have been shipped back to Ireland at the earliest convenience in the event of a breakdown in Anglo-Spanish relations and when Spanish interests were directly involved. It was to be Tyrone's misfortune that his very presence on the continent was a powerful factor in ensuring that Anglo-Spanish relations remained on a relatively even keel. (A new Anglo-Spanish war broke out in 1624, eight years after the earl's death.)[112] In the end the threatened withdrawal of his Spanish pension and the outright refusal of his request to return to Flanders in July 1615 played a part in scuppering his plans to return to Ireland and take his chances in one final all-out attempt to regain his lands.[113] In his own expressive phrase, Tyrone had suffered 'destruction by peace'.[114]

Despite his persistent determination to die in battle in Ireland, the reality was that old age and infirmity were beginning to take a serious toll on Tyrone. By the early summer of 1615 he had become seriously ill, being confined to bed for several months under the care of Dr Bernardini, the Pope's physician, well skilled in the remedies of the period. However, as C. P. Meehan so aptly remarked, 'Tyrone's sickness was of a character which none of these nostrums could cure; and we can readily fancy that a breach between the Dutch provinces and Spain would have done more for his restoration than all the phials on Bernardini's shelves.'[115] Tyrone was later visited by another physician, a Dr Doyne, who recorded his observations on what he had witnessed in Tyrone's household over a period of two months. He reported that while the earl was

> an old man, by sight; yet he is lusty and strong, and well able to travel: for a month ago, at evening, his friar and his gentlemen were all with him. They were talking of England and of Ireland; he drew out his sword and said 'The Emperor [King of England] thinks that I am not strong. I would he that hates me most in England were with me to see whether I am strong or no.'

This was the earl's aggressive demeanour despite the fact that Dr Doyne had had to extract sixteen ounces of blood from his legs.[116] Despite his infirmities, it was reported that Tyrone was kept up to date with developments in Ireland, reputedly having spies in the inner sanctum of the viceregal court in Dublin. Seán Crón Mac Dhaibhéid, who had accompanied Tyrone at the time of the Flight, a confidant of the earl described as a 'politic fellow', had recently travelled to Bordeaux and then Spain, bringing back reports which apprised the earl of developments in Ireland. It was even reported that Tyrone had received letters from a senior figure in the English navy.[117] This is a fascinating assertion that raises the possibility that some of the piratical activity that had been ongoing on the coasts of Ireland for several years may well have involved followers of the Earl of Tyrone. As early as 1608 the Venetian ambassador in London suspected as much, when he commented that 'the number of pirates who are collected in that island [Ireland] awake a suspicion that they have been sent there by others on a more dangerous enterprise than piracy'.[118] Then, in 1611, rumours that a pirate fleet had departed Irish shores bound for Italy raised the spectre that pirates were possibly in league with the Earl of Tyrone.[119] What is not in doubt is that disillusionment with the plantations in Ireland resulted in some locally based piracy. For example, opponents of the Wexford settlement resorted to piracy in 1612.[120] During the spring of 1616 the English Privy Council signified their concern about the 'spoils committed of late by certain pirates and rebels in the north'.[121] What is more, Sorley MacDonnell, one of those implicated in the 1615 Ulster Conspiracy, later seized a vessel and operated as a pirate on the Irish Sea before sailing to Dunkirk and ultimately joining the Irish regiment in Flanders.[122]

Having missed, partly through illness, an opportunity to return to Ireland during the summer of 1615, the earl would have to wait for the good weather of the following summer before another attempt could be made. But when the long-awaited summer of 1616 finally arrived, Tyrone was on his deathbed. He remained active almost to the last, conspiring all the time; but the final months of the earl's life were to bring further heartache and disappointment. Having plotted to have his son Conn spirited out of English captivity in Ireland, he learned that Conn had been transported to England, 'which news grieved' him.[123] (The English sent Conn to Eton College, but fearing that the youngster could later become a figurehead for Irish rebels, he was transferred to the Tower of London.)[124] To make matters worse, an unseemly controversy erupted when Peter Lombard, the Catholic Archbishop of Armagh, who for seven years had shared the earl's residence in Rome, the Salviati palace, moved out. Dr Doyne's contemporary reference to the affair contains a hint of scandal involving the Countess of Tyrone, described as 'young and fair', and Robert Lombard, the archbishop's nephew.[125] Significantly, Robert Lombard, who had been an English spy for some time, boasted in March 1614 that he had access to 'secret information', having ingratiated himself intimately in the countess's favours. Sir Dudley Carleton, the English ambassador at Venice, found his information 'not unprobable', citing Lombard's 'youth, and the wantonness with which she [the Countess of Tyrone] is commonly noted'.[126] In a possible further development in this sensational affair, it is intriguing to note that in January 1616 the Earl of Tyrone was seeking to make formal arrangements for his wife to be permitted to live by herself in Flanders, citing 'how the air of this city [Rome] disagrees with the countess his wife, and how weakened her health is'.[127] If Robert Lombard and Carleton were telling the truth, however, she was much more vigorous than Tyrone was claiming, and the plan to send the countess to Flanders may have been linked to her alleged infidelity. It is a matter of speculation whether the supposed licentious activities of his nephew may have had some bearing on Archbishop Lombard's concurrent reorientation of the Catholic Church in Ireland away from supporting the plots and conspiracies of Irish *émigrés* and towards seeking some sort of *modus vivendi* with the English crown.[128]

In the end, several months before he died in 1616, the old earl lost his sight and was intermittently convulsed by attacks of fever.[129] Tyrone finally passed away on 20 July 1616 in Rome 'after exemplary penance for his sins, and gaining victory over the world and the Devil'. The Four Masters, the seventeenth-century Gaelic chroniclers, reflected on his demise with the epitaph that the 'person who here died was a powerful, mighty lord, [endowed] with wisdom, subtlety, and profundity of mind and intellect; a warlike, predatory, enterprising lord, in defending his religion and his patrimony against his enemies'.[130] His funeral was a grand affair, attended by the Spanish ambassador, cardinals, foreign ambassadors and Roman dignitaries.[131] An English diplomat wrote to the Earl of Somerset: 'I may now safely and truly by these confirm the news I wrote unto your honour by my last letters, concerning the late Earl of Tyrone, who died at Rome the 20th of July, of a fever, and was there buried with great pomp and solemnity, at the charges of the Spanish ambassador.'[132] The diplomat's employment of the term 'safely' betrays the lingering English apprehension at the very mention of the dead earl. Such reticence about making a definitive declaration, it is worth noting, reflected the contemporary English caricature of the Irish view of death, as portrayed in Webster's *The White Devil* where the character Francisco remarks:

> Like the wild Irish, I'll ne'er think thee dead
> Till I can play at football with thy head.[133]

And yet, even with the Earl of Tyrone dead and gone, the English continued to dread the fact that one day one of his descendants would return to Ireland to lead a new revolt. As a result, the earl's children on the continent remained the targets of suspicion as well as assassination. Thus allegations of English foul play surround the murder of Bernard O'Neill, the earl's son, in Brussels in 1617. The young boy was found strangled with his hands tied behind his back.[134] Commenting on the ensuing controversy, the English ambassador in Brussels, remarked on how the 'Irish friars in Louvain have launched the lying rumour that His Majesty [James I] was responsible, but the absurdity of their falsehood will become evident when it is considered that the king would have been most ill-advised to have assassinated the youngest brother and left the two eldest alive, one [Conn O'Neill] in his own custody'.[135] Indeed, it was with great delight that the ambassador reported that a relative of Bernard's had been 'brought under guard from Flanders to Brussels on suspicion of having committed the murder'.[136] As for Tyrone's elder remaining sons, the English ambassador informed some members of the archduke's council that 'His Majesty held these two to be persons of no importance whatsoever'.[137] That these latter remarks were disingenuous casts doubt on the overall reliability of the ambassador's account of the murder. The fact was that the children of the Earl of Tyrone — or indeed any relative who could raise the standard of revolt as the departed earl had once done — posed a serious threat to the English government.

The powerful resonance of the name of O'Neill continued to reverberate through Irish history in the seventeenth century. In 1623 there were reports of seditious activities in Ulster, particularly in County Cavan. John O'Neill, Hugh O'Neill's successor as Earl of Tyrone, was reported to be on the verge of landing 'to the destruction of the plantations and the restitution of all men to their lands'.[138] A similar report of John O'Neill's return also circulated in 1627: 'It is given out amongst them that Tyrone hath his crown already delivered to him, not now of peacock's feathers as his father's was, but all of pure gold, and lies constantly upon his table by his bedside in his chamber in Brussels, under the continual guard of his own eye.'[139] On this occasion the claimant had the enthusiastic backing of Philip IV of Spain, who warmly commended the expedition as being in defence of Catholicism in Ireland, signifying that he was 'firmly resolved to sacrifice all his possessions to advance the cause of his religion'.[140] All this, of course, would have been music to the ears of the old Earl of Tyrone, had he been alive. Interestingly, though, the Spanish noted that the successors of Hugh O'Neill and Rory O'Donnell as Earls of Tyrone and Tyrconnell were rivals to lead the proposed expedition in 1627 to establish a 'Republic ... of Ireland' — a title devised to prevent jealousies arising among the earls themselves and between the earls and the leading lords and citizens of Ireland on their return. Hugh O'Donnell, the claimant to the earldom of Tyrconnell, was not prepared to play second fiddle to an Earl of Tyrone as his father had done. Thus it was observed: 'If it be undertaken in the name of the Earl of Tyrone, the friends of the Earl of Tyrconnell will take no part in it; and if in the name of Tyrconnell, the friends of Tyrone will disagree.'[141] In the end the projected invasion of Ireland never took place, and John O'Neill, like his father before him, never returned to the land of his birth.

In 1642, however, following the outbreak of a major new revolt in Ireland, Owen Roe O'Neill, Hugh O'Neill's nephew and the 'prime upholder of the expatriate tradition',[142] did return to Ireland. Owen Roe emulated his uncle's triumph at the Yellow Ford by achieving a striking military victory close to the same River Blackwater, at the battle of Benburb in 1646. For the second time in less than fifty years an O'Neill had come tantalisingly close to ejecting the Protestant colonists from Ireland. In recognition of Owen Roe's achievements, the old Earl of Tyrone's sword was brought from Rome and presented to him.[143] The sword had passed on.

ABBREVIATIONS

A.F.M.	*Annála Ríoghachta Éireann: Annals of the Kingdom of Ireland by the Four Masters from the earliest period to the year 1616*, ed. and trans. John O'Donovan (3rd ed., 7 vols, Dublin, 1990)
Acts Privy Council	*Acts of the Privy Council of England* (46 vols, London, 1890–1964)
Anal. Hib.	*Analecta Hibernica*
B.L.	British Library, London
Cal. Carew MSS	*Calendar of the Carew Manuscripts preserved in the Archiepiscopal Library at Lambeth* (6 vols, London, 1867–73)
Cal. Pat. Rolls Ire., Jas I	*Irish Patent Rolls of James I: facsimile of the Irish Record Commissioners' calendar prepared prior to 1830*, with foreword by M. C. Griffith (Irish Manuscripts Commission, Dublin, 1966)
Cal. S.P. Dom.	*Calendar of State Papers, Domestic Series* (81 vols, London, 1856–1972)
Cal. S.P. Ire.	*Calendar of State Papers relating to Ireland* (24 vols, London, 1860–1911)
Cal. S.P. Venice	*Calendar of State Papers and Manuscripts, relating to English Affairs, existing in the archives and collections of Venice …* (London, 1864–)
Desid. Cur. Hib.	[John Lodge (ed.)], *Desiderata Curiosa Hibernica: or a select collection of state papers* (2 vols, Dublin, 1772)
H.M.C.	Historical Manuscripts Commission [Source references to H.M.C. publications are given in short form in the Notes section (e.g. H.M.C., *Salisbury*). Full bibliographical descriptions are entered in the Bibliography under the name of the collection as given in the title (e.g. Salisbury).]

I.H.S.	*Irish Historical Studies*
N.H.I., iii	T. W. Moody, F. X. Martin and F. J. Byrne (eds), *A New History of Ireland*, vol. iii: *Early Modern Ireland, 1534–1691* (Oxford, 1976; 2nd ed., Oxford, 1989)
N.L.I.	National Library of Ireland, Dublin
P.R.O.	Public Record Office of England
P.R.O., SP	Public Record Office of England, State Papers series
T.C.D.	Trinity College, Dublin

NOTES

Introduction (pp 1–7)

1. *Cal. S.P. Ire., 1606–8*, pp 270–4, 275–7. There is a lingering belief that the term 'the Flight of the Earls' was coined by historians: see James L. Sanderson, *Sir John Davies* (Boston, 1975), p. 32; Murray Smith, 'Flight of the Earls? Changing views on O'Neill's departure from Ireland', *History Ireland*, iv, no. 1 (1996), pp 17–20.
2. N. P. Canny, 'The Flight of the Earls', *I.H.S.*, xvii (1971), p. 380.
3. C. P. Meehan, *The Fate and Fortunes of Hugh O'Neill, Earl of Tyrone, and Rory O'Donnel, Earl of Tyrconnell, their flight from Ireland and death in exile* (3rd ed., Dublin, 1886), p. 81n.
4. Micheline Kerney Walsh, *Destruction by Peace: Hugh O'Neill after Kinsale* (Monaghan, 1986), document 211.
5. Ibid., *passim.*
6. John McCavitt, 'The Flight of the Earls', *I.H.S.*, xxix (1994), pp 159–73.
7. *Cal. S.P. Ire., 1606–8*, pp 259–62.
8. Ibid., pp 270–4.
9. Ibid., pp 374–83.
10. Ibid., pp 511–14.
11. John McGurk, 'The Dead, Sick and Wounded of the Nine Years War (1594–1603)', *History Ireland*, iii, no. 4, (1995), p.19.
12. Richard Bagwell, *Ireland under the Stuarts* (3 vols, London, 1909–16), i, 34.
13. Charles Hughes (ed.), *Shakespeare's Europe* (London, 1903), p. 240.
14. Ibid., p. 210.
15. John McCavitt, *Sir Arthur Chichester, Lord Deputy of Ireland, 1605–16* (Belfast, 1998), p. 23.
16. Ibid., p. 170.
17. *Cal. S.P. Ire., 1608–10*, pp 470–3.
18. N. P. Canny, 'The Treaty of Mellifont and the Reorganisation of Ulster, 1603', *Irish Sword*, ix (1969), p. 262.
19. Ibid.
20. Sean O'Faolain, *The Great O'Neill* (repr., Dublin, 1981), p. 240.
21. Pirate fleets alternated between Ireland and the Barbary coast during the early seventeenth century. See J. C. Appleby, 'The "Affairs of Pirates": the surrender and submission of Captain William Baugh at Kinsale, 1611–1612', *Journal of the Cork Historical and Archaeological Society*, xci (1986), pp 68–84.

22. Joyce Lorimer (ed.,) *English and Irish Settlement on the River Amazon, 1550–1646* (Hakluyt Society, London, 1989), pp 43–5.

Chapter 1: 'Better hang at home than die like a dog in Ireland' (pp 8–28)

1. Hiram Morgan, *Tyrone's Rebellion: the outbreak of the Nine Years War in Tudor Ireland* (Woodbridge, Suffolk, 1993), p. 166.
2. Ibid., p. 94.
3. *A.F.M.*, vi, 2367.
4. Morgan, *Tyrone's Rebellion*, p. 75.
5. Cyril Falls, *Elizabeth's Irish Wars* (London, 1950), pp 138–44.
6. John McGurk, *The Elizabethan Conquest of Ireland* (Manchester, 1997), p. 220.
7. Morgan, *Tyrone's Rebellion*, p. 79.
8. Ibid.
9. O'Faolain, *The Great O'Neill*, p. 90; Cyril Falls, *The Birth of Ulster* (London, 1936), pp 42–3.
10. Morgan, *Tyrone's Rebellion*, p. 216.
11. Nicholas Canny, *Reformation to Restoration: Ireland, 1534–1660* (Dublin, 1987), p. 139.
12. O'Faolain, *The Great O'Neill*, p. 90; Falls, *Birth of Ulster*, pp 42–3.
13. Richard Bagwell, *Ireland under the Tudors* (repr., 3 vols, London, 1963), iii, 223–5.
14. *Cal. S.P. Ire., 1606–8*, pp 374–83.
15. Quoted in *A.F.M.*, vi, 1944–5.
16. Morgan, *Tyrone's Rebellion*, p. 71.
17. Ibid., p. 143.
18. McGurk, *Elizabethan Conquest*, p. 243.
19. Falls, *Elizabeth's Irish Wars*, pp 174–6.
20. *A.F.M.*, vi, 1941.
21. Falls, *Elizabeth's Irish Wars*, p. 176.
22. Morgan, *Tyrone's Rebellion*, p. 155.
23. Falls, *Elizabeth's Irish Wars*, pp 176–7.
24. Lughaidh Ó Cléirigh, *The Life of Aodh Ruadh Ó Domhnaill*, ed. Paul Walsh (2 pts, Dublin, 1948–57), i, 65.
25. Falls, *Elizabeth's Irish Wars*, p. 177.
26. Morgan, *Tyrone's Rebellion*, pp 139–40.
27. Kerney Walsh, *Destruction by Peace*, document 43a.
28. Falls, *Elizabeth's Irish Wars*, pp 181–2.
29. O'Faolain, *The Great O'Neill*, p. 148.
30. Morgan, *Tyrone's Rebellion*, pp 181–3.
31. Graham Kew (ed.), 'The Irish Sections of Fynes Moryson's Unpublished Itinerary', *Anal. Hib.*, xxxvii (1998), pp 69–70.
32. *A.F.M.*, vi, 1959.
33. Jonathan Bardon, *A History of Ulster* (Belfast, 1992), p. 96.
34. *A.F.M.*, vi, 1987.
35. McGurk, *Elizabethan Conquest*, p. 243.
36. Quoted in O'Faolain, *The Great O'Neill*, p. 163.
37. Ibid., p. 164.
38. McGurk, *Elizabethan Conquest*, pp 43–4. English troops dressed in 'red coats' were not the norm in the late sixteenth century (see ibid., p. 61).
39. Kew (ed.), 'Moryson's Unpublished Itinerary', p. 72.
40. Hughes (ed.), *Shakespeare's Europe*, p. 237.

41. Kew (ed.), 'Moryson's Unpublished Itinerary', p. 87.
42. Ibid., p. 70.
43. Ibid., p. 102.
44. O'Faolain, *The Great O'Neill*, p. 169.
45. *A.F.M.*, vi, 1973; Falls, *Elizabeth's Irish Wars*, p. 188.
46. *A.F.M.*, vi, 1969.
47. Ibid.
48. Ibid., p. 1971.
49. Ibid.
50. Falls, *Elizabeth's Irish Wars*, p. 189.
51. *A.F.M.*, vi, 1971.
52. Morgan, *Tyrone's Rebellion*, p. 208.
53. Ibid., p. 209.
54. Hiram Morgan, 'Hugh O'Neill and the Nine Years War in Tudor Ireland', *Historical Journal*, xxxvi, (1993), pp 26–7.
55. *Cal. S.P. Ire., 1606–8*, pp 270–4.
56. Bardon, *History of Ulster*, p. 99.
57. Falls, *Elizabeth's Irish Wars*, p. 175.
58. Morgan, *Tyrone's Rebellion*, p. 131.
59. *A.F.M.*, vi, 1913–17.
60. Morgan, *Tyrone's Rebellion*, p. 132.
61. *A.F.M.*, vi, 1917.
62. Ibid., pp 1919, 1927.
63. Ibid., p. 1923; Morgan, *Tyrone's Rebellion*, p. 132.
64. O'Faolain, *The Great O'Neill*, p. 123.
65. *A.F.M.*, vi, 1927.
66. McGurk, 'Dead, Sick and Wounded of the Nine Years War', p. 17.
67. *A.F.M.*, vi, 2013; see also *Cal. S.P. Ire., 1596–7*, p. 252.
68. Falls, *Elizabeth's Irish Wars*, p. 207.
69. Ibid.
70. Fynes Moryson, *A History of Ireland from the year 1599 to 1603* (2 vols, Dublin, 1735), i, 58.
71. Falls, *Elizabeth's Irish Wars*, pp 213–14.
72. Ibid., p. 173.
73. *Cal. S.P. Ire., 1598–9*, pp 232.
74. Kew (ed.), 'Moryson's Unpublished Itinerary', pp 113–14.
75. *A.F.M.*, vi, 2061.
76. Ó Cléirigh, *Life of Aodh Ruadh*, p. 171.
77. Ibid., p. 167. An English account confirms that there were dispositions on the flanks (*Cal. S.P. Ire., 1598–9*, pp 277–8).
78. *A.F.M.*, vi, 2061.
79. *Cal. S.P. Ire., 1598–9*, pp 227–8.
80. Ibid., pp 227–8, 236–7.
81. Moryson, *History of Ireland*, i, 58–9.
82. Ó Cléirigh, *Life of Aodh Ruadh*, p. 173.
83. *Cal. S.P. Ire., 1598–9*, pp 235–6.
84. Ibid., pp 237–8, 243–4, 253–4, 277–8.
85. Ó Cléirigh, *Life of Aodh Ruadh*, p. 173.
86. Kerney Walsh, *Destruction by Peace*, document 227.

87. Ó Cléirigh, *Life of Aodh Ruadh*, p. 177.
88. Ibid., p. 169.
89. *Cal. S.P. Ire., 1598–9*, p. 244; Ó Cléirigh, *Life of Aodh Ruadh*, p. 175.
90. Ó Cléirigh, *Life of Aodh Ruadh*, p. 175; *A.F.M.*, vi, 2073, 2075.
91. Moryson, *History of Ireland*, i, 59.
92. *Cal. S.P. Ire., 1598–9*, pp 224, 236–7, 244.
93. Ibid., pp 262, 319–22; Falls, *Elizabeth's Irish Wars*, p. 219. Some Irish troops in the English army had deserted.
94. Kew (ed.), 'Moryson's Unpublished Itinerary', p. 94.
95. *Cal. S.P. Ire., 1598–9*, pp 231–4.
96. H.M.C., *Salisbury*, viii, 318–9.
97. Morgan, *Tyrone's Rebellion*, pp 23, 86–7.
98. William Camden, *Britannia* (London, 1610), p. 117.
99. Quoted in O'Faolain, *The Great O'Neill*, p. 156.
100. Canny, *Reformation to Restoration*, p. 144.
101. Kew (ed.), 'Moryson's Unpublished Itinerary', p. 71.
102. Falls, *Elizabeth's Irish Wars*, p. 220; *Cal. S.P. Ire., 1598–9*, p. 260; *A.F.M.*, vi, 2075.
103. *Cal. S.P. Ire., 1598–9*, p. 321.
104. Ibid., p. 320.
105. Falls, *Elizabeth's Irish Wars*, p. 220.
106. Canny, *Reformation to Restoration*, p. 143.
107. Ibid., pp 143–4.
108. Ibid., p. 144.
109. Falls, *Elizabeth's Irish Wars*, p. 229.
110. Kew (ed), 'Moryson's Unpublished Itinerary', p. 72.
111. Ibid.
112. Bardon, *History of Ulster*, p. 102.
113. Faithful Fortescue, *An Account of the Rt Hon. Sir Arthur Chichester*, ed. Lord Clermont (London, 1858), pp 11–12.
114. G. A. Hayes-McCoy, 'The Completion of the Tudor Conquest, and the Advance of the Counter-Reformation' in *N.H.I.*, iii, 128.
115. O'Faolain, *The Great O'Neill*, p. 213.
116. Falls, *Elizabeth's Irish Wars*, pp 242–3.
117. *A.F.M.*, vi, 2127–31.
118. Falls, *Elizabeth's Irish Wars*, pp 242–3.
119. *A.F.M.*, vi, 2136n, 2137.
120. Falls, *Birth of Ulster*, p. 56.
121. Ibid., p. 57.
122. Falls, *Elizabeth's Irish Wars*, p. 244.
123. O'Faolain, *The Great O'Neill*, p. 216.
124. *Cal. S.P. Ire., 1599–1600*, pp 98–101.
125. *A.F.M.*, vi, 2143.
126. Quoted in Hiram Morgan, 'Faith and Fatherland in Sixteenth Century Ireland', *History Ireland*, iii, no. 2 (1995), p. 17.
127. Ibid.
128. Morgan, 'Hugh O'Neill and the Nine Years War', p. 25.
129. Ibid., pp 25–6.
130. Ibid., p. 31.

131. O'Faolain, *The Great O'Neill*, p. 175.

132. Tyrone denied that he was seeking the kingship of Ireland (see Morgan, 'Faith and Fatherland', p. 17).

133. *The Letters of John Chamberlain*, ed. N. E. McClure (2 vols, Philadelphia, 1939), i, 99–102.

134. G. A. Hayes-McCoy, *Irish Battles* (London, 1969), p. 148.

135. O'Faolain, *The Great O'Neill*, p. 214.

136. Russell, one of Essex's predecessors in Ireland, had received short change from the queen when he paraded the heads of a number of minor Gaelic captains in a basket at court (see O'Faolain, *The Great O'Neill*, p. 149).

137. Meehan, *Fate and Fortunes*, p. 67n.

138. Quoted in McGurk, 'Dead, Sick and Wounded of the Nine Years' War', p. 17.

Chapter 2: 'Received to grace and mercy, even out of the jaws of death' (pp 29–50)

1. Hayes-McCoy, *Irish Battles*, p. 149.

2. England, it is worth noting, had only itself emerged from a period of prolonged political fragmentation with the conclusion of the Wars of the Roses at the end of the fifteenth century.

3. At the time, as for much of subsequent history, England's strength was its navy, not its land forces.

4. Falls, *Elizabeth's Irish Wars*, p. 254.

5. Ibid.

6. A sickly figure, Mountjoy did not long survive his flirtations with death in Ireland. Reprimanded by James I for his 'heavy use of tobacco', he died in 1606 following prolonged bouts of serious illness. Interestingly, his symptoms included 'acute inflammation of the lungs', suggesting that Mountjoy was perhaps an early victim of a tobacco-related illness following Sir Walter Raleigh's discovery of the tobacco plant (see F. M. Jones, *Mountjoy, 1563–1606, the last Elizabethan deputy* (Dublin, 1958), pp 180–1).

7. Falls, *Elizabeth's Irish Wars*, pp 262–3; Canny, *Reformation to Restoration*, p. 145.

8. Sir Henry Docwra, 'A Narration of the Services done by the Army ymployed to Lough-Foyle' in *Miscellany of the Celtic Society*, ed. John O'Donovan (Dublin, 1849), p. 238.

9. Falls, *Elizabeth's Irish Wars*, p. 262.

10. Fynes Moryson, *An Itinerary containing his ten yeeres travell through … Germany, Bohmerland, Sweitzerland, Netherland, Denmark, Poland, Italy, Turkey, France, England, Scotland and Ireland* (4 vols, Glasgow, 1907–8), ii, 336–7.

11. *Cal. S.P. Ire., 1600*, pp 522–4.

12. Lord Ernest Hamilton, *Elizabethan Ulster* (London, 1919), pp 271–2.

13. *Cal. S.P. Ire., 1600–1*, pp 27–31.

14. Ibid.

15. *Cal. S.P. Ire., 1600*, pp 524–30.

16. Ibid.

17. Ibid.; *Cal. S.P. Ire., 1600–1*, pp 27–31. Sir Christopher St Lawrence, who was later to play a key role in the Flight of the Earls, was wounded in the neck fighting on the English side at the engagements at the Moyry Pass. The English were inclined to play down their own casualties, while exaggerating Irish dead and wounded. In this respect it has been well remarked that 'What Bagenal said after the battle [of Clontibret 1595] about the alleged Irish dead was also true of the living: "They were so scattered in wood and bog that we could not see them".' (O'Faolain, *The Great O'Neill*, p. 163)

18. *Cal. S.P. Ire., 1600–1*, pp 27–31. An English officer involved in the Moyry Pass exchanges remarked on the advantage of the fortifications to the Irish: 'We had only their heads for our marks, they our whole bodies' (ibid).

19. *Cal. S.P. Ire., 1600*, p. 463.

20. Jones, *Mountjoy*, p. 82.

21. Mountjoy had a liking for bestowing placenames with a link to his own names.

22. *Cal. S.P. Ire., 1600–1*, pp 27–31.

23. Ibid.

24. *Cal. S.P. Ire., 1600*, pp 469–70. The castle built in the Moyry Pass can still be seen today close to the Belfast–Dublin railway line.

25. O'Faolain, *The Great O'Neill*, p. 191.

26. *Cal. S.P. Ire., 1600–1*, pp 27–31.

27. Moryson, *Itinerary*, ii, 339.

28. *Cal. S.P. Ire., 1600–1*, pp 27–31.

29. Moryson, *Itinerary*, ii, 341.

30. Ibid., p. 342.

31. Falls, *Elizabeth's Irish Wars*, p. 208. The MacDonnell clan had been colonising parts of Ulster for some centuries. As Catholics they sided with the Earl of Tyrone during the Nine Years War.

32. Quoted ibid.

33. Ibid.

34. McGurk, *Elizabethan Conquest*, p. 243.

35. Hans Pawlisch, *Sir John Davies and the Conquest of Ireland: a study in legal imperialism* (Cambridge, 1985), p. 86.

36. *Cal. S.P. Ire., 1596–7*, pp 450–1.

37. McCavitt, *Chichester*, p. 10.

38. *Cal. S.P. Ire., 1600*, pp 192–3.

39. Drake either constructed small vessels during his expeditions or carried prefabricated ones with him (see John Cummins, *Francis Drake* (London, 1995), pp 61, 136).

40. *Cal. S.P. Ire., 1600–1*, pp 355–8.

41. Ibid., pp 332–5.

42. P.R.O., SP 63/209i/57. The reinforcements were duly dispatched (see *Cal. S.P. Ire., 1601–3*, pp 162–3).

43. *Cal. S.P. Ire., 1601–3*, pp 63–5.

44. *Acts Privy Council, 1601–4*, pp 447–8.

45. Hayes-McCoy, *Irish Battles*, p. 149.

46. Ibid., pp 150–2.

47. *Cal. S.P. Ire., 1601–3*, pp 152–3; Hayes-McCoy, *Irish Battles*, p. 155.

48. *Cal. S.P. Ire., 1601–3*, pp 206–7.

49. P.R.O., SP 63/209ii/196.

50. Ibid.

51. Hayes-McCoy, *Irish Battles*, p. 159.

52. Ibid., p. 157.

53. Ibid., p. 156.

54. Kerney Walsh, *Destruction by Peace*, document 43a; Bardon, *History of Ulster*, p. 111.

55. Kew (ed.), 'Moryson's Unpublished Itinerary', p. 75.

56. Ibid.

57. Hayes-McCoy, *Irish Battles*, p. 159.

58. Ó Cléirigh, *Life of Aodh Ruadh*, p. 309.

59. Kew (ed.), 'Moryson's Unpublished Itinerary', p. 111. The Irish were also reputed to 'exceedingly delight in playing at cards and dice, especially at dice, and professed gamesters go about, carrying cards and dice with them, and they will not only play for all the money and clothes they have, but even for the members of their body at a rate of money, suffering themselves to be tied by those members (even the shameful parts), and so to be led about, till they can free themselves by paying the rate of money' (ibid., p. 112).

60. Ibid., p. 75. If the common soldier resorted to alcohol to numb the horror of war, Lord Mountjoy was reported to have enjoyed Irish dancing by way of entertainment. Fynes Moryson described a variety of dances including 'the Matachine dance with naked swords, which they make to meet in divers comely postures, and this I have seen them often dance before the Lord Deputy in the house of [divers] Irish lords, and it seemeth to me a dangerous sport to see so many naked swords so near the Lord Deputy and chief commanders of the army, in the hands of the Irish kern, who had either lately been or were not unlike to prove rebels' (ibid., p. 112).

61. Meehan, *Fate and Fortunes*, pp 356–7.

62. Quoted in Thomas Morrissey, *James Archer of Kilkenny* (Dublin, 1979), p. 31. While del Águila's conduct has provoked much debate, the Earl of Tyrone later singled out for praise Pedro Blanco, a Spaniard who had been in his service since being shipwrecked at the time of the Armada in 1588. During the siege of Kinsale Tyrone testified that 'there was no other but this great soldier whom I could trust' to cross back and forth repeatedly through enemy lines to bring messages to and from del Águila (see Kerney Walsh, *Destruction by Peace*, document 227).

63. *A.F.M.*, vi, 2289.

64. Falls, *Elizabeth's Irish Wars*, p. 303. Whiskey was often referred to by Englishmen by the Latin term *aqua vitae*. The Irish called it *usquebaugh*. Both mean 'water of life'.

65. E. A. D'Alton, *History of Ireland from the earliest times to the present day* (6 vols, London, 1910), iii, 178.

66. Hayes-McCoy, *Irish Battles*, p. 162.

67. Proposals to erect a bridge at Narrow Water have yet to obtain government backing.

68. Bardon, *History of Ulster*, p. 111.

69. For the 'butter captains' see p. 13 above.

70. *A.F.M.*, vi, 2289.

71. Ibid., p. 2285n.

72. Moryson, *History of Ireland*, ii, 76.

73. *A.F.M.*, vi, 2289.

74. *Cal. S.P. Ire., 1606–8*, pp 270–4.

75. *A.F.M.*, vi, 2291.

76. Ibid., p. 2295; Meehan, *Fate and Fortunes*, p. 70n.

77. *A.F.M.*, vi, 2297.

78. Ibid., p. 2325.

79. Kerney Walsh, *Destruction by Peace*, document 43a.

80. McGurk, *Elizabethan Conquest*, p. 74.

81. Moryson, *History of Ireland*, ii, 142.

82. Ibid., pp 149–50.

83. Ibid., p. 151.

84. Ibid., p. 150.

85. Ibid., p. 152.
86. Docwra, 'Narration', p. 262.
87. McCavitt, *Chichester*, p. 13.
88. *A.F.M.*, vi, 2193.
89. Docwra, 'Narration', pp 241–3. In an attempt to combat dysentery, Docwra procured large amounts of liquorice and aniseed to make medicinal drinks (see McGurk, 'Dead, Sick and Wounded of the Nine Years War', p. 17).
90. Docwra, 'Narration', p. 242; *A.F.M.*, vi, 2208–9.
91. *A.F.M.*, vi, 2209.
92. Ibid., p. 2193.
93. McGurk, *Elizabethan Conquest*, p. 221.
94. Docwra, 'Narration', pp 245–6.
95. *A.F.M.*, vi, 2211.
96. Ibid., p. 2217.
97. McCavitt, *Chichester*, p. 13.
98. P.R.O., SP 63/209ii/133.
99. *Cal. S.P. Ire., 1601–3*, pp 335–6.
100. Falls, *Birth of Ulster*, p. 67.
101. Moryson, *History of Ireland*, ii, 283.
102. C. L. Falkiner (ed.), 'William Farmer's Chronicles of Ireland', *English Historical Review*, xxii (1907), pp 129–30. Mountjoy's secretary, Fynes Moryson, provides a poignant account of the same incident. According to his version, three children, the eldest no older than ten, had been found 'eating and gnawing with their teeth the entrails of their dead mother, upon whose flesh they had fed twenty days past, and having eaten all from the feet upward to the bare bones, roasting it continually by a slow fire, were now come to the eating of her said entrails in like sort roasted, yet not divided from the body, being as yet raw' (Moryson, *History of Ireland*, ii, 283).
103. Moryson, *History of Ireland*, ii, 284.
104. Kerney Walsh, *Destruction by Peace*, document 56b.
105. Docwra, 'Narration', pp 260–1.
106. *Cal. S.P. Ire., 1601–3*, p. 414.
107. *Cal. S.P. Ire., 1606–8*, pp 215–18.
108. P.R.O., SP 63/211/60.
109. McCavitt, *Chichester*, p. 9.
110. A. B. Grosart (ed.), *The Lismore Papers*, 2nd ser. (5 vols, London, 1887–8), i, 41–2; *Cal. S.P. Ire., 1601–3*, p. 541.
111. Kew (ed), 'Moryson's Unpublished Itinerary', p. 103.
112. O'Faolain, *The Great O'Neill*, p. 267.
113. *Chamberlain Letters*, ed. McClure, i, 158–62.
114. *Cal. S.P. Ire., 1608–10*, pp 14–17. English ignorance of the physical geography of Ulster proved to be beneficial to the Irish during the war. It was an advantage the Irish were determined to keep. Towards the end of the conflict a cartographer who had been sent into Tyrconnell by Mountjoy had his head cut off (see Meehan, *Fate and Fortunes*, p. 196n).
115. Josias Bodley, 'A Visit to Lecale in the County of Down, in the year 1602–3' in C. L. Falkiner, *Illustrations of Irish History and Topography, mainly of the seventeenth century* (London, 1904), pp 329–30.
116. Ibid., p. 330.
117. *Chamberlain Letters*, ed. McClure i, 183–6.

118. Ibid., p. 186–7.
119. Ibid.
120. McGurk, *Elizabethan Conquest*, p. 15.
121. Docwra, 'Narration', pp 276–7.
122. *A.F.M.*, vi, 2338n.
123. Docwra, 'Narration', pp 274–5.
124. Ibid., p. 277.
125. Canny, 'Treaty of Mellifont', p. 250.
126. McGurk, 'Dead, Sick and Wounded of the Nine Years War', p. 17.
127. *Cal. S.P. Ire., 1606–8*, pp 511–14.
128. Kew (ed.), 'Moryson's Unpublished Itinerary', p. 7.
129. Meehan, *Fate and Fortunes*, p. 7. Another account of Tyrone's submission, written by an English eyewitness, describes how the earl 'prostrated himself grovelling to the earth, with such a dejected countenance, that the standers by were amazed. ... It was one of the deplorablest sights that ever I saw; and to look upon such a person, the author of so much trouble, and so formerly glorious, so dejected, would have wrought many changes in the stoutest heart, and did no doubt at this instant raise a certain commiseration in his greatest adversary.' (Quoted in George Hill (ed.), *The Montgomery Manuscripts, 1603–1706* (Belfast, 1869), p. 45)
130. Sir John Davies, *A Discovery of the True Causes Why Ireland Was Never Entirely Subdued ... until ... His Majesty's Happy Reign* [1612] (facsimile repr., Shannon, 1969), p. 263.

Chapter 3: The aborted flight of an earl (pp 51–72)

1. Kerney Walsh, *Destruction by Peace*, document 102a.
2. Ibid., document 56b.
3. McCavitt, *Chichester*, p. 45.
4. *Cal. S.P. Ire., 1603–6*, pp 576–7.
5. Kew (ed.), 'Moryson's Unpublished Itinerary', p. 27. Interestingly in this respect, subsequent events proved that even when the Old English gravitated much closer politically to Tyrone, there was no question that they would ever accept him as 'king' of Ireland.
6. Edmund Spenser, *A View of the Present State of Ireland*, ed. W. L. Renwick (Oxford, 1970), p. 104.
7. *Desid. Cur. Hib.*, i, 415–16.
8. Kew (ed.), 'Moryson's Unpublished Itinerary', p. 53.
9. M. J. Byrne, *Ireland under Elizabeth* (Dublin, 1903), a translation of Philip O'Sullivan Beare, *Historiae Catholicae Iberniae Compendium* (Lisbon, 1621), p. 179.
10. H.M.C., *Egmont*, i, pt 1, pp 28–9.
11. Kerney Walsh, *Destruction by Peace*, document 6.
12. Jenny Wormald, 'James VI and I: two kings or one?', *History*, lxviii (1983), pp 187–209.
13. Ibid., p. 187.
14. Thomas Gainsford, *The True and Exemplary and Remarkable History of the Earle of Tirone* (London, 1619).
15. Falls, *Birth of Ulster*, p. 84.
16. *Cal. S.P. Venice, 1607–10*, pp 287–8.
17. Quoted in Falls, *Birth of Ulster*, p. 85.
18. Canny, 'Treaty of Mellifont', p. 261.
19. Falls, *Birth of Ulster*, pp 86–7.

20. *Cal. S.P. Ire., 1611–14*, pp 392–9. Four 'agents' from the nobility and gentry of Ireland were committed to the Tower of London in August 1603 for their part in these proceedings, not least because of the alleged intimidatory manner in which the petition was presented to the king. See *The Journal of Sir Roger Wilbraham, Solicitor General in Ireland and Master of Requests for the years 1594–1616 ...*, ed. H. S. Scott, Camden Miscellany, 3rd ser., vol. x (London, 1902), p. 62.

21. *Cal. S.P. Ire., 1603–6*, pp 108–9.

22. Ibid., pp 158–62.

23. McCavitt, *Chichester*, p. 130.

24. Docwra, 'Narration', p. 276. Tyrone's participation in a volatile binge–drinking session with some prominent former rebel allies during the spring of 1604 also raised some eyebrows. 'The Earl of Tyrone, the Viscount Mountgarrett, Phelim McFeaugh, Redmond McFeaugh, and, as it would seem, Donel Spaniagh too, met all together at Carlow, and in their riot and drinking swords were drawn, and mischief was like to be done. And yet of themselves they grew friends again, and had conference together, though to what end he [Davies] knows not; only this he dares affirm, that it was not to this end that religion and peace might be established in this kingdom.' (*Cal. S.P. Ire., 1603–6*, pp 158–62)

25. Carey was sixty-eight years old at the time of his appointment (see *Cal. S.P. Ire., 1603–6*, pp 243–5).

26. Ibid., pp 300–1.

27. Cecil received this title in 1603 (see Kerney Walsh, *Destruction by Peace*, p. 32).

28. *Cal. S.P. Ire., 1603–6*, p. 264.

29. McCavitt, *Chichester*, p. 71.

30. *Cal. S.P. Ire., 1608–10*, pp 532–46.

31. *Cal. S.P. Ire., 1603–6*, pp 300–1.

32. McCavitt, *Chichester*, p. 6.

33. *The Poems of Sir John Davies*, ed. Robert Krueger (Oxford, 1975), p. xxxv.

34. Robert Steele, *Tudor and Stuart Proclamations* (2 vols, Oxford, 1910, ii, 17.

35. *Cal. S.P. Ire., 1603–6*, pp 243–5, 261–2.

36. Ibid., pp 259–60.

37. Ibid., p. 334.

38. Ibid., pp 338–44.

39. McCavitt, *Chichester*, p. 95.

40. *Cal. S.P. Ire., 1603–6*, pp 328–30.

41. Robert Steele, *Tudor and Stuart Proclamations* (2 vols, Oxford, 1910), ii, 17.

42. *Cal. S.P. Ire., 1603–6*, pp 512–13.

43. Ibid., pp 370–3.

44. Ibid., pp 355–8.

45. P. J. Corish, *The Irish Catholic Experience: a historical survey* (Dublin, 1985), p. 97. Castle Chamber was the equivalent of Star Chamber in England.

46. In one letter Chichester acknowledged that he received news of the Gunpowder Plot on 22 November 1605 (*Cal. S.P. Ire., 1603–6*, pp 355–8), whereas in another letter he recorded that he received this information on 20 November (ibid., pp 359–62).

47. *Cal. S.P. Ire., 1603–6*, pp 359–62; Bagwell, *Stuarts*, i, 23.

48. *Cal. S.P. Ire., 1603–6*, pp 355–8.

49. *Cal. S.P. Ire., 1608–10*, pp 141–5.

50. McCavitt, *Chichester*, p. 1.

51. Quoted in P. F. Moran, *History of the Catholic Archbishops of Dublin since the Reformation* (Dublin, 1864), p. 232.
52. Bagwell, *Stuarts*, i, 25.
53. *Cal. S.P. Ire., 1603–6*, pp 373–4.
54. McCavitt, *Chichester*, pp 117, 120.
55. P.R.O., SP 63/218/1.
56. *Cal. S.P. Ire., 1603–6*, pp 580–3.
57. *Cal. S.P. Ire., 1606–8*, pp 152–3.
58. Falls, *Birth of Ulster*, p. 91.
59. McCavitt, *Chichester*, pp 6–7.
60. Ibid., pp 131–2.
61. *Cal. S.P. Ire., 1603–6*, pp 408–10.
62. *Cal. S.P. Ire., 1606–8*, pp 89–90.
63. Kerney Walsh, *Destruction by Peace*, document 43a.
64. Ibid., document 72a.
65. McCavitt, 'Flight of the Earls', p. 160.
66. As with his three previous wives, relations between the Earl of Tyrone and his fourth wife, Catherine Magennis, were at times tempestuous.
67. *Cal. S.P. Ire., 1603–6*, pp 568–9.
68. Ibid., pp 408–10. While often acting in unison in the period 1603–7, the two northern earls did not see eye to eye on all matters. In 1605, for instance, the Earl of Tyrconnell opposed the appointment of the Earl of Tyrone's son as colonel of the Irish regiment in Flanders (Jerrold Casway, 'Henry O'Neill and the Formation of the Irish Regiment in the Netherlands, 1605', *I.H.S.*, xviii (1973), p. 484).
69. O'Faolain, *The Great O'Neill*, p. 272.
70. Meehan, *Fate and Fortunes*, p. 44.
71. Falls, *Birth of Ulster*, p. 102n.
72. *Cal. S.P. Ire., 1603–6*, pp 406–8.
73. John McCavitt, 'Lord Deputy Chichester and the English Government's "Mandates Policy" in Ireland, 1605–7', *Recusant History*, xx (1991), pp 320–35.
74. *Cal. S.P. Ire., 1603–6*, p. 503.
75. Ibid., p. 534. Tyrone was noted for resorting to bribery, and it is highly likely that he had bargained for something in exchange for his act of generosity. Tyrone's reputation for using bribery has been well documented: numerous instances are detailed in Morgan, *Tyrone's Rebellion*.
76. Canny, 'Flight of the Earls', p. 388. As a reminder of his Irish service, Mountjoy had kept at his home in Wanstead for amusement an Irishman in 'fool's apparel' who was known as 'His Lordship's fool' (Jones, *Mountjoy*, p. 179).
77. McCavitt, *Chichester*, pp 25, 106.
78. *Cal. S.P. Ire., 1603–6*, pp 568–9.
79. *Cal. S.P. Ire., 1601–3*, pp 555–7.
80. McCavitt, *Chichester*, pp 24–5.
81. Moryson, *Itinerary*, iii, 337.
82. *Cal. S.P. Ire., 1603–6*, p. 549.
83. Ibid., pp 548–9.
84. Sir John Davies, *Historical Tracts* (London, 1786), p. 227.
85. Ibid.
86. Ibid., p. 239.

87. Ibid., p. 235.
88. See Chapter 4.
89. Robert Wyse Jackson, *Archbishop Magrath: the scoundrel of Cashel* (Dublin, 1974), p. 72.
90. *Cal. S.P. Ire., 1603–6*, pp 558–62.
91. Ibid., pp 566–7.
92. Falls, *Birth of Ulster*, p. 183.
93. *Cal. S.P. Ire., 1603–6*, pp 463–77; Falls, *Birth of Ulster*, p. 183.
94. Wyse Jackson, *Archbishop Magrath*, p. 69.
95. Falls, *Birth of Ulster*, p. 183.
96. *Cal. S.P. Ire., 1606–8*, pp 364–74.
97. Ibid., pp 92–5.
98. McCavitt, 'Flight of the Earls', p. 160.
99. Nicholas Canny has suggested that such financial concerns were crucial in precipitating the Flight of the Earls in 1607: see Canny, 'Flight of the Earls', pp 380–99.
100. *Cal. S.P. Ire., 1603–6*, pp 562–6.
101. Ibid.
102. *Cal. S.P. Ire., 1606–8*, pp 374–83.
103. *Cal. S.P. Ire., 1603–6*, pp 569–71.
104. *Cal. S.P. Ire., 1606–8*, pp 364–74.
105. *Cal. S.P. Ire., 1603–6*, pp 570–1; *Cal. S.P. Ire., 1606–8*, p. 26.
106. *Cal. S.P. Ire., 1606–8*, pp 487, 490.
107. Meehan, *Fate and Fortunes*, p. 46; Kew (ed.), 'Moryson's Unpublished Itinerary', p. 62.
108. Davies, *Historical Tracts*, p. 253.
109. Kew (ed.), 'Moryson's Unpublished Itinerary', p. 59.
110. Davies, *Historical Tracts*, pp 253–4.
111. Ibid., p. 269.
112. Quoted in Meehan, *Fate and Fortunes*, pp 130–9. This version of Tyrconnell's grievances contains some details not included in the published *Calendar of State Papers* version (see *Cal. S.P. Ire., 1606–8*, pp 364–74). Official records show that one Richard Ellis, described as a fisherman from Dublin, received a 'general pardon' in 1606 (*Cal. Pat. Rolls Ire., Jas I*, p. 87). By 1606 a substantial number of officers and soldiers had been demobilised in Ireland, so it is possible, though by no means certain, that the Richard Ellis referred to in the pardon was the same person that the Earl of Tyrconnell had accused of rape.
113. *Cal. S.P. Ire., 1606–8*, pp 53–5.
114. Quoted in W[illiam] McD[onald] (ed.), 'Irish Ecclesiastical Colleges since the Reformation', *Irish Ecclesiastical Record*, 1st ser., x (1874), p. 181.
115. Quoted ibid., p. 459.
116. Ibid.
117. *Cal. S.P. Ire., 1606–8*, pp 374–83.
118. Margaret MacCurtain, 'The Flight of the Earls' in Liam de Paor (ed.), *Milestones in Irish History* (Dublin, 1986), p. 57.
119. Kerney Walsh, *Destruction by Peace*, document 43a.
120. O'Faolain, *The Great O'Neill*, pp 272–3.
121. McCavitt, 'Flight of the Earls', p. 160.
122. H.M.C., *Salisbury*, xviii, 254–6.
123. *Cal. S.P. Ire., 1606–8*, pp 14–21.
124. Ibid.

125. Ibid., pp 374–83.
126. Pawlisch, *Davies*, p. 31; Davies, *Poems*, ed. Krueger, p. xxxiv.
127. Quoted in Davies, *Poems*, ed. Krueger, p. xxxiii.
128. George Carleton, *A Thankful Remembrance of God's Mercy* (London, 1624), p. 232.
129. *Cal. S.P. Ire., 1606–8*, pp 155–7.
130. Ibid., pp 215–18.
131. Ibid., pp 155–7.
132. McCavitt, *Chichester*, pp 83–4.
133. Davies, *Historical Tracts*, p. 241.
134. Carleton, *A Thankful Remembrance of God's Mercy*, p. 232.
135. Docwra, 'Narration', p. 277.

Chapter 4: The 'passion' of Tyrone (pp 73–91)

1. Meehan described O'Cahan as Tyrone's 'Iscariot' (see Meehan, *Fate and Fortunes*, p. 14).
2. Pawlisch, *Davies*.
3. H.M.C., *Salisbury*, xviii, 254–6.
4. Cecil was created Earl of Salisbury in 1605 (see Kerney Walsh, *Destruction by Peace*, p. 32).
5. James I nicknamed Cecil his 'little beagle' (ibid.).
6. *Cal. S.P. Ire., 1603–6*, pp 548–9.
7. W. C. Trevelyan and C. E. Trevelyan (eds), *Trevelyan Papers*, Camden Society, 2nd ser., vol. iii (London, 1872), pp 95–6.
8. *Cal. S.P. Ire., 1606–8*, pp 14–21.
9. Ibid., p. 27.
10. Ibid., pp 89–90.
11. Ibid., pp 92–5. Tyrone's rendition of events lends considerable credence to his wife's contention that Tyrconnell and Maguire were 'altogether' dependent on 'his council'. See Chapter 3.
12. Ibid., pp 90–1.
13. McCavitt, *Chichester*, pp 122–3.
14. *Cal. S.P. Ire., 1606–8*, p. 107.
15. P.R.O., AO1/289/1085.
16. *Cal. S.P. Ire., 1606–8*, pp 108–9.
17. Ibid., pp 151–2. See also Chapter 3.
18. *Cal. S.P. Ire., 1606–8*, pp 92–5.
19. See Chapter 1.
20. *Cal. S.P. Ire., 1603–6*, pp 576–7.
21. Ibid., p. 519.
22. *Cal. S.P. Ire., 1606–8*, pp 92–5.
23. *Cal. S.P. Ire., 1603–6*, pp 365–6.
24. Ibid., p. 519; Meehan, *Fate and Fortunes*, pp 67–71.
25. Antonia Fraser, *The Gunpowder Plot: terror and faith in 1605* (London, 1996).
26. McCavitt, *Chichester*, pp 122–3.
27. Quoted in McD[onald] (ed.), 'Irish Ecclesiastical Colleges', p. 519.
28. Quoted ibid., pp 519–20.
29. Henry Fitzsimon, *Words of Comfort … letters from a cell … and diary of the Bohemia war of 1620*, ed. Edmund Hogan (Dublin, 1881), pp 64–6.
30. *Cal. S.P. Ire., 1608–10*, pp 269–70.
31. McCavitt, *Chichester*, pp 121–4.

32. McD[onald] (ed.), 'Irish Ecclesiastical Colleges', p. 210.
33. Ibid., p. 522.
34. *Cal. S.P. Ire., 1606–8*, p. 26.
35. Quoted in McD[onald] (ed.), 'Irish Ecclesiastical Colleges', p. 522.
36. *Cal. S.P. Ire., 1606–8*, pp 101–2.
37. Moran, *Archbishops of Dublin*, p. 235.
38. *Cal. S.P. Ire., 1606–8*, p. 188.
39. McCavitt, *Chichester*, p. 120.
40. David Edwards, 'The Butler Revolt of 1569', *I.H.S.*, xxviii (1993), p. 247.
41. *Cal. S.P. Ire., 1606–8*, pp 124–5.
42. Ibid., pp 129–31, 137–8.
43. Meehan, *Fate and Fortunes*, p. 10.
44. Kew (ed.), 'Moryson's Unpublished Itinerary', p. 101.
45. *Cal. S.P. Ire., 1606–8*, pp 125–7.
46. Ibid.
47. Ibid.
48. Ibid., pp 143–4.
49. Ibid., pp 200–1.
50. Ibid., pp 374–83.
51. Ibid., pp 199–200; *Cal. Carew MSS, 1603–23*, p. 384. Bishop Montgomery suspected that an attempt had been made to kidnap O'Cahan on his way to the council meeting in Dublin. The bishop recorded an incident near Dungannon when a party of armed men attempted to seize O'Cahan, who was travelling with the bishop's military escort: 'Tyrone's son came forth with sixteen horsemen, but finding the bishop well appointed and guarded with men, told him that he came forth only to attend his lordship some part of the way' (Carleton, *A Thankful Remembrance of God's Mercy*, p. 233).
52. *Cal. S.P. Ire., 1606–8*, p. 151.
53. H.M.C., *Salisbury*, xix, 146.
54. Ibid., pp 156–7.
55. P.R.O., SP 63/221/57.
56. Ibid.
57. Ibid.
58. *Cal. S.P. Ire., 1606–8*, pp 152–3. After Chichester's campaign of ruthless persecution in Drogheda during the early months of 1607 it is not unimaginable that a desperado, a religiously inspired fanatic, had volunteered to assassinate him.
59. Meehan, *Fate and Fortunes*, pp 65–6.
60. *Cal. S.P. Ire., 1603–6*, pp 490–3, 531–3, 580–3.
61. P.R.O., SP 63/221/57.
62. Ibid.
63. *Cal. S.P. Ire., 1606–8*, pp 209–13.
64. H.M.C., *Salisbury*, xix, 150–1.
65. *Cal. S.P. Ire., 1606–8*, p. 194.
66. Ibid., pp 199–200.
67. P.R.O., 31/8/201, ff 242–7.
68. McCavitt, *Chichester*, p. 136.
69. P.R.O., 31/8/199, ff 236–9.
70. Ibid.
71. *Cal. S.P. Ire., 1606–8*, pp 302–3.

72. H.M.C., *Salisbury*, xix, 315–17; *Cal. S.P. Ire., 1606–8*, pp 356–7.

73. *Cal. S.P. Ire., 1606–8*, pp 227–30.

74. Meehan, *Fate and Fortunes*, pp 71, 147.

75. *Cal. S.P. Ire., 1606–8*, pp 227–30.

76. H.M.C., *Salisbury*, xix, 63, 500–1.

77. Ibid., pp 500–1.

78. Ibid., p. 63.

79. H.M.C., *Downshire*, ii, 25–7; *Cal. S.P. Ire., 1606–8*, p. 147.

80. *Cal. S.P. Ire., 1606–8*, pp 203–4.

81. Kew (ed.), 'Moryson's Unpublished Itinerary', p. 43; McCavitt, *Chichester*, ch. 5.

82. *Cal. S.P. Ire., 1606–8*, pp 226–7. Chichester did not normally doubt his ability to cope alone with such a crisis. A contemporary noted that he was more inclined to 'grip all things in his own fist, to heap all things into his own bosom, to swallow all things down his own throat, having that confidence in himself that the River Jordan might flow into his mouth' (N.L.I., MS 6453, f. 51).

83. *Cal. S.P. Ire., 1606–8*, pp. 231–2.

84. Ibid., pp 264–6.

85. P.R.O., 31/8/199, f. 240.

86. This argument was most recently advanced in Kerney Walsh, *Destruction by Peace*, p. 50.

87. P.R.O., 31/8/199, ff 236–9.

88. *Cal. S.P. Ire., 1606–8*, pp 192–3, 244–8.

89. H.M.C., *Salisbury*, xix, 207.

90. *Cal. S.P. Ire., 1606–8*, pp 259–62.

91. Meehan, *Fate and Fortunes*, pp 150–1; *A.F.M.*, vi, 2381.

92. See Chapter 6.

93. McCavitt, 'Flight of the Earls', p. 171.

94. Kerney Walsh, *Destruction by Peace*, documents 12, 22a, 30. The Earl of Tyrconnell made the initial overtures for financial assistance to the Spanish ambassador in London in December 1604. Initially the Spanish were guarded in their response, fearing that Tyrconnell (married to a grandchild of the English Lord High Admiral: see p. 94 below) was being 'used as an instrument to penetrate the [Spanish] royal intentions' (ibid., documents 11, 12). The earls were eventually granted 4,000 ducats p.a. each.

95. Meehan, *Fate and Fortunes*, pp 247–9; Kerney Walsh, *Destruction by Peace*, pp 52–3. The earls fled to the continent at a time when their material well-being had improved considerably. In addition to the Spanish pension which they were on the verge of receiving, it was noted by several observers that the north had begun to 'grow rich again', with plentiful supplies of corn and cattle and other goods. See *Cal. S.P. Ire., 1606–8*, pp 274–5, 280–1.

96. Kerney Walsh, *Destruction by Peace*, document 36. Sir Christopher St Lawrence was aware that the Spanish were furnishing the Earl of Tyrconnell with money, reckoning the sum to be in the region of £5,000 or £6,000. It is possible that he had obtained this information from Henry O'Neill, his 'intimate' friend. (See Meehan, *Fate and Fortunes*, pp 67–71.)

97. The original version of the letter, dated 8 September 1607, makes it clear that it was Howth who put the 'buzzes' in Tyrone's head rather than the Baron of Delvin (P.R.O., SP 63/222/128; *Cal. S.P. Ire., 1606–8*, pp 264–6.

98. *Cal. S.P. Ire., 1606–8*, pp 275–7.

99. Ibid., pp 270–4.

100. Ibid., pp 374–83.
101. Ibid., pp 259–62, 374–83.
102. Ibid., pp 270–4.
103. Ibid.
104. P.R.O., SP 63/222/128.
105. *Cal. S.P. Ire., 1606–8*, pp 374–83.

Chapter 5: On a wing and a prayer (pp 92–112)
1. *Cal. S.P. Ire., 1606–8*, pp 374–83.
2. Hiram Morgan, 'Extradition and Treason-Trial of a Gaelic Lord: the case of Brian O'Rourke', *Irish Jurist*, new ser., xxii (1987), pp 285–301.
3. *Cal. S.P. Ire., 1606–8*, pp 266–8.
4. P.R.O., SP 14/28/65.
5. Davies, *Discovery*, p. 271.
6. Tadhg Ó Cianáin, *The Flight of the Earls*, ed. Paul Walsh (Dublin, 1916), p. 17.
7. *Cal. S.P. Ire., 1606–8*, pp 301–2, 297–300, 314–15.
8. Ibid., pp 301–2; Ó Cianáin, *Flight of the Earls*, p. 3 n. 5.
9. *Cal. S.P. Ire., 1606–8*, pp 270–4.
10. Ibid., pp 297–300.
11. Ibid., p. 322.
12. Meehan, *Fate and Fortunes*, pp 150–1; George Hill, *An Historical Account of the MacDonnells of Antrim* (Belfast, 1873), p. 213.
13. *Cal. S.P. Ire., 1606–8*, pp 259–62; Meehan, *Fate and Fortunes*, pp 67–71. Hugh O'Donnell had yet to reach his first birthday (see Kerney Walsh, *Destruction by Peace*, p. 57).
14. See Chapter 6.
15. *Cal. S.P. Ire., 1606–8*, pp 305–6.
16. Quoted in Meehan, *Fate and Fortunes*, p. 156. After Tyrconnell's death Brigid married Viscount Kingsland (ibid., pp 156–7).
17. Brendan Jennings (ed.), *Wild Geese in Spanish Flanders, 1582–1700* (Dublin, 1964), pp 100–1.
18. *Cal. S.P. Ire., 1606–8*, p. 649.
19. Kerney Walsh, *Destruction by Peace*, pp 29–30.
20. *Cal. S.P. Ire., 1608–10*, p. 117. For evidence of payment of the pension see B.L., Lansdowne MS 164, ff 35–7.
21. *Cal. S.P. Ire., 1606–8*, pp 264–6.
22. Ibid., pp 259–62.
23. F. W. Harris, 'The State of the Realm: English military, political and diplomatic responses to the Flight of the Earls, autumn 1607 to spring 1608', *Irish Sword*, liv (1980), p. 60.
24. *Cal. S.P. Ire., 1608–10*, pp 169–71.
25. *Cal. S.P. Ire., 1606–8*, pp 270–4.
26. Harris, 'State of the Realm', p. 60.
27. *Cal. S.P. Ire., 1606–8*, pp 270–4.
28. Ibid., pp 259–62; *Cal. S.P. Ire., 1615–25*, pp 38–9.
29. *Cal. S.P. Ire., 1606–8*, pp 259–62.
30. Harris, 'State of the Realm', p. 60.
31. *Cal. S.P. Ire., 1606–8*, p. 270–4.
32. Ibid.

33. Ibid.; Ó Cianáin, *Flight of the Earls*, p. 9; Harris, 'State of the Realm', p. 60.
34. *Cal. S.P. Ire., 1606–8*, pp 297–300.
35. Ibid., pp 270–4.
36. Ó Cianáin, *Flight of the Earls*, p. 9. Cúchonnacht Ó Cianáin, a brother of Tadhg, was to be implicated in the 1615 Ulster Conspiracy (see Raymond Gillespie, *Conspiracy: Ulster plots and plotters in 1615* (Belfast, 1987), p. 9).
37. *Cal. S.P. Ire., 1606–8*, pp 555–6.
38. Ibid., pp 364–74.
39. Ibid., pp 259–62.
40. Ibid., pp 259–62, 278.
41. Ó Cianáin, *Flight of the Earls*, p. 11.
42. Ibid., pp 11–13; Kerney Walsh, *Destruction by Peace*, document 40.
43. Ó Cianáin, *Flight of the Earls*, pp 11–15.
44. Ibid., pp 16–19.
45. Meehan, *Fate and Fortunes*, p. 182.
46. Canice Mooney, 'A Noble Shipload', *Irish Sword*, ii (1954–6), pp 195–204. For an English translation of this list see Kerney Walsh, *Destruction by Peace*, document 40a.
47. *Cal. S.P. Ire., 1606–8*, pp 259–62, 270–4.
48. Ibid., pp 435–6. A report in the Spanish records indicated that the earls brought with them twenty gentlemen and twelve servants (Jennings (ed.), *Wild Geese*, pp 483–4). One Owny ny Shyle who had accompanied the Countess of Tyrone was granted permission to return to Ireland in 1614 (ibid., p. 555).
49. *Cal. S.P. Ire., 1606–8*, pp 301–2. The English ambassador in Brussels estimated that the earls' party travelling to the archduke's court in October 1607 comprised about sixty people in total (see ibid., pp 627–8). It would not be unreasonable to suggest that some of the marines from the earls' ship provided a form of military escort from France to Flanders.
50. *A.F.M.*, vi, 2359.
51. Ó Cianáin, *Flight of the Earls*, p. 19.
52. Ibid., pp 19–21.
53. Ibid., pp 21–3.
54. Ibid., pp 22–5n; Meehan, *Fate and Fortunes*, p. 81; Kerney Walsh, *Destruction by Peace*, p. 62.
55. Ó Cianáin, *Flight of the Earls*, p. 25.
56. Ibid.
57. *Cal. S.P. Ire., 1606–8*, pp 624–5.
58. Ó Cianáin, *Flight of the Earls*, p. 25.
59. Penry Williams, *The Later Tudors: England 1547–1603* (London, 1995), pp 347–8.
60. Quoted in Meehan, *Fate and Fortunes*, p. 81n.
61. McCavitt, *Chichester*, p. 7.
62. *Cal. S.P. Venice, 1607–10*, pp 52–3.
63. Ibid., p. 42.
64. Ibid., pp 46, 70–1.
65. *Cal. S.P. Ire., 1606–8*, pp 285–6. Likening the earls to 'so many fleas', Cornwallis duly did his best to blacken their name, placing great weight, for instance, on the allegation that the Earl of Tyrone had been guilty of multiple homicide (see Sir Ralph Winwood, *Memorials of Affairs of State in the reigns of Q. Elizabeth and James I*, ed. Edward Sawyer (3 vols, London, 1725, ii, 386–8).

66. *Cal. S.P. Venice, 1607–10*, p. 42.
67. Quoted in Conrad Russell, *The Crisis of Parliaments: English history, 1509–1660* (Oxford, 1971), p. 258.
68. Kerney Walsh, *Destruction by Peace*, document 39.
69. *Cal. S.P. Ire., 1606–8*, pp 646–8.
70. Jennings (ed.), *Wild Geese*, pp 109–11.
71. *Cal. S.P. Ire., 1606–8*, pp 632–3.
72. Ibid., pp 633–5. James Bath was a brother of Captain John Bath (see p. 90 above).
73. Ibid., p. 635.
74. Ibid., p. 641.
75. Ibid., p. 669.
76. Kerney Walsh, *Destruction by Peace*, document 42.
77. At the end of the Nine Years War Mountjoy had been keen to prevent Tyrone escaping abroad, fearing that he would 'become a pawn in the hands of the Spanish' (see Canny, 'Treaty of Mellifont', p. 252).
78. Kerney Walsh, *Destruction by Peace*, document 42.
79. Ó Cianáin, *Flight of the Earls*, pp 31–3.
80. Ibid., pp 37–49.
81. *Cal. S.P. Ire., 1606–8*, pp 631–2; Jennings (ed.), *Wild Geese*, p. 101.
82. Ó Cianáin, *Flight of the Earls*, pp 55–7.
83. The King of France was perhaps unwilling to offend English sensibilities twice in such a short period of time, having 'forbidden their journey through his lands' to Spain (see Kerney Walsh, *Destruction by Peace*, document 46).
84. Ibid., document 43.
85. Ó Cianáin, *Flight of the Earls*, p. 59.
86. Kerney Walsh, *Destruction by Peace*, document 45. Spinola gave the earls 5,000 crowns each on their arrival in Flanders, while 2,000 crowns was given to the Countess of Tyrone and other relatives (Jennings (ed.), *Wild Geese*, pp 483–4).
87. Kerney Walsh, *Destruction by Peace*, document 58.
88. Ibid., document 43a.
89. Ibid., document 49.
90. Ibid., document 52.
91. Ibid., document 44.
92. Ibid., document 55. The English ambassador to Spain characterised the expatriate Irish as 'good scarecrows for England' (Winwood, *Memorials of Affairs of State*, iii, 66–9).
93. Ó Cianáin, *Flight of the Earls*, p. 59.
94. *Cal. S.P. Ire., 1606–8*, p. 642.
95. Ó Cianáin, *Flight of the Earls*, p. 65.
96. *Cal. S.P. Ire., 1606–8*, pp 648–50.
97. Ibid., pp 652–3.
98. Ó Cianáin, *Flight of the Earls*, p. 73; Kerney Walsh, *Destruction by Peace*, documents 56, 59.
99. The English Privy Council agreed that they had embarked on a 'pilgrimage', though they considered that their hosts in Flanders were glad to see the back of them, 'having left so good a memory of their barbarous life and drunkenness where they were' (*Cal. S.P. Ire., 1606–8*, pp 434–5).
100. Ó Cianáin, *Flight of the Earls*, pp 73–89.
101. Ibid., pp 78–9.

102. Jennings (ed.), *Wild Geese*, p. 544. James I was to be so incensed by the reception afforded the earls by the Duke of Lorraine that when the duke died shortly afterwards, he refused to send a representative to the funeral. The French ambassador in London recorded the response of the King of England to the death of the Duke of Lorraine: 'The king said he would have more regret for the loss of that old man and would send messages of condolence to his children, had he not, before dying, caused him such grave displeasure by receiving the earl and the manner in which he did so. In fact he is sending no one.' (Quoted in Micheline Kerney Walsh, *An Exile of Ireland: Hugh O'Neill, Prince of Ulster* (Dublin, 1996), p. 75. I am grateful to Dr Mary Ann Lyons for this reference.)

103. Ó Cianáin, *Flight of the Earls*, p. 83.

104. Ibid., p. 85.

105. Ibid., pp 87–9.

106. Ibid., p. 95.

107. *Cal. S.P. Ire., 1606–8*, pp 397–9.

108. Ibid., p. 651.

109. Kerney Walsh, *Destruction by Peace*, documents 42, 48, 50.

110. Ibid., document 50.

111. Ibid., document 56.

112. Ó Cianáin, *Flight of the Earls*, p. 95.

113. *Cal. S.P. Ire., 1606–8*, p. 651.

114. Ó Cianáin, *Flight of the Earls*, p. 99.

115. Ibid., p. 101.

116. *Cal. S.P. Ire., 1606–8*, pp 657–9.

117. Kerney Walsh, *Destruction by Peace*, document 58.

118. *Cal. S.P. Ire., 1606–8*, p. 649.

119. Jennings (ed.), *Wild Geese*, p. 546.

120. Kerney Walsh, *Destruction by Peace*, document 63. It is worth drawing the tentative conclusion that the annual sum received by Tyrconnell from the Spanish government would have been 400 ducats greater if he had remained in Ireland.

121. Ibid., document 56.

122. *Cal. S.P. Ire., 1606–8*, pp 653–4.

123. An English observer noted how Tyrone had previously slowed down his progress in the Spanish Netherlands to a snail's pace to 'put himself and his company in some good order' before reaching his final destination (see ibid., pp 627–8).

124. Ó Cianáin, *Flight of the Earls*, pp 169–71. Wotton, the English ambassador in Venice, reported that eight coaches were sent (*Cal. S.P. Ire., 1606–8*, p. 654).

125. *Cal. S.P. Ire., 1606–8*, p. 654.

126. Ibid., p. 655.

127. Ó Cianáin, *Flight of the Earls*, pp 171–3.

128. Ibid., p. 175.

129. Ibid.

130. *Cal. S.P. Ire., 1606–8*, pp 655–6.

131. Ó Cianáin, *Flight of the Earls*, p. 189.

132. Ibid.

133. *Cal. S.P. Ire., 1606–8*, pp 655–6.

134. Ó Cianáin, *Flight of the Earls*, pp 189–91.

135. Ibid., pp 193–201.

136. *Cal. S.P. Ire., 1606–8*, p. 662.

137. Ibid., pp 664–5.
138. Kerney Walsh, *Destruction by Peace*, pp 88–9.
139. *A.F.M.*, vi, 2367.
140. Ó Cianáin, *Flight of the Earls*, pp 239–41.
141. *A.F.M.*, vi, 2365–7.
142. *Cal. S.P. Ire., 1606–8*, pp 468–71.
143. Ó Cianáin, *Flight of the Earls*, p. 243.

Chapter 6: Robin Hood and his not-so-merry men (pp 113–134)

1. *Cal. S.P. Ire., 1606–8*, p. 263.
2. P.R.O., SP 63/222/128.
3. *Cal. S.P. Ire., 1606–8*, p. 269.
4. Ibid., pp 345–6, 534–7.
5. Meehan, *Fate and Fortunes*, p. 150.
6. *Cal. S.P. Ire., 1606–8*, pp 295–7, 649.
7. P.R.O., 31/8/199, ff 245–7.
8. Howth's split personality may perhaps be explained in part by his disillusionment with problems caused by his Anglo-Irish identity. At the time of the Essex plot in England he bemoaned: 'I am sorry that when I am in England I should be esteemed to be an Irishman, and in Ireland an Englishman' (quoted in McGurk, *Elizabethan Conquest*, p. 47).
9. *Cal. S.P. Ire., 1606–8*, pp 356–7.
10. Ibid., pp 320–1. Delvin, while admitting complicity in treason, did not seek to ingratiate himself with his captors by incriminating others.
11. Ibid., pp 347–8.
12. Ibid., pp 348–50.
13. Meehan, *Fate and Fortunes*, pp 145–9.
14. *Cal. S.P. Ire., 1606–8*, pp 333–4, 405–9.
15. Ibid., pp 333–4, 418–19.
16. Ibid., pp 335–6.
17. Ibid., pp 414–16.
18. *Cal. S.P. Ire., 1608–10*, pp 384–7.
19. Meehan, *Fate and Fortunes*, p. 184.
20. Docwra, 'Narration', p. 262.
21. Meehan, *Fate and Fortunes*, p. 183.
22. McCavitt, *Chichester*, pp 141–2. In his own account of his visit to Burt, Paulet confirmed that he intended to have 'surprised' the castle but for the fact that he found it well manned (*Cal. S.P. Ire., 1606–8*, pp 316–17). Some years later a government agent confirmed that O'Doherty had secured a 'safe-conduct' for his journey to Dublin from Sir Richard Hansard, governor of Lifford (*Cal. S.P. Ire., 1615–25*, pp 179–81).
23. *Cal. S.P. Ire., 1606–8*, p. 288.
24. Ibid., p. 360.
25. Ibid., pp 405–9.
26. *Cal. S.P. Dom., 1603–10*, p. 358. The enlistment of vagrants and criminals was a common practice during the Nine Years War (see McGurk, 'Dead, Sick and Wounded of the Nine Years War', p. 17).
27. Bagwell, *Stuarts*, i, 51.
28. *Cal. S.P. Ire., 1606–8*, pp 111–13.
29. Bagwell, *Stuarts*, i, 51.

30. P.R.O., SP 63/222/184.
31. P.R.O., SP 63/222/175; *Cal. S.P. Ire., 1606–8*, pp 336–7.
32. McCavitt, *Chichester*, p. 143; B.L., Add. MS 19838, f. 159.
33. *Cal. S.P. Ire., 1606–8*, pp 389–93.
34. McCavitt, *Chichester*, p. 143.
35. *Cal. S.P. Ire., 1606–8*, pp 336–7.
36. *Cal. S.P. Ire., 1601–3*, p. 414.
37. *Cal. S.P. Ire., 1606–8*, pp 418–19.
38. Ibid., pp 389–93.
39. Ibid., pp 336–7. For his 'extraordinary pains' in discovering the 'plots and bad pur-
    poses' of O'Cahan and for travelling to Dublin to pursue his allegations, Bishop
    Montgomery was given £100 reward (P.R.O., AO1/290/1088, f. 50).
40. *Cal. S.P. Ire., 1606–8*, pp 558–60.
41. Ibid.
42. Ibid., pp 405–9.
43. Ibid., pp 418–19.
44. Winwood, *Memorials of Affairs of State*, ii, 390–2.
45. Kerney Walsh, *Destruction by Peace*, document 67; McCavitt, *Chichester*, p. 41.
46. McCavitt, *Chichester*, p. 42.
47. E. R. Foster, (ed.), *Proceedings in Parliament, 1610*, vol. i: *House of Lords* (New Haven,
    1986), pp 3–8.
48. McCavitt, *Chichester*, p. 33.
49. S. R. Gardiner, *History of England from the accession of James I to the outbreak of the Civil War,
    1603–1642* (new ed., 10 vols, London, 1883–4), ii, 112.
50. *Cal. S.P. Venice, 1607–10*, p. 71.
51. *Cal. S.P. Ire., 1606–8*, pp 347–8.
52. Ibid., pp 334–5; McCavitt, *Chichester*, p. 81.
53. *Cal. S.P. Ire., 1606–8*, pp 336–7.
54. Ibid., pp 337–8.
55. Ibid., pp 534–7.
56. Ibid., p. 338.
57. Ibid., pp 352–4.
58. Ibid., pp 348–50.
59. Ibid., p. 360.
60. Ibid., pp 348–50.
61. Ibid., pp 352–4.
62. Ibid., pp 354–5.
63. Ibid., pp 350–1.
64. Kew (ed.), 'Moryson's Unpublished Itinerary', p. 57.
65. *Cal. S.P. Ire., 1606–8*, pp 244–8.
66. Ibid. Chichester's fears were far from groundless. An illegitimate son of Brian MacArt
    set out with sixty followers in a vain attempt to rescue his father from Dublin Castle
    (see Harris, 'State of the Realm', p. 58).
67. *Cal. S.P. Ire., 1606–8*, pp 244–8.
68. Ibid., pp 354–5.
69. P.R.O., SP 63/223/68.
70. *Cal. S.P. Ire., 1606–8*, pp 259–62.
71. Ibid., pp 270–4.

72. Ibid., pp 314–15.
73. Ibid., pp 356–7. A merchant spirited Sir Cormac's son John out of Ireland (see Jennings (ed.), *Wild Geese*, p. 485).
74. Harris, 'State of the Realm', p. 53.
75. McCavitt, *Chichester*, p. 140.
76. *Cal. S.P. Venice, 1607–10*, pp 109–10.
77. Ibid., pp 92–3.
78. Ibid., pp 96–7.
79. Ibid., pp 131–2.
80. *Cal. S.P. Ire., 1606–8*, pp 405–9.
81. Ibid., pp 507–8.
82. Ibid., pp 499–502.
83. *Cal. S.P. Ire., 1608–10*, pp 141–5.
84. Marc Caball, 'Providence and Exile in Early Seventeenth-Century Ireland', *I.H.S.*, xxix (1994), p. 181.
85. *Cal. S.P. Ire., 1606–8*, p. 642.
86. Ibid., pp 639–41.
87. Gráinne Henry, *The Irish Military Community in Spanish Flanders, 1586–1621* (Dublin, 1992), p. 143.
88. *Cal. S.P. Ire., 1606–8*, p. 643.
89. Ibid., pp 641–2; Ó Cianáin, *Flight of the Earls*, p. 55.
90. *Cal. S.P. Ire., 1606–8*, pp 414–16.
91. Ibid., pp 646–8.
92. Ibid., pp 414–16.
93. Roger Lockyer, *The Early Stuarts: a political history of England, 1603–42* (London, 1989), p. 14.
94. See Kerney Walsh, *Destruction by Peace, passim*.
95. *Cal. S.P. Ire., 1606–8*, p. 648.
96. Ibid., p. 650.
97. *Cal. S.P. Venice, 1607–10*, p. 115.
98. *Cal. S.P. Ire., 1606–8*, pp 414–16.
99. Ibid., pp 476–7.
100. Ibid., pp 264–6.
101. Ibid., p. 553.
102. Ibid., pp 520–1.
103. Delvin had become thoroughly disillusioned with the politics of conspiracy. He was to die in 1642 'having been roughly handled by the insurgents of the period' (see Meehan, *Fate and Fortunes*, p. 146n.).
104. P.R.O , SP 63/224/107.
105. *Cal. S P. Ire., 1606–8*, p. 551.
106. Ibid., pp 520–1.
107. *Cal. S.P. Ire., 1608–10*, pp 113–14.
108. Ibid.
109. Ibid., p. 25.
110. McCavitt, *Chichester*, p. 82.
111. As late as 1612 Howth was to complain that Moore was hounding him (see *Cal. S.P. Ire., 1611–14*, pp 290–1).
112. McCavitt, *Chichester*, p. 86.

113. *Cal. S.P. Ire., 1606–8*, pp 458–61.
114. Ibid., pp 461–4.
115. Ibid.
116. Ibid., pp 534–7
117. Ibid., pp 458–61.
118. Ibid., pp 534–7; P.R.O., SP 63/224/97.
119. Ibid., pp 461–4.
120. Ibid., pp 458–61.
121. P.R.O., SP 63/223/68.
122. *Cal. S.P. Ire., 1606–8*, pp 270–4.
123. O'Faolain, *The Great O'Neill*, pp 272–3.
124. *Cal. S.P. Ire., 1608–10*, pp 81–3.
125. Ibid., p. 115.
126. Kerney Walsh, *Destruction by Peace*, document 56b.
127. Ibid., p. 45.
128. P.R.O., SP 63/224/97.
129. *Cal. S.P. Ire., 1606–8*, pp 461–4.
130. *Cal. S.P. Ire., 1608–10*, pp 81–3. Two military officials received special payments to cover the costs of spies and messengers at this time (see P.R.O., AO1/290/1088).
131. *Cal. S.P. Ire., 1606–8*, pp 259–62, 270–4.
132. Ibid., pp 259–62.

Chapter 7: Rebellion (pp 135–153)

1. *Cal. S.P. Ire., 1606–8*, pp 389–93.
2. Ibid., pp 488–9.
3. P.R.O., SP 63/223/79.
4. *Cal. S.P. Ire., 1606–8*, p. 414.
5. Jane H. Ohlmeyer, *Civil War and Restoration in the Three Stuart Kingdoms: the career of Randal MacDonnell, Marquis of Antrim, 1609–1683* (Cambridge, 1993), p. 21.
6. T. M. Healy, *Stolen Waters: a page in the conquest of Ulster* (London, 1913), p. 124.
7. See A. P. B. Chichester, *History of the Family of Chichester* (London, 1871), p. 53.
8. *Cal. S.P. Ire., 1606–8*, pp 475–6.
9. Ibid., pp 480–3.
10. Ibid., pp 499–502.
11. *A.F.M.*, vi, 2359–61.
12. *Cal. S.P. Ire., 1606–8*, pp 530–4.
13. Seán Ó Domhnaill, 'Sir Niall Garbh O'Donnell and the Rebellion of Sir Cahir O'Doherty', *I.H.S.*, iii (1942), pp 34–8.
14. *Cal. S.P. Ire., 1606–8*, pp 503–5.
15. P.R.O., A01/289/1087; McCavitt, *Chichester*, p. 99.
16. *Cal. S.P. Ire., 1606–8*, pp 485–7. A fledgling network of biannual assize circuits dispensing English-style justice for the first time ever in many parts of the country, particularly Ulster, began to be implemented shortly after the end of the Nine Years War (see John McCavitt, '"Good Planets in Their Several Spheares": the establishment of assize circuits in early seventeenth-century Ireland', *Irish Jurist*, new ser., xxiv (1989), pp 248–78).
17. *Cal. S.P. Ire., 1606–8*, pp 485–7.
18. Docwra, 'Narration', p. 261.

19. *Cal. S.P. Ire., 1606–8*, pp 494–6, 503–5.
20. Ibid., pp 480–3.
21. Ibid., pp 499–502.
22. P.R.O., SP 63/224/93.
23. *Cal. S.P. Ire., 1606–8*, pp 494–6.
24. Ibid., pp 503–5.
25. Ibid., pp 494–6.
26. Ibid., pp 494–6, 599–605.
27. Ibid., pp 505–7; Brian Bonner, *That Audacious Traitor* (Dublin, 1975), p. 160.
28. Bagwell, *Stuarts*, i, 54.
29. *Cal. S.P. Ire., 1606–8*, pp 480–3.
30. Ibid., pp 434–5.
31. Ibid., pp 448–53.
32. Ibid., pp 480–3.
33. Ibid., pp 528–9.
34. Ibid., pp 499–502.
35. Ibid.
36. Ibid., pp 505–7. According to the Four Masters, Paulet was killed by Owen O'Doherty (*A.F.M.*, vi, 2363).
37. *Cal. S.P. Ire., 1606–8*, pp 494–6.
38. P.R.O., SP 63/224/93.
39. Bagwell, *Stuarts*, i, 55.
40. Bonner, *That Audacious Traitor*, p. 161.
41. *Cal. S.P. Ire., 1606–8*, pp 494–6.
42. Ibid., pp 524–7.
43. *Cal. S.P. Ire., 1608–10*, pp 2–3.
44. *Cal. S.P. Ire., 1606–8*, pp 524–7, 541–5.
45. *Cal. S.P. Venice, 1607–10*, pp 132–3.
46. Meehan mistakenly believed Eoghy Óg was captured and executed after the rebellion, whereas in fact he was transported to Sweden (see Meehan, *Fate and Fortunes*, p. 194; Jennings (ed.), *Wild Geese*, p. 153).
47. P.R.O., SP 63/224/93.
48. *Cal. S.P. Venice, 1607–10*, p. 138; *Cal. S.P. Ire., 1608–10*, pp 30–1.
49. McCavitt, *Chichester*, p. 145.
50. *Cal. S.P. Ire., 1606–8*, pp 480–3.
51. Farmer, 'Chronicles', p. 537.
52. *Cal. S.P. Ire., 1606–8*, pp 494–6.
53. Ibid., pp 499–502.
54. Ibid., pp 541–5.
55. Ibid., pp 524–7.
56. Ibid., pp 499–502.
57. *Cal. S.P. Venice, 1607–10*, pp 132–3.
58. *Cal. S.P. Ire., 1606–8*, pp 547–9.
59. B.L., Stowe MS 170, ff 47–8.
60. Farmer, 'Chronicles', p. 538.
61. *Cal. S.P. Ire., 1606–8*, pp 499–502.
62. Ibid., pp 567–8.
63. Ibid., pp 597–8.

64. Ibid., pp 606–8.
65. Ibid., pp 567–8.
66. Ibid., pp 606–8.
67. Ibid., pp 599–605.
68. Ibid.
69. T.C.D., Early printed books, Press A.2.43, no. 2.
70. *Cal. S.P. Ire., 1608–10*, p. xlix.
71. Farmer, 'Chronicles', p. 538.
72. *Cal. S.P. Ire., 1606–8*, pp 606–8.
73. T.C.D. Early printed books, Press A.2.43, no.2.
74. *Cal. S.P. Ire., 1606–8*, pp 606–8.
75. *Cal. S.P. Ire., 1611–14*, pp 392–9.
76. T.C.D., Early printed books, Press A.2.43, no. 2. It has been remarked that the 'arms of the city of London-Derry commemorate this event: the escutcheon shews a skeleton, the head leaning on the hand, the figure resting on a stone, which is said to have been the position in which O'Dogherty was found' (G. V. Sampson, *A Memoir, explanatory of the Chart and Survey of the County of London-derry, Ireland* (London, 1814), p. 6). It should be noted, however, that other, perhaps more plausible, explanations have been given for the skeleton in the city arms.
77. T.C.D., Early printed books, Press A.2.43, no. 2.
78. *Cal. S.P. Ire., 1608–10*, pp 26–9.
79. Lord Ernest Hamilton, *The Irish Rebellion of 1641, with a history of the events which led up to and succeeded it* (London, 1920), p. 30.
80. James Wills (ed.), *Lives of Illustrious and Distinguished Irishmen* (6 vols, Dublin, 1890), ii, pt 2, pp 393–4.
81. Farmer, 'Chronicles', p. 539.
82. P.R.O., AO1/290/1089, f. 39.
83. *Cal. S.P. Ire., 1606–8*, pp 606–8.
84. *Cal. S.P. Ire., 1608–10*, pp 225–35.
85. Hamilton, *Irish Rebellion*, p. 31.
86. Farmer, 'Chronicles', p. 540.
87. *Cal. S.P. Ire., 1608–10*, pp 5–10.
88. Ibid.
89. Ibid., pp 5–10, 26–9.
90. Gillespie, *Conspiracy*, p. 48.
91. *Cal. S.P. Ire., 1608–10*, pp 5–10.
92. T.C.D., Early printed books, Press A.2.43, no. 2.
93. *Cal. S.P. Venice, 1607–10*, pp 96–7.
94. Ibid., p. 137.
95. Ibid., pp 139–40.
96. Gardiner, *History of England*, ii, 30; Kerney Walsh, *Destruction by Peace*, document 75.
97. Barnaby Rich, *A New Description of Ireland* (London, 1610), p. 106.
98. McCavitt, *Chichester*, p. 257 n. 66.
99. B.L., Stowe MS 170, ff 39–40.
100. *Cal. S.P. Venice, 1607–10*, pp 131–2.
101. Ibid., pp 132–3.
102. *Cal. S.P. Ire., 1606–8*, p. 662.
103. Meehan, *Fate and Fortunes*, p. 187.

104. Ibid., pp 183–5.
105. Kerney Walsh, *Destruction by Peace*, document 69.
106. Ibid.
107. *Cal. S.P. Venice, 1607–10*, pp 142–3.
108. Kerney Walsh, *Destruction by Peace*, document 69. Similar sentiments were expressed in document 72a.
109. *Cal. S.P. Ire., 1606–8*, pp 660–1.
110. Ibid., pp 663–4.
111. Ibid., 665–6.
112. *Cal. S.P. Ire., 1608–10*, p. 120.
113. *Cal. S.P. Ire., 1606–8*, pp 595–6.
114. Tristram Marshall, 'James VI and I: three kings or two?', *Renaissance Forum*, v, no. 1 (2000) (http://www.hull.ac.uk/renforum/v5no1/marshall.htm).
115. Kerney Walsh, *Destruction by Peace*, document 72. S. R. Gardiner has argued that while the Spanish were inclined to renew hostilities against England in 1613, sober reflection on their 'poverty' persuaded them to avoid warfare (Gardiner, *History of England*, ii, 165).
116. Kerney Walsh, *Destruction by Peace*, document 74.
117. Ibid., document 76.
118. Ibid., p. 231. Tyrconnell died on 18 July (old style); 28 July (new style).
119. *Cal. S.P. Ire., 1606–8*, p. 665.
120. Kerney Walsh, *Destruction by Peace*, documents 69, 72a, 78.
121. *Cal. S.P. Ire., 1608–10*, p. 120.
122. *Cal. S.P. Ire., 1606–8*, pp 303–4, 430, 524–7, 541–5; *Cal. S.P. Ire., 1608–10*, p. 40.
123. *Cal. S.P. Ire., 1608–10*, pp 46–7.

Chapter 8: Plantation and transportation (pp 154–174)

1. *Cal. S.P. Ire., 1606–8*, pp 612–13.
2. H.M.C., *Salisbury*, xxi, 121.
3. *Cal. S.P. Ire., 1608–10*, pp 26–9, 34–7.
4. *Cal. S.P. Ire., 1606–8*, p. 608.
5. *Cal. S.P. Ire., 1608–10*, pp 14–17.
6. Kew (ed.), 'Moryson's Unpublished Itinerary', p. 50.
7. *Cal. S.P. Ire., 1608–10*, pp 141–5.
8. Ibid.
9. Ibid., pp 85–8. Chichester was no stranger to resorting to radical measures in an attempt to resolve perennial security problems. He had already arranged the transplantation of the O'Mores, considered to be a threat to the Pale, from Laois to Kerry (see McCavitt, *Chichester*, pp 97, 156, 223).
10. *Cal. S.P. Ire., 1608–10*, pp 251, 270–4, 343.
11. Ibid., pp 270–4. One John Cusack was paid £933 for supplying clothing for the transportees (P.R.O., AO1/290/1088, f. 47).
12. *Cal. S.P. Ire., 1608–10*, pp 251, 270–4.
13. B.L., Stowe MS 171, ff 130–2.
14. *Cal. S.P. Venice, 1607–10*, pp 325–6.
15. *Cal. S.P. Ire., 1608–10*, pp 285–7.
16. Ibid., p. 290.
17. Ibid., pp 285–7.

18. Ibid., pp 292–3.
19. Ibid., pp 296–7.
20. Ibid., p. 300.
21. Ibid.
22. Ibid., pp 240–1.
23. Henry, *Irish Military Community in Spanish Flanders*, p. 41.
24. *Cal. S.P. Ire., 1608–10*, pp 303–4.
25. Ibid., pp 304–5.
26. Ibid.; P.R.O., SP 63/227/150.
27. *Cal. S.P. Ire., 1608–10*, pp 305–6.
28. P.R.O., SP 63/227/150.
29. H.M.C., *Downshire*, ii, 195–6.
30. P.R.O., SP 14/49/81.
31. H.M.C., *Salisbury*, xxi, 162–3.
32. *Cal. S.P. Ire., 1608–10*, pp 415–16, 420–4. The Earl of Salisbury agreed that Russia would be a suitable destination. The Earl of Tyrone later testified that some of the levies had served in Russia (see Kerney Walsh, *Destruction by Peace*, document 158).
33. *Cal. S.P. Ire., 1608–10*, pp 193–7, 334.
34. Ibid., p. 334.
35. *Register of the Privy Council of Scotland, 1607–10* (Edinburgh, 1887), p. 393.
36. P.R.O., SP 14/52/45.
37. *Cal. S.P. Ire., 1608–10*, pp 496–7.
38. *Cal. S.P. Ire., 1611–14*, pp 479–80.
39. Henry, *Irish Military Community in Spanish Flanders*, p. 107.
40. Kerney Walsh, *Destruction by Peace*, document 158.
41. Ibid., document 143a.
42. Henry, *Irish Military Community in Spanish Flanders*, p. 107.
43. Kerney Walsh, *Destruction by Peace*, document 211. There were instances in which drownings had occurred (see Henry, *Irish Military Community in Spanish Flanders*, p. 107). Perhaps the 'shipwreck' incident involving the vessel which departed in 1610 was portrayed as a deliberate exercise in 'scuttling'.
44. *Cal. S.P. Ire., 1647–60*, pp 86–7. I am grateful to Dr John Appleby for this reference.
45. R. D. Fitzsimon, 'Irish Swordsmen in the Imperial Service in the Thirty Years War', *Irish Sword*, ix (1969), pp 22–31.
46. *Cal. S.P. Ire., 1608–10*, pp 213–15.
47. Ibid., pp 68–9.
48. Ibid., pp 362–5.
49. *Cal. S.P. Ire., 1611–14*, pp 44, 284.
50. Falls, *Birth of Ulster*, p. 234.
51. P. J. Corish, 'The Rising of 1641 and the Catholic Confederacy, 1641–5' in *N.H.I.*, iii, 291–2.
52. F. W. Harris, 'The Rebellion of Sir Cahir O'Doherty and its Legal Aftermath', *Irish Jurist*, new ser., xv (1980), p. 308.
53. *Cal. S.P. Ire., 1606–8*, pp 558–60.
54. *Cal. S.P. Ire., 1608–10*, pp 306–7.
55. *Cal. S.P. Ire., 1606–8*, pp 599–605.
56. Ibid., pp 587–8.
57. Ibid., pp 508–11.

58. Ibid., pp 546–7.
59. Ibid., pp 129–31.
60. *Cal. S.P. Ire., 1608–10*, pp 141–5.
61. Ibid., pp 176–9.
62. Ibid., pp 204–5.
63. Ibid., pp 222–5.
64. Ibid., pp 453–4.
65. Ibid., pp 222–5.
66. H.M.C., *Egmont*, i, pt i, p. 35.
67. *Cal. S.P. Ire., 1606–8*, pp 546–7; *Cal. S.P. Ire., 1608–10*, pp 240–1.
68. *Cal. S.P. Ire., 1608–10*, p. 266.
69. Ibid., pp 240–1.
70. Ibid., p. 263.
71. Meehan, *Fate and Fortunes*, p. 222. 'Imprisonment in the Tower was not a sign of ignominy, rather the reverse. It was a recognition of their nobility. A list of the prisoners in the Tower in 1612 included one pretender to the throne, Lady Arabella Stuart, four peers, including the Earl of Northumberland and the Countess of Shrewsbury, and a number of knights, the most prominent being Sir Walter Raleigh' (Gillespie, *Conspiracy*, p. 28).
72. *Cal. S.P. Ire., 1603–6*, pp 558–62.
73. Davies, *Historical Tracts*, p. 244.
74. Ibid., p. 255.
75. Ibid., p. 259.
76. *Cal. S.P. Ire., 1608–10*, pp 157–61.
77. Ibid., pp 479–80.
78. Ibid., pp 497–501.
79. McCavitt, *Chichester*, p. 158.
80. Ibid.
81. Ibid., pp 151–2.
82. *Cal. S.P. Ire., 1606–8*, pp 480–3.
83. Ibid., pp 524–7.
84. P.R.O., SP 63/229/135.
85. *Cal. S.P. Ire., 1606–8*, pp 287–8.
86. Ibid., pp 281–2.
87. *Cal. S.P. Venice, 1607–10*, pp 181–2.
88. T.C.D., Early printed books, Press A.2.43, no. 2.
89. Ibid.
90. *Cal. S.P. Venice, 1607–10*, pp 184–5.
91. *Cal. S.P. Ire., 1615–25*, pp 220–6.
92. *Cal. S.P. Ire., 1608–10*, pp 213–15.
93. Ibid., pp 269–70.
94. Ibid., pp 280–1.
95. As with Adam and Eve, the London companies' succumbing to the temptation of taking the rich pickings on offer in O'Cahan's country was later to rebound on them when the colonisation project encountered serious problems.
96. P.R.O., 31/8/199, ff 500–1.
97. *Cal. S.P. Ire., 1608–10*, pp 285–7.
98. Ibid., pp 280–1. Ireland had a reputation as being unhealthy for Englishmen, not least during the Nine Years War. See Chapter 2.

99. *Cal. S.P. Ire., 1608–10*, pp 304–5; P.R.O., SP 63/227/150.
100. Bardon, *History of Ulster*, p. 133.
101. Michael Perceval-Maxwell, *The Scottish Migration to Ireland in the Reign of James I* (2nd ed., London, 1990), pp 80–8.
102. Aidan Clarke, 'Pacification, Plantation and the Catholic Question, 1603–23' in *N.H.I.*, iii, 197.
103. *Cal. S.P. Venice, 1607–10*, pp 325–6.
104. *Cal. S.P. Ire., 1608–10*, pp 211–12.
105. Ibid., pp 191–3.
106. Kerney Walsh, *Destruction by Peace*, document 240.
107. *Cal. S.P. Venice, 1607–10*, p. 302.
108. The Countess of Tyrconnell was believed by the English to be in receipt of an annuity of 200 crowns from the Spanish (see Winwood, *Memorials of Affairs of State*, ii, 386–8, 420–1, 456–60).
109. See Kerney Walsh, *Destruction by Peace, passim.*
110. Ibid., document 240.
111. Ibid., document 73.
112. *Cal. S.P. Ire., 1608–10*, pp 532–46.
113. Kerney Walsh, *Destruction by Peace*, document 90.
114. Ibid., document 97. The first direct correspondence which Philip III was prepared to address to Tyrone concerned the proposed reconciliation. For diplomatic reasons the Spanish king had previously preferred to conduct his correspondence by more indirect means. Tyrone was appalled to learn that the king preferred a reconciliation rather than supporting a military expedition to restore him to his patrimony. Tyrone felt aggrieved that the king had not informed him of this position in the early days after the Flight when the English were more anxious to discuss a rapprochement (see ibid., document 114).
115. Ibid., document 98.
116. Ibid., document 99.
117. H.M.C., *De L'Isle and Dudley*, iv, 165.
118. J. K. Graham, 'The Birth-Date of Hugh O'Neill, Second Earl of Tyrone', *I.H.S.*, i (1938), pp 58–9; *Cal. S.P. Venice, 1607–10*, pp 287–8.
119. *Cal. S.P. Venice, 1607–10*, pp 287–8.
120. B.L., Stowe MS 171, ff 130–2.
121. H.M.C., *Salisbury*, xxi, 121.
122. *Cal. S.P. Ire., 1608–10*, pp 521–2; Philip Robinson, *The Plantation of Ulster: British settlement in an Irish landscape, 1600–70* (Dublin, 1984), p. 77.
123. *Cal. S.P. Ire., 1608–10*, pp 14–17.
124. Perceval-Maxwell, *Scottish Migration*, p. 75.
125. *Cal. S.P. Ire., 1608–10*, p. 129.
126. McCavitt, *Chichester*, p. 160.
127. Clarke, 'Pacification', p. 202.
128. Robert Dunlop (ed.), *Ireland under the Commonwealth: being a selection of documents relating to the government of Ireland, 1651–9* (2 vols, Manchester, 1913), i, p. lxxii.
129. *Cal. S.P. Ire., 1608–10*, pp 474–5.
130. Falls, *Birth of Ulster*, p. 196.
131. Perceval-Maxwell, *Scottish Migration*, p. 80 n. 34.
132. *Cal. S.P. Ire., 1608–10*, pp 193–7, 334.

133. Ibid., pp 474–5.
134. *Cal. S.P. Ire., 1606–8*, p. 263. The exact date of the Act of Oblivion is uncertain (see J. J. Silke, 'Bishop Conor O'Devanney, O.F.M., *c.* 1533–1612', *Seanchas Ard Mhacha*, xiii (1988), p. 25).
135. *Cal. S.P. Ire., 1608–10*, pp 474–5.
136. Ibid.
137. Robinson, *Plantation of Ulster*, p. 75.
138. *Cal. S.P. Ire., 1608–10*, pp 501–4.
139. B.L., Cotton MSS, Titus, B.X. 202.
140. P.R.O., SP 63/229/135.
141. *Cal. S.P. Ire., 1608–10*, pp 496–7.
142. Kerney Walsh, *Destruction by Peace*, p. 113.
143. While Tyrone's eyesight had undoubtedly deteriorated, he was not completely blind at this time (see ibid., p. 141).
144. *Cal. S.P. Ire., 1608–10*, pp 530–1.
145. McCavitt, *Chichester*, p. 159.
146. B.L., Cotton MSS, Titus, B.X. 189.

Chapter 9: 'For they would have Barabbas' (pp 175–199)

1. *Cal. S.P. Ire., 1608–10*, pp 500–1. For an English translation of Davies's Latin quotation from *The Aeneid* see Virgil, *The Aeneid*, trans. W. F. Jackson Knight (London, 1958), p. 41.
2. Dominic O'Daly, *The Earls of Desmond and the Persecution of the Irish Catholics*, ed. and trans. from the original Latin edition (Lisbon, 1665) by C. P. Meehan (Dublin, 1847), p. 177.
3. *Cal. S.P. Dom., 1611–18*, p. 23.
4. *Cal. S.P. Ire., 1611–14*, pp 59–60.
5. *Cal. S.P. Ire., 1608–10*, pp 521–2.
6. McCavitt, *Chichester*, ch. 9.
7. *Cal. Carew MSS, 1603–23*, pp 68–9.
8. Ibid., pp 75–9, 220–30.
9. *Cal. S.P. Ire., 1611–14*, pp 63–7.
10. Ibid., pp 145–7.
11. H.M.C., *Salisbury*, xxi, 307–8. If Tyrone had approached the Italian nobility in this regard, it is possible that the Italians recollected events at Smerwick in 1580, when almost 700 of their fellow-countrymen had been massacred in Ireland.
12. Kerney Walsh, *Destruction by Peace*, document 136.
13. H.M.C., *Egmont*, i, pt i, p. 37.
14. For an elaboration of this concept see Brendan Bradshaw, 'Sword, Word and Strategy in the Reformation in Ireland', *Historical Journal*, xxi (1978), pp 475–502.
15. *Cal. S.P. Ire., 1608–10*, pp 141–5.
16. P.R.O., SP 63/229/91.
17. McCavitt, *Chichester*, p. 174.
18. *Cal. S.P. Ire., 1611–14*, pp 166–7.
19. Quoted in McD[onald] (ed.), 'Irish Ecclesiastical Colleges', pp 196–201.
20. McCavitt, *Chichester*, p. 175.
21. Maurice Lenihan, *Limerick: its history and antiquities* (repr., Cork, 1967), p. 138.
22. *Acts Privy Council, 1615–16*, pp 689–90.
23. Michael MacCarthy-Morrogh, *The Munster Plantation: English migration to southern Ireland, 1583–1641* (Oxford, 1986), p. 195.

24. *Cal. S.P. Ire., 1611–14*, pp 306–7.

25. M. V. Ronan, *The Irish Martyrs of the Penal Laws* (London, 1935), p. 91.

26. H.M.C., *Franciscan Manuscripts*, pp 67–8. An early seventeenth-century source reported that 5,000 recusants were prosecuted at a single assize in County Cork (George O'Brien (ed.), *Advertisements for Ireland, being a description of the state of Ireland in the reign of James I* (Dublin, 1923), pp 15–16).

27. McCavitt, *Chichester*, p. 175.

28. Ibid., p. 253 n. 106.

29. *Cal. S.P. Ire., 1615–25*, pp 22–5.

30. P. F. Moran, *Spicilegium Ossoriense: being a collection of original letters and papers illustrative of the history of the Irish church from the Reformation to the year 1800* (3 vols, Dublin, 1874–84), i, 119–23.

31. O'Brien (ed.), *Advertisements for Ireland*, p. 16.

32. Ronan, *Irish Martyrs*, p. 91.

33. *Cal. S.P. Ire., 1611–14*, pp 3–5.

34. Quoted in McD[onald] (ed.), 'Irish Ecclesiastical Colleges', p. 295. 'Redshanks' was the name originally given to Scottish mercenary soldiers serving in Ireland.

35. *Cal. S.P. Ire., 1611–14*, p. 315.

36. Quoted in McD[onald] (ed.), 'Irish Ecclesiastical Colleges', pp 295–6.

37. Ibid.

38. *Cal. S.P. Ire., 1611–14*, p. 103.

39. Moran, *Spicil. Ossor.*, i, 119–23.

40. Kerney Walsh, *Destruction by Peace*, documents 139a, 156, 164.

41. *Cal. S.P. Ire., 1603–6*, pp 65–8.

42. *Cal. S.P. Ire., 1606–8*, pp 479–80.

43. *Cal. S.P. Ire., 1611–14*, p. 186; B.L., Cotton MSS, Titus B.X. 288.

44. Kerney Walsh, *Destruction by Peace*, documents 215, 156, 164.

45. Ibid., p. 4.

46. McCavitt, *Chichester*, p. 175. Chichester was particularly concerned about the activities of Jesuit priests whom he believed were swarming into Ireland. However, Catholic records indicate that in 1610 there were few as twelve Jesuits in Ireland (see McD[onald] (ed.), 'Irish Ecclesiastical Colleges', p. 530).

47. *Cal. S.P. Ire., 1608–10*, pp 141–5.

48. McCavitt, *Chichester*, p. 170.

49. Silke, 'O'Devanney', p. 24.

50. Meehan, *Fate and Fortunes*, p. 238.

51. Peter Lombard, *De Regno Hiberniae Sanctorum Insula Commentarius*, ed. P. F. Moran (Dublin, 1868), pp xlix–li.

52. Silke, 'O'Devanney', p. 24.

53. *Cal. S.P. Ire., 1608–10*, pp 461–2.

54. Moran, *Spicil. Ossor.*, i, 123–6.

55. Ibid.

56. Silke, 'O'Devanney', p. 13.

57. Ibid., p. 32.

58. Moran, *Spicil. Ossor.*, i, 123–6.

59. Ibid.

60. Barnaby Rich, *A Catholicke Conference betweene Syr Tady Mac Mareall, a popish priest of Waterford, and Patrick Plaine, a young student in Trinity College by Dublin in Ireland*

(London, 1612), p. 5.

61. Kew (ed.), 'Moryson's Unpublished Itinerary', p. 103.

62. Lombard, *De Regno Hiberniae*, pp xlix–li.

63. Moran, *Spicil. Ossor.*, i, 123–6.

64. Rich, *Catholicke Conference*, pp 5–6.

65. Moran, *Spicil. Ossor.*, i, 123–6; Ronan, *Irish Martyrs*, p. 101.

66. *A.F.M.*, vi, 2373.

67. Moran, *Spicil. Ossor.*, i, 123–6. The 'hangman of Dublin', an Irishman, was said to have fled the city on hearing news that Bishop O'Devany had been condemned to death. No manner of inducement could entice anyone in Ireland to carry out the sentence, an English murderer being reputedly released from jail and pardoned to execute the sentence (see *A.F.M.*, vi, 2370–1).

68. Moran, *Spicil. Ossor.*, i, 123–6.

69. Farmer, 'Chronicles', p. 544.

70. *Cal. S.P. Ire., 1611–14*, p. 244; Moran, *Spicil. Ossor.*, i, 123–6.

71. R. D. Edwards (ed.), 'Chichester Letter-Book', *Anal. Hib.*, viii (1938), pp 125–7.

72. *Cal. S.P. Ire., 1611–14*, p. 246. In England during March 1612 James I ordered the burning at the stake of two prominent non-conforming Protestants (see Gardiner, *History of England*, ii, 128–30).

73. Corish, *Irish Catholic Experience*, p. 98.

74. Quoted in Meehan, *Fate and Fortunes*, p. 248.

75. Appleby, 'Affairs of Pirates'.

76. H.M.C., *Downshire*, iii, 138.

77. H.M.C., *Buccleuch and Queensberry*, i, 152–5. The reference is to the proverb *In vino veritas* [In wine is truth revealed].

78. Kerney Walsh, *Destruction by Peace*, documents 150, 154.

79. Ibid., document 154.

80. Ibid., document 160.

81. Gardiner, *History of England*, ii, 163–5.

82. McCavitt, *Chichester*, p. 182.

83. *Cal. S.P. Venice, 1610–13*, p. 491; *Cal. S.P. Dom., 1611–18*, p. 169.

84. *Cal. S.P. Venice, 1610–13*, pp 506–7.

85. Quoted in Meehan, *Fate and Fortunes*, pp 250–3.

86. Kerney Walsh, *Destruction by Peace*, document 156.

87. Gillespie, *Conspiracy*, p. 11.

88. Kerney Walsh, *Destruction by Peace*, document 156a.

89. H.M.C., *Downshire*, iii, 425–8; *Cal. S.P. Venice, 1610–13*, pp 469–70, 471–3, 477–8, 488–9, 491, 506–7; *Cal. S.P. Dom, 1611–18*, p. 167, 169; H.M.C., *Downshire*, iv, 13–14, 28.

90. *Cal. S.P. Venice, 1610–13*, pp 506–7.

91. H.M.C., *Downshire*, iii, 425–8.

92. Ibid., iv, 83.

93. Clarke, 'Pacification', pp 214–16.

94. T. W. Moody, 'The Irish Parliament under Elizabeth and James I: a general survey', *Proceedings of the Royal Irish Academy*, xlv (1939), sect. C, p. 54.

95. Ibid.

96. *Desid. Cur. Hib.*, i, 158–62.

97. Ibid.

98. *Cal. Carew MSS, 1603–23*, p. 281.

99. *Desid. Cur. Hib.*, i, 200.
100. *Cal. S.P. Ire., 1611–14*, p. 288.
101. H.M.C., *Egmont*, i, pt i, p. 42.
102. *Cal. Carew MSS, 1603–23*, p. 284.
103. *Desid. Cur. Hib.*, i, 157; *Cal. S.P. Ire., 1611–14*, pp 360–4.
104. McCavitt, *Chichester*, p. 182.
105. *Cal. S.P. Ire., 1611–14*, pp 443.
106. *Desid. Cur. Hib.*, i, 421.
107. *Cal. S.P. Ire., 1611–14*, pp 399–405.
108. Unless otherwise stated, the source for the bizarre events during the election to the Speakership is based upon John McCavitt, 'An Unspeakable Parliamentary Fracas: the Irish House of Commons, 1613', *Anal. Hib.*, xxxvii (1998), pp 223–35.
109. McCavitt, *Chichester*, p. 98.
110. Clarke, 'Pacification', p. 214.
111. *Cal. S.P. Ire., 1611–14*, pp 354–5; *Desid. Cur. Hib.*, i, 392–3.
112. Brian Jackson (ed.), 'Document on the Irish Parliament of 1613', *Anal. Hib.*, xxxiii (1986), p. 53; see also *Desid. Cur. Hib.*, i, 199, 223.
113. Jackson (ed.), 'Document on the Irish Parliament of 1613', p. 53.
114. *Desid. Cur. Hib.*, i, 422.
115. Ibid., i, 187.
116. *Cal. Carew MSS, 1603–23*, pp 278–85.
117. *Desid. Cur. Hib.*, i, 392.
118. *Cal. S.P. Ire., 1611–14*, pp 354–5.
119. H.M.C., *Downshire*, iv, 128–9.
120. McCavitt, *Chichester*, p. 184.
121. H.M.C., *Downshire*, iv, 124–5, 128–9.
122. Kerney Walsh, *Destruction by Peace*, document 174.
123. Farmer, 'Chronicles', p. 546.
124. McCavitt, *Chichester*, p. 184.
125. *Desid. Cur. Hib.*, i, 429.
126. Ciaran Brady, 'Conservative Subversives: the community of the Pale and the Dublin administration, 1556–86' in P. J. Corish (ed.), *Radicals, Rebels and Establishments: Historical Studies XV* (Belfast, 1985), pp 11–32.
127. P.R.O., SP 63/232/17 (*Cal. S.P. Ire., 1611–14*, p. 407).
128. *Desid. Cur. Hib.*, i, 209.
129. Ibid.; Robinson, *Plantation of Ulster*, pp 199–200.
130. O'Daly, *Earls of Desmond*, ed. and trans. Meehan, p. 181.
131. *Cal. S.P. Ire., 1611–14*, pp 429–31.
132. *Desid. Cur. Hib.*, i, 394–6.
133. *Cal. S.P. Ire., 1611–14*, p. 431.
134. *Cal. Carew MSS, 1603–23*, p. 285.
135. *Cal. S.P. Ire., 1611–14*, pp 381–2.
136. Kerney Walsh, *Destruction by Peace*, document 211.

Chapter 10: The sword passes on (pp 200–222)
1. Kerney Walsh, *Destruction by Peace*, document 169b.
2. *Cal. S.P. Ire., 1615–25*, pp 95–7.
3. McCavitt, *Chichester*, p. 186.

4. *Desid, Cur. Hib.*, i, 362–4.
5. McCavitt, *Chichester*, pp 186–7.
6. H.M.C., *Downshire*, iv, 143–5.
7. *Cal. S.P. Venice, 1610–13*, pp 553–4; H.M.C., *Downshire*, iv, 168.
8. *Acts Privy Council, 1613–14*, pp 159–61.
9. *Cal. S.P. Venice, 1613–15*, pp 31–2.
10. *Cal. S.P. Ire., 1611–14*, pp 309–11.
11. Ibid., pp 311–12.
12. Ibid., pp 435–6.
13. Kerney Walsh, *Destruction by Peace*, document 169a.
14. *Cal. S.P. Ire., 1611–14*, pp 357–8.
15. Kerney Walsh, *Destruction by Peace*, document 169b.
16. Ibid., document 175a.
17. H.M.C., *Downshire*, iv, 165–6. Henry's premature death engendered a wave of emotion in England. 'Throughout the whole of England the sad news was received with tears and lamentations. Never in the long history of England had an heir to the throne given rise to such hopes, or had, at such an early age, inspired every class of his countrymen with love and admiration.' Popular grief spilled over 'in the foolish outcry that their beloved Prince had been murdered' by prominent courtiers (see Gardiner, *History of England*, ii, 158).
18. Kerney Walsh, *Destruction by Peace*, document 172.
19. Ibid., document 167.
20. Ibid., document 137.
21. Ibid., document 176.
22. Ibid., document 178.
23. Ibid., document 183.
24. H.M.C., *Downshire*, iv, 348.
25. Kerney Walsh, *Destruction by Peace*, document 183.
26. H.M.C., *Downshire*, iv, 232.
27. Kerney Walsh, *Destruction by Peace*, document 184.
28. H.M.C., *Downshire*, iv, 272.
29. Marshall, 'James VI and I' (see p. 250 n. 114 above); *Cal. S.P. Dom., 1611–18*, p. 219.
30. H.M.C., *Downshire*, iv, 366–9.
31. McCavitt, *Chichester*, p. 195.
32. Kerney Walsh, *Destruction by Peace*, document 184.
33. *Lismore Papers*, ed. Grosart, 2nd ser., i, 174–6.
34. Kerney Walsh, *Destruction by Peace*, document 188; *Desid. Cur. Hib.*, i, 321.
35. *Cal. Carew MSS, 1603–23*, pp 288–92.
36. *Cal. S.P. Ire., 1611–14*, pp 476–7.
37. *Trevelyan Papers*, ed. Trevelyan, pp 127–8; *Lismore Papers*, ed. Grosart, 2nd ser., i, 207–8.
38. *Acts Privy Council, 1613–14*, pp 433–4; H.M.C., *Downshire*, iv, 407–8.
39. *Cal. S.P. Ire., 1611–14*, pp 481–4; *Cal. S.P. Ire., 1615–25*, pp 53–4.
40. McCavitt, *Chichester*, p. 194.
41. Ibid., p. 195.
42. R. M. Young, *Historical Notices of Old Belfast and its Vicinity* (Belfast, 1896), p. 38.
43. McCavitt, *Chichester*, pp 196, 203.
44. H.M.C., *Downshire*, iv, 449.
45. Ibid., 457–8.

46. Ibid., 511–15; Henry, *Irish Military Community in Spanish Flanders*, p. 115.
47. Gardiner, *History of England*, ii, 262–4.
48. Quoted in Meehan, *Fate and Fortunes*, p. 277.
49. Ibid.
50. Kerney Walsh, *Destruction by Peace*, document 199a. Spain's determination to frustrate the return of Tyrone, or indeed that of any soldiers of the Irish regiment, even if they arranged their own transport, is readily explicable. The English had made it clear in the early days after the Flight of the Earls that they would treat it as an act of war 'when he [James I] shall see any troops transported from Spain or Dunkirk, under whose name or banner soever it be covered, than for a breach of amity; yea, tho' it be but by suffering them to use the vessels or assistance of any of his subjects' (Thomas Birch, *An Historical View of the Negotiations between the Courts of England, France and Brussels, from the year 1592 to 1617* (London, 1749), pp 303–6).
51. Meehan, *Fate and Fortunes*, p. 280.
52. H.M.C., *Downshire*, v, 78.
53. P.R.O., SP 63/232/60.
54. Young, *Historical Notices*, p. 38.
55. T. W. Moody, *The Londonderry Plantation, 1609–41: the city of London and the plantation in Ulster* (Belfast, 1939), p. 329; Gillespie, *Conspiracy*, p. 10.
56. Gillespie, *Conspiracy*, p. 10.
57. J. T. Gilbert (ed.), *A Contemporary History of Affairs in Ireland* (3 vols, Dublin, 1879), i, 319.
58. *Cal. S.P. Ire., 1611–14*, p. 504.
59. McCavitt, *Chichester*, p. 51.
60. Ibid., pp 198–9.
61. Kerney Walsh, *Destruction by Peace*, document 185.
62. H.M.C., *Downshire*, v, 147–8.
63. Ibid., p. 86.
64. Kerney Walsh, *Destruction by Peace*, document 218.
65. Ibid., document 201.
66. Lockyer, *Early Stuarts*, pp 20–4.
67. H.M.C., *Downshire*, v, 165.
68. Kerney Walsh, *Destruction by Peace*, documents 214–15.
69. Ibid., document 192.
70. Ibid., document 204.
71. *Cal. S.P. Ire., 1615–25*, pp 19–20.
72. Ibid., p. 22.
73. Kerney Walsh, *Destruction by Peace*, document 215.
74. H.M.C., *Downshire*, v, 185.
75. Ibid., pp 173–4.
76. P.R.O., SP 63/233/13.
77. *Cal. S.P. Ire., 1615–25*, pp 89–91.
78. McCavitt, *Chichester*, pp 201–4.
79. *Cal. S.P. Ire., 1615–25*, pp 85–6.
80. McCavitt, *Chichester*, p. 204.
81. Gillespie, *Conspiracy*, p. 60. The challenged physical qualities of the conspirators may be explained in part by the fact that thousands of able-bodied 'swordsmen', semi-professional soldiers, had been transported to Sweden in the years previously.
82. Meehan, *Fate and Fortunes*, p. 318.

83. Gillespie, *Conspiracy*, p. 17.
84. McCavitt, *Chichester*, p. 202.
85. Ibid., p. 103.
86. Gillespie, *Conspiracy*, p. 9.
87. *Cal. S.P. Ire., 1615–25*, pp 78–9.
88. Gillespie, *Conspiracy*, p. 22.
89. *Cal. S.P. Ire., 1615–25*, pp 53–4.
90. Kerney Walsh, *Destruction by Peace*, document 219a.
91. *Cal. S.P. Ire., 1611–14*, pp 333–5, 481–4. The youngsters were not only to be hostages for the good behaviour of their relatives, but were being targeted for conversion to Protestantism. Lord Power, for example, was reported to be at Lambeth Palace with the Archbishop of Canterbury in 1615: 'His being here is an exemplary and leading case unto the young noblemen that are expected from Ireland next spring; my Lord's Grace doth with more solicitous care and circumspection carry an eye over him, and with all gentle and ingenious usage endeavoureth first to win him to think well of his entertainment and of the conversation of us Protestants, and then by degrees drop in such soft and insensible distillation of virtue and religion, that if he be not of too rugged a nature, he will in the end comply to our religion and to a true obedience to His Majesty and his government' (H.M.C., *Franciscan Manuscripts*, pp 70–1).
92. McCavitt, *Chichester*, pp 228–9.
93. *Acts Privy Council, 1615–16*, pp 689–90.
94. Brendan Fitzpatrick, *Seventeenth-Century Ireland: the war of religions* (Dublin, 1988), p. 33.
95. Kerney Walsh, *Destruction by Peace*, document 215.
96. Ibid., p. 107. Bath is not to be confused with the ship's captain of the same name who also became an English agent (see p. 90 above).
97. Ibid., document 214; Meehan, *Fate and Fortunes*, p. 305.
98. Kerney Walsh, *Destruction by Peace*, document 211.
99. Ibid., pp 52–3, 107.
100. Ibid., document 215.
101. Ibid.
102. Ibid., document 211a.
103. Ibid., document 215.
104. Ibid. The Irish merchants referred to were more than likely Old English. Their involvement suggests that Tyrone was not depending on the Spanish to finance his personal return to Ireland.
105. Ibid., document 214.
106. Ibid., document 213.
107. Ibid., document 208.
108. Jennings (ed.), *Wild Geese*, p. 144.
109. Kerney Walsh, *Destruction by Peace*, document 207.
110. Ibid., documents 202, 218.
111. Ibid., document 226.
112. Lockyer, *Early Stuarts*, pp 24–5.
113. Kerney Walsh, *Destruction by Peace*, document 218.
114. Ibid., p. vi.
115. Meehan, *Fate and Fortunes*, pp 307–8.
116. *Cal. S.P. Ire., 1615–25*, pp 89–91.
117. Ibid. The implication is that the letters had been received from Charles Howard, Earl

of Nottingham, the Lord High Admiral of England. Nottingham, it is worth recalling, was the grandfather of the former Countess of Tyrconnell, and it is possible that the countess had played some role in arranging this channel of communication.

118. *Cal. S.P. Venice, 1607–10*, pp 180–1.
119. H.M.C., *Downshire*, iii, 138.
120. McCavitt, *Chichester*, p. 169.
121. *Acts Privy Council, 1615–16*, pp 529–30.
122. Gillespie, *Conspiracy*, p. 34.
123. *Cal. S.P. Ire., 1615–25*, pp 89–91.
124. Meehan, *Fate and Fortunes*, pp 321–2.
125. *Cal. S.P. Ire., 1615–25*, pp 89–91.
126. H.M.C., *Buccleuch and Queensberry*, i, 152–5.
127. Kerney Walsh, *Destruction by Peace*, document 228. Controversy continued to plague the Countess of Tyrone after her husband's death in 1616. She was accused by discontented elements among the Irish expatriate community in Rome of 'appropriating more than her fair share of her late husband's property … and that the money was ill–spent'. The countess, for her part, complained in June 1618 that her allowance had not been paid for seventeen months and that the Spanish king was 'without concern for this afflicted and unprotected widow, who was his [Tyrone's] wife, but leaves her and his family to die of hunger'. The countess claimed that this situation subjected her to the 'ridicule of the English enemies'. She died in 1619. See Micheline Walsh, 'Some Notes towards a History of the Womenfolk of the Wild Geese', *Irish Sword*, v (1961–2), pp 104–6.
128. P. J. Corish, *The Catholic Community in the Seventeenth and Eighteenth Centuries* (Dublin, 1981), p. 20.
129. Meehan, *Fate and Fortunes*, p. 315.
130. *A.F.M.*, vi, 2373–5. Tyrone died on 10 July (old style); 20 July (new style).
131. Meehan, *Fate and Fortunes*, pp 315–16.
132. Ibid., pp 317–18n.
133. Quoted in Marshall, 'James VI and I' (see p. 250 n. 114 above).
134. Meehan, *Fate and Fortunes*, pp 322–4.
135. H.M.C., *Downshire*, vi, 296.
136. Ibid.
137. Ibid.
138. *Cal. S.P. Ire., 1615–25*, p. 432.
139. Quoted in Meehan, *Fate and Fortunes*, p. 327.
140. Jennings (ed.), *Wild Geese*, pp 228–35.
141. Ibid.
142. Aidan Clarke, 'The Genesis of the Ulster Rising of 1641' in Peter Roebuck (ed.), *Plantation to Partition* (Belfast, 1981), p. 34.
143. Meehan, *Fate and Fortunes*, p. 333.

BIBLIOGRAPHY

Acts of the Privy Council of England, 1532–1631 (46 vols, London, 1890–1964), vols: *1601–4, 1613–14, 1615–16*

Appleby, J. C., 'The "Affairs of Pirates": the surrender and submission of Captain William Baugh at Kinsale, 1611–1612', *Journal of the Cork Historical and Archaeological Society*, xci (1986), pp 68–84

Bagwell, Richard, *Ireland under the Stuarts* (3 vols, London, 1909–16), vol. i

—— *Ireland under the Tudors, with a succinct account of the earlier history* (3 vols, repr., London, 1963), vol. iii

Bardon, Jonathan, *A History of Ulster* (Belfast, 1992)

Birch, Thomas, *An Historical View of the Negotiations between the Courts of England, France and Brussels, from the year 1592 to 1617* (London, 1749)

Bodley, Josias, 'A Visit to Lecale in the County of Down, in the year 1602–3' in C. L. Falkiner, *Illustrations of Irish History and Topography, mainly of the seventeenth century* (London, 1904), pp 326–44

Bonner, Brian, *That Audacious Traitor* (Dublin, 1975)

Bradshaw, Brendan, 'Sword, Word and Strategy in the Reformation in Ireland', *Historical Journal*, xxi (1978), pp 475–502

Brady, Ciaran, 'Conservative Subversives: the community of the Pale and the Dublin administration, 1556–86' in P. J. Corish (ed.), *Radicals, Rebels and Establishments: Historical Studies XV* (Belfast, 1985), pp 11–32

Buccleuch and Queensberry: *Report on the Manuscripts of the Duke of Buccleuch and Queensberry* (6 vols, H.M.C., London, 1897–1926), vol. i

Byrne, M. J., *Ireland under Elizabeth* (Dublin, 1903), a translation of Philip O'Sullivan Beare, *Historiae Catholicae Iberniae Compendium* (Lisbon, 1621)

Caball, Marc, 'Providence and Exile in Early Seventeenth-Century Ireland', *I.H.S.*, xxix (1994), pp 174–88

Calendar of the Carew Manuscripts preserved in the Archiepiscopal Library at Lambeth (6 vols, London, 1867–73), vol.: *1603–23w*

Calendar of State Papers, Domestic Series (81 vols, London, 1856–1972), vols: *1603–10, 1611–18*

Calendar of State Papers relating to Ireland (24 vols, London, 1860–1911), vols: *1596–7, 1598–9, 1599–1600, 1600, 1600–1, 1601–3, 1603–6, 1606–8, 1608–10, 1611–14, 1615–25*

Calendar of State Papers and Manuscripts, relating to English Affairs, existing in the archives and collections of Venice … (London, 1864–), vols: *1607–10, 1610–13, 1613–15*

Camden, William, *Britannia* (London, 1610)

Canny, N. P., 'The Treaty of Mellifont and the Reorganisation of Ulster, 1603', *Irish Sword*, ix (1969), pp 249–62

—— 'The Flight of the Earls', *I.H.S.*, xvii (1971), pp 380–99

—— *Reformation to Restoration: Ireland, 1534–1660* (Dublin, 1987)

Carleton, George, *A Thankful Remembrance of God's Mercy* (London, 1624)

Casway, Jerrold, 'Henry O'Neill and the Formation of the Irish Regiment in the Netherlands, 1605', *I.H.S.*, xviii (1973), pp 481–8

Chamberlain, John, *The Letters of John Chamberlain*, ed. N. E. McClure (2 vols, Philadelphia, 1939), vol. i

Chichester, A. P. B., *History of the Family of Chichester* (London, 1871)

Clarke, Aidan, 'The Genesis of the Ulster Rising of 1641' in Peter Roebuck (ed.), *Plantation to Partition* (Belfast, 1981)

—— 'Pacification, Plantation and the Catholic Question, 1603–23' in *N.H.I.*, iii, 187–232

Corish, P. J., *The Catholic Community in the Seventeenth and Eighteenth Centuries* (Dublin, 1981)

—— *The Irish Catholic Experience: a historical survey* (Dublin, 1985)

—— 'The Rising of 1641 and the Catholic Confederacy, 1641–5' in *N.H.I.*, iii, 289–316

Cummins, John, *Francis Drake* (London, 1995)

D'Alton, E. A., *History of Ireland from the earliest times to the present day* (6 vols, London, 1910), vol. iii

Davies, Sir John, *A Discovery of the True Causes Why Ireland Was Never Entirely Subdued ... until ... His Majesty's Happy Reign* [1612] (facsimile repr., Shannon, 1969)

—— *Historical Tracts* (London, 1786)

—— *The Poems of Sir John Davies*, ed. Robert Krueger (Oxford, 1975)

De L'Isle and Dudley: *Report on the Manuscripts of Lord De L'Isle and Dudley* (6 vols, H.M.C., London, 1925–66), vol. iv

Docwra, Sir Henry, 'A Narration of the Services done by the Army ymployed to Lough-Foyle' in *Miscellany of the Celtic Society*, ed. John O'Donovan (Dublin, 1849)

Downshire: *Report on the Manuscripts of the Marquis of Downshire preserved at Easthampstead Park, Berks* (6 vols, H.M.C., London, 1924–96), vols ii–vi

Dunlop, Robert (ed.), *Ireland under the Commonwealth: being a selection of documents relating to the government of Ireland, 1651–9* (2 vols, Manchester, 1913)

Edwards, David, 'The Butler Revolt of 1569', *I.H.S.*, xxviii (1993), pp 229–55

Edwards, R. D. (ed.), 'Chichester Letter-Book', *Anal. Hib.*, viii (1938), pp 3–177

Egmont: *Report on the Manuscripts of the Earl of Egmont* (2 vols, H.M.C., London, 1905–9), vol. i

Falls, Cyril, *The Birth of Ulster* (London, 1936)

—— *Elizabeth's Irish Wars* (London, 1950)

Farmer, William, 'Chronicles of Ireland', ed. C. L. Falkiner, *English Historical Review*, xxii (1907), pp 104–30, 527–52

Fitzpatrick, Brendan, *Seventeenth-Century Ireland: the war of religions* (Dublin, 1988)

Fitzsimon, Henry, *Words of Comfort ... letters from a cell ... and diary of the Bohemia war of 1620*, ed. Edmund Hogan (Dublin, 1881)

Fitzsimon, R. D., 'Irish Swordsmen in the Imperial Service in the Thirty Years War', *Irish Sword*, ix (1969), pp 22–31

Fortescue, Faithful, *An Account of the Rt Hon. Sir Arthur Chichester*, ed. Lord Clermont (London, 1858)

Foster, E. R. (ed.), *Proceedings in Parliament, 1610*, vol. i: *House of Lords* (New Haven, 1966)

Four Masters, *Annála Ríoghachta Éireann: Annals of the Kingdom of Ireland by the Four Masters from the earliest period to the year 1616*, ed. and trans. John O'Donovan (3rd ed., 7 vols, Dublin, 1990), vol. vi

Franciscan Manuscripts: *Report on the Franciscan Manuscripts preserved at the Convent, Merchants' Quay, Dublin* (H.M.C., Dublin, 1906)

Fraser, Antonia, *The Gunpowder Plot: terror and faith in 1605* (London, 1996)

Gainsford, Thomas, *The True and Exemplary and Remarkable History of the Earle of Tirone* (London, 1619)

Gardiner, S. R., *History of England from the accession of James I to the outbreak of the Civil War, 1603–1642* (new ed., 10 vols, London, 1883–4), vol. ii

Gilbert, J. T. (ed.), *A Contemporary History of Affairs in Ireland* (3 vols, Dublin, 1879), vol. i

Gillespie, Raymond, *Conspiracy: Ulster plots and plotters in 1615* (Belfast, 1987)

Graham, J. K., 'The Birth-Date of Hugh O'Neill, Second Earl of Tyrone', *I.H.S.*, i (1938), pp 58–9

Grosart, A. B. (ed.), *The Lismore Papers*, 2nd ser. (5 vols, London, 1887–8), vol. i

Hamilton, Lord Ernest, *Elizabethan Ulster* (London, 1919)

—— *The Irish Rebellion of 1641, with a history of the events which led up to and succeeded it* (London, 1920)

Harris, F. W., 'The State of the Realm: English military, political and diplomatic responses to the Flight of the Earls, autumn 1607 to spring 1608', *Irish Sword*, liv (1980), pp 47–65

—— 'The Rebellion of Sir Cahir O'Doherty and its Legal Aftermath', *Irish Jurist*, new ser., xv (1980), pp 298–325

Hayes-McCoy, G. A., *Irish Battles* (London, 1969)

—— 'The Completion of the Tudor Conquest, and the Advance of the Counter-Reformation' in *N.H.I.*, iii, pp 94–141

Healy, T. M., *Stolen Waters: a page in the conquest of Ulster* (London, 1913)

Henry, Gráinne, *The Irish Military Community in Spanish Flanders, 1586–1621* (Dublin, 1992)

Hill, George (ed.), *The Montgomery Manuscripts, 1603–1706* (Belfast, 1869)

—— *An Historical Account of the MacDonnells of Antrim* (Belfast, 1873)

Hughes, Charles (ed.), *Shakespeare's Europe* (London, 1903)

Irish Patent Rolls of James I: facsimile of the Irish Record Commissioners' calendar prepared prior to 1830, with foreword by M. C. Griffith (Irish Manuscripts Commission, Dublin, 1966)

Jackson, Brian (ed.), 'Document on the Irish Parliament of 1613', *Anal. Hib.*, xxxiii (1986), pp 47–58

Jennings, Brendan (ed.), *Wild Geese in Spanish Flanders, 1582–1700* (Dublin, 1964)

Jones, F. M., *Mountjoy, 1563–1606, the last Elizabethan deputy* (Dublin, 1958)

Kerney Walsh, Micheline, *Destruction by Peace: Hugh O'Neill after Kinsale* (Monaghan, 1986)

—— *An Exile of Ireland: Hugh O'Neill, Prince of Ulster* (Dublin, 1996)

Kew, Graham (ed.,) 'The Irish Sections of Fynes Moryson's Unpublished Itinerary', *Anal. Hib.*, xxxvii (1998), pp 3–137

Lenihan, Maurice, *Limerick: its history and antiquities* (repr., Cork, 1967)

Lockyer, Roger, *The Early Stuarts: a political history of England, 1603–42* (London, 1989)

[Lodge, John (ed.)], *Desiderata Curiosa Hibernica: or a select collection of state papers* (2 vols, Dublin, 1772), vol. i

Lombard, Peter, *De Regno Hiberniae Sanctorum Insula Commentarius*, ed. P. F. Moran (Dublin, 1868)

Lorimer, Joyce (ed.,) *English and Irish Settlement on the River Amazon, 1550–1646* (Hakluyt Society, London, 1989)

MacCurtain, Margaret, 'The Flight of the Earls' in Liam de Paor (ed.), *Milestones in Irish History* (Dublin, 1986), pp 52–61

MacCarthy-Morrogh, Michael, *The Munster Plantation: English migration to southern Ireland, 1583–1641* (Oxford, 1986)

McCavitt, John, '"Good Planets in Their Several Spheares": the establishment of the assize circuits in early seventeenth-century Ireland', *Irish Jurist*, new ser., xxiv (1989), pp 248–78

—— 'Lord Deputy Chichester and the English Government's "Mandates Policy" in Ireland, 1605–7', *Recusant History*, xx (1991), pp 320–35

—— 'The Flight of the Earls, 1607', *I.H.S.*, xxix (1994), pp 159–73

—— *Sir Arthur Chichester, Lord Deputy of Ireland, 1605–16* (Belfast, 1998)

—— 'An Unspeakable Parliamentary Fracas: the Irish House of Commons, 1613', *Anal. Hib.*, xxxvii (1998) pp 223–35

McD[onald], W[illiam] (ed.), 'Irish Ecclesiastical Colleges since the Reformation', *Irish Ecclesiastical Record*, 1st ser., x (1874), pp 167–81, 196–211, 449–63, 519–31

McGurk, John, 'The Dead, Sick and Wounded of the Nine Years War (1594–1603)', *History Ireland*, iii, no. 4 (1995), pp 16–22

—— *The Elizabethan Conquest of Ireland* (Manchester, 1997)

Marshall, Tristram, 'James VI and I: three kings or two?', *Renaissance Forum*, v, no. 1 (2000) (http://www.hull.ac.uk/renforum/v5no1/marshall.htm)

Meehan, C. P., *The Fate and Fortunes of Hugh O'Neill, Earl of Tyrone, and Rory O'Donel, Earl of Tyrconnell, their flight from Ireland and death in exile* (3rd ed., Dublin, 1886)

Moody, T. W., 'The Irish Parliament under Elizabeth and James I: a general survey', *Proceedings of the Royal Irish Academy*, xlv (1939), sect. C, pp 41–81

—— *The Londonderry Plantation, 1609–41: the city of London and the plantation in Ulster* (Belfast, 1939)

Mooney, Canice, 'A Noble Shipload', *Irish Sword*, ii (1954–6), pp 195–204

Moran, P. F., *History of the Catholic Archbishops of Dublin since the Reformation* (Dublin, 1864)

—— *Spicilegium Ossoriense: being a collection of original letters and papers illustrative of the history of the Irish church from the Reformation to the year 1800* (3 vols, Dublin, 1874–84), vol. i

Morgan, Hiram, 'Extradition and Treason-Trial of a Gaelic Lord: the case of Brian O'Rourke', *Irish Jurist*, new ser., xxii (1987), pp 285–301

—— *Tyrone's Rebellion: the outbreak of the Nine Years War in Tudor Ireland* (Woodbridge, Suffolk, 1993)

—— 'Hugh O'Neill and the Nine Years War in Tudor Ireland', *Historical Journal*, xxxvi (1993), pp 21–37

—— 'Faith and Fatherland in Sixteenth-Century Ireland', *History Ireland*, iii, no. 2 (1995), pp 13–20

Morrissey, Thomas, *James Archer of Kilkenny*, (Dublin, 1979)

Moryson, Fynes, *A History of Ireland from the year 1599 to 1603* (2 vols, Dublin, 1735)

—— *An Itinerary containing his ten yeeres travell through … Germany, Bohmerland, Sweitzerland, Netherland, Denmark, Poland, Italy, Turkey, France, England, Scotland and Ireland* (4 vols, Glasgow, 1907–8), vols ii–iii

O'Brien, George (ed.), *Advertisements for Ireland, being a description of the state of Ireland in the reign of James I, contained in a manuscript in the library of Trinity College Dublin* (Dublin, 1923)

Ó Cianáin, Tadhg, *The Flight of the Earls*, ed. Paul Walsh (Dublin, 1916)

Ó Cléirigh, Lughaidh, *The Life of Aodh Ruadh Ó Domhnaill*, ed. Paul Walsh (2 pts, Dublin, 1948–57), pt i

O'Daly, Dominic, *The Earls of Desmond and the Persecution of Irish Catholics*, ed. and trans. from the original Latin edition (Lisbon, 1655) by C. P. Meehan (Dublin, 1847)

Ó Domhnaill, Seán, 'Sir Niall Garbh O'Donnell and the Rebellion of Sir Cahir O'Doherty', *I.H.S.*, iii (1942), pp 34–8

O'Faolain, Sean, *The Great O'Neill* (repr., Dublin, 1981)

Ohlmeyer, Jane H., *Civil War and Restoration in the Three Stuart Kingdoms: the career of Randal MacDonnell, Marquis of Antrim, 1609–1683* (Cambridge, 1993)

Pawlisch, Hans, *Sir John Davies and the Conquest of Ireland: a study in legal imperialism* (Cambridge, 1985)

Perceval-Maxwell, Michael, *The Scottish Migration to Ireland in the Reign of James I* (2nd ed., London, 1990)

Register of the Privy Council of Scotland, 1607–10 (Edinburgh, 1887)

Rich, Barnaby, *A New Description of Ireland* (London, 1610)

—— *A Catholicke Conference betweene Syr Tady Mac Mareall, a popish priest of Waterford, and Patrick Plaine, a young student in Trinity College by Dublin in Ireland* (London, 1612)

Robinson, Philip, *The Plantation of Ulster: British settlement in an Irish landscape, 1600–70* (Dublin, 1984)

Ronan, M. V., *The Irish Martyrs of the Penal Laws* (London, 1935)

Russell, Conrad, *The Crisis of Parliaments: English history, 1509–1660* (Oxford, 1971)

Salisbury: *Calendar of the Manuscripts of the … Marquess of Salisbury … preserved at Hatfield House* (24 vols, H.M.C., London, 1883–1976), vols viii, x, xviii–xix, xxi

Sampson, G. V., *A Memoir, explanatory of the Chart and Survey of the County of Londonderry, Ireland* (London, 1814)

Sanderson, James L., *Sir John Davies* (Boston, 1975)

Silke, J. J., 'Bishop Conor O'Devanney, O.F.M., *c.* 1533–1612', *Seanchas Ard Mhacha*, xiii (1988) pp 9–32

Smith, Murray, 'Flight of the Earls? Changing views on O'Neill's departure from Ireland', *History Ireland*, iv, no. 1 (1996), pp 17–20

Spenser, Edmund, *A View of the Present State of Ireland*, ed. W. L. Renwick (Oxford, 1970)

Steele, Robert, *Tudor and Stuart Proclamations, 1485–1714* (2 vols, Oxford, 1910), vol. ii

Trevelyan, W. C., and Trevelyan, E. C. (eds), *Trevelyan Papers* (Camden Society, 2nd ser., vol. iii (London, 1872)

Walsh, Micheline, 'Some Notes towards a History of the Womenfolk of the Wild Geese', *Irish Sword*, v (1961–2), pp 98–106

Wilbraham, Sir Roger, *The Journal of Sir Roger Wilbraham, Solicitor General in Ireland and Master of Requests for the years 1594–1616, together with notes in another hand for the years 1642–1649*, ed. H. S. Scott, Camden Miscellany, 3rd ser., vol. x (London, 1902), pp 3–139

Williams, Penry, *The Later Tudors: England 1547–1603* (London, 1995)

Wills, James (ed.), *Lives of Illustrious and Distinguished Irishmen* (6 vols, Dublin, 1890), vol. ii

Winwood, Sir Ralph, *Memorials of Affairs of State in the Reigns of Q. Elizabeth and James I*, ed. Edward Sawyer (3 vols, London, 1725), vols ii–iii

Wormald, Jenny, 'James VI and I: two kings or one?', *History*, lxviii (1983), pp 187–209

Wyse Jackson, Robert, *Archbishop Magrath: the scoundrel of Cashel* (Dublin, 1974)

Young, R. M., *Historical Notices of Old Belfast and its Vicinity* (Belfast, 1896)

INDEX